KU-274-118

LOCAL FAMILY, TANNA,
VANUATU P63

Welcome to Vanuatu & New Caledonia

Tropical weather, sandy beaches and turquoise waters await you. Locals welcome visitors, with dazzling grins and a chance to peek into their unique Melanesian cultures.

Life in the Tropics

In Vanuatu and New Caledonia you'll find a touch of the exotic in the everyday. Life here is always entertaining, whether you're being surprised by turtles peeking out of the sea, sidestepping crabs at the market, or eyeing up unruly mounds of kava before they get pounded up at a kava bar. Wherever you go, take in the little pleasures that pop up each day, whether it's bright flowers strewn on your bed, fresh coconut milk ready for drinking, or being in town during a harvest festival.

Something for Everyone

Take the kids to Vanuatu; the ni-Van children are a lot of fun, and there's always beachside hermit-crab action for entertainment. Peering into a live volcano will give a whole new meaning to future geography classes. There's plenty to do for adults, too. Party in Noumea and practise your French. Discover one of the world's largest reefs on a diving trip. Yachties flock to the Pacific, and the ni-Van in particular know how to extend a warm welcome. Sound like too much work? These countries are also ideal for anyone keen on doing nothing but relaxing.

A French Twist

Noumea, especially around Baie des Citrons and Anse Vata, is decidedly French. Its food, language and architecture may make you wonder exactly which hemisphere you're in. Port Vila crouches around a bay which, on cruise-ship days (and there are plenty of those), is a hive of adrenaline-boosting activity. It doesn't have the la-di-da factor of neighbouring Noumea; instead, it's a down-to-earth collection of dusty, low-rise buildings where carvings and boar tusks jostle for space with bright Mother Hubbard dresses, and fresh raspberries are lined up invitingly at the fruit and vegetable market.

Offshore Islands Await

Finding island paradise is a frangipani-scented breeze in New Caledonia and Vanuatu. Less than half an hour after arriving in Vanuatu you could be chilling in your lagoon-facing room and settling into island life with an icy welcome cocktail. In New Caledonia, even the cheapest island bungalows are charming. Getting around is easy too, with reliable flights, ferries and roads making connections from coast to mountain to atoll simple. Off the main islands, Vanuatu's bungalows are basic affairs, but who needs electric lights when they just dull the glow of the stars?

30119 028 063 49 5

WA

Vanuatu &
New Caledonia

Vanuatu
p46

**New
Caledonia**
p128

THIS EDITION WRITTEN AND RESEARCHED BY

Paul Harding, Craig McLachlan

Contents

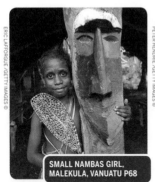

SMALL NAMBAS GIRL,
MALEKULA, VANUATU P68

ÎLOT MAÎTRE, NEW
CALEDONIA P132

LONDON BOROUGH OF SUTTON LIBRARY SERVICE (WAL)

30119 028 063 49 5	
Askews & Holts	Feb-2017
919.595	

Why I Love Vanuatu & New Caledonia

By Craig McLachlan, Writer

I love colour, especially those hues of aquamarine that dominate the lagoons and seas around Vanuatu and New Caledonia. And it gets better. Those waters are full of a kaleidoscope of technicolour tropical fish that are quite happy to eyeball me through my mask as I snorkel around their paradise. Out of the water, the skies are a stunning blue, rainforests a brilliant green, sandy beaches white or black, and my cocktail can be virtually any colour I choose.

For more about our authors, see page 224

Above: *Pirogue* (outrigger canoe) approaching New Caledonia's Île des Pins (p163)

Vanuatu & New Caledonia

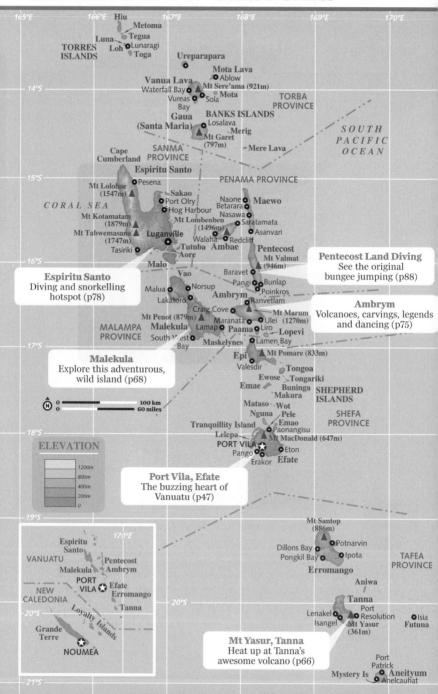

TORRES ISLANDS
Hiu
Metoma
Luna
Tegua
Loh Lunaragi
Toga

Ureparapara

Mota Lava
Ablow
Vanua Lava Mt Sere'ama (921m)
Waterfall Bay Mota
Vureas Sola
Bay **BANKS ISLANDS**
Gaua Losalava
(Santa Maria) Merig
Mt Garet
(797m) Mere Lava

TORBA PROVINCE

SOUTH PACIFIC OCEAN

Cape
Cumberland **SANMA PROVINCE**
Espiritu Santo **PENAMA PROVINCE**
Mt Lolohoe Pesena
(1547m)
CORAL SEA Sakao Naone **Maewo**
Port Olry Betarara
Mt Kotamatam Hog Harbour Nasawa
(1879m) Mt Lombenben Saratamata
Mt Tabwemasana (1496m) Asanvari
(1747m) **Luganville** Walaha Redcliff Asanvari
Tasiriki **Tutuba** **Ambae**
Aore **Pentecost**
Malo Mt Valmat
(946m)

Espiritu Santo
Diving and snorkelling
hotspot (p78)

Vao Baravet
Malua Norsup Pangi Bunlap
Lakatoro Poinkros
Ambrym Ranvetlam
Craig Cove Mt Marum
Mt Penot (879m) Maranata Ulei (1270m)
MALAMPA **Malekula** Lamap **Paama** Liro **Lopevi**
PROVINCE South West Maskelynes Lamen Bay
Bay

Pentecost Land Diving
See the original
bungee jumping (p88)

Ambrym
Volcanoes, carvings, legends
and dancing (p75)

Malekula
Explore this adventurous,
wild island (p68)

Epi Mt Pomare (833m)
Valesdir **Tongoa**
Ewose Tongariki
Emae Buninga
Makura **SHEPHERD**
Mataso Wot **ISLANDS**
Nguna Pele **SHEFA**
Tranquillity Island Emao **PROVINCE**
Lelepa Paonangisu
PORT VILA Mt MacDonald (647m)
Pango Eton
Erakor **Efate**

N 0 — 100 km
0 — 60 miles

ELEVATION

1200m
800m
400m
200m
0

Port Vila, Efate
The buzzing heart of
Vanuatu (p47)

VANUATU
Espiritu Santo
Pentecost
Malekula Ambrym
NEW
CALEDONIA **PORT** Efate
VILA Erromango
Loyalty Islands Tanna
Grande
Terre
NOUMEA

Mt Santop
(886m)
Dillons Bay Potnarvin
Pongkil Bay Ipota
Erromango

Aniwa

TAFEA
PROVINCE

Tanna
Port
Lenakel Resolution Isia
Isangel Mt Yasur Futuna
(361m)

Mt Yasur, Tanna
Heat up at Tanna's
awesome volcano (p66)

Port
Patrick
Mystery Is **Aneityum**
Anelcauhat

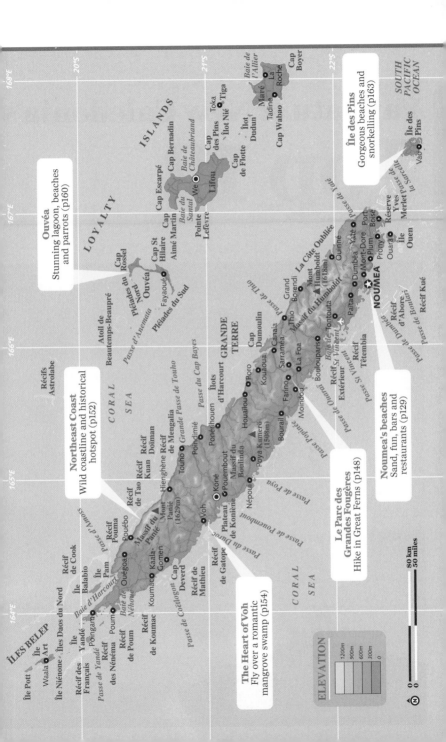

Ouvéa
Stunning lagoon, beaches and parrots (p160)

Northeast Coast
Wild coastline and historical hotspot (p152)

The Heart of Voh
Fly over a romantic mangrove swamp (p154)

Le Parc des Grandes Fougères
Hike in Great Ferns (p148)

Noumea's beaches
Sand, fun, bars and restaurants (p129)

Île des Pins
Gorgeous beaches and snorkelling (p163)

ÎLES BELEP

île Pott
île Art
Waala
îles Nienone
île Yandé
île Nénéma
île Daos du Nord
Pöingam
Poum
Arama
Ouégoa
Pam
Balabio
île Baaba
île Cook
Pouébo
Mandjélia
Gomen
Koumac
Kaala-
Gomen
Cap
Deverd
Hienghène
Touho
Poindimié
Voh
Koné
Pouembout
Népoui
Poya
Bourail
Moindou
Farino
Houaïlou
Poro
Kouaoua
Canala
Sarraméa
La Foa
Thio
Boulouparis
Paîta
Dumbéa
Mont-Dore
NOUMEA
Plum
Prony
Port
Boisé
Yaté
Goro
Ouara
île
Ouen
Vao
île des
Pins
Waho
Tiwaka
Ponérihouen
Grand
Borendi
Quinne

Récifs Astrolabe
Récif des Français
Récif de Poum
Récif de Koumac
Récif de Mathieu
Récif de Gatope
Récif Pouma
Récif de Tao
Récif Kuan
Récif Doïman
Récif de Mengalia
Récif Doïman
Récif Tétembia
Récif St Vincent
Récif Extérieur
Récif d'Aboré
Récif Kué
Récif de Boularí

Massif du
Panié
Mont
Panié
(1629m)
Plateau
de Koniène
Massif du
Kaala
Mont
Humboldt
(1618m)
Massif du
Humboldt
Poya Kaméré
(1508m)
Réserve
Yves
Merlet

GRANDE
TERRE

La Côte Oubliée

CORAL
SEA

SOUTH
PACIFIC
OCEAN

LOYALTY
ISLANDS

Cap Roussel
Ouvéa
Fayaoué
Pléiades du Nord
Pléiades du Sud
Atoll de
Beautemps-Beaupré

Cap St Hilaire
Cap
Aimé Martin
Pointe
Lefevre
Baie du
Santal
Lifou
We
Baie de
Châteaubriand
Cap Escarpé
Cap Bernadin
Cap
de Flotte

îlot
Dudun
Cap
des Pins
îlot Nié
Toka
Tiga
Tiga
Tadine
Maré
La
Roche
Cap Wabao
Baie de
l'Allier
Cap
Boyer

Passe de Thio
Passe de Toutouta
Passe de Dumbéa
Passe de Boulari
Passe de la Sarcelle
Passe de Yaté
Passe St Vincent
Passe d'Ouarail
Passe de Poya
Passe de Pouembout
Passe du Duroc
Passe de Coëtlogon
Passe d'Amos
Passe d'Harcourt
Passe d'Anemata
Grande Passe de Touho
Passe de Touho
Passe du Cap Bayes

îlots
d'Harcourt

20°S
21°S
22°S

164°E
165°E
166°E
167°E
168°E
169°E

N

0   80 km
0   50 miles

ELEVATION

1200m
900m
600m
300m
0

Vanuatu & New Caledonia's
Top 12

Mt Yasur, Tanna

1 Staring down into the cauldron of Mt Yasur (p66) as the magma boils, spits and periodically explodes is a surreal – some say scary – experience. The fact that it is only a five-minute walk to get here makes it all the more amazing: welcome to the world's most accessible active volcano. You can even 'ashboard' down the side of the crater, if you choose. Away from Yasur, Tanna island is an extraordinary place, with primitive villages, white- and black-sand beaches, rustic island bungalows and Vanuatu's most potent kava.

Île des Pins

2 Known as Kunié to the Melanesians, Île des Pins (Isle of Pines; p163) is a tranquil paradise of turquoise bays, white-sand beaches and tropical vegetation 110km southeast of Noumea. There's plenty of fun to be had, from snorkelling at La Piscine Naturelle and Baie de Kanuméra, to exploring Queen Hortense's cave, taking part in a *pirogue* (outrigger canoe) excursion or heading out on a day trip to spectacular Nokanhui Atoll. The island is known for its seafood and delectable Île des Pins snails. Try them at your resort or local accommodation. Below right: Kanak totem poles

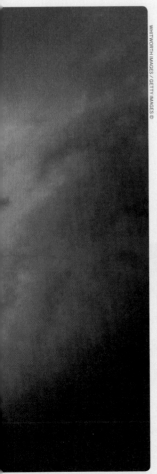

WHITWORTH IMAGES / GETTY IMAGES ©

BLAINE HARRINGTON III / GETTY IMAGES ©

Espiritu Santo

3 Want to experience outer island life but with a healthy dose of comfort and plenty of adventure? Vanuatu's largest island (p78) offers a lively main town, island resorts, dazzling white-sand beaches and a rugged interior where mountain treks and caving adventures await. Scuba diving and snorkelling are major attractions. The wreck of the ocean liner USS *President Coolidge* is the world's most accessible, while Million Dollar Point is a real eye-opener. Experienced dive operators will take you out, then swap stories at a local bar or restaurant. Top left: Wreck diving, Million Dollar Point (p81)

Noumea's Beaches

4 Cosmopolitan Noumea (p129) has gorgeous beaches 10 minutes' drive from the city centre. Trendy Baie des Citrons attracts locals and visitors alike. The beach is great for swimming, while the strip of restaurants, bars and nightclubs along the main road could well pull you in from breakfast until the wee hours. Just around the corner, Anse Vata (bottom left) is a hotspot for visitors to Noumea, who come for hotels, restaurants, shopping and other attractions. Locals relax here, too, especially on the *petanque* courts next to the beach.

Port Vila, Efate

5 Vanuatu's capital (p47) is the buzzing heart of the archipelago. Some say this is far removed from the 'real' Vanuatu, but what it lacks in island culture, Port Vila more than makes up for with good food, luxury resorts, adventure activities, markets and ease of transport. Set around a pretty harbour and two lagoons, Vila has beach bars, movie nights and every conceivable activity above and below water. Hire a car or quadbike and tour Efate on the sealed Ring Rd. Above: Port Vila market vendor

Malekula

6 One of Vanuatu's wildest islands, Malekula (p68) abounds with stories of tribal warfare and cannibalism. Visit the intriguing Big Nambas and Small Nambas tribes, burial sites of chiefs or trek with a local guide deep into the highlands of the Dog's Head. If you're not feeling that adventurous, Malekula has some excellent offshore islands where you'll probably be the only guest, and you can spend lazy days on the beach or snorkelling in marine reserves. In the Far South, the Maskelyne islands are just such a place. Below: Big Nambas men calling for dancers

Ouvéa

7 Think 25km of perfect white beach backed with grass, tropical flowers and thick forest inhabited by the protected Ouvéa green parrot. Look out over an exquisite turquoise lagoon that stretches as far as you can see. Add a chain of tiny islets, the Pléiades. Sound unreal? Ouvéa (p160) may leave you shaking your head in wonder. The Ouvéa lagoon was one of six marine areas in New Caledonia to be listed as a Unesco World Heritage site. It's stunning, and there's plenty to do in it, on it and around it. Top right: Lekiny, Ouvéa

DE AGOSTINI PICTURE LIBRARY / GETTY IMAGES ©

Ambrym

8 Smoking Ambrym (p75) is famous for its twin active volcanoes: reasonably fit hikers can traverse the island in several directions via the calderas of Mt Marum and Mt Benbow, camping at the base. Finish your trek with a soak in one of the many hot springs that mix with seawater in secluded bays around the island. Ambrym is also known for its *tamtams* (which in these parts are tall, elaborately carved slit drums valued by collectors worldwide; pictured left), mysterious black-magic legends and black-sand-thumping Rom dances – a cultural trifecta.

Grande Terre's Northeast Coast

9 North of Hienghène (p154) is the wildest stretch of Grande Terre's coastline. It's covered in vegetation, and waterfalls and streams rush down the mountains. You'll discover the captivating ferry across the Ouaième River, stalls selling fruit and carvings, lots of one-lane bridges, and dogs and chickens wandering out onto the road. The area around Balade is a fascinating hotspot. This is where Captain Cook landed and gave New Caledonia its name, and where the French took possession in 1853.

Top: Lindéralique Rocks (p153)

The Heart of Voh

10 This mangove swamp north of Koné on Grande Terre has developed some unusual natural designs. The most intriguing is a perfect heart shape, La Cœur de Voh (p154), which features on the cover of *Earth from Above,* a book of aerial photography by renowned photographer Yann Arthus-Bertrand. It's best seen from the air. Microlight flights also take in the magnificent lagoon, let you look right into a 'blue hole', and fly low enough for you to spot stingrays, turtles and sharks.

Pentecost Land Diving

11 Each year the stages are selected, towers painstakingly built from local timbers and the vines carefully chosen. Then, during the *naghol* (land diving) season (April until June), the jumping begins. This is bungee jumping Vanuatu style (p88) – and it's what started the bungee phenomenon worldwide. There are several levels to dive from, with the youngest boys (and the occasional tourist) often leaping from the lowest rung. Day trippers fly in from Port Vila. Stay a while to get to know Pentecost and its people a little better.

Le Parc des Grandes Fougères

12 The lovely 4500-hectare Park of the Great Ferns (p148), in the mountains near La Foa in central Grande Terre, features tropical rainforest with rich and varied flora and fauna. As the name suggests, tree ferns are in abundance, and most examples of New Caledonia's native birdlife can be spotted. A number of well-signposted hiking tracks range from 45 minutes to six hours, plus there are trails for mountain-bike enthusiasts.

Need to Know

For more information, see each country's Directory A-Z (p118, p195)

Currency
Vanuatu: Vatu (VT)
New Caledonia: Pacific
Franc (CFP)

....

Language
Vanuatu: Bislama,
French
New Caledonia: French,
Melanesian-Polynesian
dialects

....

Visas
Vanuatu: 30-day visas
issued at the border for
most nationalities.
New Caledonia: Not
needed for stays of up to
three months for most
nationalities.

....

Money
ATMs available on main
islands only in Vanuatu
but widely available in
New Caledonia. Take
cash to outer islands.

....

Mobile Phones
Local SIM cards are
cheap in Vanuatu,
expensive in New
Caledonia.

....

Time
GMT/UTC plus 11 hours

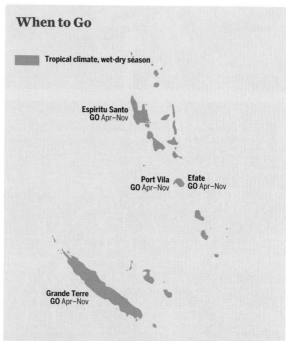

When to Go

Tropical climate, wet-dry season

Espiritu Santo
GO Apr–Nov

Port Vila
GO Apr–Nov

Efate
GO Apr–Nov

Grande Terre
GO Apr–Nov

High Season
(May–Aug)

➡ Throughout the
region life is gearing
up again after the
cyclone season.

➡ The only time
to see Vanuatu's
Pentecost land
divers.

➡ Tropical heat dips
in the cool season.

Shoulder
(Sep–Oct)

➡ Both countries
can be popular
during nearby
countries' school
holiday periods and
may be busy.

➡ Expect pleasant,
warm weather and
some good deals.

Low Season
(Nov–Apr)

➡ Cyclone season
for both countries;
it's possible to get
excellent deals on
accommodation.
Some places may
close up.

➡ Expect tropical
heat and humidity.

Useful Websites

Office de Tourisme (www.office-tourisme.nc) New Caledonia tourism office.

Vanuatu Tourism Office (http://vanuatu.travel) Tourist info for Vanuatu.

Wantok Environment Centre (www.positiveearth.org) Good online resource for all things in Vanuatu.

Loyalty Islands (www.iles-loyaute.com) Loyalty Islands info.

Lonely Planet (www.lonely planet.com/vanuatu; www.lonely planet.com/new-caledonia) Destination info, hotel bookings, traveller forum and more.

Important Numbers

Vanuatu country code	☏678
New Caledonia country code	☏687
Vanuatu police	☏111
New Caledonia police	☏17
International access code	☏00

Exchange Rates

Australia	A$1	82VT	81 CFP
Canada	C$1	8VT	83 CFP
Europe	€1	121VT	119 CFP
Japan	¥100	103VT	102 CFP
NZ	NZ$1	77VT	76 CFP
UK	£1	144VT	143 CFP
US	US$1	110VT	109 CFP

For current exchange rates, see www.xe.com.

Daily Costs

**Budget:
Less than A$100**

➡ Stay in bungalows or basic accommodation: A$15–25

➡ Ride local buses: A$2 per trip

➡ Grab a simple take-out sandwich for lunch: A$5

**Midrange:
A$100–A$200**

➡ Stay in a decent hotel: A$70

➡ Hire a car: A$40

➡ Eat a meal at a midrange restaurant: A$20

**Top End:
More than A$200**

➡ Stay at a resort: A$150

➡ Go on a single dive: A$100

➡ Eat out for lunch and dinner: A$60

Opening Hours

May vary outside Noumea and Port Vila, especially in rural areas and outer islands. Sundays are extremely quiet throughout the islands.

Government offices 7.30–11.30am and 1.30–4.30pm Monday to Friday; some open Saturday mornings

Banks 8am–4pm Monday to Friday

Shops 7.30am–6pm Monday to Friday; Saturday mornings; some close for lunch

Cafes 6am–6pm Monday to Saturday

Arriving in Vanuatu & New Caledonia

Bauerfield International Airport (Port Vila, Vanuatu; p124) is 6km from central Port Vila. Late arrivals should prebook a shuttle service. Local buses depart from the domestic terminal next door until around 5pm.

Pekoa International Airport (Santo, Vanuatu; p124) Taxis service the airport, 3km from Luganville, and resorts offer pick-up services.

Tontouta International Airport (Noumea, New Caledonia; p199) International flights arrive here, 45km (one hour) northwest of Noumea. Public buses service the airport during the day, as do more-expensive shuttle-bus services.

Getting Around Vanuatu

Air Light planes cover most of the archipelago reasonably efficiently.

Boat Passenger boats, speed-boats and canoes reach the outer islands.

Bus Minibus services are limited to Efate, Santo and West Tanna.

Car The only places you can hire a car, scooter or quad bike are Port Vila and Luganville.

Getting Around New Caledonia

Air Very efficient service to northern Grande Terre, the Loyalty Islands and Île des Pins.

Boat The Betico fast ferry links Noumea to the Loyalty Islands and Île des Pins.

Bus Regular daily services on Grande Terre, limited on outer islands.

Car Rental vehicles are available everywhere. Excellent roads throughout the islands.

For much more on **getting around**, see p124 and p199

PLAN YOUR TRIP NEED TO KNOW

If You Like...

Beaches

This is one of the main reasons you're here, right?

Champagne Beach This crescent of white sand and luminous blue water is a beauty on Vanuatu's Santo. (p86)

Port Resolution On Tanna's southeastern tip, Port Resolution overlooks a popular anchorage and a dazzling white-sand beach. (p65)

Port Olry Fishing village in Santo with bungalows, turquoise waters and a glorious squeaky white beach. (p86)

Baie des Citrons This lovely Noumea beach is lined with popular bars and restaurants. (p131)

Yedjele Beach A stunner on the southwest coast of Maré, Loyalty Islands, with amazingly clear waters. (p156)

Fayaoué Beach This sandy white beach stretches for 25km along Ouvéa's World Heritage–listed lagoon. (p161)

Baie de Kanuméra Lined with pines on legendary Île des Pins, Kanuméra Bay is a real beauty. (p166)

Isolation

While untouched spaces are more common in Vanuatu, in both countries peaceful spots with simple accommodation are easy to find.

Maskelynes Enjoy the private bay and plenty of quiet just a local boat ride from Malekula, Vanuatu. (p74)

Ratua Private Island Resort This might just be the Vanuatu private island you've been dreaming of. (p84)

Relais de Poingam At the northern tip of Grande Terre, this superb spot is fabulously isolated. (p152)

Jokin Cliffs This cliff-top hang-out in northern Lifou has stunning views and access to the reef below. (p158)

Relais de Ouane Batch For an out-of-the-way experience on Grande Terre's northeast coast, head north from Hienghène. (p155)

Diving & Snorkelling

Dive centres make it easy to access the deep. Bring your own gear if you're planning lots of underwater time.

Million Dollar Point Check out what the US army left behind after WWII. It was dumped underwater here. (p81)

USS President Coolidge Explore this luxury-liner wreck that's been resting underwater since 1942. (p81)

Hideaway Island With an underwater post office, this is a favourite with newbie snorkellers. (p47)

Grande Terre New Caledonia's main island has dive centres operating on its east and west coasts. (p129)

La Piscine Naturelle Brilliant snorkelling at Île des Pins' 'natural swimming pool'. (p167)

Baie de Jinek An active snorkelling route in a fabulous coral-filled bay in northern Lifou, Loyalty Islands. (p158)

Hiking

Get deep into Vanuatu and New Caledonia by setting off on foot. It's relatively easy to find local guides. Vanuatu's volcanoes make for popular, challenging (and hot) hikes.

Malekula Trekking in the highlands of Malekula is some of the wildest in Vanuatu. (p70)

Ambrym Traverse the island on foot, crossing paths with active volcanoes on a two- to five-day hike. (p75)

GRNC1 Walking Track Hike Grande Terre's Far South on this 123km marked and signposted track. (p145)

Shabadran Hike with a guide to find this otherwise inaccessible beach on Maré's southeast coast. (p156)

Le Parc des Grandes Fougères Head to the Park of the Great Ferns near La Foa for superb day hiking. (p148)

Culture

French influence shows in Noumea, while Kanaks in New Caledonia and ni-Van in Vanuatu brighten up all islands and towns with song, dance and sculpture.

National Museum of Vanuatu Combines a bunch of facilities to show off Vanuatu's ni-Van culture. (p99)

Ambrym Watch a Rom dance and gaze at amazing carvings on this volcanic island. (p75)

Malekula See traditional dances by the Big and Small Nambas and visit the Lakatoro Cultural Centre. (p68)

Tjibaou Cultural Centre Sculpture, paintings and photographs representing Kanak culture in an architectural masterpiece. (p131)

Musée de Nouvelle-Calédonie Noumea's Museum of New Caledonia is an excellent introduction to traditional Kanak and regional culture. (p129)

Top: Ratua Private Island Resort (p84), Vanuatu
Bottom: Hikers at Mt Marum volcano (p76), Vanuatu

Month by Month

Fest' Napuan,
November
Naghol, April
Port Vila Race Day,
July
Foire de Bourail,
August
Loyalty Islands Fair,
September

January

It's hot, humid and cyclone season in the South Pacific. Nearby countries such as Australia and New Zealand are in their summer holiday period, so there are still people around.

☆ New Year Fireworks

Noumea greets the New Year with a huge fireworks display and concert at the harbour.

☆ ATP Challenger Tennis

Noumea hosts an ATP Challenger tennis tournament in early January, with many top pros turning up to play before heading to the Australian Open.

February

Cyclone season is still in full swing, and it's mighty hot with plenty of rain in New Caledonia – getting up to 35°C in Noumea. It's also the hottest month in Vanuatu.

🎎 John Frum Day

Prayers and flowers are offered in John Frum communities on the east coast of Tanna. Part of the celebration is a flag-raising ceremony and military parade in which men march with bamboo rifles. It's held on 15 February. (p69)

🎎 Festival of the Yam

This Kanak festival marks the beginning of the yam harvest and is held in New Caledonia's southern Grande Terre town of Yaté.

March

Although temperatures are dipping slightly, it's still hot, still cyclone season and this is the rainiest month of the year for New Caledonia.

April

Cyclone season is over; yachts are making their way to Vanuatu and New Caledonia. Tanna's Mt Yasur volcano is particularly active as it works to unclog the wet season's debris.

🎎 Yam Festival

Come and witness dancing and feasting on the volcanic island of Tanna to praise the yam harvest. The island has a number of *kastom* (traditional) villages where you can see dancing and the customary way of life year-round.

✖ Giant Omelette Festival

This festival is held around Easter in Dumbéa, near Noumea. It involves some dozen chefs using 7000 eggs to make one free-for-all omelette, 3.5m in diameter. There's also dance, music and crafts.

🎎 Naghol

The spectacular ritual of *naghol* (land diving) is held in several villages on Pentecost. It's very well organised, with dates and venues planned months in advance so travellers don't miss out.

It runs almost daily from April to the end of June.

May

The dry season arrives in Vanuatu, which actually means it's cooler, too. It begins heating up again in October. New Caledonia is particularly photogenic from now until November.

✖ Stag & Prawn Festival

Held in central Grande Terre, New Caledonia's cowboy country, in mid-May, this festival incorporates the best of festival fun; think sausage-eating and stag-calling competitions.

☆ New Caledonia Car Rally

The Asia Pacific Rally Championship comes to New Caledonia in mid-May. See local and international drivers rev their engines and compete on New Caledonian roads.

☆ New Caledonia Great Lagoon Regatta

This celebration of the biodiversity of the lagoon takes place at the end of May, and is open to all types of yachts, no matter how small or large.

✖ Avocado Festival

Held in Nece on the New Caledonian Loyalty Island of Maré, this celebration includes weaving classes and plenty of papayas, bananas, apples, yams, sweet potatoes and, of course, avocados. Fishers also show off their catches.

June

It's cooling down in New Caledonia; expect fresh breezes and cold patches. Water temperatures may go as low as 21°C. As compensation, it is usually dry.

✖ Fete du Lagon

Celebrates the natural heritage of Ouvéa over three days in early June. Taste the seafood of the Loyalty Islands and join in the fishing contest.

✖ Vanuatu Open Water Swim

In Port Vila, competitors can choose either the 3.2km Iririki Swim or the 1.5km Harbour Swim. The next race, a few days later on Santo, has swimmers paddling fast from the channel to Aore Island (2.6km). See www.vanuatuswim.com.

☆ La Foa Film Festival

Bringing famous film folk to La Foa, this week-long festival celebrates film. It runs into July, and also takes place in cinemas in Noumea. Films are in French. See www.festival-cinemalafoa.com.

July

This is a busy time at Vanuatu's resorts as Australian families come to enjoy the sun. For locals it's still pretty cool, with temperatures an average 23°C. Rainfall is near its lowest annual level, too.

☆ Port Vila Race Day

Port Vila Race Day is a big annual charity event, with races including the Vanuatu Cup. It's the one race of the year. The week around it also features a regatta and charity ball.

✖ Ruan Cultural Festival

Spanning five days in July, this festival is held in Nobul in north Ambrym. It is a festival of initiation rites, which involve mask dances for boys and men, and ceremonial dances for women.

☆ Bastille Day

New Caledonia celebrates France's national day with fireworks on the 13th and a military parade in Noumea on the 14th. Families carry candle-lit red, blue and white lanterns on an evening walk that ends at Noumea's Place des Cocotiers.

✖ Kastom Magic Festival

This festival is held over a few days in late July on the volcanic and ultramagical island of Ambrym. Expect music, plenty of Rom dance and, yes, magic.

☆ Independence Day

Every village in Vanuatu celebrates Independence Day. Port Vila has the widest range of activities: sporting events, a military parade and fun stalls at Independence Park; canoe and yacht races in the bay; string-band competitions; and *kastom* dancing. It's held on 30 July.

August

Expect fresh nights and hot days in New Caledonia. Whale watching is in full swing. It's the coolest and driest month in Vanuatu, with Port Vila chilling out to an average temperature of 23°C.

☆ Vanuatu Golf Open

This week of golf brings together professionals and amateurs from around the South Pacific. See www.vanuatugolfopen.com for more information. It's held at the Port Vila Golf and Country Club.

🎎 Back to My Roots

North Ambrym's villages of Fanla and Olal come to life during this three-day festival in late August. See chiefs passing their ranks and witness the Rom dance. It's a popular event with yachties.

🎎 Foire de Bourail

Held in Bourail on New Caledonia's Grande Terre, this is a true cowboy fest. Complete with rodeo, lumberjack contests and the 'Miss Bourail Fair', it's a side of New Caledonia that visitors might not even know exists.

🎎 Noumea Carnival

New Caledonia's capital celebrates Carnival with a parade and all sorts of fun events in late August.

September

Temperatures are on the rise in New Caledonia and this is also the driest month of the year. Accommodation on the main islands can be busy in Vanuatu due to Australian school holidays.

🎎 Nekowiar & Toka Ceremony

A three-day extravaganza of dancing and feasting on Tanna, during which villagers cement relationships and arrange marriages. The place and date is only announced close to the time. Held in September or October every three years.

🎎 Loyalty Islands Fair

Enjoy all things Loyalty during three days of activities at this fair that is held in turn by Lifou, Maré and Ouvéa. There's dancing, art, fishing and agricultural goodies plus a Miss Loyalty Islands competition.

October

The dry season continues in New Caledonia; watch for bushfires. The cold season is about to end in Vanuatu.

🎎 Vanilla Festival

Lifou in the Loyalty Islands holds its Vanilla Festival in mid-October. Vanilla first arrived with an English missionary in 1860 and is now described as Lifou's gold. Head here for everything vanilla.

☆ Touques Regatta

This festive sporting event involves teams on vessels made with the same number of *touques* (floats). They can use any kind of propulsion as long as it's not motorised. Held in Anse Vata, Noumea, in late October.

November

Cyclone season begins in Vanuatu and New Caledonia and the yachties are gone. Vanuatu is heading into its hottest and wettest season, which lasts until April.

☆ Fest' Napuan

This is a major five-day outdoor music concert with big-name local bands and international guests held in Port Vila. Visit www.festnapuan.org for details. A sister concert in Luganville, Santo, is called the Lukaotem Gud Santo Festival.

🎎 Beef Festival

Greater Noumea's Païta township holds its Beef Festival in early November. There's rodeo, music, food tasting and all sorts of farming fun.

December

It's hot, rainfall is increasing, and locals are thinking of Christmas. New Caledonia starts to get visitors from France who are escaping the northern-hemisphere winter.

☆ Christmas Lights

Noumea gets ready for Christmas with a month of lights, children's activities and a Santa's post office in the Place des Cocotiers.

Itineraries

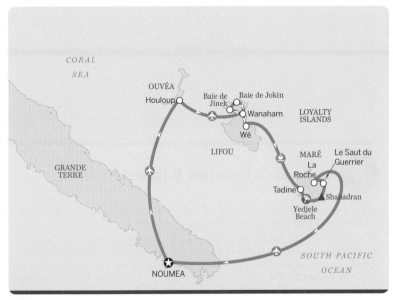

Exploring the Loyalty Islands

You can explore New Caledonia's three very different, isolated and fascinating Loyalty Islands in a week.

Fly from Magenta domestic airport in **Noumea** to **Houloup** airport on Ouvéa. Stay three nights, soaking up the sun on the island's magnificent white-sand beaches. Take an organised day trip that offers snorkelling off an uninhabited island, a barbecue and a peek at the local shark population. Check out the turtles from Ouvéa's only bridge.

Fly to **Wanaham** airport on Lifou and enjoy more island life, spotting turtles in its southeastern bays, visiting stunning beaches and snorkelling at **Baie de Jinek** in its northwest. After staying at the nearby cliff-top spot of **Baie de Jokin**, head down to **Wé** to catch the ferry to **Tadine** on little-explored Maré. Pick up a hire car from Tadine's ferry port and head south to lovely **Yedjele Beach**. Overnight before heading to the island's east and hiking **Shabadran** with a guide. Gaze at spectacular **Le Saut du Guerrier** near **La Roche** before dropping off your hire car and catching a flight back to Noumea.

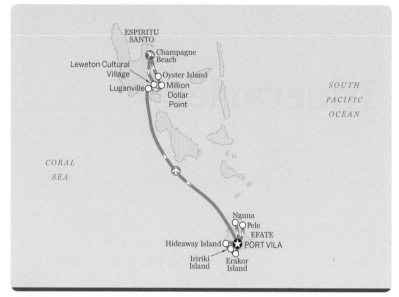

Vanuatu's Beaches & Islands

5 DAYS

If you like gorgeous beaches, playing both in and on the water, and small islands, give yourself five days for the following itinerary.

Start exploring Vanuatu's watery delights with a visit to all three of the almost football-field-sized islands off **Port Vila**. On day one, don a snorkel and fins and send a postcard from the underwater mailbox at **Hideaway Island**. Spend day two enjoying lunch on **Erakor Island**, followed by a paddle in its calm shallow waters. Then, as the sun goes down, hop on the regular ferry to **Iririki Island** for dinner. Each island has its own resort but you don't need to stay at them to visit. If manicured-resort fatigue kicks in, travel north by public transport or hire car and take the short boat trip to the islands of **Nguna** or **Pele**. Experience hospitality ni-Van style while staying in a rustic bungalow by the beach.

Head back to Port Vila to catch a plane north to **Luganville**, the capital of Santo. Get straight into the action by exploring the underwater WWII dumping ground of **Million Dollar Point** and dive the wreck of the luxury liner USS *President Coolidge*. Once the diving's done, make your way north to recover on comfortable and fun **Oyster Island**. For a change from beaches, borrow one of the resort's kayaks and paddle your way to its nearby blue hole. You won't be able to resist diving into the luminous bright-blue water once you get there.

Return the kayak and venture further north by road to **Champagne Beach**, which is one of Vanuatu's most impressive strands. Its cuticle shape holds whiter-than-white sand and clear turquoise waters. It's a cruise-ship favourite but, if you're lucky, you'll have it all to yourself. Before you bother to get all the sand out from between your toes, you might be tempted by yet more blue holes along the road back south. To finish off the watery Vanuatu experience stop at **Leweton Cultural Village** in time to see women and children from the northern island of Gaua perform water music. The soothing sounds and images will stick with you as you board your flight from Luganville back to Port Vila.

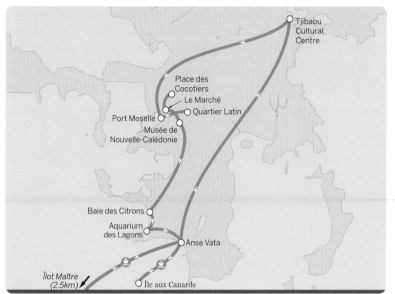

 **Noumea**

This itinerary will suit those with a day to explore Noumea, whether coming in on a cruise ship or staying in the city.

If you arrive by cruise ship you're in luck: the terminal is right in the middle of Noumea waterfront. It's just a short stroll into the city. Start your day with a bit of shopping and people-watching around **Place des Cocotiers**. Drop off your purchases and walk south to the multi-hexagonal municipal city market, **Le Marché**. Stand and drink your coffee like a local; buy fresh fruit; then walk up Rue Eugéne Porcheron for some of the best pastries in the country. **Musée de Nouvelle-Calédonie** is nearby; spend an hour here exploring Kanak culture and Melanesian artefacts.

Hop on the local bus to **Baie des Citrons** and settle onto your patch of sandy beach (there are grassed bits, too). Have a swim and chill out on the floating pontoons, just as the locals do. There are plenty of restaurants, cafes and bars just over the road if you feel like refreshments. Also nearby is the impressive **Aquarium des Lagons**. Spend at least an hour here, admiring the sharks and lagoon-dwelling sea life. Continue with a stroll to **Anse Vata**, a beachside hive of shopping and eating. Adventurous types can depart here for some kitesurfing on the windy but pretty **Îlot Maître** (book ahead), or you can just take the taxiboat out to **Île aux Canards**, the cute little island offshore. The snorkelling is great.

Then it's time to make your way (phone for a taxi) to the architecturally amazing **Tjibaou Cultural Centre**. The walk around it, complete with informative plaques, is impressive, as are the exhibitions inside. Call for another taxi or wait for the local bus to take you back to the city centre. Watch the yachting life while unwinding with an aperitif at a waterfront bar at **Port Moselle**, before ending your day with a wander through the historic and character-filled **Quartier Latin** (Latin Quarter). There are plenty of eating and drinking options here to finish off your day.

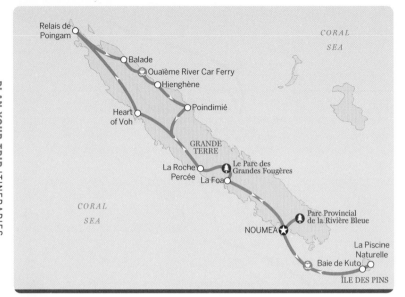

 Grande Terre & Île des Pins

A good itinerary for those who want see what New Caledonia really has to offer. Tack on another week to head out to the Loyalty Islands and you'll have pretty much covered the country.

Spend a few days in **Noumea**, swimming at the beaches of Anse Vata and Baie des Citrons and practising your French. Loll around the hotel pool, but take time for the gorgeous Aquarium des Lagons and the Tjibaou Cultural Centre.

On day four, get up early and catch a ferry to Île des Pins. On arrival at the wharf in **Baie de Kuto**, pick up your waiting rental car and stop at all the sights en route to **La Piscine Naturelle**. Stay the night on the island, explore some more, then return the car and jump back on the ferry to **Noumea**. Dance like there's no tomorrow at an over-water nightclub. Recover, then hire another car and head north along the west coast for a week of cultural exploration. The roads are excellent, so no worries there.

Take a day out and head inland near **La Foa** for a walk at **Le Parc des Grandes Fougères** (Park of the Great Ferns) and stay in the bush at Refuge de Farino. Return to the west coast road and head north again. Wander along the beach at **La Roche Percée**, near Bourail, and check out the intriguing rock formations.

Further north, at Koné, make sure to take a microlight flight to see the **Heart of Voh** and the 'blue hole' in the lagoon before heading up to the Far North for a magical time at **Relais de Poingam**, right at the tip of Grande Terre. Next, head across and down the northeast coast, exploring historical hotspots near **Balade**, buying up Kanak carvings and fresh fruit from roadside stalls, and taking the **Ouaïème River car ferry** on your way to **Hienghène**. After exploring **Poindimié**, cross back to the west on the RPN2 and retrace your path back down the west coast to Noumea.

Still time? Duck down to the Grande Terre's Far South and explore **Parc Provincial de la Rivière Bleue**, on foot or by canoe.

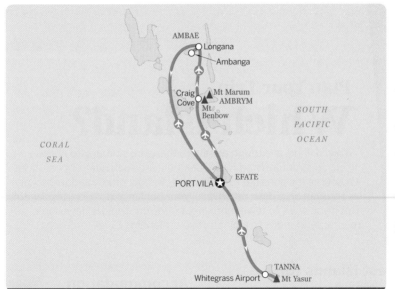

Volcanic Vanuatu

This is the way to go if you are into volcanic landscapes. We're talking active volcanoes, ash plains, lava explosions, crater lakes and sulphur galore.

Take the early morning flight from **Port Vila** straight to Whitegrass airport on the island of **Tanna**. Choose your accommodation from the resort or bungalows nearby and hang out in the blue pools filled with coral and fish. Join a tour to a *kastom* (traditional) village to see how Tanna's tribes have been living for centuries; if you're lucky you'll get a peek at some black magic – it's particularly strong on this island.

Rest up and prepare to cross a vast ash plain by 4WD truck in the late afternoon. Stop and take photos of this moon-like surface, with **Mt Yasur** rising in the background. The 4WD drops you a few minutes' walk from this active volcano's lip. Settle into your viewing position, and when dusk approaches witness the fireworks as lava and smoke spit out. Stay in a tree house beneath the volcano – you'll hear the rumbles and lava explosions all night. Climb back up in the morning if you want to get another sulphur fix before crossing the island again and flying back to **Port Vila**.

From Port Vila, fly to **Craig Cove** on the island of Ambrym. The island has several routes to **Mt Benbow** and **Mt Marum** volcanoes; each community has its own paths and guides to help get you there, and each involves a different degree of difficulty. Reaching the volcanoes requires a four- to eight-hour walk and incorporates an overnight stay camping by the rim (only if it's safe to do so – check the warnings first).

Finally, fly from Craig Cove to **Longana** on the island of Ambae. Once there, head up to **Ambanga** (a two-hour 4WD journey) and in the morning set off to visit Ambae's three crater lakes with a guide. The lakes are accessible on foot, though it's fairly dense forest you'll be making your way through. Take camping gear and overnight by one of the lakes before returning to Longana for your flight back to **Port Vila**.

Plan Your Trip
Which Island?

'Which island' is a tough question: there are so many to choose from, and Vanuatu and New Caledonia are such different countries. Of course it's possible to book flight-and-accommodation packages through an airline, or leave all your bookings up to a travel agent. But if you want to have more input into your trip, we have some recommendations to kick-start your planning.

Best Islands for....

Romantic Getaways
Ratua Private Island Resort (p84), Bokissa Eco Island Resort (p84) and Oyster Island (p87) in Vanuatu

Îlot Maître (p132), Île des Pins (p163) and Ouvéa (p160) in New Caledonia

Hiking & Adventuring
Tanna island (p63), Ambrym (p75) and Ambae (p90) in Vanuatu

Grande Terre (p129), Maré (p156) and Lifou (p157) in New Caledonia

Diving & Snorkelling
Espiritu Santo (p78), Efate (p47) and Malekula (p68) in Vanuatu

Île des Pins (p163), Ouvéa (p160) and Amédée Islet (p131) in New Caledonia

Village Life
Tanna (p63), Malekula (p68), Nguna (p61) and Pele (p61) in Vanuatu

Lifou (p157), Maré (p156) and the northeast coast of Grande Terre (p152) in New Caledonia

Rugged Isolation
Ambrym (p75), Ambae (p90) and Malekula (p68) in Vanuatu

Grande Terre's Far North (p152) and Far South (p143) and Maré (p156) in New Caledonia

Accommodation

First up, you'll need to decide what kind of experience you're after.

If it's to have a luxurious, relaxing holiday, then you may want to book a resort. You'll pay accordingly, but you'll enjoy an appealing room, a swimming pool, quality meals in the resort restaurant and a variety of optional tours to keep you entertained should you wish to do something other than loll by the pool.

If your goal is to do some exploring, without doing away with comfort, then both Vanuatu and New Caledonia can cater to your needs. There's more 'mid-level' accommodation in New Caledonia and good roads make it easy to get around all the islands in rental vehicles. Destinations in Vanuatu are limited to Efate (around Port Vila), Santo and West Tanna.

If you want to explore, meet the locals and stay in budget-friendly local accommodation, there's plenty to meet your needs in both countries. You're bound to have some unforgettable experiences. Bear in mind that while your accommodation costs may be low, this style of visit in Vanuatu can see a hike in your overall costs as you'll spend more on transport between the islands.

There are also plenty of options for the budget-conscious traveller, with camping a viable form of accommodation in both Vanuatu and New Caledonia. Many local places with bungalow accommodation also offer camping on the grounds, with use of bathroom facilities for a fee. You'll want to ask permission before putting up your tent just anywhere, though.

Resorts

Both Vanuatu and New Caledonia are home to terrific resorts; most are spread in arcs around the capitals of Port Vila and Noumea. Both countries also have entire islands dedicated to just one resort.

Some are more glamorous than others, but generally resorts come complete with at least one restaurant, some kind of water-based activity program (which can vary from snorkel and fins hire to glass-bottomed boat use) and most have swimming pools. Vanuatu's big resorts often have kids clubs and beauty spas.

Many resorts offer good deals on flight and accommodation packages, on sale through airlines or travel agents.

In New Caledonia, the over-water bungalows of L'Escapade (p138) are a 20-minute boat ride from Noumea on Îlot Maître and surrounded by turquoise waters.

The new Sheraton Déva Resort & Spa (p151) near Bourail on Grande Terre boasts the country's top golf course, while there are Méridien resorts in Noumea (p137) and on Île des Pins, the latter a short walk from spectacular La Piscine Naturelle. Each of the Loyalty Islands boasts a decent resort also.

In Vanuatu the best resorts are around Efate (Port Vila) and Santo. Standouts include Havannah (p60), Erakor Island (p55) and Eratap Beach Resort (p55) on Efate; and island resorts Aore (p84), Bokissa (p84) and Ratua (p84) across the channel from Luganville on Santo.

Hotels

Hotels are a viable and relatively inexpensive option, especially in New Caledonia, for those who wish to move around rather than base themselves at a resort. These range from simple, good-value places to large operations with upmarket rooms, quality furnishings, pools and appealing restaurants. The greatest range is in Noumea. Many visitors hire rental cars and drive around the islands, exploring at their own pace. This is the best way to see Grande Terre, and most country towns of any size have a reasonable hotel that can be prebooked. All three Loyalty Islands as well as Île des Pins can also be explored in this fashion. Most hotels also have a restaurant attached that is open for breakfast and dinner.

In Vanuatu you'll really only find hotels in Port Vila (which has the widest range) and Luganville. Choices range from budget rooms with shared facilities to motel-style rooms with satellite TVs, fridges and en suite bathrooms, up to spacious self-contained studios and family apartments.

Local Accommodation

Bungalows and gîtes are budget, family-run affairs, and offer particularly good value in New Caledonia. *Accueil en Tribu* (tribal lodgings) are the best places to meet Kanak people and learn about their culture. Accommodation is usually within a family compound in thatched-roof huts with separate bathroom facilities, and if you prebook, meals are available. Local accommodation is often found in spectacular locations, all over Grande Terre, on each of the Loyalty Islands and on Île des Pins.

In Vanuatu's outer islands (everywhere outside Efate, Santo and Tanna), accommodation is limited to bamboo-and-palm-thatch bungalows and the occasional 'cyclone-proof' concrete guesthouse. The bungalows offer little in terms of comfort and facilities, with thin mattresses, shared bathroom facilities and limited electricity (by generator or solar power), but there's beauty in their simplicity and isolation, and the owners are very welcoming. Such accommodation is often set in terrific by-the-beach locations or close to attractions such as volcanoes or waterfalls. They can be good places to meet other travellers, though in remote locations the owner

PLAN YOUR TRIP WHICH ISLAND?

OVER-WATER BUNGALOWS

New Caledonia and Vanuatu both have a set of gorgeous over-water resort bungalows. Those at New Caledonia's L'Escapade (p138) resort on Îlot Maître, a 20-minute boat ride from Noumea, have private access down to the water. They sleep no more than two, so families are relegated to the rooms on the island itself.

may have only one or two bungalows in total. Where travellers gather, such as Mt Yasur on Tanna, expect to find plenty of bungalow operations, some approaching a decent level of sophistication.

Hostels & Camping

Camping is very popular on all of New Caledonia's islands and there are plenty of campgrounds. These are often on land attached to local accommodation offering thatched huts or bungalows, and there's a good chance that meals will be available if that's the case. There is usually a separate building with toilet and shower facilities and, in many cases, hot water. Campgrounds generally charge per tent site and per adult. Hostels are not huge in New Caledonia, although Noumea's Auberge de Jeunesse (p135) is incredibly popular and there is a new purpose-built hostel at Poé Beach (p151) on Grande Terre.

Vanuatu has few official campgrounds, but almost any bungalow operation with a spare patch of land will allow you to pitch a tent (usually for around 1000VT) and will sometimes have tents available. On Efate there's a campground at Havannah Harbour and camping is available on Tranquillity Island Resort (p60). If you're embarking on an overnight trek, camping may be necessary. Your guide will organise it for you and obtain the required permission – don't set up a tent without asking permission first. On Ambrym there are dedicated campsites at the base of the volcanoes. The only hostels in Vanuatu are in Port Vila and Luganville, where several places have dorm beds, self-catering kitchens and common areas.

Activities

Countless square kilometres of warm tropical water, pristine lagoons and long stretches of beach are the most obvious attractions, but there's more to Vanuatu and New Caledonia than just watery pursuits.

Diving & Snorkelling

Vanuatu is a world-class choice for divers and snorkellers. Resorts in Santo's Luganville and on its surrounding islands are particularly focused on satisfying the travelling diver. Most islands with resorts off Santo also operate their own dive centres. Check out any packages on offer before booking your room; it may be cheaper to book a room and a dive package at the same time. On Santo, even some of the simpler resorts offer smart, clean accommodation with secure rooms for washing and storing dive gear. Wrecks include the USS *President Coolidge,* and there's great diving at Million Dollar

---

THE FRENCH FACTOR

If you're not travelling on a flights-and-accommodation package and the French language is not one of your strong points, you may like to get organised before heading out from Noumea on your voyage of exploration around New Caledonia.

English is not commonly spoken once you are out of Noumea, so getting your point across may not be easy. As well as French, there are 28 Kanak languages spoken in New Caledonia, including different languages on each of the Loyalty Islands and two on Ouvéa. Everyone can speak French, but learning English has never been a priority.

Organising a flight or boat, accommodation and rental car by yourself when you can't speak or read French can be difficult. Think about getting a local Noumea travel agency (p202) to book everything for you, especially if you're heading out to the Loyalty Islands or Île des Pins. Being prepared will not kill the adventure.

French is one of Vanuatu's official languages but English is more widely spoken on the islands, especially among people involved with visitors (bungalow owners, guides etc). The national language is Bislama, a form of pidgin English. There are numerous Francophone pockets throughout the islands, including Malekula and Santo, where French schools and churches have been based.

Top: Diving the SS
President Coolidge
(p81), Vanuatu

Bottom: Local men on
Vanuatu's Manbush
Trail (p70)

GRANT DIXON / GETTY IMAGES ©

Point, off Aore Island, and snorkelling at Champagne Beach and Port Olry.

Other superb islands for divers include Efate's nearby Hideaway Island, Tranquillity Island, and Pele and Ngunu. Established operators in Port Vila can take you to these and dozens more reef and wreck sites. Off Malekula the vehicle-free Maskelynes, home to coral reefs and marine conservation areas, and the Uri Marine Protected Area are great snorkelling destinations. Tanna's west coast dive sites are now accessible thanks to a new outfit based at White Grass Ocean Resort (p68).

Resorts offering scuba diving are less common in New Caledonia. Most dive places are attached to budget camping or bungalow accommodation, or run as independent businesses. Such dive clubs can be found on all coasts of Grande Terre, on each of the Loyalty Islands and at Île des Pins. With Grande Terre and Ouvéa's lagoons both World Heritage-listed, diving is becoming a popular activity in New Caledonia.

Water Sports

You could get dizzy with all the water sports on offer in Port Vila; lagoon-located resorts often offer guests the use of glass-bottomed boats, kayaks, snorkelling gear and occasionally even small fishing boats. Resorts can also arrange more-advanced water activities such as diving, jet-boat rides and parasailing; resort pick-up is usually free.

Every water sport imaginable is available in New Caledonia. Being on the coast, with gorgeous beaches at Baie des Citrons and Anse Vata, Noumea offers water activities from jet skiing to kitesurfing, wakeboarding, windsurfing and sailing, and it has taxiboats. Near Bourail, La Roche Percée is known for its surfing and Poé Beach for all sorts of water sports. Head out to the Loyalty Islands and Île des Pins for more water-bound adventures. On Ouvéa's magnificent lagoon, Canio (p162) water sports centre has windsurfers, small yachts, hobie cats and kayaks for hire. And of course, there is spectacular snorkelling all over the place.

Adventure

One of Vanuatu's most popular adventures is the trip to Tanna's bubbling and exploding active volcano, Mt Yasur. It can be done on a long day or overnight package trip from Port Vila, but the best idea is to stay at one of the budget island bungalows at the volcano's base and hike up for sunrise and/or sunset. Other volcanic adventures include the much more arduous Ambrym hike and the crater-lake trek on Ambae.

Organised adventures include the full-day Millennium Cave tour on Santo, kayaking and mountain-biking tours and jungle ziplining. Hire a quad-bike or all-terrain buggy and go off-road in Port Vila and Luganville.

Likewise, New Caledonia offers its share of adventure sports, from mountain biking in Grande Terre's Parc Provincial de la Rivière Bleue and Le Parc des Grandes Fougères to flying in a microlight over the Heart of Voh and the massive blue hole in the lagoon. Whale-watching excursions head out from mid-July to mid-September.

In the Loyalty Islands you can join Charly Aema Tours (p162) to uninhabited islands on Ouvéa; get a guide to lead you to magnificent Shabadran on Maré; or head to Lifou and explore caves. On Île des Pins you can join a *pirogue* (outrigger canoe) adventure, followed by a walk to La Piscine Naturelle, or head out on an unforgettable Nokanhui Atoll boat excursion.

Hiking

Hiking or trekking opportunities abound in Vanuatu. Take a volcano trek on Ambrym; hike to the volcanic lakes on Ambae; mountain-trek on Santo; and hike to remote villages on Malekula, as just a few starting options. All of these treks require a guide, road or boat transfers and usually the payment of *kastom* (traditional ownership) fees, all of which can easily be organised locally.

The great hike in New Caledonia is the five-day, 123km Grande Randonnée in southern Grande Terre, but if you are after something less intensive, head to Parc Provincial de la Rivière Bleue in southern Grande Terre or Le Parc des Grandes Fougères near La Foa. Both parks offer hikes ranging from 45 minutes up to seven hours. The popular Plateau de Dogny hike from Sarraméa takes six to eight hours, while the Sentier de la Petite Cascade (Little Waterfall Walk) is one for families from nearby Farino.

Horse Riding

Vanuatu offers riders the choice of horse-riding ranches in Port Vila and Santo, where you can arrange beach and forest trail rides. Ratua Private Island Resort (p84) also has horse riding. Tanna is famous for its horses, but you'll need to ask around at your resort or bungalow to see if there are any available for riding.

Horse riding is popular in New Caledonia, particularly on the western coastal plains of Grande Terre, which is cowboy country. Sarraméa, near La Foa, has excellent riding opportunities and there are companies operating tours further up the island at Bourail, Koné and Koumac. While you can't ride them, horse enthusiasts will want to keep their eyes open for wild horses when driving in Grande Terre's Far North.

Local Culture

In Vanuatu you only need to travel to any outer island and stay in a village bungalow to experience local culture. For a fee, villages on some islands can organise traditional dances and cultural demonstrations at short notice: some of the best are the Big Nambas and Small Nambas of Malekula, the Rom dance on Ambrym, the Snake Dance on Motalava and the traditional village ceremonies on Tanna.

A popular cultural experience is to try kava. In Port Vila and Luganville the many kava bars are less-than-traditional affairs where women and visitors are welcome, and there's a social atmosphere. If you're visiting a village as part of a cultural tour, kava tasting may be included. Many of Port Vila's resorts have some kind of 'Melanesian' night, with dancing, opportunities to try local food and, of course, taste kava. All island villages have at least one – usually many – *nakamals* (kava bars), which open at 5pm; ask locally about joining in.

In New Caledonia your best way to interact with Kanak people is by staying at tribal lodgings. This is easy to do on all the Loyalty Islands, on Île des Pins and in a number of areas on Grande Terre, particularly at Hienghène on the northeast coast. Keep in mind that there is still a huge cultural and economic divide between New Caledonia's Kanaks and the Caldoche (locally born descendants of Europeans). A referendum on independence from France is to be held by the end of 2018, and the Loyalty Islands and Province Nord are heavily Kanak and pro-independence. Province Sud, in particular Greater Noumea, which is home to 64% of the country's population, is staunchly pro-France and anti-independence. It would be fair to say that Kanaks feel particularly hard done by in their own lands. That said, many are very friendly and welcoming to visitors.

Day Spas

Most resorts in Vanuatu and New Caledonia offer some kind of massage service. Vanuatu's Santo has a couple of good boutique resorts offering day-spa facilities, including Moyyan House by the Sea (p88) and Aore Island (p84). Many of Port Vila's resorts have full day spas, including Erakor Island Resort (p55) and Poppy's on the Lagoon (p55), and there are several Thai massage places in town.

New Caledonia's big new addition, the Sheraton Déva Resort & Spa on Grande Terre's west coast near Bourail, offers all sorts of creature comforts and a brand-new golf course.

Plan Your Trip

Diving

The waters surrounding Vanuatu and New Caledonia provide divers with impressive stories to tell of awesome walls, high-voltage drift dives, close encounters with sharks and manta rays, luscious soft and hard corals, iconic wrecks and gorgeous reefs replete with multi-hued tropical fish.

Shipwrecks

Vanuatu's Wrecks

MV Konanda This former island trader sits on a sandy bottom 26m down near Port Vila.

Star of Russia Built in 1874 by the builders of the *Titanic*, this ship now rests 36m down in Port Vila harbour.

Tasman Flying Boat This Qantas S26 flying boat is located 40m down in Port Vila harbour.

WWII Corsair fighter plane This intact relic of WWII sits in 30m of water in northern Efate.

USS President Coolidge Sunk by a friendly mine in 1942, this is the largest, most accessible shipwreck in the world.

USS Tucker This destroyer struck a friendly mine off Santo in 1942.

New Caledonia's Wrecks

Dieppoise This wooden patrol boat is 26m underwater off the coast of the Grande Terre.

Snark A Panamanian cargo ship sunk off Noumea in 1942, where there are frequent sightings of leopard and black spotted rays.

Humboldt This Palangrier was sunk near Noumea in 1993.

Planning Your Dive

The best and most popular spots in both Vanuatu and New Caledonia are serviced by first-rate dive centres. The most popular dive towns (such as Luganville, Santo) have diver-friendly accommodation with secure scuba-gear wash and storage facilities. There are several islands off Vanuatu that have their own dive centres.

When to Go

Waters are warm year-round and magnificent at most times – think turquoise coral shallows, inky-blue seas and idyllic backdrops as you travel to and from the sites.

Diving is possible year-round, although conditions vary according to the season and location. Visibility is reduced in the wet season (which is also the cyclone season, from November to March), as the water is muddied by sediments brought into the sea by the rivers. Areas that are exposed to currents might also become heavy with particles. On average, visibility ranges from 15m to 50m.

The water temperature peaks at a warm 29°C during the rainy season, but can drop to 20°C in New Caledonia from July to September. Vanuatu's waters are warmer; water temperatures peak at 30°C but can drop to 26°C between April and October. Though it's possible to dive without a wetsuit, most divers wear at least a Lycra wetsuit to protect themselves from abrasions. A 3mm tropical wetsuit is most appropriate.

Where to Go

New Caledonia

New Caledonia's main claim to fame is its lagoon – which, at 24,000 sq metres, is the largest natural lagoon in the world. It's protected by a barrier reef that extends more than 1600km. There are dive sites and dive centres off the north and east coast of Grande Terre, and sites on the islands of Île des Pins, Ouvéa and Lifou.

Off Noumea, Passe de Boulari is an excellent site. Coral is not the strong point of the dive, but for fish and manta-ray action it's unbeatable. Passe de Dumbéa is also exciting; it plays home to schools of groupers from October to December.

In Hienghène, on the northeast coast of Grande Terre, you can't help but be impressed by Tidwan, Cathédrale and Récif de Kaun; all boast an outstanding topography comprising canyons, chasms and fissures, plus prolific marine life, including parrotfish in October and November.

The area off Poindimié, also on the northeast coast of Grande Terre, is more renowned for reef life, soft corals and nudibranches. There are some 50 dive sites with canyons and arches around here, and many are loaded with colourful gorgons. Sharks, including whale sharks, are frequently seen.

Île des Pins features some stunning sites. Vallée des Gorgones, off Gadji's reef, is a killer, with an excellent drop-off adorned with a profusion of graceful sea fans and a dense array of reef fish. Récif de Kasmira is another superb site, featuring a coral mound ranging from 3m to 17m, and plenty of fish and leopard sharks. If you're after something unusual, try Grotte de la Troisième (Cave of the Third). About 8km north of Kuto, it features an inland cave filled with crystal-clear fresh water. You'll navigate inside the cave, at about 6m, wending your way among stalactites and stalagmites. Beware of silt build-up, though.

The sites in the Loyalty Islands are also well worth bookmarking. Lifou's signature dives are Gorgones Reef and Shoji Reef, where delicate sea fans wafting in the current are the main attraction. Keep your eyes peeled for pelagic sightings, including tuna, sharks, rays and barracudas. Tomoko Point, also off Lifou, is a grotto and tunnel-filled spot. It's a hotspot for lobsters and features the occasional shark. Ouvéa offers pristine drift-diving sites, protected from trade winds, south of the atoll.

Vanuatu

Vanuatu's diving spots are based around the main islands of Efate and Santo. A few strokes from Santo's shore, the legendary USS *President Coolidge* is trumpeted as the best and most accessible wreck dive in the world. The sheer proportions of this behemoth are overwhelming: resting on its side in 21m to 67m of water off Luganville, the *Coolidge* is 200m long and 25m wide. It's shrouded with a palpable aura, and much has been written about its history. Amazingly, more than 50 years after its demise it's still in very good shape. It's not heavily overgrown with marine life, so you will see numerous fittings and artefacts, including weaponry, gas masks, trenching tools, trucks, rows of toilets, a porcelain statue (the 'Lady'), a pool, personal belongings abandoned by 5000 soldiers, and all the fixtures of a luxury cruise liner. In 1983 the Vanuatu government declared that no salvage or recovery of any artefact would be allowed from this wreck. A minimum of five to 10 dives is recommended to get a glimpse of the whole vessel. Although nearly all dives on the *Coolidge* are deep (more than 30m), it is suitable for novice divers. You'll start at shallower depths (about 25m) and go progressively deeper as you become more familiar with the diving.

The only downside is that the *Coolidge* has overshadowed other dive sites in Vanuatu. In Santo, other wrecks worthy of exploration include the USS *Tucker,* a destroyer that struck a friendly mine in 1942.

ISLAND RESORT DIVING IN VANUATU

• •

Island resorts with in-house diving centres:

Tranquillity Island Resort (p60), off Efate

Aore Island Resort (p84), off Luganville, Santo

Bokissa Island Dive (☑30030; www.bokissa.com), between Aore and Tutuba

Hideaway Island Resort (p54), off Efate

PLAN YOUR TRIP DIVING

If you need a break from wreck dives, don't miss the opportunity to sample some truly excellent reef dives off Santo, including Cindy's Reef and Tutuba Point. That said, Santo's prominent dive site is Million Dollar Point, where thousands of tonnes of military paraphernalia were discarded by the US Navy when it left the country post WWII. Divers swim among the tangle of cranes, bulldozers, trucks and other construction hardware in less than 30m and finish their dive by exploring a small shipwreck in the shallows.

Efate has plenty of good reef and wreck dives, many a short boat ride off outlying islands, and there are numerous dive operators based in Port Vila. Worthwhile sites include Hat Island and Paul's Rock, both off the north side of Efate, Tranquillity Island, Hideaway Island and Pango Wall. Wreck dives include the *Corsair,* a WWII fighter plane in 30m of water near Pele Island, the trading ship *Konanda,* the cargo vessel *Semele Federesen* and the 19th-century sailing ship *Star of Russia,* in 35m of water.

Vanuatu's newest dive adventure is on Tanna's west coast, where blue holes, reefs, caves and drop-offs offer plenty of adventure.

DIVING COSTS

The prices below give a general gauge as to the costs of diving in Vanuatu and New Caledonia. Prices may be higher or lower, depending on the dive centre.

➡ Introductory dive in New Caledonia with equipment 8000 CFP

➡ Single dive with equipment 8000 CFP

➡ 10-dive package with equipment 56,000 CFP

➡ Introductory dive in Vanuatu with equipment 8000VT

➡ Single dive with equipment 8000VT

➡ 10-dive package with equipment 54,000VT

Dive Centres

In most cases, the standards of diving facilities are high in the South Pacific. You'll find professional and reliable dive centres staffed with qualified instructors catering to divers of all levels.

New Caledonia has its own regulations in regard to underwater diving, as professional dive centres must also hold a tourist licence to operate; these outfits conform to international courses and qualifications. The majority of dive centres are affiliated with an internationally recognised diving organisation – eg PADI, SSI, NAUI and CMAS. They are mostly hotel or island based, but welcome walk-in guests. The staff members usually speak English, and Japanese-speaking instructors can be found in New Caledonia.

In Vanuatu, check your dive operator's qualifications and safety equipment, as maintenance and adherence to safety standards might not be met.

Centres are open year-round, most of them every day, but it's best to reserve your dive a day in advance. Depending on the area, centres typically offer two-tank dives (usually in the morning) or single dives (one in the morning and one in the afternoon). Many sites are offshore and involve a boat ride.

Be aware that even if common standards apply, each dive centre has its own personality and style. It's a good idea to visit the place first to get the feel of the operation.

How Much?

Diving in the South Pacific is expensive in comparison to most destinations in Asia, the Caribbean or the Red Sea. In Vanuatu, dive packages (eg five or 10 dives) are usually cheaper than in New Caledonia. In New Caledonia, buy a Carte Plongée for 5000 CFP, which is valid for one year and gives holders a minimum 15% discount at 10 dive centres around the country.

Gear hire may or may not be included in the price of the dive, so it's not a bad idea to bring your own equipment (though not weights) if you plan to dive a lot.

SAFETY GUIDELINES FOR DIVING

Before embarking on a scuba diving, skin diving or snorkelling trip, carefully consider the following points to ensure a safe and enjoyable experience:

➡ Possess a current diving certification card from a recognised scuba diving instructional agency (if scuba diving).

➡ Be sure you are healthy and feel comfortable diving.

➡ Obtain reliable information about physical and environmental conditions at the dive site (eg from a reputable local dive operation).

➡ Be aware of local laws, regulations and etiquette about marine life and the environment.

➡ Dive only at sites within your realm of experience; if available, engage the services of a competent, professionally trained dive instructor or dive master.

➡ Be aware that underwater conditions vary significantly from one region, or even site, to another. Seasonal changes can significantly alter any site and dive conditions. These differences influence the way divers dress for a dive and what diving techniques they use.

➡ Ask about the environmental characteristics that can affect your diving and how local trained divers deal with these considerations.

Required Documents

If you're a certified diver, don't forget to bring your C-card and logbook with you. Dive centres welcome divers regardless of their training background, provided they can produce a certificate from an internationally recognised agency.

Responsible Diving

In order to preserve the ecology and beauty of reefs, there are a number things you can do to make a difference when diving. Firstly, while on the boat you should never use anchors on the reef, and take care not to ground boats on coral. Once you're in the water, avoid touching or standing on living marine organisms or dragging equipment across the reef. Polyps can be damaged by even the gentlest contact. If you must hold on to the reef, only touch exposed rock or dead coral. Also be conscious of your fins.

Even without contact, the surge from fin strokes near the reef can damage delicate organisms. Take care not to kick up clouds of sand, which can smother organisms. Maintaining proper buoyancy control is also something you should practise, as major damage can be done by divers descending too fast and colliding with the reef.

If diving in underwater caves, take great care. Try to spend as little time within them as possible as your air bubbles may be caught within the roof and thereby leave organisms high and dry. Take turns to inspect the interior of a small cave.

Resist the temptation to collect or buy corals or shells or to loot marine archaeological sites (mainly shipwrecks). You'll also need to ensure that you take home all your rubbish and any litter you may find as well. Plastics in particular are a serious threat to marine life.

Finally, minimise your disturbance of marine animals. Do not feed fish and *never* ride on the backs of turtles.

Plan Your Trip
Travel with Children

Few regions of the world are as family-friendly as the South Pacific. With endless sunshine, sandy beaches, swimming, snorkelling and more on offer, kids will find plenty to keep them active and interested, and you're likely to have an unforgettable family holiday.

Best Regions for Children

Port Vila
From sedate snorkelling to speedy jet-boat rides, you can book an activity that suits your family from one of the waterfront 'activity huts'.

Noumea
Your resort will probably have a luxurious pool, but nothing beats the family atmosphere of the city beaches of Anse Vata and Baie des Citrons.

Amédée Islet
A day trip to this island off Noumea involves a boat ride; a French lighthouse to climb; snorkelling; dancing; and seeing stripy sea snakes.

Tanna
If you think the kids can handle the dangers of visiting an active volcano, take a trip to Mt Yasur. Some resorts won't let children under seven go on the trip.

Loyalty Islands
Great for kids. Consider staying in traditional tribal accommodation; while basic, it's almost always clean and comfortable.

Vanuatu for Kids

Children and their parents will love Vanuatu; ni-Van kids are outgoing, smiling and welcoming, and so are their parents. Vanuatu has catered for visiting children for decades, so resorts are usually well equipped to look after them. Some in Port Vila have kids clubs, family apartments and lots of activities. Others are child-free or only allow children during Australian and New Zealand school holidays, so plan to meet your needs. Port Vila has plenty of kid-friendly activities. If your children are sand-castle fanatics, keep in mind that not all beaches in Vanuatu are covered in white sand; quite a few are coral or black-sand beaches.

Where in Vanuatu?

Where you take the kids in Vanuatu will depend on your level of adventurousness, but there are a couple of points to keep in mind. Most of the resorts are around Port Vila and Luganville on Santo, which are relatively easy to get to. Tanna also has some good resorts near the airport, so that trip to Mt Yasur is certainly on the cards, and older kids will be in awe of the volcano. Outer island travel is often slow-going in the back of trucks on rough roads or by speedboats that may or may not have life jackets, or on foot. Some consideration should be given to the risks or difficulty of travelling to outer islands with young children.

New Caledonia for Kids

New Caledonia is quite different to Vanuatu: don't expect your children to be cheek-pinched or whisked away from you to be treated like little kings and queens. They'll still have plenty of fun interactions with the locals; they just won't be as intense and gushing as they can be on other islands in the South Pacific. New Caledonia is a little more formal, too, with Noumea's better restaurants requiring a certain level of decorum. Noumea's aquarium, museum and cultural centre are of a high standard, while touristy highlights such as the Tchou Tchou Train are just plain great fun.

Where in New Caledonia?

New Caledonia's transport infrastructure has been built and maintained with support from France. Domestic air and boat travel is extremely efficient, the roads are amazing, and rental vehicles are available everywhere. While everything you need for a fun family holiday is in or around Noumea, exploring Grande Terre, Île des Pins and the three Loyalty Islands is very feasible as a family. If you're heading to the Loyalties or Île des Pins, it would pay to prebook your transport out there, a rental car and accommodation.

Children's Highlights

Snorkelling

Hideaway Island (p47) With some guidance, kids will love posting a letter at Hideaway Island's underwater post office. It's in Mele Bay, near Port Vila in Vanuatu.

Big Blue Vanuatu (p51) Children aged five and up (with their parents) can join an organised snorkelling safari that includes a lesson and a floating device if necessary.

Île aux Canards (p132) Known in English as Duck Island, this great spot is a five-minute taxiboat ride from Noumea's Anse Vata beach and features an underwater snorkelling path.

La Piscine Naturelle (p167) Head to Île des Pins in New Caledonia and take the kids snorkelling in its natural, protected aquarium. If they've not snorkelled before, see how they handle the resort's pool first.

Adventure

Mele Cascades (p47) Climbing and swimming at the Mele Cascades in Port Vila is terrific natural fun (though it involves a bit of a walk to the top).

Mt Yasur (p66) Nothing will beat looking into a real live volcano. Give tweens and teens a new appreciation of geography with a visit to Vanuatu's Tanna. They'll be driven over an ash plain and up a steam-spouting road, before seeing a fireworks display of real live lava. Cool.

Remote Islands Show kids how simple life can be by swapping the luxury resort for a bungalow on a remote island. In Vanuatu almost any island is remote but try Port Olry (p86) or Lonnoc Beach (p85) on Santo. In New Caledonia, try Moague (p162) 'tribal lodging' on Ouvéa in New Caledonia's Loyalty Islands.

Le Parc des Grandes Fougères (p148) For a break from the beach, head to the Park of the Great Ferns near La Foa on Grande Terre for a walk in the bush. Half the fun is driving there.

Dance

Rom dance (p39) Children will be entranced by the islanders' dancing, singing and chanting; in Vanuatu, see the Rom dance on Ambrym.

Leweton Cultural Village (p81) If you're visiting, take the kids to a dance at this cultural centre near Luganville on Santo.

Ekasup Cultural Village (p50) If you're sticking to Port Vila, you can see dancing at this cultural village.

Tjibaou Cultural Centre (p131) It's a little bit more difficult to see dance in New Caledonia, but there's a Kanak dance at this cultural centre in Noumea each Tuesday and Thursday.

Markets

Port Vila (p56) Kids love the colour, smells and sounds of Vanuatu's wonderful produce markets. Port Vila's waterfront market in particular is bright, loud and jam-packed with goodies.

Noumea (p129) Visit Le Marché on a lazy weekend and your troop might happen upon a musical combo playing by the fish section. Even better, there are circus-type fair rides in the parking lot.

DON'T LEAVE HOME WITHOUT

You'll find the usual supplies you might need in supermarkets and pharmacies in New Caledonia's main towns, but you may want to plan ahead for Vanuatu:

➡ Disposable nappies are available at supermarkets and stores in Port Vila and Luganville in Vanuatu, and can sometimes be found in shops on smaller islands; however, buy up in Port Vila just in case. If you can, buy biodegradable nappies and nappy wipes in your own country, as rubbish disposal is a problem in Vanuatu and disposable nappies take decades to decompose.

➡ Baby food can be purchased in Port Vila's supermarkets but take your own to other islands.

➡ It's often cheaper to bring your own insect repellent to Vanuatu.

➡ To avoid malaria, consider bringing insecticide-impregnated mosquito nets to Vanuatu. It can also be a good idea to impregnate your children's clothing with permethrin insecticide before you leave.

Planning

Before You Go

If you're looking for some parental time out while on your family holiday, make enquiries about the kids club at your resort before you book. Confirm that it will be operating when you are there; some of Vanuatu's kids clubs only operate during Australian school-holiday periods (a good time to go, as there will be plenty of other children around).

Teach your children a few words of French for New Caledonia, and some common words of Bislama for Vanuatu.

Accommodation

Families often book into Vanuatu and New Caledonia's large resorts for that 'family-holiday experience' complete with kids club, kids meals and so on, but smaller family-run hotels and bungalows are worth a look, too. Accommodation on Vanuatu's outer islands can be challenging for kids; basic bungalow accommodation often doesn't come with flush toilets, running water or electricity. In contrast, even the cheapest bungalow in New Caledonia will have clean sheets and electricity, with a clean bathroom not too far away.

Health

New Caledonia has well-stocked pharmacies on all of its islands that can offer basic healthcare advice. In Vanuatu, pharmacies and large hospitals are limited to Luganville and Port Vila.

Dehydration develops very quickly in children when a fever and/or diarrhoea and vomiting occur. Bottled water is available in both countries, though tap water can be drunk in most areas of New Caledonia.

The presence of malaria in Vanuatu is a concern on outer islands; dress children in long-sleeved tops and long pants during the times when mosquitoes are biting, and keep them covered in insect repellent. Malaria and dengue fever are much more dangerous to children than to adults.

There is no malaria in New Caledonia, and no rabies in either country.

Regions at a Glance

These two different Pacific countries, located a hop, skip and jump away from each other, both offer travellers excellent experiences. Decide what you're looking for – volcanoes? dugongs? adventure? – and suss it out island by intoxicating island. Vanuatu, away from its smooth-faced resorts, has a rugged side to it; get dirty in its black-sand earth and explore its smiling culture, red-hot volcanoes and unique underwater worlds. Similarly, behind New Caledonia's glossy brochures is an intriguing interior of waterfalls, rainforests, mountains, dry coastal plains and distinctive wildlife. Its lagoon is the biggest in the world and, thanks to the country's top-notch infrastructure, it's easy to explore. Visit the Loyalty Islands to enjoy the vibrant Kanak way of life.

Efate

Wining & Dining
Adventure
Islands

Wining & Dining
Port Vila and Havannah Harbour have the best restaurants, bars and shopping in Vanuatu. Dine on island seafood and sink a beer or cocktail at a waterfront bar as the sun sets.

Adventure
Try a scuba dive in the morning, a climb up a cascading waterfall in the afternoon and an evening excursion to an island for dinner. You'll have options to zipline, parasail or hire an all-terrain buggy.

Islands
The choice is here: go for very basic island accommodation in northern Efate or step up a notch and stay at resorts on the islands of Iririki, Erakor, Hideaway and Tranquillity.

p47

Epi

Dugongs
Island Life
Fishing

Dugongs
Sure, you might have to spend a while underwater, but Lamen Bay on Epi is a hotspot for dugong sightings. If they're not there when you are, be consoled by the presence of giant turtles.

Island Life
Stay at inviting guesthouses in Lamen Bay and Valesdir, where you can enjoy island hospitality and a taste of village life.

Fishing
Watch as locals bring in the morning's fishing haul, and see if they'll take you out with them next time they sail. Or borrow an outrigger canoe or kayak and try reef fishing for yourself.

p62

Tanna

Volcanoes
Cargo Cults
Culture

Volcanoes

It's smoking, it's spitting lava and you can walk to its edge in some 45 minutes (or get there in five minutes by 4WD): Mt Yasur is one of the world's most accessible volcanoes and, even when napping, it's seriously spectacular.

Cargo Cults

Cargo cults are a thing of legend (and documentaries) but they are alive and well (and chanting loudly) on Tanna. The main cargo cult on Tanna is John Frum.

Culture

There's a certain magic on this island, and a day trip to a *kastom* (traditional) village will give you the chance to learn more about it.

p63

Malekula

Hiking
Island Paradise
Cannibal Life

Hiking

Organised hikes in Malekula's northern highlands will take you to *kastom* villages and the domain of the infamous Big Nambas and Small Nambas tribes.

Island Paradise

Down in southern Malekula, near Lamap airport, the Maskelyne Islands are perfect for spending a couple of days surrounded by mangroves and reefs and not much else. Bring your snorkelling gear, a torch, a good book and chill out.

Cannibal Life

Hire a guide to visit the cannibal sites and burial grounds of chiefs in northern Malekula and hear haunting stories of tribal warfare, skulls and conch shells.

p68

Ambrym

Dance
Volcanoes
Carvings

Dance

The island's signature dance, the Rom dance, is entrancing. Hike to a small village and witness the combination of foot thumping and chanting.

Volcanoes

Ambrym's two volcanoes glow red in the night's clouds. Guides throughout the island can take you to the source. If camping by a volcano is your kind of thing, this is the place to do it.

Carvings

The performance space of the Rom dance becomes a mini market when the dancing is over; expect to see a huge variety of sleek carvings for sale. The larger-than-life *tamtam* (slit drum) carvings are amazing.

p75

Espiritu Santo

Scuba Diving
Blue Holes
Beaches

Scuba Diving

The wreck of the luxury liner USS *President Coolidge* is lauded as one of the most accessible wreck dives in the world. Plenty of other great dives, too.

Blue Holes

These lovely deep pools of blue water and fish are dotted around Santo; dive in and relax in the exhilarating pools just as WWII soldiers did half a century ago.

Beaches

Champagne Beach alone is almost reason enough to go to Santo; it's certainly why cruise ships dock here (yes, at the beach itself!). If the beach is packed, head north to Port Olry.

p78

Pentecost

Land Diving
Adventure
Waterfalls

Land Diving

The spectacle of *naghol* (land diving) has become so popular that it's performed almost daily during the season (April to June). Watch local boys and men jump from carefully constructed towers with nothing but vines to stop them hitting the ground.

Adventure

You might want to tackle a hike on this mountainous island. Hiring a guide is a great idea for exploring the south; try heading over to the east coast from Pangi.

Waterfalls

The name Waterfall Village says it all; swim in the cascading pools that form the end of Waterfall Falls, north of Lonorore airfield.

p88

Noumea

French Culture
Food
Sights

French Culture

Antipodeans rejoice: just three hours from Brisbane you can find a completely French experience. The language, the folk, the niceties and even the rather Mediterranean weather all scream France.

Food

Food-wise, Noumea is outstanding, with wonderful bakeries, beautiful bistros and waterside bars serving up aperitifs and champagne. Hit the fresh-food market for wonderful delights; even the supermarkets have a certain French flair.

Sights

Noumea packs a punch with its sights and activities, from a world-class aquarium to well-preserved historic buildings and the astounding Tjibaou Cultural Centre. Baie des Citrons and Anse Vata are lovely beaches.

p129

Grande Terre

Nature
Scuba Diving
Open Roads

Nature

There is so much to explore here from Parc Provincial de la Rivière Bleue in the Far South to hiking in Le Parc des Grandes Fougères near La Foa, to flying over the Heart of Voh and the lagoon from Koné.

Scuba Diving

With dive centres and sites on the east and west coasts, Grande Terre is a great island for diving in and around the World Heritage-listed lagoon.

Open Roads

Grande Terre's superb roads must rank as the best bitumen in the region. Take it slow and divert into the interior whenever you get the chance.

p129

Loyalty Islands

Island Culture
Lagoon Life
Food

Island Culture

There's a relaxed vibe on these islands. Most of the bungalow accommodation is Kanak-owned, so you'll get to know the culture as well as the islands themselves.

Lagoon Life

There are myriad ways to explore the waters around the Loyalties; scuba dive, head out on a snorkelling day trip or simply swim. Unique experiences include seeing turtles from bridges and feeding fish in enclosed natural aquariums.

Food

From fish barbecued on a deserted island to the traditional underground-oven-cooked *bougna* (yam, taro and sweet potatoes with chicken, fish or crustaceans), exploring the local menu won't disappoint. Even the islands' 'fast food' is often delectable.

p155

Île des Pins

Seafood
Bays
Boating

Seafood

There's a tradition of feasting on seafood on this island; book ahead and indulge in freshly cooked lobster or try seafood *bougna*. The island's other speciality is Île des Pins snail.

Bays

Discover natural pools embedded in coral and chill out on sunny white-sand beaches, with outstanding snorkelling just offshore. Baie de Kuto and Baie de Kanuméra are superb, as is the snorkelling at La Piscine Naturelle.

Boating

Each morning *pirogues* (outrigger canoes) head out from Baie de St Joseph; get yourself on one for a wonderful traditional-style boating excursion. Another superb day trip heads out to Nokanhui Atoll.

p163

On the Road

Vanuatu

📞 678 / POP 281,500

Best Places to Stay

➡ Rocky Ridge Bungalows (p68)

➡ Havannah (p60)

➡ Traveller's Budget Motel (p54)

➡ Espiritu (p83)

➡ Lope Lope Adventure Lodge (p87)

Best Places to Eat

➡ Oyster Island (p87)

➡ Market Meal Booths (p84), Luganville

➡ Kesorn's Exotic Thai Kitchen (p57)

➡ L'Houstalet (p57)

Why Go?

Vanuatu is a Pacific island adventure far beyond any notions of cruise-ship ports and flashy resorts. Deserted beaches, ancient culture, remote and rugged islands and world-class diving are just a small part of the magnetism of this scattered 80-plus island archipelago.

Where else can you hike up a crater to stare down into a magma-filled active volcano then ashboard back down, snorkel in a blue hole and drink kava with the local village chief – all in the same day? The resorts and restaurants of Port Vila have little in common with traditional *kastom* (custom) village life in the outer islands, but it's contrasts like these that make Vanuatu a surprise and a challenge.

Vanuatu was slammed by Cyclone Pam in 2015, but its people, resilient and laid-back as ever, take life in smiling strides.

It takes a little time, effort and a healthy sense of adventure to truly explore Vanuatu's islands, but it's worth every bit of it.

When to Go
Port Vila

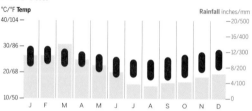

May–Jul Warm and dry; high season. Pentecost's land diving is in full swing.

Aug–Oct Avoid Australian school holidays and enjoy mostly dry sunny days.

Nov–Mar Wet (cyclone) season, so accommodation is plentiful but transport may be delayed.

EFATE

POP 66,000 / AREA 915 SQ KM

Efate is Vanuatu's main island, politically, economically, industrially and in terms of population and tourism. Even so, outside of the capital Port Vila it's pretty low-key, with some of the village life you'll find on other islands.

Efate has two of Vanuatu's best deep-water anchorages in Vila Bay and the expanding Havannah Harbour, as well as the principal airport. Drive around the island's sealed ring road (opened in 2011) to explore its bays and beaches, islands and inlets. It's also easy to access remote-feeling offshore islands such as Pele, Nguna, Moso and Lelepa.

Port Vila & Around

POP 44,000

Set around pretty Vila Bay and a series of lagoons, beaches and offshore islands, Port Vila is a surprisingly compact but energetic town. It's a little rough around the edges, with a few traffic-clogged main streets offering up a supply of souvenirs, markets, and waterfront restaurants and cafes with some lingering French influences. Beneath this veneer is an odd mix of holidaymakers, cruise-ship day trippers, expats and yachties, along with ni-Vanuata (local people) drawn from all over the archipelago.

This is the liveliest town in Vanuatu, with a mind-boggling array of tours and adventure activities, some excellent restaurants, bars, supermarkets, banks and markets. Vila is a place for comfort over culture, beach bars over basic bungalows – and that's reason enough to stay a while.

◉ Sights

★ **National Museum of Vanuatu**   MUSEUM
(Map p53; ☑22129; Rue d'Artois; 1000VT, with guided tour 1500VT; ☺9am-4.30pm Mon-Fri, to noon Sat; P) This excellent museum, in a soaring traditional building opposite the parliament, has a well-displayed collection of traditional artefacts such as *tamtam* (slit gongs or slit drums), outrigger canoes, ceremonial headdresses, shell jewellery and examples of Lapita and Wusi pottery. There's an interesting photographic display on the unearthing of Chief Roi Mata's burial site. One-hour guided tours include a traditional instrument demonstration and sand drawing.

Hideaway Island   ISLAND
(Map p50; ☑22963; http://hideaway.com.vu; opposite Mele Beach; marine park adult/child 1250/600VT; ☺24hr; 🖮) Just 100m or so offshore from Mele Beach, Hideaway Island isn't all that hidden but it's one of Vila's favourite spots for snorkelling, diving or just enjoying lunch at the island's resort (nonguests can access the marine park until 4pm). The free ferry putts out from in front of the Beach Bar (p56) regularly, and once on the island you can snorkel in the marine sanctuary, join a dive tour and send a waterproof postcard from the world's only underwater post office.

Erakor   ISLAND
(Map p50; www.erakorislandresort.com; adult/child day pass 1000/500VT; ☺24hr; 🖮) Erakor is one of Vila's excellent resort islands. Day trippers can swim and snorkel at the shallow white-sand beach, kayak around the island or dine in the Aqua Restaurant (the day pass is redeemable for food and drinks). The 24-hour ferry leaves from the end of the road past Nasama Resort.

★ **Mele Cascades**   WATERFALL
(Map p50; adult/child 2000/1000VT; ☺8.30am-5pm; P 🖮) This popular and photogenic swimming spot is 10km from Port Vila. A series of clear aquamarine pools terrace up the hillside, culminating in an impressive 35m waterfall flowing into a natural plunge pool. A slippery path with guide ropes directs you to the top. There are toilets, change rooms and a cafe-bar with free wifi at the entrance. Go out by local minibus (250VT), or take a guided tour with **Evergreen** (Map p56; ☑23050; www.evergreenvanuatu.com; Lini Hwy; tours 3000VT).

Tanna Coffee Factory   FACTORY
(Map p50; ☑23661; Devil's Point Rd, Mele; ☺8am-5pm Mon-Fri, to 1.30pm Sat; P) 🗨**FREE** Watch the roaster at work and learn the story of Tanna coffee over a strong brew (350VT) at this welcoming coffee-roasting factory and cafe.

Secret Garden   CULTURAL CENTRE
(Map p50; ☑26222; www.vanuatusecretgarden.com; adult/child 1000/500VT; 🖮) The beautiful botanic gardens here help bring some of Vanuatu's island flora and its cultural uses to life. There's a *kastom* magic show (adult/child 1500/750VT) on Friday morning and a popular 'Island Feast' (3500/1750VT) on Tuesday and Thursday evening.

VANUATU PORT VILA & AROUND

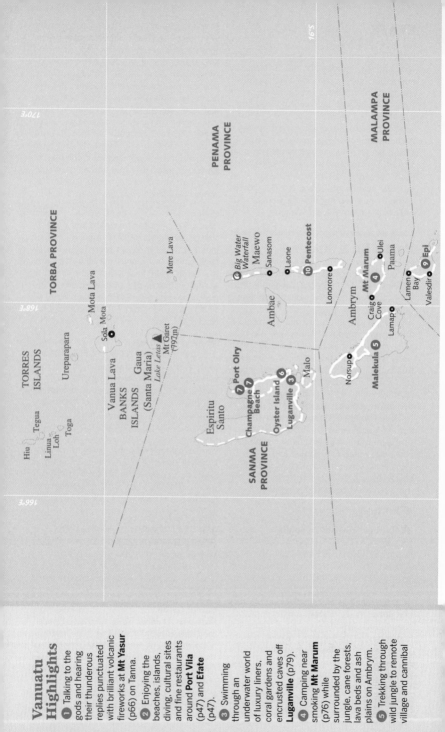

Vanuatu Highlights

1 Talking to the gods and hearing their thunderous replies punctuated with brilliant volcanic fireworks at **Mt Yasur** (p66) on Tanna.

2 Enjoying the beaches, islands, diving, cultural sites and fine restaurants around **Port Vila** (p47) and **Efate** (p47).

3 Swimming through an underwater world of luxury liners, coral gardens and encrusted caves off **Luganville** (p79).

4 Camping near smoking **Mt Marum** (p76) while surrounded by the jungle, cane forests, lava beds and ash plains on Ambrym.

5 Trekking through wild jungle to remote village and cannibal

---

170°E

TORBA PROVINCE

Hiu
Tegua
Loh
Toga
Linua

TORRES ISLANDS

Ureparapara

Mota Lava

Sola Mota

Vanua Lava

BANKS ISLANDS

Gaua (Santa Maria)

Lake Letas
Mt Garet (797m)

Mere Lava

Mota Mota

PENAMA PROVINCE

16°S

168°E

Big Water Waterfall

Maewo

Sanasom

Laone

10 Pentecost

Lonororo

Ambae

Ambrym

Mt Marum

Craig Cove

Lamap

Paama

Ulei

4

Lamen Bay

Valesdir

9 Epi

MALAMPA PROVINCE

Norsup

Malekula

5

Espiritu Santo

Port Oly

7

Champagne Beach

Oyster Island

6

Luganville

3

Malo

SANMA PROVINCE

166°E

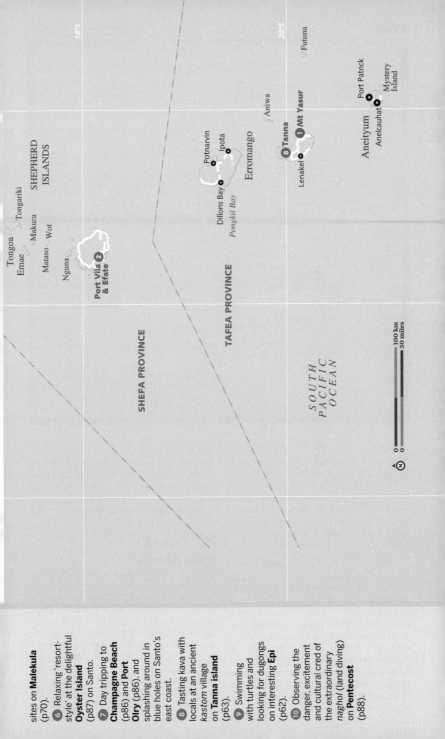

18°S

20°S

**SHEPHERD
ISLANDS**

Tongoa ∘Tongariki
Emae ∘
∘ Makura ∘ Wot
Mataso
Nguna

**Port Vila
& Efate** ❷

SHEFA PROVINCE

Potnarvin
∘ Ipota
Dillons Bay ∘
Pongkil Bay
Erromango

TAFEA PROVINCE

∘ Aniwa

❽ **Tanna** ❶ **Mt Yasur**

Lenakel ∘

∘ Futuna

Port Patrick
∘
Aneityum ∘ Mystery
Anelcauhat Island

*SOUTH
PACIFIC
OCEAN*

Ⓝ

0 ⊢━━━━━━━ 100 km
0 ⊢━━━━━━━ 50 miles

sites on **Malekula**
(p70).

❻ Relaxing 'resort-
style' at the delightful
Oyster Island
(p87) on Santo.

❼ Day tripping to
Champagne Beach
(p86) and **Port
Olry** (p86), and
splashing around in
blue holes on Santo's
east coast.

❽ Tasting kava with
locals at an ancient
kastom village
on **Tanna island**
(p63).

❾ Swimming
with turtles and
looking for dugongs
on interesting **Epi**
(p62).

❿ Observing the
danger, excitement
and cultural cred of
the extraordinary
naghol (land diving)
on **Pentecost**
(p88).

Efate

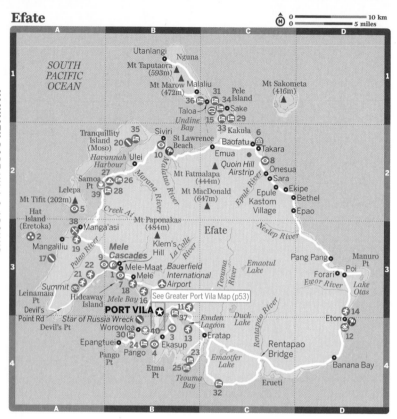

Summit
VIEWPOINT, GARDENS

(Map p50; ☑5660713; www.thesummitvanu
atu.com; off Devil's Point Rd; ⊙9am-4pm; Ⓟ)
FREE Take the winding road up to the Summit to visit these botanic gardens offering
wonderful views over Mele Bay. There's a
plant distillery producing essential oils such
as sandalwood, which you can buy in the
nearby shop. The attached cafe has more of
those views from the patio.

Ekasup Cultural Village
VILLAGE

(Map p50; adult/child 4000/2000VT; ⊙9am &
2pm Mon-Sat; 🛉) Futuna islanders talk about
and demonstrate their traditional lifestyle at
their *kastom* village. If you're not heading out
to other islands, this is an excellent cultural
experience close to Port Vila. Book through
Nafonu Tatoka Tours (☑24217, 7746734; tato
katours@vanuatu.com.vu). Friday night is 'Feast
Night' (adult/child 3100/1550VT), with shells
of kava, entertainment and buffet food. Book
a day in advance.

Iririki
ISLAND

(Map p53; www.iririki.com; opposite Grand Hotel &
Casino; ⊙24hr) Iririki is the green, bungalow-
laden island right across from Port Vila's
waterfront; it was closed following Cyclone
Pam in 2015 but should have reopened by the
time you read this..

🏃 Activities

Diving & Snorkelling
Local dive sites feature wrecks, reefs, drop-
offs, thermal vents, caverns and swim-
throughs. These include the Cathedral, a
warren of holes, stipples and tunnels; Paul's
Rock, with sheer walls of coral down an extinct submarine volcano; small plane wrecks;
and the *Star of Russia,* an iron-hulled schoon-
er with masts and hull still intact that's home
to thousands of colourful fish. Hideaway and
Tranquillity are popular island dive sites.

Introductory dives start at 8000VT, double
dives for certified divers from 11,000VT and

Efate

gear hire from 1500VT per dive. Transfers, boat trips and meals are extra. All operators offer Professional Association of Diving Instructors (PADI) courses from 32,000VT.

Big Blue Vanuatu DIVING, SNORKELLING
(Map p56; ☑27518; www.bigbluevanuatu.com; single/double dive 6400/11,900VT, gear hire per dive 1500VT; ☺8am-4pm) PADI five-star operator with twice-daily dives in Port Vila Harbour and Mele Bay. Discover Scuba courses are 9500VT (free pool session first); Open Water course 42,500VT.

Nautilus Watersports DIVING
(Map p53; ☑22398; nautilus@vanuatu.com.vu; Lini Hwy) Great resources: five-star PADI dive centre, dive boat and skills pool. Discover Scuba 8000VT; Open Water course 31,500VT.

Fishing
Vanuatu has some fabulous game-fishing opportunities and there are numerous experienced operators who will take you out for a half-day, full-day or liveaboard charter. Most big game fishing is on a tag-and-release basis.

Crusoe Fishing Adventures FISHING
(Map p56; ☑7745490; www.crusoefishing.com.vu; half/full day 22,500/30,000VT) Fishing charters aboard the 34ft *Nevagivup* or *Reel Capture*, both fitted out for cruising and deep-sea fishing. Prices are for minimum four people.

Sportfish Vanuatu FISHING
(Map p50; ☑7752433; www.sportfishvanuatu.com; half/full day maximum 3 people 40,000/70,000VT) Russ Housby holds many game-fishing records and will take you out on his 7m (23ft) customised fishing boat. He's based at the Wahoo Bar in Havannah Harbour.

Harbour Fishing Charters FISHING
(Map p50; ☑7739539; www.melebeach.com.vu; 4/6/8 hours 48,000/65,000/85,000VT) Head out with Mitch and fish for marlin on the 6.7m Stabicraft *Dorado*. Trips over six hours' duration include lunch.

Lelepa Island Fishing Charters BOAT TOUR
(☑22714; www.lelepaislandtours.com; half-/full-day charter 45,000/55,000VT) Albert Solomon operates a 7m banana boat; the price includes snorkelling and island tour.

Light-tackle and reef fishing costs from around 7000VT per person.

Scenic Flights

Vanuatu Helicopters
SCENIC FLIGHTS
(Map p56; ☑7744106, 25022; www.vanuatu helicopters.com; scenic flights 9000-38,000VT) Everything from a seven-minute whirl over Vila to a full circuit of Efate or a half-day flight over Ambrym's volcanoes.

Port Vila Parasailing
ADVENTURE SPORTS
(Map p56; ☑5563288, 22398; www.portvila parasailing.com; single flight per person 9000VT) Parasail over the harbour. No experience necessary.

Swimming & Surfing

Surfers can get up-to-date info on www.surf-forecast.com. The best surf is down Pango way (between Breakers Beach Resort and Pango Point), along Devil's Point Rd or at Erakor. There's good swimming at Hideaway Island and Erakor.

Saltwater Players
SURFING
(☑7775875; www.vanuatu-kitesurfing.com; 1hr/half-day per person 3000/4500VT) Learn to surf, kitesurf or stand-up paddleboard with this outfit. Rates include equipment and transport, or you can just hire boards for 3000VT per day.

Water Sports

U-Power Zego Sea Adventures
WATER SPORTS
(Map p56; ☑7760495; www.upowerzegovanu atu.com; Vila Outdoor Market; 30/60min tours per person from 4000/6500VT; ⊙hourly 10am-4pm) Hit the bay in a high-speed Zego sports boat. Prices are for two people per boat but you can pay extra to ride solo.

Vila Flyboard
WATER SPORTS
(Map p53; ☑7778007; Lini Hwy; adult/child 30min 14,000/12,500VT) Take water sports to another level with these space-age jet propulsion packs that can raise you up to 9m above the surface, or shoot you through the water like a human jet ski.

Tropic Thunder Jet
BOATING
(Map p56; ☑5544107; http://tropicthunder jet.com; adult/child 6100/4700VT; ⊙8am-5pm) Experience the high-speed 'Thrilla in Vila' 30-minute jet-boat ride around Vila Harbour, with 360s and other tricks. The one-hour tour (adult/child 6900/5500VT) goes further to Coco Beach Resort.

Land-Based Activities

Bellevue Ranch Equestrian Club
HORSE RIDING
(Map p50; ☑7747318; www.bellevue-ranch.com; Montmartre; 2hr trail ride adult/child 5000/2500VT) Bellevue Ranch is run by experienced Tanna horseman Tom Nangam. Trail rides catering to all levels range from a two-hour rainforest ride to waterfall and sunset rides.

Club Hippique
HORSE RIDING
(Map p50; ☑23347, 5566947; 1hr 4000VT; ⊙9.30am & 2.30pm) Offers morning and afternoon horse rides by the lagoon and Erakor Beach.

Wet 'n' Wild Adventure Park
ADVENTURE SPORTS
(Map p50; ☑5564353; www.wetnwildvanuatu. com; Devil's Point Rd; 2000-5000VT; ⊙10am-4pm; ⊕) Downhill zorbing, a giant waterslide, go-karting and the 'human slingshot'. Great fun for kids.

Vanuatu Jungle Zipline
ADVENTURE SPORTS
(Map p50; ☑5550423; http://vanuatujungle zipline.com; off Devil's Point Rd; adult/child 9000/4000VT; ⊙10.45am & 2pm; ⊕) One of Vila's newest adventure thrills is the dramatic zip line from the Summit, about 13km from the town centre (book ahead for a pick-up). Once you're harnessed you can ride six lines through the jungle canopy.

Port Vila Golf & Country Club
GOLF
(Map p50; ☑7710779; www.pvgcc.club; Rte de Mele; 18 holes 3500VT, club & buggy hire 2000VT, caddie 1000VT) A challenging course with palm-tree and ocean-front hazards, and an excellent 19th hole overlooking Mele Bay.

⌖ Tours

Native Round Island Tour
BUS TOUR
(☑5450253; nativetours@hotmail.com; adult/child 7500/3500VT; ⊙8.30am-5pm) This full-day tour includes swimming stops, nature walks, hot springs, Taka *kastom* village and lunch.

Vanuatu Ecotours
ECOTOUR
(☑5403506; www.vanuatu-ecotour.com.vu; half-day tours 5900VT) Pascal Guillet leads you through lush gardens, down cascades, into rock pools and along riverbanks with three half-day tours: river kayaking, cycling or bushwalking. You can also hire bikes (per day 2500VT, free delivery). Book ahead.

Greater Port Vila

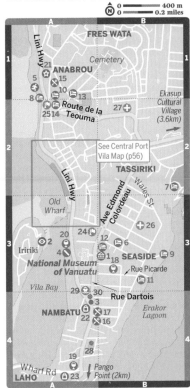

Greater Port Vila

Coongoola Day Cruise CRUISE
(Map p56; ☑ 25020; www.southpacdivecruise.com.vu; adult/child 10,800/5400VT; ☑) Sail to Tranquillity Island on *Lady of the Sea*, a romantic sailing ketch. Picnic on the beach, visit the turtle sanctuary and snorkel or dive in crystal-clear waters.

Buggy Fun Adventures TOUR
(Map p53; ☑ 22775, 7744092; www.buggyfunrental.com.vu; safari rides 7000-8500VT) Guided half-day all-terrain buggy adventures include the jungle safari and beach tours.

Vanuatu Adventures in Paradise TOUR
(Map p56; ☑ 25200; www.adventuresinparadise.vu; Anchor Inn, Lini Hwy) Local tours as well as Tanna overnight and full-day Pentecost land-diving packages.

Reef Explorer BOAT TOUR, SNORKELLING
(Map p56; ☑ 23303; http://thereefexplorervnuatu.com; Lini Hwy; adult/child 3500/2500VT;

☑ 10.30am & 2pm; ☑) The semisubmersible *Reef Explorer* is a good way to see marine life without getting wet, but you can also snorkel. Departs from Cafe du Village and moors off Iririki island.

🛏 Sleeping

Port Vila has by far the greatest range of accommodation in Vanuatu, from backpacker boltholes to five-star resorts.

★ Traveller's Budget Motel   HOTEL $

(Map p53; ☑ 23940, 7756440; www.thetravellersmotel.com; Ave du Stade; dm/d 3300/9500VT, d with air-con 9800VT; ❄🎧🏊) Owners Jack and Janelle have created a hostel/guesthouse you'll fall for, with spotless motel-style rooms orbiting a small pool and convivial bar area where you write down your drinks and food and pay later. It's a great place to meet other travellers and chat about onward plans. The dorm beds and vibe drag it back to the budget category.

Sportsmen's Hotel   HOTEL $

(Map p53; ☑ 25550; www.thesportsmenshotelvanuatu.com; Rue d'Artois; d per person with/without bathroom 3000/2000VT; ❄) Rooms at this budget hotel-bar-restaurant cater to visiting islanders as well as frugal travellers. The downstairs rooms share bathroom facilities, but the larger upstairs rooms with en suite are a steal. Great location (opposite the parliament building), well-kept and Emily's Cafe & Takeaway is on site. The owner is larger-than-life Aussie Bob.

Room with a View   B&B $

(Map p53; ☑ 7763860, 7793407; www.roomwithaview-vanuatu.com; Rue Renee Pujol; d/tw incl breakfast 5500/6700VT; 🎧) This lovely colonial building on a hilltop overlooking the harbour just north of town has three charming rooms and an expansive balcony. There's also a self-catering kitchen and guest piano.

★ Hideaway Island Resort   RESORT $$

(Map p50; ☑ 22963; www.hideaway.com.vu; dm 3750VT, d 8500-21,500VT, villas from 25,000VT; ❄🎧🏊) Hideaway is a favourite with day trippers but also a great place to stay. Spacious, well-designed rooms and bungalows are all on the waterfront, while the luxurious one-bedroom villas come with private pool. The cheapest rooms have shared bathroom, and the dorm-style quad-share rooms are a good deal for backpackers.

Moorings Hotel   RESORT $$

(Map p53; ☑ 26800; www.mooringsvanuatu.com; Lini Hwy; d 15,000-17,000VT, f 18,000VT; ❄🎧🏊) Moorings enjoys an excellent waterfront location with cute, chalet-style bungalows facing the harbour or orbiting a large pool. The restaurant is good and Wednesday is movie night.

Coconut Palms Resort   HOTEL $$

(Map p53; ☑ 23696; www.coconutpalms.vu; Rue Cornwall; d/apt 13,500/15,000VT, s/d without bathroom 6300/9500VT, all incl breakfast; ❄🎧🏊) Coconut Palms has a wide range of rooms, from small but tidy singles and budget doubles with shared facilities to spacious self-contained family apartments. Facilities are good too, with engaging communal areas, restaurant, the Wild Pig bar, swimming pool, kitchen and barbecue area. Location is central but no water views.

Seachange Lodge   APARTMENT $$

(Map p53; ☑ 26551; www.seachangelodge.com; Captain Cook Ave, Seaside; studios/cottages/lodges 8000/15,000/23,000VT; ❄🎧🏊) Orchids line the path as you meander down to the lovely cottages and studio apartments arranged around the garden or facing Erakor Lagoon.

VILA'S MARKETS

Vila Outdoor Market (Map p56; Lini Hwy; ⊙ open 24hr 6am Mon–noon Sat; 🚻) Vila's colourful waterfront covered market (also known as the Mama's Market) is open round the clock from Monday morning to noon on Saturday with women from all over the country wearing beautiful island dresses selling their fruit and vegetables. There's also a whiffy fish market here.

Hebrida Market Place (Map p56; Lini Hwy; ⊙ 8am-1pm & 2-5pm Mon-Fri, 7.30am-12.30pm Sat) Hebrida Market Place buzzes with the sound of sewing machines, as local women make island dresses to order. There's a range of hand-painted clothes, handmade souvenirs, woven bags, mats and trinkets for sale.

Vanuatu Handicraft Market (Map p53; ☑ 22277; www.vanuatuhandicraftmarket.com; Wharf Rd; ⊙ 8am-5pm Mon-Sat, plus Sun cruise-ship days; 🎧) With more than 140 stalls packed with traditional handicrafts, T-shirts, surf wear, jewellery and duty free, this giant shed is a one-stop souvenir shopping experience. Money exchange and ATM on-site, as well as cafes.

Cottages, sleeping up to five, are spacious and self-contained with kitchenette and TV.

Ripples on the Bay
BUNGALOW $$

(Map p50; ☑7758080; www.ripplesresortva nuatu.com; Lot 19, Narpow Point; d incl breakfast 12,500VT; ⓟ⊛☎) In a secluded oceanfront location about 14km from Vila, Ripples is a boutique miniresort consisting of four private bungalows with sea views from their hammock-strewn verandahs. Apart from the serenity (strictly no kids) and opportunities for swimming and snorkelling, there's an excellent little restaurant serving local seafood and Asian dishes.

Vila Chaumières
RESORT $$

(Map p50; ☑22866; www.vilachaumieres.com; Rte de la Teouma; r 10,500-14,000VT; ⊛☎☎) This romantic child-free resort has three private octagonal bungalows enshrouded in lush gardens and two upper-floor hotel-style rooms with spacious balcony overlooking Emten Lagoon. Absorb the ambience from the highly regarded lagoonside restaurant and take a kayak out for a paddle.

★Eratap Beach Resort
RESORT $$$

(Map p50; ☑5545007; www.eratap.com; Eratap; d incl breakfast from 47,000VT, 2-/3-bedroom villas 50,000/60,000VT; ⓟ⊛☎☎) This is one of Vila's top resorts, set on a secluded peninsula 12km from town and boasting honeymoon rooms with private plunge pools and baths with views. The 16 waterfront villas have flat-screen TVs, fridge and open-air showers. Take a boat or kayak out on the lagoon or relax in the excellent restaurant.

Erakor Island Resort
RESORT $$$

(Map p50; ☑26983; www.erakorislandresort. com; Erakor; d 17,500-28,500VT, spa bungalows 28,500-32,800VT, 4-bedroom houses 66,000VT; @☎) Reached by a 24-hour ferry, Erakor is a stunning 6.5-hectare island with an air of exclusivity (although day visitors are welcome). There's a fine range of accommodation here, from motel-style rooms to beachfront spa villas and the deluxe four-bedroom Aqua Blue Beach House, plus catamarans, water sports, a day spa and the sublime Aqua restaurant.

Paradise Cove
Resort & Restaurant
RESORT $$$

(Map p50; ☑22701; www.paradisecoveresort. net; 1-/2-bedroom bungalows incl breakfast 26,500/32,800VT; ☎☎) This boutique resort has 10 self-contained, spacious and luxurious bungalows in a lovely waterfront garden out

Pango way. The popular poolside restaurant beneath a traditional *nakamal* (men's clubhouse) oozes romance and offers an international menu (mains 2500VT to 5000VT).

Poppy's on the Lagoon
APARTMENT $$$

(Map p53; ☑23425; www.poppys.com.vu; d 18,000-29,500VT, 2-/3-bedroom apt 30,000/ 47,500VT; ⓟ⊛☎) The absolute waterfront location on Erakor Lagoon is the big attraction at Poppy's, but there's also a lot to like about the various apartments and bungalows. All rooms have a kitchen and balcony; some have disabled access. The family cottages boast soaring ceilings and loads of space. Sea kayaks and kids' activities are free, and there's a day spa on-site.

Breaka's Beach Resort
RESORT $$$

(Map p50; ☑23670; www.breakas.com; garden/ beachfront bungalows 22,400/29,600VT; ⓟ⊛☎) On a sublime piece of Pango surf beach, Breaka's is an intimate child-free resort. Traditional individual bungalows in the garden or facing the beach have open-sky bathrooms and king-sized beds. There's a good poolside restaurant and bar and a regular program of cultural and feast nights.

Aquana Beach Resort
RESORT $$$

(Map p50; www.aquana.com.au; Eratap; d incl breakfast 24,500-28,500VT, tr/q 27,500/31,000VT; ⓟ⊛☎☎) Aquana is a gorgeous little family-friendly resort with 16 one- and two-bedroom beachfront bungalows, all equipped with aircon, flat-screen TV and bar fridge. With easy access to ocean, reefs and islands but in a secluded location, Aquana is a cool little retreat. There's a great little restaurant, kids club and regular cultural entertainment.

✗ Eating

★Jill's Cafe
AMERICAN $

(Map p56; ☑25125; mains 350-900VT; ⊙7am-5pm Mon-Fri, to 1.30pm Sat; ☎⊞) This bustling American-style diner is always buzzing with expats, tourists and locals, seeking out waffles, burgers, burritos and chilli cheese fries. Try Jill's homemade earthquake chilli and famous Port Vila thickshakes.

★Nambawan Cafe
CAFE, PIZZA $

(Map p56; ☑7714826, 25246; mains 500-1600VT; ⊙6.30am-8pm; ☎⊞) A great place to hang out by the harbour, this popular cafe has free wi-fi, snacks, tapas, pizzas, all-day breakfast and a full bar. The cafe is usually open from sunrise to sunset but Wednesday,

Central Port Vila

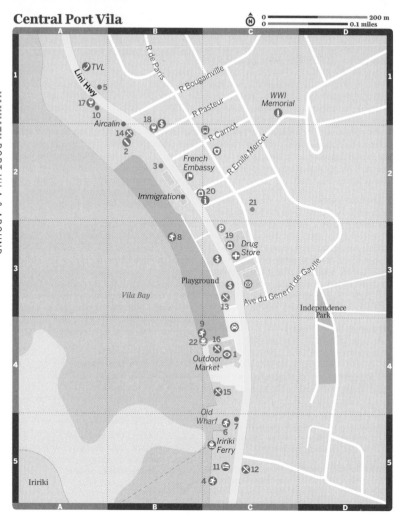

0   200 m
0   0.1 miles

Saturday and Sunday are outdoor movie nights (from 6.45pm).

Vila Outdoor Market   HAWKER $
(Map p56; Lini Hwy; meals 400VT; ⊙ food stalls 11am-3pm Mon-Fri, to noon Sat) Join the locals on the communal benches to the side of the main market, where chicken, beef and fish meals piled with rice and vegetables are cooked to order.

Beach Bar   PIZZA $
(Map p50; ☑ 5601132; www.vanuatubeachbar. com; pizzas 1000-1450VT, mains 850-1850VT; ⊙ 8.30am-9pm; ☎ ⓓ) Facing across to Hide-

away Island, Beach Bar is a fun place with Tuesday movie nights (the screen is set up on the beach), a free (very popular) Friday night fire show, a Sunday circus and excellent wood-fired pizzas.

Emily's Cafe & Takeaway   CAFE $
(Map p53; Rue d'Artois; mains 600-1500VT; ⊙ 24hr; ☎) Emily's offers some of the best-value meals around. The 1000VT lunch specials – fish and chips, rump steak or chicken – are a steal and there are some good noodle dishes too.

Central Port Vila

★ Kesorn's Exotic Thai Kitchen THAI $$
(Map p53; ☑ 7731751, 29994; www.exotic-thai.
com; mains 1500-2200VT; ☉ 10.30am-2.30pm &
5.30-10pm, dinner only Sun) Spicy aromas waft
from the kitchen onto the breezy elevated
deck at this authentic Thai place. Alongside
the fragrant curries (red curry duck, Penang
prawn curry) are pan-Asian dishes prepared
with fresh local ingredients. Book ahead for
the Thursday night buffet (2200VT).

★ L'Houstalet FRENCH $$
(Map p53; ☑ 22303; mains 890-2700VT; ☉ 5-
10pm Mon-Sun, plus noon-2pm Wed) Still going
strong after more than 40 years, L'Houstalet is famous for its offbeat French creations
including stuffed flying fox, wild pigeon and
garlic snails. Simpler fare such as pizza and
pasta (from 900VT) is also available. It's well
worth a splurge for the rustic gastronomic
atmosphere.

**Brewery Bar
& Restaurant** INTERNATIONAL, PIZZA $$
(Map p56; ☑ 28328; Lini Hwy; mains 800-
2000VT; ☉ 10am-11pm; ☜) The street-front
deck at the Brewery usually attracts a crowd.
Try a pint of the local Nambawan draught
and peek into the open kitchen to see what's
cooking: there's a predictable menu but the
wood-fired pizzas are reliable (1000VT on
Monday and Tuesday).

Spice INDIAN $$
(Map p53; ☑ 7766373; Lini Hwy; mains 1000-
2500VT; ☉ 7.30am-3pm & 6-9pm Mon-Thu,
7.30am-3pm Fri, 6-10pm Sat, 6-9pm Sun) Spice

serves authentic and reasonably priced
Indian food in cosy surrounds. It's mostly
north Indian fare with chicken tikka masa-
la, rogan josh and aromatic Punjabi chicken
curry. There's a kids' menu (hold the spice!)
and a full bar with cocktails such as Bengali
booze.

Au Faré FRENCH $$
(Map p53; ☑ 25580; Lini Hwy; mains 1300-
3200VT; ☉ 9am-10pm Mon-Sat; ☜) A little bit
French, a little bit Pacific, Au Faré is a breezy
waterfront restaurant under an open-sided
thatched 'nakamal' with central bar. Sample
fresh local fish in ginger sauce, beef carpaccio
or Gallic steak dishes from the blackboard
menu. Saturday night sees fire dancing.

Chill SEAFOOD $$
(Map p56; ☑ 22578; mains 1500-4000VT;
☉ 11am-9pm; ✹☜⚐) Chill enjoys a good
waterfront location, next to the market and
looking through large windows out to Iririki. It's a family friendly place specialising in
seafood: try the impressive seafood platter
or lobster pizza. The 1200VT lunch special is
a good deal until 5pm.

🍷 Drinking

Port Vila has a few atmospheric waterfront
bars and an abundance of kava bars with
bamboo walls and earthen floors; unlike on
some outer islands women are usually wel-
comed. The sunset kava cup (small/large
50/100VT), served in a coconut shell or plastic
bowl, is a ritual.

Bamboo Nakamal
KAVA BAR

(Map p53; Rue Picarde; cup from 50VT; ⊙5-10pm) With its colourful murals, this is one of the numerous welcoming kava bars in Port Vila's Nambatu area, on the hill near the hospital.

War Horse Saloon
BAR

(Map p53; ☑26670; Wharf Rd; ⊙11am-late; 🔊) There's more than a hint of a Wild West theme at this popular expat bar and brewery. With a range of beers on tap (including Vanuatu Bitter), wagon wheels for chandeliers, bison heads on the wall and live music, it's a fun night out. Also a good place for burgers, ribs and Tex-Mex (mains 950VT to 6000VT).

Banyan Beach Bar
BAR

(Map p53; ☑7114689; Lini Hwy; ⊙noon-11pm) With fire pits and sunloungers on the beach, cocktails and shooters at 10 paces and a true beach bar close to the town centre, the Banyan makes for a fun night out.

Waterfront Bar & Grill
BAR

(Map p53; ⊙11am-late) A popular spot for yachties and expats (Yachting World is next door), the Waterfront is a fun place to kick back with a sunset cocktail and a seafood platter. Live music usually plays under the flag-strewn thatch roof.

Anchor Inn
BAR

(Map p56; ⊙10am-9pm Mon-Sat, 4-8pm Sun; 🔊) The timber deck of the Anchor Inn is a great place for a sundowner, and there's a welcoming local pub atmosphere, with draught beer, televised sports, live music on Friday nights, free wi-fi and good food.

Voodoo Bar
CLUB

(Map p56; Main St; ⊙9pm-late Wed-Sat) Port Vila's favourite nightclub and sports bar, Voodoo fills up with locals and expats after 11pm. Next door is Elektro, another late-night music venue.

☆ Entertainment

Most large resorts feature a Melanesian show at least once a week that includes buffet meal, kava tasting, string bands and *kastom* dancers. Prices range from 2400VT to 4500VT. The tourist office has a list.

There are casinos at the **Grand Hotel** (Map p56; ☑27344; www.grandvanuatu. com; Lini Hwy) and **Holiday Inn** (Map p53; ☑22040; www.ichotelsgroup.com/holidayinnresorts; Tassiriki Park; ❄🔊🏊).

Tana Cine
CINEMA

(Map p53; ☑7770444; Lini Hwy; tickets from 600VT, gold class from 1850VT; ⊙10am-10.30pm; 🎦) Vila's brand-new cinema complex shows mainstream movies in modern comfort; Gold Class features reclining seats and food and drink service.

🛍 Shopping

Apart from the markets, you'll find a number of shops selling duty-free products on Lini Hwy. They're reasonable for alcohol, perfume, fine china and jewellery. On cruise-ship days, prices at souvenir shops are known to unofficially increase.

Au Bon Marché
FOOD & DRINK

(Map p53; ⊙7.30am-10pm) There are several Au Bon Marché supermarkets around Vila, but the biggest and best is at the southern end of town. Good range of camping gear, books, groceries and alcohol.

Kava Emporium
DRINK

(Map p56; ☑26964; www.thekavaemporium. com; ⊙9am-5pm Mon-Fri, to noon Sat) Billed as the 'happiest shop in the world', this cool place deals in kava products from coconut drinks to kava chocolate and powdered kava. Even if you don't like the muddy stuff, this is worth a visit.

ℹ Information

MEDICAL SERVICES

Drug Store (Map p56; ☑22789; ⊙7.30am-6pm Mon-Fri, to noon Sat, 8.30am-noon Sun) A well-stocked central pharmacy.

Port Vila Central Hospital (Map p53; ☑22100; ⊙emergency 24hr, outpatients 9am-6pm Mon-Fri) Has a dentist, private practitioners and dispensary; open for outpatients during business hours.

ProMedical (Map p53; ☑26996, 25566; www.promedical.com.vu; ⊙24hr) A 24-hour paramedic service with Vanuatu's only hyperbaric chamber.

MONEY

Upmarket resorts, restaurants and car hire companies accept credit cards (with a 4% to 5% surcharge), but cash (in vatu) is still king, especially outside Port Vila. Foreign exchange is provided by the following:

ANZ (Map p56; ☑22536; Lini Hwy; ⊙8am-3pm Mon-Fri) and **Westpac** (Map p56; ☑22084; Lini Hwy; ⊙9am-3.30pm Mon-Fri). Both have ATMs.

Goodies Money Exchange (Map p56; ☑23445; cnr Lini Hwy & Rue Pasteur; ⊙8am-

5.30pm Mon-Fri, 8am-1pm Sat, 8.30am-noon Sun) Generally gives the best rates. Has three offices on Lini Hwy in the centre of town.

POST
Post Office (Map p56; ☑ 22000; Lini Hwy; ⊙7.30am-5pm Mon-Fri, 8am-noon Sat) Poste restante; card-operated phones outside.

TOURIST INFORMATION
Vanuatu Tourism Office (VTO; Map p56; ☑ 22813; www.vanuatu.travel; Lini Hwy; ⊙ 8am-5pm Mon-Fri, to noon Sat, to 2pm weekends on cruise-ship days) Helpful staff; free maps and information about accommodation, activities, tours and the outer islands.

❶ Getting There & Away

AIR
Air Vanuatu (Map p56; ☑ 23848; www.air vanuatu.com; Rue de Paris; ⊙7.30am-4.30pm Mon-Fri, 8-11am Sat) Staff at this busy office book international and domestic flights.

BOAT
Big Sista (Map p56; ☑ 5683622) The Big Sista ferry departs from the harbour in front of the main market on its weekly run between Port Vila and Santo. The booking office is also here.
Vanuatu Ferry (Map p53; ☑ 26999; www. facebook.com/Vanuatu-Ferry-Limited-690422517676564/; Lini Hwy) Vanuatu Ferry operates between Port Vila and Santo weekly. Check the Facebook page for updated schedules.

❶ Getting Around

TO/FROM THE AIRPORT
Taxis charge around 1500VT from the airport. Several tour companies offer reliable pick-ups and drop-offs (1000VT per person), which are good for early or late flights. Try **Atmosphere** (☑ 7751520, 27870; www.atmosphere-vanuatu.com). If you don't have much luggage and arrive during the day, you can catch any minibus (300VT) from outside the neighbouring domestic terminal.

CAR & MOTORCYCLE
Major car-hire companies such as Budget, Hertz and Avis have offices in Port Vila.
Go2Rent (Map p53; ☑ 22775, 7744092; www. go2rent.com.vu; Nambatu; ⊙7.30am-5.30pm Mon-Sat, to 10am Sun) This is the place to go if you're after more than a car. Rents scooters (5000VT per day), motorbikes (7500VT), quad bikes (6500VT) and beach buggies (11,500VT), including mandatory insurance. All come with unlimited kilometres and discounts for two or more days. Credit cards accepted.
World Car Rentals (Map p53; ☑ 26515; www.vanuaturentalcars.com; Rue d'Artois, Nambatu; ⊙7.30am-5pm) Good-value car

rental with compact cars and 4WDs from 6500VT per day and larger 4WDs from 9500VT.

MINIBUS & TAXI
The main roads are usually thick with minibuses between 6am and 7.30pm – this is the only place in Vanuatu where you can get stuck in traffic. In most cases, it's first in, first dropped off. Fares are a uniform 150VT around town. To travel further afield to, say, Hideaway Island or the Mele Cascades, costs 250VT.

Taxis, by contrast, cost around 500VT for a short trip across town and are only really worth using at night. Vila's main taxi stand is beside the outdoor market.

Efate Ring Road

Efate's sealed ring road (about 122km in total) makes a great day trip, with lots of interesting stopovers and jumping off points for offshore islands. Head anticlockwise east out of Port Vila. Past Teouma River (Efate's largest), take the dirt road detour down to the coastal road where the Pacific Ocean is fringed with screw-trunked pandanus palms and several waterfront restaurants.

❂ Sights & Activities

Blue Lagoon   SWIMMING
(Map p50; Eton; admission 500VT; ⊙7.30am-5pm) Near Eton village, the Blue Lagoon is a popular swimming hole with ropes, swings and canoes. It's more green than blue but there's a pleasant garden with picnic tables, toilets and change rooms.

Eton Beach   BEACH
(Map p50; admission 500VT) About 2km on from the Blue Lagoon, Eton Beach is a dazzling white-sand, family-friendly beach with rock pools, safe swimming and a small river inlet.

Taka Kastom Village   VILLAGE
(Map p50) This cultural village near Takara welcomes visitors (it's on most round-island tours). A traditional buffet meal is 700VT per person and you can see music, dancing and weaving.

Matanawora WWII Relics   HISTORIC SITE, MUSEUM
(Map p50; ☑ 5427057; boat tour 2000VT) Two US WWII fighter planes lie in the shallows near Baofatu. They ran out of fuel coming in to land at Quoin Hill. If he's around, Erik will take you out in a boat to see them. The small museum of relics was closed at the time of writing.

Valeva Cave
CAVE

(Map p50; Siviri; 500VT) Turn off the Ring Rd to fragrant Siviri village (signposted), from where you can explore Valeva Cave in a kayak (1000VT). It has chambers, tunnels and an underground lake.

Havannah Harbour

Around 30km north of Port Vila via Klem's Hill, a soaring section of the Ring Rd, Havannah Harbour is a beautiful corner of Efate, with a handful of places to stay and eat and boats heading out to offshore islands.

🛏 Sleeping & Eating

Havannah Beach & Boat Club CAMPGROUND $
(Map p50; ☑5553578; www.havannahbeach andboatclub.com; Havannah Harbour; day use 1000VT, powered campsites per person 1000VT; P) Campers can pitch a tent in this grassy picnic area and marina with free barbecues. Tent hire available.

Havannah Eco Lodge BUNGALOW $$
(Map p50; ☑5419949; www.havannahecolodge. com; d 9000-10,000VT; P) There are four original bungalows here with kitchen facilities, bathroom and verandah, and two newer bungalows facing Havannah Harbour. All are on the waterfront and the excellent Gideon's Restaurant & Bar is on-site.

⭐**Havannah** RESORT $$$
(Map p50; ☑5518060; www.thehavannah.com; Efate Ring Rd; garden/pool villas 43,700/53,000VT, waterfront villas 64,000-95,000VT; P❋🌐🏊) The Havannah is a luxurious child-free resort with 20 villas. Choose from the cosy garden villas or go all out on the deluxe waterfront ones with elevated king-sized bed and private infinity plunge pool overlooking Havannah Bay. All have polished floors, ice-cold air-con and spacious bathrooms.

Resort facilities include a tennis court, free kayaks and stand-up paddleboards, a day spa, the top-class Point restaurant (dress code applies; guests can dine on the beach), and a free sunset catamaran cruise.

⭐**Wahoo Bar** INTERNATIONAL $$
(Map p50; Efate Ring Rd; mains 1500-3000VT; ⊙10am-4pm Mon-Fri, to 8pm Sat & Sun) This laid-back bar and restaurant with a deck overlooking Havannah Harbour is a fine spot to stop for fresh fish or a cold beer. The fisherman's basket is a sight to behold and the steaks and burgers are good. Free snorkelling gear if you feel like a swim straight off the deck.

Francesca's ITALIAN $$$
(Map p50; ☑24733; www.francescas.com.vu; Havannah Harbour; mains 2200-3400VT; ⊙11am-8pm Tue-Sun) Romantic waterfront dining at Havannah Harbour is the draw here and the food is upmarket Italian with a range of pizza, pasta and risotto dishes backed by local steak, seafood and fine wine.

West Coast Offshore Islands

Three very different islands opposite Havannah Harbour offer an interesting range of activities. Tranquillity Island (Moso) has a turtle sanctuary, dive base and rustic resort; Lelepa has spectacular Feles Cave, cave drawings and fishing adventures; and Hat Island (Eretoka) is the burial ground of Chief Roi Mata, a sacred place.

👁 Sights & Activities

Chief Roi Mata
Burial Site ARCHAEOLOGICAL SITE
(Map p50; 2hr/half-/full-day tour 2000/7500/9800VT) Chief Roi Mata's domain and burial site became Vanuatu's first World Heritage site in 2008. Roi Mata was a powerful 17th-century chief who, as legend has it, created peace among the islands of Efate. He died on Lelepa island and was buried, along with family and entourage (thought to be still alive at the time) at a mass funeral site on Hat Island. Local guides conduct tours; ask at tour operators in Port Vila.

Tranquillity Island Dive DIVING
(Map p50; ☑25020, 27211; www.tranquillitydive. com) Dive some 20 sites around Tranquillity Island (Moso); expect to see turtles and the occasional dugong. A two-dive day package, including transfers and lunch, is 11,500VT.

Lelepa Island Day Tours TOUR
(☑7763516, 7742714; www.lelepaislandtours.com; adult 9800VT; ⊙8am Sun-Fri) An all-inclusive family-friendly adventure with fishing, snorkelling, BBQ lunch and village visit.

🛏 Sleeping

Tranquillity Island Resort RESORT $$
(Map p50; ☑27211, 25020; www.tranquil litydive.com; dm 3900VT, s bungalows/lodges 8500/11,900VT, d bungalow/lodge 11,250/12,750VT; 🌐) There are just eight traditional bungalows

here, fronting a private beach on rambling Tranquillity Island, all with comfy beds and thatched roofs; two (lodges) have en suites, while the others have private bathrooms outside. There's also a 10-bed dorm and a campsite (1600VT for two people). Accommodation packages usually include transfers and meals.

Nguna & Pele

NGUNA POP 1200; PELE POP 300

Only 45 minutes' drive from Port Vila at Emua village is the wharf leading to these two beautiful islands. Both have protected marine reserves (www.marineprotected area.com.vu), excellent snorkelling and a laid-back castaway vibe. Both islands were hard hit by Cyclone Pam but are steadfastly rebuilding. There's no mains electricity and not much running water.

⊙ Sights & Activities

Nguna has a village feel, some nice stretches of beach, snorkel trails through exotic coral gardens and a couple of extinct volcanoes. Pele feels more remote with scattered villages, sublime beaches, a marine protected area and a **Giant Clam Garden**. The two islands are so close at one point that it's possible to swim between them.

Both islands are car-free and easily walkable. On Nguna, guides (1500VT) will take you up the island's extinct **volcano** (Mt Marou); the climb takes about three hours return and rewards with superb panoramas over the Shepherd Islands and much of Efate.

On Pele, head out in an outrigger canoe to see the villagers turtle tagging. Sponsor your own turtle, name it and see it back into the ocean.

⟑ Tours

Evergreen   TOUR
(☑ 25418, 23050; www.evergreenvanuatu.com; adult/child 9360/4680VT; ⊗ 8.30am) Evergreen offers a day tour to Pele island, which includes transfers from Port Vila, barbecue lunch, a village visit and time for snorkelling and swimming.

⛏ Sleeping & Eating

★**Uduna Cove**
Beach Bungalows   BUNGALOW $
(Map p50; ☑ 5497449; Taloa, Nguna; s/d without bathroom incl meals 3000/5000VT) Emma runs these five bright blue-and-yellow bunga-

lows in a landscaped garden facing a decent grey-sand beach. Clean bathrooms (bucket water), and there's a kitchen guests can use (otherwise meals are 500VT). Snorkel in the marine reserve right off the beach.

Paunvina Guesthouse   GUESTHOUSE $
(Map p50; ☑ 7766263, 5348523; Unakapa, Nguna; per person incl meals 3000VT) This friendly guesthouse is in Unakapa village, facing across to Pele. There are three cramped rooms at the side but much better is the large double in the main house with verandah, well-stocked library and tile floor.

Napanga Bungalows   BUNGALOW $
(Map p50; ☑ 5630315, 7787853; Pele; per person incl meals 3500VT) Kenneth has a very colourful bungalow set on a cute little bay on Pele's east side. Snorkel in crystal-clear waters off the rocky beach and look out for turtles and dugongs.

Sunset Frangipani Bungalow   BUNGALOW $
(Map p50; ☑ 5348534; Pele; per person incl meals 3500VT) This single two-room bungalow (sleeps five) has a brilliant white-sand beachfront location on Pele's western tip across from Nguna.

Senna Papa Beach Bungalow   BUNGALOW $
(Map p50; ☑ 5424728; Pele; per person incl meals 3500VT) Frank runs this colourful bungalow with floor matting, solar lighting and a shady verandah. It's in a garden setting just above the beach.

SPOTTING DUGONGS

Dugongs (also known as sea cows) inhabit warm tropical and subtropical coastal waters. But populations are declining worldwide due to hunting, drowning in fishing nets, pollution and loss of food resources, to the point of being considered vulnerable to extinction.

Dugongs can occasionally be seen around Lamen Bay and Lamen Island, as well as Malekula and the Maskelynes, and off Santo. Bondas, Lamen Bay's resident dugong, has been going to sea for months at a time so sightings are unpredictable, but if he's around you may find yourself snorkelling near him, watching his fat little snout swishing around on the ocean floor as he separates out his food.

Epi

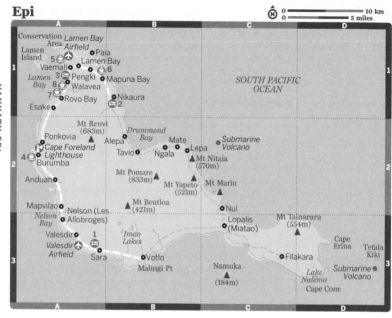

Epi

🛌 Sleeping
1 Epi Island Guesthouse A3
2 Nikaura Sunrise Bungalows B1
3 Paradise Sunset Bungalows A1

🚍 Transport
4 Cape Foreland Anchorage A2
5 Lamen Bay Anchorage A1
6 Mapuna Anchorage A1
7 Rovo Bay Anchorage A1
8 Walavea Anchorage A1

Serety Sunset   BUNGALOW $
(Map p50; ☑5630979, 7717113; Pele; per person incl meals 3500VT) On its own crescent of beach in front of the marine protected reserve, this place has a private and enviable location (it's a short walk to Piliura village). Solar lighting and flush toilet. Owner Charles is planning more bungalows.

Wora-Namoa Bungalow   BUNGALOW $
(Map p50; ☑7790881; Laonama, Pele; per person incl meals 3500VT) This grand two-room beach bungalow is very much part of the community in Laonama village on Pele's eastern point. It was built by Australian secondary-schoolers as a school project and is made from local timbers and decorated with hand-dyed materials.

🛈 Getting There & Around

Transport trucks to Emua Wharf depart from the bus stop near Port Vila's police station around 11am from Monday to Saturday (500VT); ask locals to point out the bus stop or ring ahead (☑7757410). The truck connects with an often-crowded boat to Nguna (500VT). The return trip departs at 5am.

If you're not arriving on the public truck, ask your accommodation host on Pele or Nguna about organising a private boat transfer, or just ask around Emua village; it's usually 2000VT to Pele, 3000VT to Nguna (one way) and 1000VT between the two islands.

EPI

POP 5200 / AREA 444 SQ KM

A 40-minute flight from Port Vila, Epi is an agreeably rugged and remote-feeling island where days can be spent snorkelling in search of dugongs or sampling ni-Van village life. Lamen Bay in the north is the main destination, from where you can head across by boat to Lamen Island (about 1km west) to spot turtles and lots of marine life in the fringing reef. An alternative entry point is Valesdir in the southwest.

🛏 Sleeping & Eating

Paradise Sunset Bungalows BUNGALOW $
(Map p62; ☑5649107; Lamen Bay; per person incl breakfast & dinner 3500VT) This relaxed and friendly place is 15 minutes' walk from the Lamen Bay airfield. The rooms and shared facilities are basic, but the food and bay views are fine. Owner Tasso has snorkel gear and kayaks, and can arrange tours to Lamen Island. The restaurant is often busy with visiting yachties.

★ Epi Island Guesthouse LODGE $$
(Map p62; ☑5528225; www.facebook.com/epiguesthouse; Valesdir Plantation; adult/child incl meals 15,000/7500VT; �🛜) Organic food and the relaxed lodge life of Epi Island Guesthouse draws people south to Valesdir. This arty ecolodge run by Alix and Rob Crapper features a large central room full of fascinating things (such as 1865–75 Enfield guns once owned by blackbirders) where you can chat with the family.

🛈 Getting There & Around

AIR

For a full Epi experience a good plan is to fly to Lamen Bay, make your way down the west coast by truck (8000VT) and then fly out of Valesdir (or vice versa). Epi's west coast road is rough, and there are only walking tracks in the east.

Air Vanuatu flies from Port Vila to Lamen Bay (8500VT) and Valesdir (7400VT) three or four times a week.

Air Taxi (☑5544206; http://airtaxivanuatu.com) runs full-day tours including a landing and lunch at Lamen Bay and a flight over Ambrym's volcanoes.

BOAT

Big Sista (☑23461, 5663851) stops at Epi (5500VT) on its weekly Port Vila–Santo run. Cargo ships also stop at Lamen Bay once or twice a week.

TANNA

POP 29,000 / AREA 565 SQ KM

If you visit only one island outside of Efate, this should be it. Tanna is an extraordinary place with the world's most accessible active volcano, sublime secluded beaches and some of Vanuatu's most intriguing traditional village life.

Apart from the fuming, furious Mt Yasur, the landscape features undisturbed rainforests, coffee plantations, mountains,

hot springs, blue holes and waterfalls, with some areas formed into marine and wildlife sanctuaries by local chiefs. *Kastom* is important in traditional villages, where all natural phenomena have a fourth dimension of spirituality and mystique, while strange cargo cults (John Frum and Prince Philip, in particular) still hold sway in some villages.

Lenakel is the main town with a market, port, several shops and a hospital, and it's near here that Tanna's more upmarket accommodation is located. The volcano and most of the island's basic bungalow accommodation is about 30km southeast on the rugged cross-island road via a central fertile, dense forest, aptly called Middlebush. The 'road' crosses Mt Yasur's remarkable ash plain on its way to Port Resolution.

🛈 Tours

You can get package deals in Vila that typically include airfares, transfers, accommodation, meals and visits to Mt Yasur and a *kastom* village (from 45,000VT), but if time isn't a factor it's cheaper to fly in and organise things yourself. Tours around the island can be arranged through your accommodation.

Air Safaris ADVENTURE TOUR
(☑7745206; www.airsafaris.vu; half-day tour 46,500VT) Air Safaris has a whirlwind half-day tour from Port Vila, flying past the crater and landing on the ash plain.

Air Taxi ADVENTURE TOUR
(☑5544206; http://airtaxivanuatu.com; day tour adult/child 39,000/26,000VT; overnight 46,000/31,000VT) Air Taxi flies to Tanna from Port Vila and offers a day tour with scenic flight over the volcano and 4WD trip across the island, and an overnight tour staying at Tanna Evergreen Bungalows.

🛈 Information

Take enough cash (vatu) for your whole time here. Credit cards are accepted at the large resorts with the usual 5% surcharge.

Tanna Evergreen Bungalows has free wi-fi if you're dining there.

Hospital (Map p64; ☑88659) At Lenakel.

NBV (Map p64; ◔8.30am-3.30pm Mon-Thu, to 4pm Fri) The NBV bank in Lenakel will change cash only.

Tafea Tourism (http://tafeatourismcouncil.com) There's no tourist office but the website for Tafea Tourism (covering Tanna, Aniwa, Futuna, Erromango and Aneityum) is a useful resource.

Tanna

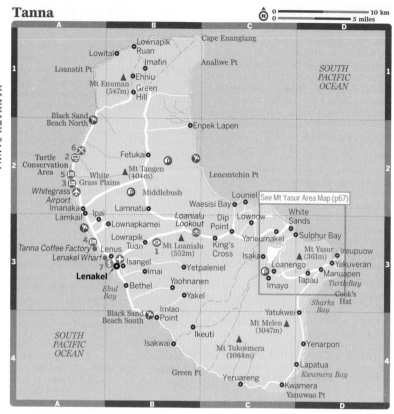

Tanna

◎ Sights
1 Giant Banyan..B3

✿ Activities, Courses & Tours
2 Blue Hole...A2

🛏 Sleeping
3 Tanna Evergreen Bungalows..............A2
4 White Beach Bungalows.....................A3
5 White Grass Ocean Resort.................A2

✦ Eating
6 White Grass Restaurant......................A2

ℹ Information
7 NBV..B3
TVL Internet...................................(see 7)

TVL Internet (Map p64; Lenakel; per hour 500VT; ⊙8-11.30am & 1.15-4pm Mon-Fri; 🛜) No computers, just a wi-fi hot spot.

ℹ Getting There & Around

Air Vanuatu (www.airvanuatu.com) flies between Vila and Tanna daily (13,000VT) except Friday and Saturday. If there are any spare seats, Air Taxi (p63) has standby fares for 10,000VT one way. Taxis (4WD trucks) and the odd minibus meet incoming flights. The fare to Lenakel from the airport is 2000/300VT by truck/bus (the truck price is for the whole truck).

For yachts, the official port of entry is at Lenakel (anchorage at Port Resolution is only possible after you've cleared immigration), and there are anchorages at Sulphur Bay and Waesi-si Bay. Immigration and **Customs & Quarantine** (⊙7.30am-noon & 1.30-4.30pm) are in Lenakel, opposite Lenakel Wharf.

The island's two main resorts are located just north of the airport; if you're staying in east Tanna, ask your bungalow to organise transport, or ask at the airport as soon as you arrive. Expect to pay 5000VT for the transfer for one or two people. The road is rough in places and the trip takes about an hour and a half.

East Tanna

East Tanna is the 'active' part of the island, in more ways than one. Mt Yasur dominates the landscape, its ash-laden smoke smothering the vegetation and creating a surreal monochrome scene on the western ash plain. There was once a large lake here, but following heavy rains in 2000 it burst its banks and drained out to sea through Sulphur Bay.

Along the coast to the north and east of Yasur are a string of black-sand and white-sand beaches, best explored from the headland of Port Resolution. Several *kastom* villages put on traditional dances for visitors and there are opportunities for jungle hikes and bathing in hot springs. If you're happy to stay in basic island bungalow accommodation, spending the night near Yasur (and climbing at sunrise) is an experience not to be missed.

◉ Sights & Activities

Bungalow owners and tour operators can arrange trips to: local villages to see *kastom* dancing; hot springs; surf beaches around Port Resolution; and Sharks Bay to see sharks feeding from the cliff-top.

Port Resolution   HARBOUR
(Map p67) Tanna's best anchorage is this beautiful bay with magnificent cliffs and easy access to east Tanna's best beaches. The Ireupuow village has a basic shop, a market and a couple of simple restaurants. To the left, a road leads up to the local cliff-top 'yacht club' and to a marine sanctuary at Yewao Point where you can snorkel in the calm water just before the coral reef finishes. Another path reaches a glorious white-sand beach and a top surf beach, with deep swells along 2.5km to Yankaren Para.

Port Resolution is 8km from the volcano entrance. A truck makes a return trip on Monday, Wednesday and Friday mornings from Port Resolution to Lenakel (2000VT), otherwise organise a charter.

John Frum Village   VILLAGE
(Map p67; Namakara; ⊘ Fri night) **FREE** At Namakara, this is one of the biggest John Frum villages on Tanna. Dances are held on Friday nights, when songs of praise are sung to the tunes of American battle hymns. It's free to attend but you'll need a local guide and transport from most bungalows is 2000VT.

Ashboarding   ADVENTURE SPORTS
(board hire 1000VT, guide 1000VT) Fancy boarding (like snowboarding or sandboarding) down the side of an active volcano? On Yasur's western side, where most of the ash clouds settle, it's possible to board from crater rim to ash plain in an exhilarating matter of minutes. It looks steep but the ash is far softer than snow! Ask at your bungalow about board hire.

🛏 Sleeping

Although most of the accommodation around Mt Yasur was flattened by Cyclone Pam, numerous operators have rebuilt and a few new ones have taken the opportunity to start up. Most offer meals and basic bungalow or tree-house accommodation, as well as camping. Generators usually provide electricity in the evenings (but don't expect it). If you can't get through by phone don't worry: just arrive and you'll find a bed.

★ **Jungle Oasis**   BUNGALOW $
(Map p67; ☑ 5448228, 7754933; camping per person 1000VT, s/d bungalows 2500/3500VT) Established 30 years ago, this was one of the original bungalow set-ups close to the volcano entrance and owner Kelson is still very active in the local tourism industry. Rebuilt from scratch after Cyclone Pam and set in black-sand gardens, the simple but quirky bungalows have shared bathroom and generator power (usually only in the evening).

A stilted restaurant-bar was under construction when we last visited.

Yasur View Lodge   BUNGALOW $
(Map p67; ☑ 7795634, 5686025; www.yasur viewlodge.com; camping per person 1000VT, s/d bungalows 1500/2500VT, s/d tree houses 2500/3500VT) Directly opposite the entrance to Mt Yasur (location, location!), the tree house here is good value. Owner Thomas has worked hard to restore his bungalows, garden and restaurant to a reasonably good standard.

Tanna Treetop Lodge   BUNGALOW $
(☑ 5417737; camping/tree houses per person 1000/2500VT) In a jungly garden setting just off the main road and about 500m from the Yasur entrance, this place does indeed have a head-spinning tree house atop a huge banyan tree (33 steps up!). Unfortunately the volcano views are

MT YASUR

Peering down into the rumbling, exploding lava storm of **Mt Yasur** (Map p67; 3350VT) is a sight you won't soon forget. The active volcano is so accessible that 4WD vehicles can get to within 150m of the crater rim. There are many tours up to see the old man, and although you can walk up without a guide (around 45 minutes from the entrance), or join a vehicle going up, it's still best to go with a guide.

Be sure to heed local warnings and take care around the crater rim – there are no safety rails or barriers. At the time of writing a new visitor centre was under construction at the entrance to the volcano road.

Although the ash plain to the west is desolate, the trip up to the crater from the entry gate on the southern slopes is through lush tree ferns and jungle. Along the path to the crater rim, there are whiffs of sulphur and whooshing, roaring sounds. Ahead are the silhouettes of people on the rim, bright orange fireworks periodically exploding behind them. Walk around to the west side of the central crater (furthest from the car park), which offers the best view into three smaller vents that take turns to spit rockets of red-molten rock and smoke. All is relatively calm until the ground trembles and the inevitable fountain of fiery magma shoots up with a deafening roar and spreads against the sky, sending huge boulders somersaulting back down into the broiling hole in the earth. Wait five minutes and it all happens again.

Some visitors find Yasur terrifying; others captivating. Photographers are beside themselves at the opportunity to capture nature at its most furious from such a vantage point. A sturdy tripod is essential for the best shots. The best times to visit Yasur are just before sunrise and for an hour or two after sunset. Absolute darkness is the ultimate thrill.

The level of activity within Yasur fluctuates between dangerous and relatively calm, but when it's hot, it's hot. It's often more active after the wet season; check www.geohazards. gov.vu and locals for the latest alert level. If the volcano is reaching activity levels three and four, entry to it won't be permitted. Take good walking shoes and a torch (flashlight), and bring a postcard to post at Volcano Post (www.vanuatupost.vu), the world's only post-box on top of a volcano. Vanuatu Post sells special 'singed' postcards for 200VT.

obscured by huge branches and the verandah is a bit pokey, but it's big enough for two double beds.

On the ground is a double-storey bungalow.

Port Resolution Yacht Club BUNGALOW **$**
(Map p67; ☑ 5376209, 5416989; wnarua@gmail. com; camping per person 1500VT, bungalows incl breakfast 3000-4000VT) Up on a bluff next to Ireupuow village, the grounds here overlook Port Resolution Bay, and one bungalow, with attached bathroom, tiled floor and balcony, has ocean views. The other two in the garden are cramped but sturdy, with shared bathroom.

It's not fancy as far as yacht clubs go, but the simple open-sided restaurant is strewn with international yachtie flags and pepped up by some threadbare but comfy old couches, and the bar serves the only cold beer for miles around. Owner Werry turns on the power in the evenings.

Island Dream BUNGALOW **$**
(Map p67; ☑ 5358595, 5621036; tannaisland dreambungalow@gmail.com; camping per person 1000VT, s/d 2000/4000VT, stilt huts d 5000VT, d with bathroom 8000VT,) Island Dream is in an interesting and slightly secluded location overlooking a small lake and Port Resolution on one side, mountains on the other. There are two basic bamboo-and-thatch bungalows, a nicer raised hut with mountain views, and a larger bungalow with tiled floor and attached bathroom.

There's a camping area if you have your own tent. The simple restaurant serves meals (from 800VT) and free breakfast.

Friendly Beach BUNGALOW **$$$**
(Map p67; ☑ 26856; www.friendlybeachvanu atu.com; d incl breakfast 18,800-28,000VT) The most upmarket accommodation in east Tanna, these three brand-new villas (well, fancy bungalows) face a lovely, secluded black-sand beach. They come with open-sky en-suite, queen-sized bed and airport transfers. Volcano tours and other activities are on offer. It's hard to justify the price tag, but if you can afford the extra style, this is your place.

✕ Eating

Ianiuia Surf Beach Restaurant CAFE $
(Map p67; ☑547990; Port Resolution; meals 750VT; ☺by arrangement) Chef Lea serves a range of chicken and vegetable dishes using a huge array of local produce, fresh herbs and flair. Book a day in advance (ask someone to help you find Lea).

Avoca Restaurant CAFE $
(Map p67; ☑5633504; Port Resolution; lunch & dinner 700VT, coffee 300VT; ☺by arrangement) This cute spot in Ireupuow village serves simple but delicious meals: chicken or fish with rice and vegetables or pancake fritters, and local Tanna coffee. Owner Serah lives next door so you can usually get a meal anytime.

West Tanna

All flights arrive at the coastal airstrip on west Tanna, 10km north of Lenakel, so this is likely to be your first view as you wing in. Tanna's upmarket resorts are a few minutes north of the airport.

Many travellers base themselves here and take a day trip to Mt Yasur (although we recommend at least one night in east Tanna). Lenakel has a lively produce market on Monday and Wednesday afternoons, and all day Friday, along with shops, mains electricity and a pretty little harbour. The kava bars offer some evening entertainment – but note that Tanna's mouth-numbing kava is regarded as the most potent in Vanuatu.

◉ Sights & Activities

Any of the accommodation places can organise a variety of adventure or cultural tours. The most obvious is the day trip to Mt Yasur volcano (adult/child from 12,000/6000VT), leaving mid-afternoon and returning at about 8pm.

Also popular are visits to traditional **kastom villages** Lowinio (Yakel) or Ipai (from 8000VT), where you'll witness village life that hasn't changed in centuries. People gather nightly under a huge banyan at Yakel to drink kava, and dancing nights occur on a regular basis. The 'Black Magic' village tour (from 7000VT) is one of the best. Jungle trails take you past villages to a **giant banyan** as big as a soccer field near Lowrapik Tuan.

There's excellent snorkelling right along the west coast, with the reef face cascading down covered in coral, in and out of its

Mt Yasur Area

Mt Yasur Area

pocketed volcanic surface. A **blue hole** just north of White Grass Ocean Resort is like a fish nursery with coral wall decorations, and there's a second blue hole in front of Rocky Ridge Bungalows.

Walk about 2km north of Rocky Ridge to a **black-sand beach** that's good for swimming. Further north the **Blue Cave** makes for an interesting boat tour (7000VT).

Volcano Island Divers DIVING
(☑30010; vanuatascuba@gmail.com; White Grass Ocean Resort; single shore/boat dive with full gear from 7000/10,500VT) This new PADI dive centre, based at White Grass Ocean Resort,

offers shore and boat dives along Tanna's west coast, as well as PADI Open Water courses.

Sleeping & Eating

★ **Rocky Ridge Bungalows** BUNGALOW $
(☎ 5417220; http://rockyridgebungalows.word press.com; camping per person 1500VT, s/d/f incl breakfast 4000/8000/10,000VT) Tom and Margaret run this friendly place. Three simple but very comfortable bungalows have en suites with hot-water showers and small sea-facing balconies, while the larger family bungalow in front of the smaller ones has uninterrupted views. Free snorkelling gear and reef shoes are supplied for the blue hole directly out front.

Tours to Mt Yasur are 12,000VT per person, airport transfers 500VT (or it's a 3km walk).

White Beach Bungalows BUNGALOW $
(Map p64; ☎ 5949220; r 2000VT, s/d 3000/4000VT, beachfront d 5000VT) Down the road past the Tanna Coffee Factory you'll find a lovely, secluded white-sand beach, pounding surf, palm trees and these simple bungalows, some with attached bathroom. A restaurant was being built at the time of writing – breakfast is included and other meals are available.

★ **Tanna
Evergreen Bungalows** BUNGALOW $$
(Map p64; ☎ 5588847; www.tannaevergreenre sorttours.com; s/d 14,000/16,000VT; ☎) These ocean-front bungalows hide in lush gardens less than 1km north of the airport. All have soft beds, hot water and verandahs. New villas at the back were being planned at the time of writing. The resort is superfriendly and offers snorkel gear, babysitting, laundry, massage and the usual range of tours.

At **Tanna Evergreen Restaurant** (mains 1500-2500VT; ⊙ 6am-10pm; ☎), the deck offers great views, free wi-fi and reliable meals from pasta to local lobster.

White Grass Ocean Resort BUNGALOW $$$
(Map p64; ☎ 30010; http://whitegrass tanna.com; d/tr/f incl breakfast 29,250/34,650/ 40,000VT; ☎ ☎) Tanna's top resort has 15 cosy bungalows with king-sized beds. Rambling grounds look out onto tiny rocky inlets, which are linked by timber bridges. There's a bar, hammocks, tennis, *pétanque* (boule) and a three-hole 'golf course'. Snorkelling gear and golf clubs are available and there's a dive outfit on site.

At **White Grass Restaurant** (Map p64; mains 2600-3800VT; ⊙ 7am-10pm; ☎) the blackboard menu changes daily, with local seafood and beef steak the highlights. The timber deck overlooks the ocean with fabulous sunset views.

MALEKULA

POP 20,000 / AREA 2023 SQ KM

Second only to Santo in size, Malekula is a wild island famed for its tribal groups, cannibal sites, highland trekking and protected marine areas.

THE NEKOWIAR

About every three years (2015 being the most recent) come August, a great restlessness spreads across Tanna. The men scour the bush and villages for pigs and kava, counting, calculating. Finally one of the chiefs announces that his village will host the Nekowiar, a three-day extravaganza of song, dance and feasting during which the leaders of neighbouring villages organise marriages.

Preparations for the Nekowiar are exhaustive. Three complex dances are practised, and beauty magic takes over. Men, women, boys and girls use powders mixed with coconut oil to colour their faces a deep red, with black and yellow stripes.

The ceremony begins with the host village's young men dancing an invitation to the women. They respond with the Napen-Napen, a spectacular dance that represents their toil in the fields, and continues throughout the first night. The male guests watch and wait for dawn, when they dance the Toka, a pounding, colourful dance that shows scenes of daily life. If the Toka dancers make a circle around a woman, she's tossed up and down between them. During this stage a man may have sex with any woman who is willing.

On the third day the chief of the host village produces the *kweriya,* a 3m bamboo pole with white and black feathers wound around it and hawks' feathers on top. It announces that the Nao – the host village's dance – is to begin. This men's dance enacts events such as hunting and wrestling, followed by triumphant feasting.

Shaped like a sitting dog, Malekula has two highland areas connected by 'the dog's neck'. The uplands are extremely rugged and inhospitable, rising to over 800m and crisscrossed by narrow valleys.

Two of Malekula's major cultural groups are the Big Nambas and Small Nambas, named because of the size of the men's *namba* (penis sheath). Small Nambas men wear one leaf of dried fibre wound around the penis and tucked into a bark belt. Their semi-*kastom* communities are built around *tamtam*, ready to beat a rhythm, and a dance area.

Big Nambas men wind large purple pandanus fibres around their penis, securing the loose ends in a thick bark belt and leaving the testicles exposed. They had such an awesome warlike reputation that no foreigner dared venture into their territory. Even police expeditions, which came to punish them for killing traders, were ambushed and dispersed. They kept a stone fireplace where unwelcome outsiders were ritually cooked and eaten.

Big Nambas' *erpnavet* (grade-taking) ceremonies are preceded by lengthy rehearsals. The men cover themselves in charcoal and coconut oil, tie nut rattles around their ankles and wear feathers in their hair. At the highest level, a man has the powerful characteristics of a hawk, and a hawk dance is performed by a spirit man.

❶ Information

Hospital (Map p72; ☑ 48410; Norsup) The provincial hospital is in Norsup, about 5km north of Lakatoro.

Malampa Travel (Map p72; ☑ 7748030, 48888; www.malampa.travel) The Malampa Travel office, near the police station in the upper part of Lakatoro, can book accommodation or organise treks and tours on Malekula, as well as to Ambrym.

NBV (Map p72; Lakatoro; ⊘ 8.30am-3.30pm Mon-Thu, to 4pm Fri) You can change major currencies (but not travellers cheques) at the bank in the LTC centre in Lakatoro, but don't count on it – bring plenty of vatu with you.

❶ Getting There & Around

AIR

There are daily flights with **Air Vanuatu** (Map p72; ☑ 23748, 23878) from Port Vila and Santo to Norsup, and three a week from Craig Cove, with usually one stopping at Lamap. The twice-weekly flight between Lamap and Norsup may be the only way to travel between these two places during the wet season, when rivers are flooded (and the flight can be cheaper than a boat or 4WD charter).

BOAT

The passenger ferry **Big Sista** (☑ 5625225; to Port Vila 7500VT, to Santo 3000VT) stops en route between Santo and Port Vila weekly, as does Vanuatu Ferry (p59). Both pick up and depart from the main wharf in Litslits, just south of Lakatoro.

VANUATU MALEKULA

THE JOHN FRUM MOVEMENT

Magic is a central force in ni-Vanuatu lives. So in 1936, when a mysterious man named John Frum came from the sea at Green Point and announced himself to some kava drinkers, they believed he was the brother of the god of Mt Tukosmera. He told the men that if the Europeans left Tanna, there would be an abundance of wealth. They spread the word. It was the beginning of a neopagan uprising, with followers doing things the missionaries had banned, such as traditional dancing – but not cannibalism, fortunately.

When US troops arrived a few years later, many Tannese went to Efate and Santo to work for them. There they met African American soldiers, who were colourful, with theatrical uniforms, decorations, badges, belts and hats. The African Americans had huge quantities of transport equipment, radios, Coca-Cola and cigarettes. But most of all, they were generous and friendly, treating the ni-Van as equals. Here was the wealth and way of life the ni-Van had been told about – John Frum was connected to America, they decided.

Some supporters made radio aerials out of tin cans and wire to contact John Frum. Others built an airfield in the bush and constructed wooden aircraft to entice his cargo planes to land. Still others erected wharves where his ships could berth. Small red crosses were placed all over Tanna and remain a feature in John Frum villages, where flags are raised daily to this god of their collective imagination.

An offshoot of John Frum, the Unity Movement, sees women in trances twirling themselves into the water at various places, such as Port Resolution, usually on a Wednesday.

A chartered speedboat ride from Wala in northern Malekula to Luganville on Santo costs around 25,000VT but will only go in calm weather. From Lamap to Craig Cove on Ambrym costs 12,000VT and takes about 90 minutes. Make sure the boat has life jackets.

All inhabited offshore islands (such as the Maskelynes) are linked to the mainland by speedboats or canoes; ask at your accommodation if you want to charter transport.

CAR, BUS & TRUCK

A dirt road runs from Lakatoro around the north coast and down the east coast to Lamap. The road south is rough and rutted and fords numerous rivers; in the wet season it's often impassable.

If you can hitch a ride on a truck it's 100VT from Norsup airport to Lakatoro, but 1000VT if you're stuck with a charter. On weekends there aren't many around; arrange a ride with your accommodation.

Jump in the tray of a truck to travel between Lakatoro and Lamap (1000VT, four hours) on weekdays. These leave Lamap between 3.30am and 5am and return from Lakatoro market at 1pm. On weekends or if you're in a hurry you'll need to charter (22,000VT). Trucks/charters run more frequently between Lakatoro and Veturah in the north (500/6500VT, one hour).

Most public transport leaves Lakatoro from the market. From Lakatoro to Lamap, you may be dropped at Black Sands, from where you can take a speedboat across to Port Sandwich or Levi's Beach Guesthouse (p502; 200VT per person). This avoids the long drive around the inlet.

Lakatoro & Around

Malekula's capital and main market town, Lakatoro is a relatively busy place with decent dirt roads, shops and power supply.

Set on two levels divided by a steep slope and a drawn-out lower main road, this is Malampa province's administrative capital. At the northern end of town is the LTC co-op, NBV bank, post office, bakery and Air Vanuatu office. The southern end has the MDC General Store and market.

About 4km north, at Norsup, is the main airstrip. A long stretch of beautiful coral reef stretches southwards from Aop Beach to Litslits, the main port for this area.

Tours to Small and Big Nambas cultural villages and to cannibal sites can be arranged through your accommodation (around 5000VT per person plus transfers), or Malampa Travel (p497).

⊙ Sights

Lakatoro Cultural Centre   CULTURAL CENTRE
(Map p72; ☑5361223, 48651; adult/child 500/100VT; ☺7.30am-4.30pm Mon-Fri) On Lakatoro's upper ridge, this small cultural centre has some fascinating exhibits such as local carvings, photos and a library.

Malampa Handicrafts Centre   ARTS CENTRE
(Map p72; ☑5398633; ☺8.30am-4pm Mon-Fri) Behind the market in Lakatoro, this small handicrafts centre and store stocks locally made baskets, hats, mats, jewellery and coconut soaps and oils. Stop by for a chat and watch the workers weaving away.

🛏 Sleeping & Eating

★**Ameltoro**
Resort & Restaurant   BUNGALOW $
(Map p72; ☑7773387, 5368944; newmanrona@ gmail.com; Norsup; bungalows incl breakfast 6500VT; 🛜) These three spacious oval-shaped

---

MALEKULA TREKKING

Malekula has some of the wildest trekking country in Vanuatu, but it's also surprisingly well organised. Malampa Travel (p69) offers a number of itineraries that include guides, porters (one for two people) and village accommodation and meals. Jeep or boat transfers are often an extra charge so are best split with a group. Prices are for a minimum of two people.

Day hikes include the strenuous **Big Nambas Trek** (5500VT per person) from Lakatoro to Tenmaru and the half-day **Losinwei Cascades & Waterfall Walk** (3500VT per person). More challenging is the three-day coast-to-coast **Dog's Head Walk** (23,500VT per person), crossing from Small Nambas territory to Big Nambas territory and experiencing traditional village life along the way.

The ultimate adventure is the four-day **Manbush Trail** (29,700VT), which includes truck transfer from Norsup/Lakatoro to Unua, guide and porter, jungle and village stays, and accommodation at Lawa in a local guesthouse. It's no picnic, with up to six hours a day spent on bush trails, but it's an adventure. See Malampa Travel's website for trek details.

Malekula

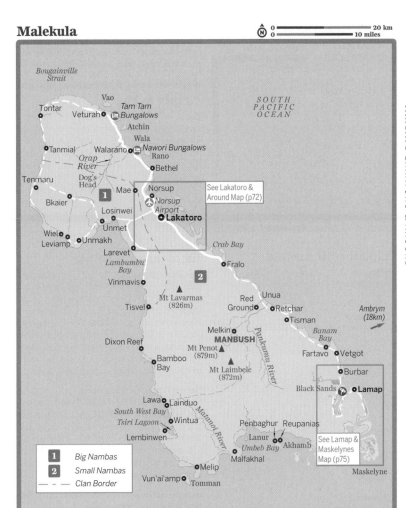

N
0 ————————— 20 km
0 ————————— 10 miles

Bougainville
Strait

SOUTH
PACIFIC
OCEAN

Vao
Tontar   Tam Tam
Veturah   Bungalows
Atchin
Wala
Tanmial   Walarano   Nawori Bungalows
Orap   Rano
River   Bethel
Tenmaru   Dog's
Head
Mae   Norsup   See Lakatoro &
1   Around Map (p72)
Bkaier   Norsup
Losinwei   Airport
Unmet   Lakatoro
Wiel
Leviamp   Unmakh
Larevet   Crab Bay
Lambumbu   Fralo
Bay
Vinmavis   2

Mt Lavarmas   Red   Unua
Tisvel   (826m)   Ground   Retchar   Ambrym
                         Tisman   (18km)
Melkin   Banam
Dixon Reef   MANBUSH   Bay
Mt Penot   Fartavo   Vetgot
Bamboo   (879m)
Bay   Mt Laimbele   Burbar
(872m)
Black Sands   Lamap
Lawa   Lainduo
South West Bay
Tsiri Lagoon   Wintua   Penbaghur   Reupanias
Lembinwen   Lanur   See Lamap &
Umbeb Bay   Akhamb   Maskelynes
Melip   Malfakhal   Map (p75)
Vun'ai'amp   Tomman   Maskelyne

1   Big Nambas
2   Small Nambas
— — —   Clan Border

bungalows on the seafront across from Norsup island come with clean attached bathrooms, 24-hour mains power and solar hot water. Rona cooks up a French-influenced storm in the gorgeous brasserie-restaurant (meals 1300VT to 2000VT; by arrangement). It's about 1km north of the airport. Wi-fi costs 500VT.

Lakatoro Palm Lodge   LODGE $

(Map p72; ☑ 5646285, 7721027; Lakatoro; r per person 2500VT, d bungalows 6000VT; ☎) A short walk from north Lakatoro on the road to Norsup, this welcoming, traditional-style

place has three rooms in the main lodge with a shared lounge and kitchen and a separate private bungalow with balcony, all set in a sloping garden. Dinner is 800VT, or you can self-cater. Wi-fi is 300VT.

LTC Holiday Units   MOTEL $

(Map p72; ☑ 549825; r 6500VT) These eight self-contained, one-bedroom units are tired looking and in an unappealing (but central) location behind the LTC co-op, but they're well-equipped with kitchenettes, white-tiled floors, attached bathroom and room enough to sleep six – good value for groups or families.

Lakatoro & Around

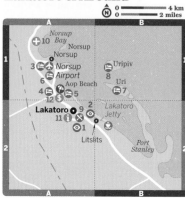

Lakatoro & Around

Nabelchel BUNGALOW $

(Map p72; ☑5456402, 7740482; nabuchel bungalows@gmail.com; Norsup; s/d incl breakfast 2500/5000VT; 🛜) These simple bungalows share a pleasant central sitting area and are conveniently located a five-minute walk north of the airport. Meals are 500VT and beer is available. Wi-fi is 500VT per day.

Lakatoro
Community Cooperative SUPERMARKET $

(LCC; Map p72; ⏱6.30am-7.30pm Mon-Fri, 6.30am-noon & 3-7.30pm Sat & Sun) Lakatoro's best-stocked store by light years (though a new shopping centre was under construction directly opposite). Has limited cold beer and wine. It's just up the hill from the market behind the football field.

Uripiv & Uri

These little islands have **marine reserves** proclaimed by the chief. They offer plenty for snorkellers, with beautiful coral, colourful fish and turtles. The sanctuary at Uri protects the mangroves and reef, and you'll see colourful giant clams.

You can get to Uripiv and Uri by speedboat from the Lakatoro (Litslits) jetty. A number of commuter boats travel across between 4pm and 4.30pm (200VT) or you can charter a speedboat for 2000VT.

🛏️ Sleeping & Eating

Nan Wat Bungalows BUNGALOW $

(Map p72; ☑5938523; Uri; per person incl breakfast 2500VT) Lines and Jake run the secluded Nan Wat Bungalows on Uri island. It's 1000VT to get a boat transfer to this peaceful little spot where there's little to do but relax, snorkel and enjoy the fresh food. The three bungalows are comfortable, with mosquito nets. Meals are 500VT.

Nawov Freswind Bungalows BUNGALOW $

(Map p72; ☑5497327, 48888; Uripiv; per person incl breakfast 2800VT) The two double bungalows and restaurant here front the Nawov Coastal Sanctuary on Uripiv island, a 25-minute boat ride from Lakatoro Wharf. Try to get a local boat (200VT, morning and afternoon) or charter one for 1000VT.

The Dog's Head

The culture-filled, francophone zone of Malekula's Dog's Head is home to several cannibal sites as well as the Big and Small Nambas tribal groups.

Kastom dancing tours go to Wala and Vao to see Small Nambas dances; to Unmet and Mae to see Big Nambas. Other tours go to the spectacular **Yalo Cavern** near Tanmial and the islets of Wala (a cruise-ship favourite) and Vao.

Accommodation places can usually arrange visits to tribal groups and the **Amelbati cannibal site** near Wala village, where piles of bones and skulls tell a story of primitive times less than a century ago. At the time of writing the cannibal site on the island of Rano was off-limits due to a land dispute.

🛏 Sleeping & Eating

★ **Nawori Bungalows** GUESTHOUSE $
(Map p71; ☑ 5471005, 5685852; etieneet iasinmal@gmail.com; Wala; s/d incl breakfast 2500/5000VT; ☎) Etienne and Lyn run this friendly place about an hour by truck north of Lakatoro. It's well placed for exploring the Dog's Head and the nearby island of Wala. There are three rooms in the main house with a communal dining room, and a separate lodge with four rooms and a sea-facing balcony.

THE SMALLER SOUTHERN ISLANDS

Aneityum & Mystery Island

Aneityum is the southernmost inhabited island in Vanuatu, but it's tiny Mystery Island just offshore – with its grass airstrip (built during WWII), glorious beaches, marine reserve and secluded bungalows – that will leave you slack-jawed. Garden paths criss-cross the island, and snorkelling is fantastic off the end of the airstrip (the island is a marine sanctuary). Aneityum people believe Mystery Island is the home of ghosts, so no one will live there. It's a favourite stopover with cruise ships, when it gets crowded and locals set up market stalls; at other times you'll probably have it to yourself.

Cross to Anelcauhat, Aneityum's main village, to see fascinating ruins of whaling-industry equipment, missionary Geddie's church and old irrigation channels. Take stunning walks from Anelcauhat to picturesque Port Patrick, impressive Inwan Leleghei Waterfall or to the top of Inrerow Atahein (853m), an extinct volcano.

Mystery Island Guesthouse (☑ 7799410; per bungalow 3000VT) has simple colourful bungalows and a basic central kitchen with a gas refrigerator (there's no electricity). You need to bring your own food and water, although someone will row across from Aneityum each day to see if you need anything. On Aneityum, Kenneth's Bungalows in the main village of Anelgauhat has two basic huts for 1500VT per person. Contact Tafea Tourism (http://tafeatourismcouncil.com) for more information.

Air Vanuatu has two scheduled flights a week from Tanna to the Mystery Island airstrip.

Erromango

The 'Land of Mangoes' is mountainous, with almost all the people living in two main villages on its rugged coast. Each village has a fertile garden, where taro, tomato, corn and sweet potato thrive among huge mango, coconut and pawpaw trees.

Dillon's Bay (Upongkor) is Erromango's largest settlement, with a huge crystal-clear swimming hole formed by the Williams River as it turns to the sea. Sandalwood trees still grow in the rainforest, and a rock displays the outline of John Williams, the first missionary here (locals laid his short, stout body on this rock and chipped around it prior to cooking and eating him in 1839).

Guided walks from Dillon's Bay include trips to a **kauri reserve** (2000VT) to see ancient 40m-high trees, and a three-day walk south and across to Ipota. At the mouth of Williams River, about 9km south of the Dillon's Bay airstrip, **Meteson's Guesthouse** (☑ 68677; Upongkor; s/d incl breakfast 2500/5000VT) sleeps eight in two rooms. Chief William arranges fishing trips and guides for treks.

Air Vanuatu flies weekly to Dillon's Bay from Port Vila and Tanna, as well as to Ipota on the remote southeastern side of the island.

Aniwa

This island is set around beautiful, clear-blue Itcharo Lagoon, with 1.5km of white-sand beach, coconut palms, a marine sanctuary and great snorkelling. The five colourful huts at **Aniwa Ocean View Bungalows** (☑ 5964778, 5616506; http://aniwaoceanviewbungalows.wordpress.com; s/d incl breakfast 2500/4000VT) are the only formal accommodation on Aniwa, and you'll get a friendly welcome (at the airstrip) from Jethro and Joshua. There's a restaurant (meals from 750VT) and island tours can be organised. Air Vanuatu flies to Aniwa from Tanna at least once a week.

Tam Tam Bungalows BUNGALOW $

(Map p71; ☎5548926; Veturah; dm 2000VT; bungalows per person 3500VT) These traditional bungalows with bathroom have been renovated and make a peaceful northern base for trekking and exploring the Small Nambas in Vao. There's snorkel gear and spear/canoe fishing, electricity from 6pm to 9pm and a restaurant. Transfers from Lakatoro are 6500VT.

Lamap

Lamap, with its nearby airstrip, is the entry point to Malekula in the south by air and boat (from Ambrym) and is the gateway to the Maskelyne islands. There's not much to the village itself: a church, school, a couple of guesthouses, dozens of kava bars and the reasonably well-stocked Levi's Store at the bottom of the hill heading into the village.

Organised activities in Lamap include *kastom* **village dances** (5000VT per person), a **dugong tour** to Gaspard Bay (2000VT) and the **Marieu Garden Tour** (2000VT per person). Ask at your accommodation or call Joseph (☎5435722) or Tito (☎5436814).

Your accommodation can organise transfers to/from the airport (1000VT) and Lakatoro (1500VT for a local truck, 25,000VT for a charter). The truck to Lakatoro departs between 3.30am and 5am on weekdays; check the night before. If you're coming to Lamap from Lakatoro, you may be dropped across the inlet at a place called Black Sands, from where a boat (200VT) will drop you at Port Sandwich or Levi's guesthouse.

🛏 Sleeping & Eating

Lamap Ocean
View Guesthouse GUESTHOUSE $

(Map p75; ☎7102018; s/d without bathroom 1800/3600VT) This neat and friendly guesthouse in the centre of Lamap village has four small rooms (three singles and a double), a sitting room with comfy couches and a kitchen. Clean shared bathrooms have flush toilet and shower. Meals are just 300VT.

Levi's Beach Guesthouse GUESTHOUSE $

(Map p75; ☎5934202, 5475656; r per person without bathroom incl breakfast 1500VT) This basic place on the waterfront next to Levi's Store has six rooms in two lodge-style buildings. The abominable shared toilet and shower were being replaced with more modern facilities at the time of writing. Lim-

ited power but comfy enough beds and Mary cooks up decent meals.

The Maskelynes

The lovely vehicle-free Maskelyne islands are only a short truck-and-boat trip from Lamap but seem a world away from mainland Malekula.

The main attractions, apart from the peaceful village life, are the coral reefs and marine conservation areas, swimming, snorkelling (BYO gear), canoeing or fishing, all of which can be experienced DIY or with organised tours.

The main island, Uliveo (Maskelyne), is a friendly place with the only accommodation – here you can watch the villagers make canoes, weave, string necklaces and hunt for edible sea creatures when the tide is out. You're welcome at the kava bars, and you can hire outrigger canoes (200/400VT half/full day or 1400VT with a guide). For tours and information, contact Sethrick at Batis Seaside Guesthouse or go online at www.maskelynetourism.blogspot.com.au.

The road from Lamap ends at a sandy beach, Point Doucere (transport from Lakatoro 1500VT), from where canoes and speedboats head out to the Maskelynes (2500VT). Point Doucere is a 20-minute walk south from the airport through coconut plantations.

◎ Sights & Activities

Ringi Te Suh
Marine Conservation Area NATURE RESERVE

(Map p75; per person 1200VT) Take a guided tour by outrigger canoe to this marine sanctuary, a 100-hectare reef protected by the villagers of Pellonk (the name itself means 'leave it alone'). You can snorkel over the beautiful **Giant Clam Garden** and picnic on an artificial island.

🛏 Sleeping & Eating

There are just three bungalow operations on Uliveo island, including two side by side (owned by brothers) on the waterfront in Pellonk village. Malaflag Beach Bungalows, in Lutes village, was closed due to cyclone damage at the time of writing but may reopen in future.

Batis Seaside Guesthouse BUNGALOW $

(Map p75; ☎7751463, 5943885; batisseaside guesthouse.vanuatu@gmail.com; Pellonk; r per person without bathroom 2500VT, bungalows

5000VT) Two lemon-yellow waterfront bungalows with verandahs on stilts have their own toilet and shower at the back, while cheaper guesthouse rooms in the garden have comfy single beds and shared bathroom. Owner Sethrick can organise any activities on the islands or arrange boat charters. Lunch and dinner are 500VT and there's a small store and 24-hour solar power.

Senelich BUNGALOW $
(Map p75; ☑7117096, 7789547; senelich@ gmail.com; Pellonk; r per person without bathroom 2500VT, bungalows 5000VT) Next to Batis Seaside Guesthouse and identical in most respects, the two sturdy waterfront bungalows have private bathrooms at the rear and verandahs over the water, and there are two more garden-facing rooms. There's also a lovely gazebo in the garden and a bar-cafe. Solar power.

Malog Bungalows BUNGALOW $
(Map p75; ☑7107905, 7783524; Peskarus; camping 500VT, dm 2000VT, s/d without bathroom incl breakfast 2800/5600VT; ☎) Owner Kalo has three traditional bungalows and a five-bed dorm on the muddy shore between the mangroves in Peskarus village, the largest on the island. The shared bathroom has flush toilets and showers and there's solar power. There are a couple of kayaks, or you can head out in an outrigger canoe. Lunch and dinner cost 700VT (1500VT if there's lobster).

AMBRYM

POP 7300 / AREA 680 SQ KM

Ambrym – called the Black Island because of its volcanic soils – has amazing twin volcanoes, Mt Marum and Mt Benbow, which keep volcanologists all over the world on the alert. Climbing one or both is the main attraction here – Ambrym isn't noted for its beaches and with few roads, getting around is mostly by boat or on foot.

Cultural attractions include Vanuatu's best tree-fern carvings and *tamtam*, and the Rom dances of northern and western Ambrym. Magic in Vanuatu is strongest on the islands with active volcanoes, and Ambrym is considered the country's sorcery centre. Sorcerers (*man blong majik* or *man blong posen*) are feared and despised. Many ni-Van have seen too many unexplained happenings, and would treat anyone who was found practising black magic severely. Tourists can visit

Lamap & Maskelynes

villages that feature traditional magic, but magic for tourists is not considered black.

Ambrym is known for sand drawings, with 180 sand designs, each referring to a specific object, legend, dance or creature.

🎭 Festivals

There are three main festivals in north Ambrym (**Fanla Art Festival** and **North Ambrym Magic Festival** in July, and **Back to my Roots** in August), each an annual extravaganza of cultural demonstrations, ceremonies, fashion shows, Rom dances, magic and cooking lessons.

ℹ Information

Malampa Travel (☑7748030, 48888; www. ambrym.travel) Malampa Travel, based in

Lamap & Maskelynes

◎ **Sights**
1 Ringi Te Suh Marine
   Conservation Area............................B3

🛏 **Sleeping**
2 Batis Seaside Guesthouse...................B3
3 Lamap Ocean View Guesthouse.........B1
   Levi's Beach Guesthouse .... (see 3)
4 Malog Bungalows..............................B3
   Senelich...(see 2)

Malekula, handles tourist information for Ambrym and is remarkably well organised. You can book guides and accommodation through here for an extra cost.

ⓘ Getting There & Around

AIR

Air Vanuatu (☏ 23748) flies between Craig Cove and Port Vila (10,000VT) and Santo (8000VT) three times a week. On Tuesday and Sunday the flight stops first at Ulei. Tour companies in Port Vila offer volcano adventure flights to Ambrym.

BOAT

The *Brisk* cargo ship makes its way from Vila to Santo on Saturdays, stopping at both Craig Cove and Ranon.

The best anchorages are at Craig Cove and Sanesup in the south (Port Vatu is OK in good weather), and Buwoma Bay, Ranvetlam, Ranon and Nobul in the north.

If you aren't concerned about deep ocean swells and fierce currents, you can travel from Ranon Beach Bungalows by speedboat from north Ambrym to Pangi in southwest Pentecost (13,000VT). You can also take a boat from Craig Cove to Lamap in Malekula (12,000VT) with Sam of Sam's Guest Bungalows. Both trips cross open oceans and are dependent on weather conditions. Speedboats also travel between Craig Cove and Ranvetlam or Ranon (12,000VT one way). Ask your bungalow host to arrange transport.

THE ROM DANCE

Ambrym's most striking traditional ceremony, the Rom dance combines *maghe* (grade-taking) elements with magic. When a man wishes to move up in the village structure, he must find someone who owns the design of a mask and ask to buy it, with pigs and cash. The owner makes his *nakamal* (men's clubhouse) *tabu* (taboo), and the buyer comes to discuss the purchase and learn the rules determining the colours and shapes of the mask. Once the design has been bought, the buyer invites men to pay to enter this *nakamal* where they practise the dance for days, cooking the food the buyer has provided. Finally there's a feast, and the next morning the dancers perform wearing the extraordinary costume: a tall, conical, brightly painted banana-fibre mask and a thick cloak of banana leaves.

TRUCK

If you're heading south from Craig Cove to Port Vatu, try to get a lift from the airport on one of the taxi trucks heading there (or hook up with other travellers), otherwise you'll need to charter (5000VT). If landing at Ulei, trucks run from Ulei to Endu (3000VT) on the east coast.

Central Ambrym

◉ Sights & Activities

The main reason to visit Ambrym is to hike up one or both of its volcanoes, preferably up one way and down another. On a clear and active night, the sky above them glows red.

Mt Benbow & Mt Marum   VOLCANO

(Map p77) The guided climb up these twin volcanoes is reasonably demanding and the view is often obscured by low cloud and volcanic smoke and ash. But on a clear day the reward for your climb will be peering into an active crater and seeing the red-hot magma boiling below like a satanic pot of tomato soup. Both volcanoes are closely monitored, climbing is occasionally suspended on high-activity days and evacuation plans are always ready.

To make the climb, you must be reasonably fit and comfortable walking on steep terrain, and you need a good guide (compulsory). Skin protection and plenty of drinking water are essential. There's a dry, slippery crust around both volcanoes so your boots need to be strong enough to kick toe holes. Ankle support is also necessary as there's some boulder hopping. Between the mountains, the walk over the razor-backed ridge gets very narrow and snakes nastily upwards, while vents all around spurt acrid smoke. Mother Nature does her best to be daunting.

The best idea is to trek up one way and down another (different guides will meet you on the caldera). There are three routes, two accessed from Craig Cove airport and one from Ulei airport:

North From Ranon or Ranvetlam, this is the only option for going up and back (Mt Marum only) in one day. From Ranon to North Camp it's two hours through jungle, then another three hours to the top. Return, or continue down (with camping) on the south or east routes.

Southwest From Port Vatu or Lalinda it's five to six hours slogging through jungle to the ash plain and the West Camp (overnight), then a steep 1½-hour trek to Mt Benbow or

Ambrym

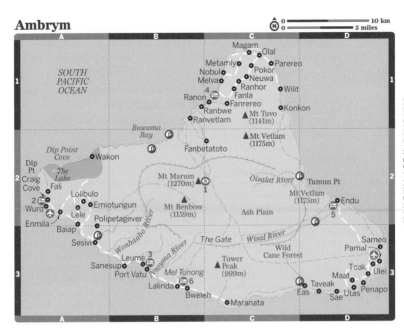

2½ hours to Mt Marum, from where you can continue down north or east.

East From Endu, 45 minutes north of Ulei airport, it's a testing 6½-hour trek to the ash plain, across Wisal River to East Camp. From there it's just 45 minutes to the top of Mt Marum. Return or continue north to Ranon or south to Port Vatu.

➡ **Tours**

Volcano tour guides usually have gear (tents, sleeping bags, hard hats, gloves, gas masks) should you want to hire anything. Ask if you need to bring extra food (meals are included).

Volcano climbs are well organised and costs for guides and transport are standardised. You can find a list of certified guides at www.ambrym.travel or posted at the airport at Craig Cove, but most travellers simply get hooked up through their accommodation.

➡ **Costs**

➡ Full Day (from Ranvetlam) – 7000VT per person (9000VT for solo travellers)

➡ Two-day return (from Port Vatu) – 11,900VT (15,850VT solo)

➡ Three-day crossover (from Ranvetlam, Port Vatu or Endu) – 21,150VT (23,100VT solo)

Ambrym

◉ **Sights**

1 Mt Benbow & Mt Marum....................C2

🛏 **Sleeping**

2 Jossie's Guesthouse............................A2
3 Karina Guesthouse..............................B3
4 Ranon Beach Bungalows....................C1
  Sam's Guest Bungalows.............(see 2)
5 Sea Roar Bungalows...........................D2
  Ter Ter Hot Spring
  Bungalows...................................(see 2)
6 Wola Volcano Guesthouse.................B3

West Ambrym

The village of **Craig Cove** is West Ambrym's tiny commercial centre, harbour and the island's main airport. It has several bungalows, a market and a few stores selling bread, canned food and hardware. From Craig Cove you can visit a number of **hot springs**; the best are at **Sesivi**, about 10km southeast.

🛏 **Sleeping**

Sam's Guest Bungalows　　　　BUNGALOW **$**
(Map p77; ☑ 5944424, 7767129; Craig Cove; per person incl breakfast 3000VT) For a family welcome and volcano information, Sam's is

hard to beat in Craig Cove. There are three tidy rooms (with attached bathroom) in a quiet area of the village and another family or group bungalow. Good meals (lunch/dinner 500/800VT) and generator power in the evening.

Ter Ter Hot Spring Bungalows BUNGALOW $
(Map p77; ☑ 5493238, 7726534; Malvert; r per person 3500VT) Away from the main village, these seafront bungalows enjoy a fabulous location overlooking a small rock-and-coral beach cove. At low tide you can relax in the hot spring pools here. There are four bungalows in a palm-filled garden but the best is the private sea-facing bungalow with views out to Malekula.

It's a 15-minute walk from the airstrip through jungle paths; call ahead and owner Freddy will meet you at the airport or harbour.

Jossie's Guesthouse GUESTHOUSE $
(Map p77; ☑ 7741186; Craig Cove; r per person incl meals 2000VT) These simple but sturdy stone and palm-thatch bungalows in a village garden include two rooms in one building and a separate bungalow sleeping three. Long-drop toilet, bucket shower and a small shop on site.

North Ambrym

Most of Ambrym's northern coast has high volcanic cliffs rising straight out of the sea. The motorboat journey north from Craig Cove burbles past sheer angled cliffs, forests, rock caves, hot pools, coral reefs, turtles, dolphins and wild ducks.

The best **Rom dances** and **magic** (per person 5000VT) can be seen inland at **Fanla**, a 45-minute walk from Ranon. An island feast can be prepared for a group, and locals will bring out a terrific array of carvings for sale. It was once prohibited to access the volcano from here during yam season, but in line with the rest of the island this is no longer taboo.

Chief Joseph at Ranvetlam is the *kastom* owner of the northern approach to the volcanoes.

🛏 Sleeping

Ranon Beach Bungalows BUNGALOW $
(Map p77; ☑ 7758941, 5637502; Ranon; per person incl meals 3000VT) If you're climbing the volcano from the north, this is where you'll stay, in traditional bungalows on the beach or up the cliff. Owners Lann and Freddie

Douglas organise volcano tours as well as Rom dances in Fanla (5000VT per person). They also run speedboat transfers to Craig Cove (12,000VT, 45 minutes) and Pangi in Pentecost (13,000VT, two hours).

East Ambrym

Ulei is also an entry point to the volcanoes. **Toak**, near the airfield, is a large village where you'll see very traditional sand drawings, magic, *kastom* stories, dances, caves and waterfalls. Volcano tours depart from **Endu**, about 45 minutes north of the airport.

🛏 Sleeping

Sea Roar Bungalows BUNGALOW $
(Map p77; ☑ 7302577, 5357584; Endu; per person 2250VT) The two excellent double-storey traditional bungalows here sleep up to eight people and are set in a lovely garden with sea views in Endu village. Host Walter can organise volcano tours from the east and cultural tours of the village. It's about 45 minutes from Ulei airport.

South Ambrym

🛏 Sleeping

Karina Guesthouse GUESTHOUSE $
(Map p77; ☑ 7742661; www.vanuatuisland experience.com; Port Vatu; per person incl meals 2000VT) John Tasso runs this simple multibed guest bungalow in Port Vatu and guides volcano tours directly from here on the southwest route. A truck charter from Craig Cove airport is 5000VT.

Wola Volcano Guesthouse BUNGALOW $
(Map p77; ☑ 5487405; Lalinda; per person incl meals 2500VT) This thatched bungalow has two rooms sleeping five, with basic shared facilites. Owner Joses Wilfred is an experienced volcano guide, so this is a good alternative starting point to climb Mts Benbow and Marum, instead of nearby Port Vatu.

ESPIRITU SANTO

POP 40,000 / AREA 3677 SQ KM

Better known simply as Santo, this is Vanuatu's largest island and one of its most enjoyable. It doesn't have quite the activities and infrastructure of Port Vila, but it does have world-class diving, some excellent upmarket island resorts and some of the most jaw-droppingly beautiful beaches in the archipelago.

Espiritu Santo hides many of its secrets away from its small capital, Luganville, but there are plenty of tour operators to help get you to every corner of the island. Big attractions include the Millennium Cave, snorkelling or diving over dumped WWII memorabilia, the stunning east coast beaches and inviting blue holes. If you scuba dive, don't miss the SS *President Coolidge*, one of the world's most accessible wrecks.

Fanafo, north of Luganville, was where, in 1963, charismatic Jimmy Stevens formed the Nagriamel movement. Then, on 27 May 1980, eight weeks before national independence, he and his supporters staged a coup known as the Coconut Rebellion. Armed mainly with bows and arrows, they occupied Luganville and proclaimed Santo's independence, calling their new country Vemarana. However, the new nation collapsed with Stevens' arrest on 1 September.

Inland, villages are isolated and the locals totally self-sufficient. Southwest Santo has Vanuatu's highest mountains: Mt Tabwemasana (1879m), Mt Kotamtam (1747m), Mt Tawaloala (1742m) and Santo Peak (1704m), all of which can be climbed with local guides.

ℹ Getting There & Away

AIR
Luganville's Pekoa International Airport receives a weekly international flight direct from Brisbane, Australia, and at least two flights daily to/from Port Vila. It's also the feeder airport for Vanuatu's northern islands, with direct flights from Santo to Malekula, Ambae, Pentecost and the Torres and Banks islands. Contact Air Vanuatu at its **Santo office** (Map p83; ☑ 37670; Main St; ⊗7.30am-4.30pm Mon-Fri, 8-11am Sat) or **airport office** (Map p86; ☑ 36506).

BOAT
Luganville has **Customs & Quarantine** (Map p83; ☑ 36225) and immigration facilities for yachts at or near the Main Wharf. Segond Channel, with its sandy bottom, is the town's main anchorage, but Aore island is the safest: 40m deep and away from the southeasterlies that hit the mainland.

Big Sista (Map p83; ☑ 23461) and Vanuatu Ferry (p59) both stop here on their weekly ferry trip between Port Vila and Santo.

ℹ Getting Around

CAR & MOTORCYCLE
Santo's East Coast Rd is sealed from Luganville to Port Olry, so it's a good opportunity to self-drive; elsewhere travel by boat, 4WD truck or foot.

Deco Stop (Map p83; ☑ 36175; www.decostop.com.vu) The best place to rent a car (from 12,000VT per day) and the only place to rent a scooter (5000VT) or wicked dune buggy (10,000VT). Also rents out mountain bikes (2500VT).

Espiritu Car Hire (Map p83; ☑ 37539; Main St) Hire compact SUVs here from 9000VT per day.

MINIBUS & TAXI
Minibuses can be found around town but compact taxis far outnumber them in Luganville and are similarly priced at around 200VT for short trips. A minibus/taxi to the airport is 200/1000VT.

A minibus runs up the east coast from Luganville to Port Olry (600VT) from Monday to Saturday, leaving Unity Pacific Garage in Luganville between 2pm and 4pm. To return, stand by the roadside in Port Olry before 6.30am.

Luganville & Around
POP 13,200

Luganville is Vanuatu's 'second city', with a long, languid main road running parallel to the waterfront. Apart from the outlook across the channel to Aore island it's not a particularly attractive town, but with a good range of accommodation, some cool cafes and kava bars, plenty of dive and tour operators and a cheerful market, it's a fun place to hang out or base yourself for trips around Santo.

◎ Sights

★ **Millennium Cave**   CAVE
(Map p80; ☑ 5470957; 7000VT; ⊗8am) Trek and trudge through the jungle, across creeks, along bamboo bridges and through cascades to this massive cave, 20m wide and 50m high, about 15km from Luganville. Climb down a bamboo ladder, and through a rocky pool dodging cascades and little bats, then out into the sunlight and into icy water to zap down the rapids past amazing towering rocks, gorgeous rainforest and waterfalls. An awesome, full-day, guided-tour experience; book through your accommodation or at the office near Sarakata Bridge.

Espiritu Santo

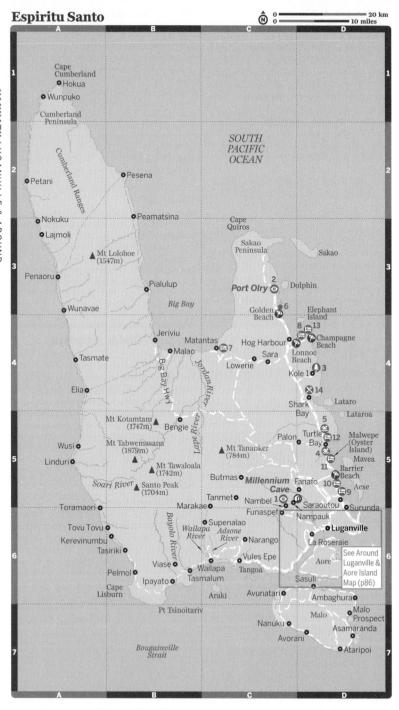

Espiritu Santo

Luganville Market　　　　　　　MARKET
(Map p83; Main St; ⊙24hr) Villagers come from all over to sell their produce here. It's near the Sarakata Bridge.

Million Dollar Point　　　　　　DIVE SITE
(Map p86; 500VT) Million Dollar Point, where hundreds of tonnes of US military equipment was dumped, now shows its coral-encrusted machinery to snorkellers and divers. At low tide you'll find metal objects littering the beach for a kilometre in either direction. Don't leave your valuables around while you dive.

Aore Island　　　　　　　　　　ISLAND
(Map p86) Across the Segond Channel, Aore island is easily reached on the free resort ferry. There's not much regular transport on the island so you're limited to short walks and hanging out at the resort for a few hours (free if you buy lunch). The ferry departs Phillips Wharf at 8am, 11.30am and 2.30pm, returning at 11am, 1.30pm and 4pm.

Leweton Cultural Village　　　VILLAGE
(Map p86; ☑5671114; 3000VT) Listen to women making water music and see other

traditions from the Banks islands. Located near the airport; book in advance.

Ransuck Cultural Village　　　VILLAGE
(Map p86; ☑5443973; 3000VT) Community members from Pentecost take you through a lush garden and show you how their beautiful mats are made. Near the airport.

⭐ Activities

Quadman Vanuatu　　ADVENTURE SPORTS
(Map p83; ☑5472051; http://quadmanvanuatu. com; half/full day 4000/7000VT) Hire a quad bike and head out for a day of adventure.

Santo Horse Adventures　　HORSE RIDING
(☑7774700; santohorseadventures@gmail.com; East Coast Rd; pony rides 4000VT, 2hr trail rides 7500VT) Experience a trail ride through jungle and along beaches. Megan's horse ranch is at Lope Lope Adventure Lodge around 11km north of Luganville.

Diving, Snorkelling & Fishing

Santo, particularly around Luganville and the offshore islands, is justifiably famous for its scuba diving, and snorkellers will find plenty to see just below the surface. Coral reefs are bright and healthy, the wrecks are world class and dive operators extremely professional, though you'll need to spend some time here to see the best of what's on offer. Look at operators' websites for some amazing images, such as MV *Henry Bonneaud*, one of the world's top night dives; SS *President Coolidge*, lying in 21m to 67m of water; and Tutuba Point, a spectacular drift dive with brilliant corals and marine life.

There are boat and offshore dives for beginners to experts. An intro dive costs about 10,000VT, single dives are 7000VT, diver certification courses cost from 48,000VT and equipment hire is 1500VT.

Allan Power Dive Tours　　　　DIVING
(Map p83; ☑36822; www.allan-power-santo. com; Main St; s/d dive 5000/10,000VT, gear hire per dive 2000VT) Allan Power is a legend in dive circles, having led more than 28,000 dives on the SS *President Coolidge* since 1969. Also dives at Million Dollar Point and other wrecks and offers PADI Open Water courses (49,000VT).

Aquamarine　　　　　　　　　DIVING
(Map p83; ☑5551555; Main St) Experienced dive outfit based at the Espiritu hotel.

Santo Island Dive & Fishing DIVING, FISHING
(Map p83; ☑7758082; www.santodive.com; Main St; per dive 7000VT, full gear hire 2000VT) This operator offers wreck and reef diving and fishing charters in search of tuna, *mahimahi* and wahoo.

Island Fishing Santo FISHING
(☑7740536; fabricemoderan@hotmail.com) Fabrice will take you out big-game fishing and snorkelling from his boat.

Hiking
Favourite Santo treks are through the Vatthe Conservation Area and the Loru Conservation Area. Wrecks to Rainforest can organise custom treks around the island.

🗘 Tours

Wrecks to Rainforest TOUR
(Map p83; ☑37365, 5547001; www.wrecksto rainforest.com; ☺7.30-11.30am & 1-5pm Mon-Fri, 7.30-11.30am Sat) With her office in front of the Espiritu hotel, owner Mayumi Green is a terrific source of knowledge and can organise custom two- to six-day treks (per day from 7000VT) through rainforest and mountains to *kastom* villages. Mayumi also runs tours with accommodation to the northern islands, Malekula and Ambrym.

Butterfly Adventure Tours TOUR
(☑5660290; tours 5000-10,000VT) Glenn runs a wide range of tours, from bushwalking to birdwatching, beaches to historic sites.

Heritage Tours TOUR
(☑36862, 7740968; www.heritagetours.com.vu) These island tours have been running for over 20 years; speak to Tim Rovu.

Paradise Tours TOUR
(☑7747159; www.paradisetourssanto.net) Luke has been running tours for years. He picks you up from your accommodation and offers a mix of one- and half-day tours.

Island Time Kayaking KAYAKING
(☑5695140; www.islandtimekayaking.net) Guided sea-kayaking tours at various locations along the east coast.

🛏 Sleeping

Luganville has a handful of good budget places and a few decent midrangers, but for the better resorts you'll need to head offshore or up the east coast.

★**Hibiscus Le Motel** MOTEL $
(Map p83; ☑36727; lemotelhac@gmail.com; Rue Dumont D'Urville; r 3500VT; ☞) Confortable rooms, all with bathrooms and kitchenettes, sleep three and are set around a cramped but sociable central area. Central but quiet location, bargain priced and friendly French hosts.

Unity Park Motel MOTEL $
(Map p83; ☑36052; www.unityparkmotel.com; Main St; s/d/tr/q 2200/3600/4500/6000, oceanview d 4000VT, with air-con 4500VT; ☀☞) Facing the park of the same name, Unity is a friendly and reliable budget hotel. Upstairs are large airy rooms along a hallway (ask for a front one with shared balcony). Downstairs is more basic but clean and cheap. The shared kitchen and bathroom facilities are great.

Aqua Backpackers HOSTEL $
(Map p83; ☑5554469; www.aquabackpack ers.com; dm 2500-3000VT, d 5000VT; ☞) This old-school backpackers has eight- and four-bed dorms and a small double in a loft-like space. Run by Mama Lou, it's built for

---

SANTO'S SUNKEN RICHES

Segond Channel was the Allies' base during WWII. For three years to September 1945, more than half a million military personnel, mainly Americans, were stationed here waiting to head into battle in the Pacific. There were sometimes 100 ships moored off Luganville. More than 10,000 ni-Van came to work for the troops. To them, the servicemen seemed fabulously wealthy and generous.

Unfortunately, **SS President Coolidge**, a luxury liner turned troopship, hit a friendly mine just offshore, where it sank with the loss of just one life. It's since become the world's largest accessible and diveable shipwreck. After the war, the USA offered the Condominium (p521) government the surplus equipment but the government didn't respond, so the lot was dumped. Everything from bulldozers, aeroplane engines and jeeps to crates of Coca-Cola went into the sea at what is now **Million Dollar Point**. The coral-encrusted equipment makes the point a popular diving and snorkelling spot.

Luganville

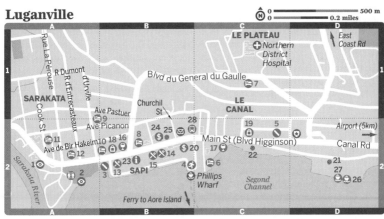

Luganville

travellers who like a good time, with a popular expat bar, pool table, live music on Fridays and a deck over the water.

Tropicana Motel & Backpackers   MOTEL **$**
(Map p83; ☑ 5372527, 36036; Cook St; dm/s/d 2000/3500/4500VT; ☎) Clean, modern rooms with en-suite bathrooms surround a courtyard garden (which acts like an echo chamber if it's busy). The industrial-sized communal kitchen is the best in Vanuatu and the dorms are only two-person bunk rooms.

★**Espiritu**   HOTEL **$$**
(Map p83; ☑ 37539; www.the-espiritu.com; Main St; d 12,000-16,000VT; ❋☎⊠) The Espiritu has transformed into an elegant boutique hotel and central Luganville's best midranger. First-floor rooms come with lounge, flat-screen TV and air-con, while the deluxe balcony rooms have king-sized beds and street views. There's a swanky pool and bar area at the back.

Deco Stop Lodge LODGE $$
(Map p83; ☎ 36175; www.decostop.com.vu; d/f incl breakfast 12,000/16,000VT; ❄ 🛜 🏊) High on the ridge behind Luganville, with views overlooking Segond Channel, Deco Stop has a convivial deck framing a pool with a view and a good restaurant. Rooms are all south-facing, some fronting the garden, others with private decks.

Beachfront Resort LODGE $$
(Map p86; ☎ 36881; www.thebeachfrontresort.com; lodge s/d/tr from 8500/11,100/13,600VT, air-con bungalows s/d from 12,600/15,900VT; ❄ 🛜 🏊) The 'budget' Starfish lodge has its own kitchen and lounge, but the best rooms at this sprawling waterfront resort are the spotless modern bungalows (garden or ocean view) with thatched roofs, verandahs, air-con and kitchenettes. There's a cool poolside area and restaurant. Cruising yachts often anchor out front.

Village de Santo APARTMENT $$
(Map p86; ☎ 5623825, 36123; www.villagede santoresort.com; d incl breakfast 13,500VT; 🛜 🏊) The 18 swish, traditionally designed, self-contained family units orbit a pool and lush gardens. It's close to the waterfront, the recommended Restaurant 1606 is on-site and it's walking distance (1.5km) to town. There's a Kids Club during school holidays.

Hotel Santo HOTEL $$
(Map p83; ☎ 36250; s/d 8200/9300VT, upstairs s/d/tr 14,700/16,300/18,100VT; ❄ 🛜 🏊) It's a bit of a time warp, but that's part of the appeal at this orange retro '70s hotel, with garden-facing units out the back and more elegant hotel-style rooms upstairs. Traditional touches include the fabulous *tamtam* in the foyer and the large *nakamal* in the back garden.

★ Aore Island Resort RESORT $$$
(Map p86; ☎ 36705; http://aoreislandresorts.com; bungalow incl breakfast from 20,000VT; 🛜 🏊) Spacious, well-designed bungalows (some in a child-free area, others for families), grassy slopes to the water, snorkel gear and kayaks: all are good, and the restaurant is a grand area (nonguests welcome). The ferry leaves from Phillips Wharf; ask for the schedule when you book. There's a dive shop and day spa.

★ Ratua Private Island Resort RESORT $$$
(Map p86; ☎ 30020; www.ratua.com; Ratua; safari tents from 37,000VT, villas from 41,000VT; ❄ @ 🏊) This private island resort some 30 minutes' speedboat ride from Santo has Bali-sourced bungalows and an eco bent (all profits go to the Ratua Foundation, to help educate children). Horse riding is popular, or laze away the day reading in the Yacht Club or being pampered at the over-water spa. The resort has its own air service (Air Ratua).

Bokissa Eco Island Resort RESORT $$$
(Map p86; ☎ 30030; www.bokissa.com; d 42,000VT; ❄ @ 🏊) This luxurious private island resort boasts bungalows just steps from astounding reef snorkelling. It's a real getaway with everything you need: day spa, dive shop and quality dining. You'll be met in Luganville for the 25-minute speedboat ride here.

✕ Eating

★ Market Meal Booths MARKET $
(Map p83; meals 400VT; ⊙ 7.30am-10pm) The best budget dining in Santo. Choose one of the bright little tables next to the orange booths and a cheery woman will appear at the window with a glass of cordial, ready to take your order. Choose from chicken, fish or steak, piled with rice and vegetables, and watch it being cooked through the window.

★ Natangora Café CAFE, JAPANESE $
(Map p83; ☎ 36811; Main St; meals 650-1500VT; ⊙ 7.30am-4.30pm Mon-Fri, 8am-1.30pm Sat; 🛜 ♿) This breezy open-air cafe (with a distant view of the water) specialises in breakfast, house-roasted coffee, hamburgers, juices and salads, but also does an interesting line in Japanese dishes: sushi, bento boxes, miso soup and Japanese curries.

Friends Cafe CAFE $
(Map p83; Main St; meals 300-1300VT; ⊙ 7.30am-4pm; 🛜) A friendly little Euro-style cafe with excellent local Aore island coffee, homemade pies, burgers and sandwiches. Great spot for breakfast.

Attar Cafe CAFE $
(Map p83; ☎ 37373; Main St; mains 500-1700VT; ⊙ 7am-5pm; 🛜) Excellent coffee, monster burgers, souvlaki and steaks – Attar does simple food with a smile.

Tu Restaurant INTERNATIONAL $$
(Map p83; ☎ 37539; Main St; pizzas 1800VT, mains 2000-2500VT; ⊙ 8am-8pm) At the Espiritu hotel, this elegant street-front restaurant serves a well-prepared local and global range of dishes from Santo scotch fillet to Thai green curry as well as all-day pizzas. Lunch features burgers and fish and chips. At the back is a stylish poolside lounge bar.

Restaurant 1606
INTERNATIONAL $$

(Map p86; Red Corner, Village de Santo; mains 1100-3400VT; ⊙7.30am-10pm) Regarded by some as Luganville's best restaurant, 1606 is worth a trip for its interesting selection of tapas (700VT to 1300VT), and mains such as seafood paella and crispy pork belly. Lunch offers the usual array of burgers and sandwiches.

Deco Stop Restaurant
INTERNATIONAL $$

(Map p83; ☑36175; Hospital Rd; mains 2200-2400VT; ⊙7am-3pm & 6-9pm) It's worth a trip up to the hilltop for the view alone, out to Segond Channel and Aore island. Dining is beside the pool with white wicker chairs on the terrace. The small but changing menu features fresh produce such as Santo scotch fillet, Thai curry, local lobster and pan-fried *poulet*. Full bar and friendly service.

Drinking & Nightlife

Luganville might be Vanuatu's second town, but it makes Vila look like Vegas. The Espiritu hotel has a very inviting poolside bar, as does Deco Stop Lodge, and there's weekly live music at Village de Santo. Kava bars are open from 5pm to 10pm – look out for a red or green light.

Seaside Kava Bar
KAVA BAR

(Map p83; Main St; cups from 50VT; ⊙from 5pm) This entertaining place has an unbeatable location with log benches right on the waterfront and other communal areas scattered around. Food is available and beer is only 300VT.

Club de Sanma
CLUB

(Map p83; ☑36039; Main St; ⊙10am-midnight Sun-Thu, to 3am Fri & Sat) Part nightclub, part sports bar and (upstairs) pokies joint, this is central Luganville's most happening nightspot. Occasional jazz and blues music on weekends.

Shopping

LCM
SHOPPING CENTRE

(Map p83; Main St; ⊙7.30am-5pm Mon-Sat) This modern shopping centre stocks a full supermarket range of groceries and liquor, as well as a surprisingly good line in fishing, camping and snorkelling gear. There's a useful noticeboard out front and credit cards are accepted.

Mama Handicrafts
SOUVENIRS

(Map p83; Main St; ⊙7.30am-5pm Mon-Sat) At the east end of town, this small shop is the best place to browse for locally made clothing, jewellery, carvings and woven bags.

Information

Luganville's main street has commercial banking facilities with ANZ and Westpac ATMs.

ANZ Bank (Map p83; ☑36711; ⊙8am-3pm Mon-Fri) Has an ATM.

Northern District Hospital (Map p83; ☑36345; ⊙24hr) Above the town in Le Plateau; usually hosts 'baby docs' (international doctors-in-training). Also has a good pharmacy.

Police (Map p83; ☑36222) Local police station.

Post Office (Map p83; Main St; ⊙8.30am-5pm Mon-Fri) Luganville's main post office.

Sanma Information & Call Centre (Map p83; ☑36616; www.santo.travel; Main St; ⊙7.30am-5pm Mon-Fri, plus weekends on cruise-ship days) Part tourist office, part private travel agency, Sanma (Santo and Malo) has helpful staff who can make local bookings.

Westpac Bank (Map p83; ☑36625; ⊙8am-4pm Mon-Fri) Has an ATM.

The East Coast Road

Santo's East Coast Rd between Luganville and Port Olry is only the second sealed road in Vanuatu (completed around the same time as the Efate Ring Rd in 2011), so it's an ideal region for a day trip. But with some excellent places to stay, play and dine, it's worth setting aside a few days.

◉ Sights & Activities

Loru Conservation Area
NATURE RESERVE

(Map p80; ☑5461731; guided tour per person 1000VT) Covering 220 hectares, Loru Conservation Area contains one of the last patches of lowland forest remaining on Santo's east coast. There are several excellent nature walks, many coconut crabs and a bat cave, which the villagers use as a cyclone shelter. Turn at the signpost off the East Coast Rd down a dirt road for 4km to Kole 1 Village. If you've come without a guide, ask for Kal. The guided walk takes about half an hour.

Lonnoc Beach
BEACH

In a beautiful coastal setting just off the East Coast Rd, this beach is all white sand and turquoise water, with views of Elephant Island. Drop into Lonnoc Beach Bungalows – day visitors can use the beach for free – and ask about kayak tours.

Around Luganville & Aore Island

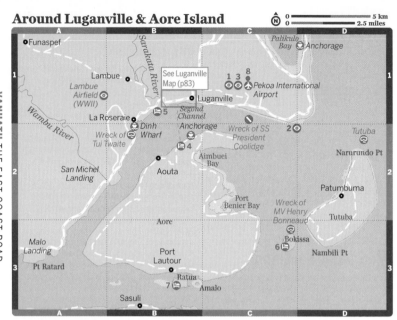

Around Luganville & Aore Island

Champagne Beach   BEACH
(per car 2000VT, or per person 500VT) Champagne Beach is a pretty horseshoe of soft white sand and turquoise water that gets rave (slightly overhyped) reviews and regular cruise-ship visitors. If you're driving, park the vehicle well back from the beach to avoid the extra charge. An impromptu souvenir market sets up when cruise ships are in.

★ **Port Olry**   VILLAGE
(Map p80) At the end of the sealed road you come to Port Olry, a small francophone fishing village with a stunning curve of white-sand beach and eye-watering shallow turquoise waters. Three offshore islands, which can be reached by kayak (500VT) or outrigger canoe (1000VT), have good reef snorkelling. There are a couple of good shack restaurants and bungalow operations here, making it a great place to chill out for a few days.

Secret Home Tour   ECOTOUR
(Map p80; ☑ 5685933, 5638219; East Coast Rd; per person 500VT) Drop in here, just before Port Olry, and local villagers will take you on this 30-minute garden and coastal walk, visiting caves, crab farms and a village garden, watching kava preparation and more.

Blue Holes
From south to north, stop at **Riri Riri Blue Hole** (Map p80; 500VT), where you can take an outrigger canoe up the river from the main road; pretty, jungle-clad **Matevulu Blue Hole** (Map p80; 500VT); or lovely **Nanda Blue Hole** (Map p80; 500VT).

DON'T MISS

OYSTER ISLAND

This small, forested island, less than 200m across from Santo's mainland, is home to a marine reserve and the excellent Oyster Island Restaurant & Resort. Take the signposted turn-off and summon the resort boat by banging on the gas cylinder – it operates on demand and nonguests are more than welcome.

The romantic **Oyster Island Restaurant & Resort** (Map p80; ☎36283; www.oyster-island.com; d units 12,500VT, d bungalows 21,000-23,000VT, family villas 30,000VT; 📶) consists of a scattering of individual traditional-style bungalows (the best are on the waterfront) and supremely comfortable units. With only 32 beds, there's a feel of exclusivity but also a welcoming, down-to-earth family vibe. A host of tours are offered, including the exclusive Mt Hope Waterfall tour (5000VT).

Much of the produce used in the **restaurant** (☎7782773; mains 1500-3000VT; ⏰7am-10pm) is sourced locally on the island – including the oysters. Call to order at least a few hours in advance for fresh oysters (1200VT for half a dozen). The Sunday lunch buffet (adult/child 2400/1200VT) is a legendary extravaganza.

Sleeping & Eating

★Port Olry Beach Bungalows & Restaurant BUNGALOW $
(Map p80; ☎5990320; portolrybeachbungalow@gmail.com; s/d/f incl breakfast 4000/6000/7000VT) The three beautifully designed traditional bungalows here are a cut above most island huts, with solid timber decks and flooring, open-sky en suite and carved furniture. The beachfront restaurant and bar is also top-notch.

Reef Resort Backpackers HOSTEL $
(Map p80; ☎7737627, 37627; www.reefresortsanto.com.vu; East Coast Rd; dm/d/f 2500/7000/10,000VT) At pretty Turtle Bay, this waterfront garden backpackers is run by Honey. Rooms range from six-bed dorms or basic rooms in the main house to spacious family rooms with en suite, fridge, TV and private balcony. Kayaks, canoes, self-catering kitchen and a restaurant. Excellent value.

Lonnoc Beach Bungalows BUNGALOW $
(Map p80; ☎5695140, 5906863; www.lonnocbeachbungalows.net; dm/s/d/f incl breakfast 2500/4500/6000/12,500VT) Fronting the captivating Lonnoc Beach, this well-organised budget resort has a dormitory lodge and a range of traditional stone and thatch bungalows with en suite. Free kayaks, generator power in the evenings and an excellent central restaurant make this a good deal.

Towoc Restaurant & Bungalows BUNGALOW $
(Map p80; ☎5636173; towoc.bungalows@hotmail.com; s/d incl breakfast 2500/5000VT, beachfront 3500/7000VT) These simple bungalows are scattered around a garden setting on pretty Towoc Beach, a few minutes' walk to Champagne Beach (free access to guests). Solar lighting but evening generator in the friendly restaurant.

Bay of Illusions Guest House BUNGALOW $
(Map p80; ☎5612525; d incl breakfast 2500VT) If you're heading inland to Big Bay or Vatthe Conservation Area, Bay of Illusions is the place to stay, with a two-room bungalow near a black-sand beach at Matantas. Meals available. Bookings and transport can also be arranged through Wrecks to Rainforest (p510) in Luganville.

Turtle Bay Lodge LODGE $$
(Map p80; ☎37988; www.turtlebaylodge.vu; dm/d/f incl breakfast 3500/7600/12,600VT; P📶🏊) With its private bit of beach, spacious units and welcoming restaurant-bar, Turtle Bay Lodge has an upmarket family feel with a reasonable price tag. Use the kayaks, rent the lodge car for a day or enjoy the serenity of Turtle Bay.

★Lope Lope Adventure Lodge LODGE $$$
(Map p80; ☎36066; www.lopelopelodge.com; d fan/air-con 38,500/41,000VT; P📶) The four luxurious, romantic bungalows here are very private and have absolute water frontage with verandahs overlooking a perfect patch of sand. Boutique-styled accommodation with elevated king-sized beds facing the water, open-sky bathrooms, wi-fi, iPod, minibar and safe. The **Slipway Sports Bar & Grill** (mains 1450-3350VT; 📶) here is one of the best places to eat in Santo.

Sunrise Beach
Cabanas Eco Resort CABAÑAS $$$
(Map p80; ☑7799927, 36060; www.sunrise
beachcabanas.com; Barrier Beach; d 18,500-
29,300VT; P🖘) The superb architect-
designed polygonal cabanas here provide a
romantic couples retreat on a private beach.
Thoughtful touches include boutique toilet-
ries, imported furniture, loaded iPod and
intercom for ordering meals. The welcoming
owners are building some cheaper guest-
house rooms, but it's strictly no kids.

Moyyan House by the Sea GUESTHOUSE $$$
(Map p80; ☑30026; www.moyyan.com; d incl
breakfast 26,000-29,000VT; P🖘) There's an
air of an old-fashioned planter's cottage
at exclusive little Moyyan, with a small
private beachfront on Barrier Beach, lush
gardens and an inviting communal deck.
Rooms are breezy but simple, focusing on
the guest experience, with privacy, free tablets, minibar and a reputable day spa.

Little Paradise Restaurant SEAFOOD $$
(Map p80; ☑5483534; Port Olry; mains 1650-
2500VT) The original shack restaurant in Port
Olry (also called Harbour Beach Restaurant).
You might find local lobster and coconut
crab on the menu or ask about cheaper local
dishes. Service can be slow. There are a few
bungalows at the back (2500VT per person).

Velit Bay Plantation & 15° South SEAFOOD $$
(Map p80; ☑5619687; www.velitbayplantation.
com; East Coast Rd; mains 1500-3000VT; ⊙7am-
4pm Mon-Fri, 9am-4pm Sat, 11.30am-4pm Sun; P)
The winding 2km drive down the rocky road
to spectacular Velit Bay is a visual sensation,
while the small, open-sided 15° South does
much to tempt the taste buds. Chill on the
private beach, where there are deckchairs
and a bunch of activities – kayaking, kitesurfing, snorkelling and beach volleyball –
or indulge in fresh seafood or pasta.

ⓘ Getting There & Away

There's a daily minibus service along the east
coast. Join the waiting crowd at Unity Pacific
Petrol Station in Luganville for the trip to Port
Olry (500VT) from around 2pm (check times in
advance). Taxis cost about 2000VT to Oyster
Island, 5000VT to Lonnoc Beach. To charter a
truck from Luganville to Matantas on Big Bay
costs around 8000VT one way. A cheaper option
is to take the local bus from Luganville, get off at
Sara village and organise a truck from there to
Matantas (around 2500VT; Monday to Friday).

PENTECOST, AMBAE & MAEWO

Pentecost

POP 16,800 / AREA 438 SQ KM

Pentecost is famously home to the *naghol*
(land diving), the most remarkable custom in
all of Melanesia, where men make spectacular leaps of courage from high towers as a gift
to the gods to ensure a bountiful yam harvest.

Pentecost is a long, thin island with a rugged interior, where truck travel can be pain-
fully slow. Most of the population lives along
the west coast, which has a high rainfall, attributed to local rainmakers. A rocky beach
extends 12km from just before Lonorore
airfield south to Ranputor. The south is the
home of the *naghol* (April to June). Pangi is
the largest village in the south but it's pretty
basic, with just a kava bar, clinic, a couple of
guesthouses and the NBV bank, which can
change foreign currency in an emergency.

⊙ Sights & Activities

Apart from the land diving, you can take
jungle walks to waterfalls and banyans and
the stone ruins of a feasting hall, where 100
people were killed by the eel spirit. Other
tours include visits to villages to see *kastom*
dances. North of the airstrip is **Waterfall
Falls** (Map p89), tumbling down behind
Waterfall Village into pretty rockpools.

★ Land Diving CULTURAL TOUR
(⊙Apr-Jun) Land-dive towers are erected
at **Lonorore Airfield**, **Londot**, **Pangi** and
Rangusuksu (Map p89), though exact sites
change and are announced annually). **Luke
Fargo** (☑7734621; Mari Bungalows) arranges
official tours to the land diving (adult/child
12,000/6000VT). Most tourists come on
day packages (per person including flights
50,000VT) with Port Vila tour companies.

🛏 Sleeping & Eating

★ Noda Guesthouse BUNGALOW $
(Map p89; ☑5473071, 7727394; www.pentecost
island.net/noda; Waterfall Village; per person incl
meals 3200VT) A great place to base yourself
in Waterfall Village (Vanu). The well-kept
house has six bedrooms and there are three
double-bed huts with shared bathroom. Silas is a great host who can organise tours to
kastom villages (7000VT), a nearby waterfall (800VT) and land diving (12,000VT),

Pentecost

and jungle treks (600VT). There's generator power in the evenings.

Mari Bungalows   BUNGALOW **$**
(Map p89; ☑ 535514, 773462; Londot; s/d incl breakfast 3000/4000VT) These traditional thatched bungalows are set into the hills beside a land-dive site and opposite Londot beach. Luke Fargo operates land-diving tours from here. It's self-catering or 600VT per meal.

River Lodge   GUESTHOUSE **$**
(Map p89; ☑ 5348846, 7723374; Baravet; d incl breakfast 3000VT) Set in a palm grove opposite a rocky beach a short drive north of the airstrip, this simple guesthouse has four rooms. Jonas arranges land diving, snorkelling, and waterfall and cave tours.

Nak Bungalow   BUNGALOW **$**
(Map p89; ☑ 3573761; Pangi; per person without bathroom incl meals 3500VT) There are 12 beds in this basic guesthouse in the heart of Pangi village. The simple rooms are dressed with colourful sarongs and the shared bathrooms have bucket showers and flush toilets.

Panliki Bungalows   BUNGALOW **$**
(Map p89; ☑ 5434412; Ranputur; per person incl meals 2500VT) In Ranputor village, Joseph runs the five simple beachfront rooms here. There's solar lighting and a friendly atmosphere.

❶ Getting There & Away

AIR

Lonorore airfield is the main point of entry for Pentecost. **Air Vanuatu** (☑ 23748) flies here from Port Vila and Santo at least twice a week. Transport from Lonorore airfield to Pangi by truck or boat is 4000VT. In the far north, Sara

Pentecost

VANUATU PENTECOST

airfield is really only useful if you're taking the boat across to Maewo island.

BOAT

Pentecost has good protection from the south-eastern trade winds along the west coast, with many anchorages and landing places. Panas and Loltong are popular. In good conditions it's possible to arrive by speedboat from Ambae, Ambrym and Maewo.

Ambae

Ambae formed as part of a dramatic semi-active shield volcano, **Mt Lombenben** (1496m), which rumbles dynamically. A cone rose out of blue **Lake Manaro Lakua**, one of its famous crater lakes, in 2005, creating world news, then went back down. Hot and lime-green **Lake Vui** also sends volcanologists into a frenzy whenever it boils. **Lake Manaro Ngoru**, the third crater lake, is mostly dry with a central cold-water spring.

Guides and entry fees to the lakes cost 1000VT each, transfers 5000VT and meals 1000VT.

⊙ Getting There & Away

Air Vanuatu flies to Longana from Santo three or four times a week and to Walaha at least once a week.

🛏 Sleeping & Eating

★**Tui Lodge** GUESTHOUSE $
(Map p90; ☑5379267; bookattuilodge@gmail.com; Saratamata; per person incl meals 3000VT) This bright, modern six-room guesthouse is at Saratamata, not far from Longana airport. There's a guest kitchen, a restaurant and hot

Ambae

water, and the hosts can organise treks to Lake Vui and Lake Manaro Lakua. A truck from the airport costs 1000VT.

Duviara Last Stop Bungalows BUNGALOW $
(Map p90; ☑5949740; Ambanga; per person 1500VT) Duviara Last Stop Bungalows is the closest place to the start of the treks to Lake Vui and Lake Manaro Lakua. Owner Paul can organise a guide (2000VT).

Toa Palms Bungalow BUNGALOW $
(Map p90; ☑5637232, 7710800; Ndui Ndui; per person 1500VT) The best bet for exploring west Ambae is Toa Palms, with three comfortable en-suite bungalows. The owners can help organise a trek to the crater lakes.

Maewo

The 'Island of Water' has rivers, hot springs, deep cold pools and magnificent waterfalls. **Big Water waterfall**, in the north, is thought of locally as the Eighth Wonder of the World.

Down south, at **Sanasom**, is magnificent **Hole of the Moon Cave** (Maewo; 1500VT) and **Malangauliuli**, a cave with spectacular petroglyphs. Chief Jonah is *kastom* owner of the caves. **Justin Ihu** (☑7742605) can get you to them on his boat (7000VT).

Near Asanvari are the **Lavoa Cascades**, where you can swim or see a cultural show.

⊙ Getting There & Away

Maewo's airstrip is located in the north, a few kilometres from Naone village. Air Vanuatu flies there once a week from Santo via Ambae. Another option is to fly into Ambae or Pentecost and take a speedboat (10,000VT) across to Asanvari in the south.

🛏 Sleeping & Eating

Mule Ocean View Guesthouse BUNGALOW $
(☑7742605; Asanvari; r per person incl breakfast 1700VT) Justin and Ericka run this simple but cosy guesthouse with two double bungalows near the fading Yacht Club in Asanvari. There's a restaurant as well as a kitchen for self-caterers, and fresh vegetables from the garden. Justin also has a boat.

Sparkling Waters
Bar & Restaurant SEAFOOD $$
(☑5442135; Asanvari; ⊙8am-8pm) Enjoy a cold beer on the verandah of this bar at Lavoa Cascades, or find out what's on the menu – seafood is the speciality.

BANKS & TORRES ISLANDS

These remote northerly groups of islands are popular with touring yachties and are accessible by Air Vanuatu, which flies from Santo to Gaua, Torres, Motalava and Vanua Lava in a loop two or three times a week.

Gaua (Santa Maria)

Gaua offers spectacular hikes, including a two-day test around the island's three major sights: pretty **Lake Letas**, one of the largest freshwater lakes in the Pacific; **Mt Garet** (797m), a semiactive volcano; and fabulous **Siri Waterfall**. Climb up to the lake (camp overnight) and canoe across to the volcano – a sulphurous mess that seeps orange into the lake. Then it's a vicious trek down to the falls, 120m of roaring power pummelling to the sea.

🛏 Sleeping

Wongrass Bungalow   BUNGALOW **$**
(☑ 5690831, 7712879; per person incl meals 3500VT) The thatched two-bedroom Wongrass, near the airport, was the first in Gaua and is still going strong. Charles can arrange tours to the crater lake (3500VT).

Vanua Lava

The largest of the Banks islands, Vanua Lava offers waterfalls and excellent trekking. **Sola**, the island's capital, is the base for walks, such as the glorious day's hike (1000VT) via Mosina across the plateau overlooking Vureas Bay, through water-taro gardens, over streams and rapids to **Waterfall Bay**, where spectacular **Sasara Falls** tumbles over the cliff into the bay.

🛏 Sleeping

Leumerous Guesthouse   GUESTHOUSE **$**
(☑ 7733426, 5391846; Sola; camping 500VT, bungalows per person incl meals 2500VT) In Sola, stay at beachfront Leumerous Guesthouse

where six thatched bungalows sit along a garden path.

Motalava & Rah

Motalava is a small island in the Banks group, famous for its snake dance and treks to Sleeping Mountain (243m). A short canoe ride off the southwestern tip is stunning Rah island.

Air Vanuatu flies to Motalava from Santo once or twice a week. Wrecks to Rainforest (p82) in Santo can organise tours.

🛏 Sleeping

Rah Paradise Beach Bungalows   BUNGALOW **$**
(☑ 7745650, 5945757; per person incl meals 4000VT) On a beautiful beach on a tiny island just off Motalava, this guesthouse is run by Father Luke and his wife Rona, who work closely with the village. Organised activities include a snake dance, treks to Sleeping Mountain, a legend tour of the Rock of Rah and reef-island trips.

Torres Islands

These are the most remote islands of Vanuatu, with some dazzling white-sand or coral beaches and good surfing. There's excellent snorkelling on most islands: **Linua**, with the Kamilisa guesthouse and the airstrip; **Loh**, across a tidal sandbank; **Tegua** and **Hiu** to the north (from where you can see the Solomon Islands on a clear day); and **Toga**, where most of the people live. Everyone gets around in outrigger canoes.

🛏 Sleeping

Kamilisa Memorial Resort   GUESTHOUSE **$**
(☑ 7114506; Linua; per person incl meals 3000VT) The delightful Kamilisa guesthouse has four bungalows in a delicate rainforest, right on the lagoon on Linua island. Phone coverage is patchy, but owner Whitely greets every flight.

PETER UNGER / GETTY IMAGES ©

1. Ashboarding, Mt Yasur (p66)
Descend from crater rim to ash plain in a matter of minutes.

2. Waterfall Falls, Pentecost (p88)
Spectacular cascades behind the aptly named Waterfall Village meet enticing rockpools.

3. Totemic carvings, Ambrym (p75)
Ambrym is home to some of Vanuatu's most impressive tree-fern carvings.

4. *Laplap* preparation, Tanna (p63)
Sharing this national, traditional dish in a *kastom* village is a Vanuatu must-do.

LIVCOOL / GETTY IMAGES ©

TOM PFEIFFER / VOLCANODISCOVERY / GETTY IMAGES ©

WILL SALTER / GETTY IMAGES ©

1. Welcoming ceremony, East Tanna (p65)
The only thing warmer than the welcome is Mt Yasur smouldering above.

2. Mele Beach, Port Vila (p47)
Heavenly sunsets abound, with Hideaway Island just 100m offshore.

3. Small Nambas Man, Malekula (p68)
This wild island is renowned for its rich tribal life.

4. Mt Benbow (p76), Ambrym
The sight of red-hot magma is a memorable reward for the somewhat demanding climb up this volcano.

PETER UNGER / GETTY IMAGES ©

Vanuatu Today

Vanuatu is often called the 'Land of Smiles'. Perhaps it's a genius marketing idea, but it was once named the 'world's happiest place' in the Happy Planet Index, and to see the beaming faces and hear the 'hellos' of the ni-Vanuatu it's hard not to agree. Paradise it may be, but it's not all smiles in these happy isles: islanders contend with frequent land disputes, lack of basic infrastructure, corrupt politicians and tropical cyclones.

Etiquette

Do Accept that landowners will want payment (from around 500VT to 2000VT) if you use their land, for instance to visit a blue hole, a snorkelling spot or a beach.

Do Check with locals to find out if the local *nakamal* (meeting house and kava bar) is female-friendly. It's rude to walk through a *nakamal* and they can be quite difficult to spot in rural villages when they're outdoors and there's no lighting.

Don't Bargain: prices are fixed, even at markets. Tipping is not expected either.

Top Website

Histri Blong Yumi Long Vanuatu (www.vanuatu.net.vu) Oral history plays a big part in Vanuatu's culture. Get a head start by reading some of the origin stories.

Best in Film

Tanna (2015) Romeo and Juliet tale set on Tanna island.

Best in Print

Getting Stoned with Savages (2006) Unfortunately titled Vanuatu travelogue by J Maarten Troost.

Bouncing Back from Pam

A global risk analysis study in 2015 reported that Port Vila (and by extension, Vanuatu) was the world's most exposed capital to natural disasters – cyclones, earthquakes, volcanic activity and drought. Not long after the report, Cyclone Pam (p105) wrought havoc across the islands, in March 2015, damaging or wiping out 95% of buildings (mostly homes) in the hardest hit areas, along with crops and plantations. Although the clean-up and rebuilding is well under way, the economic effects of one of Vanuatu's worst-ever natural disasters are far-reaching as Vanuatu's economy is largely agricultural; some 80% of the population is involved in farming and fishing. Major exports include copra (dried coconut), beef, cocoa and kava.

Tourism is also an important source of income, though little filters through to the outer islands. Cruise ships provide two-thirds of annual visitors (most coming from Australia and New Zealand), who come ashore for a few hours to buy handicrafts or take adventure tours. Many young ni-Van leave their villages to work in the tourism and service industries in Efate and Santo.

Politics Vanuatu Style

Corruption in Vanuatu politics is nothing new since independence, but a culture of backhanders and bribes was laid bare in October 2015 when 14 MPs, including Deputy Prime Minister Moana Carcasses, were found guilty of corruption and bribery and sent to prison for up to four years. Prime Minister Sato Kilman was criticised over his handling of the affair but was not among those charged. Still, with half of his People's Progress Party in jail, governing became untenable and a snap election was called by President Baldwin Lonsdale for 22 January 2016. Incredibly, more than half of the jailed MPs applied to recontest the election from prison. They were denied by the electoral commission.

By February 2016, a bloc of 36 newly elected MPs from 11 parties was attempting to establish a new coalition government.

The Times (& Kastoms) are Changing

Vanuatu is like two different countries: there are well-developed Efate and Santo, which have roads, electricity and tourism infrastructure, and then there are the other islands – all 81 of them. Outside Efate and Santo, life mostly goes on without basic infrastructure and the islanders survive on subsistence farming.

Though Vanuatu's villages can be remote, ni-Vanuatu that have eschewed modern life (by choice) are few and far between. *Kastom* (traditional) villages on the island of Tanna are the most well known, featuring in a handful of documentaries and reality TV programs. Even here, *kastom* itself is changing to meet the tourism industry's demands. What were once only ceremonial dances are now staged for tourists, while Pentecost's traditional spectacle of land diving now has an extended season and more jumps per week to cater to passing cruise ships.

My Land, My Vatu

Since independence in 1980, foreigners have been permitted to buy 75-year land leases for commercial use (50 years for residential) in Vanuatu. It's tempting for traditional owners to lease out lucrative land and buy a speedboat or 4WD truck; however, these decisions are often later regretted. The law was developed so that ni-Van could have control of their land and earn rent, but foreign investors now control some 90% of the (mostly beachfront) land around Efate, and there have been plenty of disagreements between developers and landowners when things go wrong.

Vanuatu's beauty has also created tourism opportunities for the ni-Van. The traditional owner of a tourist-friendly blue hole or stunning beach can charge between 500VT to 2000VT per visitor, even just for a look. Working out who that traditional owner is can lead to disputes that sometimes result in the complete closure of an attraction.

Cultural Landscapes

Vanuatu's population is not completely homogenous. There are hundreds of expatriates living in Vanuatu (mostly in Port Vila and mostly from Australia and New Zealand), and on most islands you'll find Australian Youth Ambassadors, American Peace Corps volunteers and New Zealand Volunteer Service Abroad participants (VSAs). There's an increasing number of Asian families running shops in Port Vila and Luganville, and projects such as the port development at Luganville have seen an influx of Chinese workers. Tanna's Lenakel is an exception, as no foreigners are allowed to own shops here.

POPULATION: **281,500**

TOTAL AREA OF VANUATU: **860,000 SQ KM**

AREA OF LAND: **12,200 SQ KM**

NUMBER OF TOURISTS (2014): **110,142 BY AIR; 221,691 DAY (CRUISE-SHIP) VISITORS**

GDP GROWTH: **2%**

UNEMPLOYMENT: **1.5%**

ARABLE LAND: **1.6%**

if Vanuatu were 100 people

98 would be Ni-Vanuatu
2 would be other

belief systems
(% of population)

56 Protestant
13 Roman Catholic
14 other Christian
5 indigenous beliefs
10 other
2 none/unspecified

population per sq km

VANUATU   NEW ZEALAND   AUSTRALIA

≈ 3 people

Vanuatu History

The many islands of Vanuatu share an ancient Pacific tribal culture dating back more than 3000 years. The more recent past of the islands, formerly known as New Hebrides (named by one James Cook in 1774), has been one of explorers, blackbirders, missionaries, colonial settlement and, finally, independence.

The First Pots

Early South Pacific travellers in their longboats had a neat navigational method: they'd jump out of the canoe and feel the current against their testicles. Then they'd know which way to go.

The history of Vanuatu begins with the Lapita people. They're easily traced because of their ability to make (and leave around) fine pottery. They also made long canoe voyages, leaving their lovely pottery at sites from northeast Papua New Guinea to Samoa. There is evidence of their occupation of Vanuatu in many places.

Pottery found on Malo, off Santo, showed they settled there about 1400 BC. In July 2004, an archaeological dig at Teouma (near Port Vila) unearthed more Lapita pottery, as well as the skeletal remains of nine Lapita people, plus chickens and pigs, dated at 3200 years ago. This was especially exciting because it shows that the people brought animals with them along with yams and taro, and a considerable appetite for shellfish.

Between the 11th and 15th centuries AD, Polynesians arrived from the central Pacific in sailing canoes holding up to 50 people plus live animals and plants. Vanuatu's oral traditions tell of cultural heroes arriving around this time from islands to the east, bringing with them new skills and customs.

Early Ni-Van Society

People lived in small clans, separated by deep ravines, impenetrable jungle and broad stretches of sea. Everyone lived in the shadow of their ancestral spirits. Some ghosts were benevolent, while others were hostile, quick to harass the living with famines, natural disasters or military defeat. When anyone suffered a serious misfortune, sorcery or spirits were blamed. Magic was widespread.

In the north, a man's status within the clan was earned through grade-taking ceremonies. Each grade took a man closer to becoming a

TIMELINE	1400 BC	11th Century AD	AD 1459
	Lapita people arrive in longboats with pottery.	Polynesians arrive from the central Pacific with animals and plants.	The volcano Kuwae erupts in Vanuatu, destroying an island in the huge explosion.

chief and finally a paramount chief. On a supernatural plane, the more grades a man had earned, the more powerful would be his defences against sorcery while alive, and the more potent his spirit after death.

Skirmishes between villages were frequent, and usually the victor captured one or two males for the men of high rank to eat. The victims' relatives would mount reprisals, so hostilities continued indefinitely.

The women attended to the gardening and cooking and, most importantly, to the husband's pigs. Men considered their pigs, which were a symbol of wealth and provided currency in the form of their tusks, more valuable than their wives.

The culture was steeped in agriculture. Yam cultivation decided the cycle of the year, with months named after yams.

Enter the Explorers

In 1605 Pedro Fernández de Quirós, a Portuguese navigator in the service of the Spanish crown, was on a voyage to find the missing southern continent, *terra australis*. The Spanish expedition left Callao in Peru on 21 December. Four months later the tall peak of Mere Lava came into view and, on 3 May 1606, the fleet sailed into Big Bay in northern Santo. Quirós believed he had at last found the great southern continent and named it Terra Australis del Espiritu Santo.

Quirós claimed Santo and *all* lands south of it to be under Spain's rule, and attempted to settle at Big Bay. This lasted 49 days. The mutinous crew, fed up with Quirós' dominating nature, used the opportunity of his ill-health to sail for Mexico.

For a modern take on *kastom* (traditional) law and how it operates within the legal framework of Vanuatu today, download *A Bird that Flies with Two Wings* by Miranda Forsyth from http://press. anu.edu.au.

VANUATU HISTORY ENTER THE EXPLORERS

CHIEF ROI MATA

Much of Vanuatu's history has been passed down in the form of oral stories, so it's always reassuring for historians to be able to match the legends with the facts.

A great example of this is the story of Chief Roi Mata, a king of Vanuatu. Legend has it that sometime around AD 1600 this chief of chiefs had the power to calm the warring tribes of Efate, and even put a (temporary) halt to cannibalism. However, sibling rivalry ended Chief Roi Mata's reign when he was shot in the neck with a poisoned arrow by his brother. Legend had it that he was buried on Hat Island with 47 others who were possibly interred alive. For 400 years few would visit the island, and it was only when a French archaeologist gained permission to dig there in 1967 that the truth was unveiled; yes, there was a mass grave, and yes, it looked like it was a voluntary live burial. There's a fascinating exhibit on this at the **National Museum of Vanuatu** (☑22129; Rue d'Artois; admission 1000VT, with guided tour 1500VT; ⊙9am-4.30pm Mon-Fri, 9am-noon Sat; ℗) in Port Vila, and locals offer guided tours of the **site** (2hr/half-/full-day tour 2000/7500/9800VT) on Hat Island.

1606	1825	1839	1865
Portuguese explorer, Pedro Fernández de Quirós, sails into Big Bay in Santo on 3 May and names the islands Terra Australis del Espiritu Santo.	European explorer Peter Dillon discovers sandalwood trees on Erromango and quickly sets up trading routes.	Missionaries begin their attempts to try to bring Christianity to the islanders. Many get eaten.	Nearly 100 years after British explorer Captain James Cook charts the islands, Europeans flock to settle them.

More than 160 years later, on 21 May 1768, the French nobleman Louis-Antoine de Bougainville sighted Maewo and Pentecost. He landed at Ambae and Malo, sailed between Malekula and Santo (proving Santo was not the fabled *terra australis*) and visited Big Bay.

In 1774 Commander (soon to be Captain) James Cook of the HMS *Resolution,* on his second Pacific expedition, mapped and gave his own names to the islands of Vanuatu. Many are still used today, including Tanna, Erromango, Ambrym and the Shepherd Islands. He named the archipelago the New Hebrides.

In 1788 the Frenchman Jean-François de Galaup La Pérouse and his two ships, *Boussole* and *Astrolabe,* passed through the New Hebrides. However, both ships were lost in the southeastern Solomons. Their wrecks were later found by Peter Dillon in 1826 on the island of Vanikoro.

The Sandalwood Trade

The best study of the turbulent times of the 19th-century sandalwood trade is Dorothy Shinberg's *They Came for Sandalwood.*

Irish explorer-trader Peter Dillon set the markets buzzing in 1825 by reporting huge numbers of sandalwood trees on Erromango (hence the name 'Dillon's Bay' on the island). There was a great demand for sandalwood in China, where it was used for incense; traders, keen to exchange sandalwood for tea, which they could then sell to the growing tea industry in England, were quickly on their way. Sandalwood became Vanuatu's first export.

Initially, traders would exchange a hooped piece of iron for a longboat full of sandalwood, which was a much better deal than they could get in Asia. There were enormous profits to be made. But as the supply of slow-growing sandalwood dwindled, islanders demanded guns, ammunition and tobacco; men from enemy villages (for eating at ceremonies); or pigs in their thousands (which usually came from Tanna or Fiji). Sometimes islanders would persuade the traders to use their ships' guns to lay waste to their enemies' villages.

There were many attacks on ships' crews, often in retaliation for previous trader atrocities. If a ship cheated some villagers or fired its cannon at them, the next Europeans could expect a violent reception.

The sandalwood trade virtually ceased in 1868 with the removal of the last accessible stands.

Blackbirding

As the sandalwood trade declined, a more insidious trade in blackbirding developed. In the 1870s, cheap labour was needed for the sugar-cane industries of Fiji and Queensland (Australia), the nickel mines of New Caledonia and the coconut plantations of Western Samoa. Blackbirders recruited shiploads of ni-Van workers, often through trickery or coercion, to work in these industries. Blackbirding vessels (the cost of which

1868	1906	1938	1942
With the last sandalwood gone from Erromango, blackbirding takes over, supplying cheap labour to nearby countries.	England and France decide to set up the Condominium government, and jointly administer it.	The John Frum cargo cult surfaces. The movement's leaders are jailed by the British and mentioning the words 'John Frum' is outlawed.	A US fleet sets up a huge base on Santo as WWII begins its final phases.

were covered within two voyages) made several trips a year, earning huge sums for their owners.

Whole villages were enticed aboard ships with the promise of trade, or a blackbirder might dress as a priest, hold a service and kidnap the worshippers. Ships were overcrowded, with poor and limited supplies of food, so many ni-Vans died at sea. If they reached Queensland or Fiji, they'd be lined up and sold to the highest bidder.

All a blackbirded islander would have after three years of overseas labour was a musket and some European clothes. Some returned labourers were dropped off at the wrong island, where they would be promptly robbed and sometimes killed and eaten.

Labour ships became targets for reprisals into the 20th century, but British and Australian officials only attempted to regulate the trafficking, not ban it. When sailors from blackbirding ships the *Carl* and the *Hopeful* were tried in Sydney for committing multiple murders in 1872 and 1874 respectively, Australian public opinion was on the sailors' side.

The most persistent and effective lobbyists against blackbirders were Presbyterian missionaries. They campaigned relentlessly in Britain and Australia. Finally – aided by the White Australia Policy of 1901 – they secured the banning of overseas labour recruitment to Queensland (in 1904), Fiji (in 1911) and Western Samoa (in 1913).

Missionaries

The first missionaries arrived in Erromango in 1839. However, after two of their number were killed and eaten, the Church decided to move carefully, depending more on Polynesian teachers, who it was hoped would be more acceptable to the islanders than Europeans. Polynesians, however, had no status in Melanesian society. Consequently, several were devoured. Others were devastated by malaria.

Presbyterianism became the major Christian denomination in Vanuatu. The missionaries took an uncompromising stand against many time-honoured Melanesian customs such as cannibalism, grade-taking, ancestor worship and polygamy. Some barred their converts from smoking, drinking kava and dancing.

The less dogmatic Anglican Diocese of Melanesia (DOM) arrived in 1860, and the Roman Catholics in 1887. Unlike the Protestants, the Catholics proved to be tolerant towards ni-Vanuatu traditions.

Ni-Vans mingled Christianity with their traditional beliefs, and found the rivalry between the various denominations hard to understand.

European Settlement

Although there was a sandalwood station on Aneityum by 1843, and missionaries were there from 1848 onwards, the first true European settler

1942	1956	1969	1972
On 26 October the troop-carrying USS *President Coolidge* is hit by a friendly mine while approaching Santo's harbour.	The Anglo-French Condominium recognises the John Frum cargo cult as a religion.	The last ritualistic cannibal killing occurs.	Cruise ships start visiting, marking the start of Vanuatu as a tourist destination.

was a cattle rancher who arrived in 1854. Other settlers from Australia followed in the 1860s to grow cotton when its price was high during the American Civil War. Cotton gave way to coconuts and cocoa when peace in America brought a slump in the price.

After France annexed New Caledonia in 1853, the Presbyterian Church unsuccessfully petitioned Britain to proclaim Aneityum a protectorate. Six years later it tried again, extending its appeal to cover all Vanuatu. But the British government refused to act.

Neglected by their government, most British settlers (including Australians) were near bankruptcy by the early 1880s. Meanwhile, large numbers of French people had settled and prospered. With the benefit of France's official support they dominated Vanuatu's fledgling economy.

In 1882 a French land speculator, the Irish-born John Higginson, founded the Compagnie Calédonienne des Nouvelles-Hébrides (CCNH) and purchased more than 20% of the country's agricultural land from settlers and local chiefs, who were not necessarily the true *kastom* (traditional) landowners but often just the first islanders who came along. Ten years later the CCNH owned 55% of Vanuatu's arable land.

French settlers now outnumbered British by three to one, and there was intense rivalry between them. Brawls were common as settlers took advantage of the absence of law and order. Islander attacks on settlers continued.

Condominium Government

In 1906 the Anglo-French Condominium of the New Hebrides was created. British and French nationals had equal rights, and retained their home country's citizenship. Ni-Vans were officially stateless. To travel abroad, they needed an identifying document signed by both the British and French resident commissioners.

Both British and French courts existed to pronounce judgments in cases involving their nationals; a joint court decided disputes between British and French, and between Europeans and ni-Vans; another court was for cases involving only ni-Vans. The British carried out their last capital punishments in 1924, when three Santo men were hanged for the murder of a British settler. The French guillotined six Tonganese men in 1931, for the murder of a French settler.

Cynics called the Condominium 'the Pandemonium', as the dual administration produced amazing duplication. There were two police forces with their own laws (including road rules), two health services, two education systems, two currencies and two prison systems.

Overseas visitors had to opt for either British or French authority. British law was stricter, but British prisons were considered more humane. French jails were very uncomfortable, but the food was better.

During the Condominium government, the English population drove on the left-hand-side of the road, the French population on the right. And yes, that caused a bit of a problem. These days it's on the right.

To Kill a Bird with Two Stones: a Short History of Vanuatu by Jeremy Mac-Clancy gives a good account of Vanuatu's earliest beginnings, through the Condominium period (the 'two stones' of the title) and right up to independence.

1980	**1980**	**1980**	**1987**
On the eve of independence, Nagriamel, a political movement led by Jimmy Stevens of Santo, declares Santo a separate nation (it's short-lived).	Independence Day – New Hebrides becomes Vanuatu on 30 July.	George Sokomanu is elected as Vanuatu's first president.	Hilda Lini and Maria Crowby are the first women elected to parliament.

War in the Pacific

Japan's lightning-fast advance through the Pacific in WWII, reaching the Solomon Islands by early 1942, convinced Vanuatu's settlers that invasion was imminent. However, in May of that year a fleet of soldiers arrived from the US, constructing bases on Efate and southeast Santo. Over three months Luganville became a city of 50,000 servicemen. In all, 500,000 Allied soldiers passed through the archipelago.

Many islanders either joined the small local regiment, the New Hebrides Defence Force, or went to work at the US bases. All were astounded by the apparent equality between white and black military personnel. Moreover, no ni-Van had ever been paid such generous wages before.

With Japan's defeat in 1945, the Americans withdrew and abandoned huge quantities of equipment, some of which was sold at bargain prices. The rest was dumped into the sea.

At almost 200m long, the USS *President Coolidge* was one of the largest luxury liners in the US when built in 1931. It was commandeered as a troop ship during the Pacific War in 1941 and promptly sank when it hit a friendly mine in Luganville harbour.

VANUATU HISTORY WAR IN THE PACIFIC

Towards Self-Rule

Land ownership became Vanuatu's central political concern in the mid 1960s. It was the spark that finally spurred the country to take the path to independence.

Europeans viewed land as a commodity. But to the ni-Vans this was contrary to ancient customs, in which land is held by the present generation in trust for future ones.

White settlers owned about 30% of the country's land, and cleared it for coconut production. When they began clearing more land for cattle ranching, it led to ni-Vanuatu protests in Santo and Malekula.

A *kastom* movement called Nagriamel arose, led by the charismatic Jimmy Stevens. Operating from Santo, its aims were to protect Melanesians' claims to their traditional land. Incensed by reports of US developers buying large blocks of land, Nagriamel expanded to other islands.

In 1971 the New Hebrides National Party, later called the Vanua'aku Party, was formed by Anglican minister Father Walter Lini. The Vanua'aku Party sent a petition for independence to the UN in 1974. It drew its support from English-speaking Protestants, whereas the Nagriamel became clearly identified with the French. The Francophones became known as the Modérés or 'Moderates'. They wanted the Condominium to remain as it was or be replaced by French rule, and they supported the idea that individual islands should have greater autonomy.

The Condominium authorities set up an assembly that allowed minority parties to govern until the first-ever election in November 1979. This election produced a clear winner: the Vanua'aku Party, with its founder, Father Walter Lini, as the chief minister.

1988	2003	2003	2005
Vanuatu sends its first athlete to the summer Olympic Games.	Teouma, the largest known cemetery in the Pacific islands, is discovered on Efate.	Vanuatu is removed from the Organisation for Economic Cooperation and Development's list of 'uncooperative tax havens'.	Vanuatu qualifies for a US Millennium Grant of US$65 million, beginning a four-year period of financial and political stability.

However, the Vanua'aku Party was extremely unpopular in some areas, particularly on Santo and Tanna. Nagriamel had been calling for the secession of Santa and Tanna since 1976 and most of Santo's French community now joined in.

Meanwhile, in 1980 independence for Vanuatu was fixed for July of the same year. The French government, seeing its influence declining, began to support the Modérés.

Independence

July was too far away. Santo and Tanna were screaming for secession. The UK wanted to send troops, but France said *non*.

In late May 1980 an insurrection on Tanna split the island between government supporters and rebel Modérés. On Santo, secessionists seized Luganville and hoisted the flag of the independent republic of Vemarana. The Lini government responded with a blockade of Santo.

Modéré supporters on northern islands proclaimed their own secessions. Jimmy Stevens brought them together and announced a provisional government for these islands. Lini's government had Papua New Guinea (PNG) troops on standby to break them up, but he wouldn't have the power to send the troops to Santo until after independence.

France and England dispatched a small joint military force to Santo, but failed even to stop the rebels from looting Luganville's shops.

The moment independence was declared on 30 July 1980, the new Vanuatu government brought in the soldiers from PNG, order was restored and the secessionist ringleaders, including Stevens, were arrested.

The New Nation

The Republic of Vanuatu. What a sweet sound for the ni-Vans. The 30th of July has since become a public holiday marked by celebrations every year in every village over the entire nation. With independence won, the ni-Vans set up a Westminster-style constitution and a 52-member parliament. Father Walter Lini became the founding prime minister, serving until 1991. He died in 1999.

The first decade of independence was reasonably stable. The next decade, however, was a very different, chaotic story and a sign of things to come. Charges of nepotism and other political crimes, rivals becoming allies and vice versa, splits within parties, leaders being ousted and police mutinies were all commonplace. Of concern in 1998 was the Vanuatu National Provident Fund (VNPF) riot, when members of the VNPF discovered that their superannuation funds were allegedly being 'borrowed' by leading politicians. A two-week state of emergency followed and more than 500 people were arrested.

Jimmy Stevens, charismatic leader of a short-lived secessionist rebellion on Santo, was thrown into jail in 1980 (allegedly escaping once) and was finally released in 1991. He died on Santo in 1994.

2005	2006	2008	2010
Ambae's Mt Manaro erupts, resulting in the evacuation of thousands of people from the island.	The New Economics Foundation declares Vanuatu to be the happiest country in the world. Part of the index measures people's impact on the environment.	Chief Roi Mata's domain (Hat Island) becomes the first Vanuatu site to be inscribed by Unesco.	The Asian Development Bank declares Vanuatu one of the fastest-growing economies in the Pacific.

CYCLONE PAM

Tropical Cyclone Pam hit Vanuatu in the early hours of 13 March 2015. Though many cyclones have threatened Vanuatu in the past, this Category 5 monster was always going to prove destructive. By the time it had petered out into the Pacific, Pam had become one of the worst natural disasters in Vanuatu's history.

Hardest hit were the southern provinces of Shefa (including the main island, Efate) and Tafea (including Tanna and Erromango). An estimated 95% of village homes were flattened, telecommunications knocked out and important food crops and plantations wiped out by sustained winds of up to 250km/h. Considering the destruction, loss of life was relatively low at an estimated 11 to 15 people.

Over the next few months, government and international aid organisations quickly set up temporary shelters, including tents for school classrooms, and delivered much needed food, water and building materials.

Although islanders have largely rebuilt their homes and *nakamals* (meeting house and kava bar) the full economic impact of the cyclone is yet to be realised. Replacing valuable crops, water sources and agricultural land is the biggest challenge for many. Encouraging visitors back to Vanuatu is another.

In 2005 Vanuatu qualified for the US Millennium Challenge (www.mcc.gov), a grant available to countries that show they will use it for sustainable economic growth. It was the only South Pacific country to be selected. The US$65 million was used to seal the Efate Ring Rd and the East Coast Rd on Santo. Recent economic growth has been attributed to the services sector (including tourism) and the growth of aid programs. Other encouraging economic trends are the 2 billion VT earned annually by ni-Van workers under New Zealand's Recognised Seasonal Employer (RSE) scheme; the rising interest in copra (coconut fibre); and the demand for Vanuatu beef, which consistently outstrips supply.

Vanuatu joined the World Trade Organization in October 2011. In 2015 work began on the US$93 million Luganville Wharf expansion project to be undertaken by China's Shanghai Construction Group. Meanwhile, Qantas, Air NZ and Virgin suspended flights into Port Vila in early 2016 due to concerns over the state of the international airport runway, despite the World Bank offering US$59.5 million in credit to fix its aviation issues.

Vanuatu's political problems resurfaced in late 2015 when 14 MPs, including the deputy prime minister, were found guilty of corruption and bribery and thrown into jail for between three and four years. A snap election called for January 2016 attracted 265 candidates from 37 political parties. By February 2016 a wobbly coalition of 36 MPs from 11 parties had been formed, with caretaker prime minister Sato Kilman retaining his seat.

Cyclone Pam in 2015 was one of the most destructive in Vanuatu's history but there have been others, notably Cyclone Lusi in 2014 and the Category 5 Cyclone Fran in 1992.

2011	**2015**	**2015**	**2016**
Vanuatu becomes a member of the World Trade Organization (WTO).	Cyclone Pam devastates much of the country in March.	Half of the serving parliament is convicted and jailed for corruption in October.	A snap election is called for January, ushering in an 11-party coaltion.

Vanuatu Environment

Vanuatu is an elongated chain of 83 Pacific islands, scattered between the equator and the Tropic of Capricorn. Most of these islands are the summits of submerged mountain ranges rising up from the mountain floor and are covered in lush forest and often impenetrable jungle, while their narrow coastal plains are dominated by coconut plantations and other agriculture.

Land Area

The best source of information on volcanic activity in Vanuatu is Vanuatu Geohazards Observatory (www.geohazards. gov.vu).

Vanuatu's total land area is around 12,200 sq km, with the largest islands being Espiritu Santo (4000 sq km), Malekula (2040 sq km) and the most populous island of Efate (900 sq km). Mt Tabwemasana (1879m) on Santo is the country's highest peak, and many other peaks are higher than 1000m.

Volcanoes & Earthquakes

Vanuatu lies squarely on top of the Pacific Ring of Fire, at its western-most edge. In fact, it is at the edge of the Pacific tectonic plate, which is being forced up and over the Indo-Australian plate. This action causes frequent earthquakes and volcanic eruptions.

Some areas of Vanuatu are being uplifted at a rate of 2cm a year, while others are subsiding. Earthquakes in 1994, 2002, 2010 and 2015 rated more than seven on the Richter scale and caused extensive damage. Others, in 1875, 1948 and 1999, created tsunamis that destroyed villages. Vanuatu has nine active volcanoes – seven on land and two under sea. The most famous is the easily accessible Mt Yasur on Tanna. Mt Garet on Gaua is potentially the most dangerous because of the thin layer of rock that separates its crater lake from magma. Both Mt Marum on Ambrym and Mt Lombenben on Ambae are monitored for activity and occasionally have locals ready to evacuate.

Wildlife

Animals

Apart from disease-carrying mosquitoes, Vanuatu is free of dangerous land creatures (no matter what they said on *Survivor: Vanuatu*). Due to the relative youth and isolation of the islands, the only native land mammals are 12 species of bat (including four species of flying fox). Only one of these – the white flying fox – is endemic.

Cats, dogs, cattle, horses, pigs and goats were all introduced to Vanuatu. Rats are the bane of village life; they cause much damage to the copra (coconut fibre) industry as well as to nesting birds.

An Australian vulcanologist and adventurer has lots of info and pictures on Vanuatu volcanoes at www.volcanolive. com.

Marine Animals

The country's largest resident mammal is the dugong. It's a relatively frequent visitor to Epi and Santo, though cyclones sometimes wipe out its food source, causing it to move elsewhere.

Several species of sea turtle (particularly hawksbill and green turtles) live and breed around the islands, but their meat and eggs are considered delicacies by the ni-Vans and turtle populations are dwindling. In most

> **PROTECTING THE SEA**
> ....
> You may find yourself being taken on a very indirect route around an island. Why? It's possible you're passing a marine conservation area. These are well looked after by local communities and the results (more fish and turtles, mostly) speak for themselves. Protected areas include Ringhi te Suh (Maskelynes), Hideaway Island (Efate), Narong Marine Reserve (Uri Island), Mystery Island Reef (Aneityum), Nguna-Pele Marine Protected Area, Epi, Lelepa Marine Protected Area, Mangaliliu Marine Protected Area, Spuaki Conservation Area (Nguna) and Nabi Protected Area (Malekula).

areas it's now taboo to eat turtle. Many chiefs have created sanctuaries, and there's an official breed-and-release program at Tranquillity Island, off Efate.

Brilliantly colourful schools of small species are a feature of the country's many coral gardens and reefs. Large fish include bonito, yellowfin tuna, sailfish, barracuda and swordfish.

Birds

Vanuatu's 121 bird species include 32 seabirds. Santo is the richest bird habitat, home to 55 species, including all seven of those endemic to Vanuatu. The Santo mountain starling is found only in Santo's higher mountains. In contrast, the native white-eye is widespread and common throughout Vanuatu.

The most interesting of the country's birds is the megapode, which lives close to active volcanic areas, and lays its eggs in the hot soil. Its young, which emerge fully feathered, can run immediately after hatching and can fly within 24 hours. The swamp hen, or purple gallinule, is the most common ground-dwelling bird. You may glimpse the bright-red beak, purplish-blue feathers and yellow feet as it scuttles off into the bush.

Heinrich Bregulla's *Birds of Vanuatu* is required reading on the country's 121 bird species, but it's too large to take with you.

Reptiles

Vanuatu has 19 lizard species including Efate's banded iguana. It grows to 1m long and has an emerald-green body with black bands.

The two types of land snake are perfectly harmless: the burrowing snake and the Pacific boa, known as the 'sleeping snake' because of its habit of lying absolutely still when threatened. The boa grows to about 2.5m and is coloured from silver to orange-brown. It's fond of rats, mice and chickens, so it lives close to villages.

The only venomous snakes are the yellow-bellied and banded sea snakes. These graceful creatures are often curious but rarely aggressive. They have small mouths and teeth that aren't at all suitable for savaging humans. Over the years saltwater (or estuarine) crocodiles have appeared around Vanuatu's northern islands. The small 'salty' population is all on Vanua Lava.

Plants

Much of the country is a botanical wonderland, with 1500 species of flowers, ferns, shrubs, vines and trees. Lord of the forest is the banyan. The largest banyans are on Tanna. There are forests of mighty kauri trees up to 4m in diameter on Erromango.

Vanuatu palms include the decorative snakeskin palm and the very beautiful carpoxylon palm; both are rare and confined to southern Vanuatu. Another is the lovely natangura palm.

Orchids festoon the trees in many areas, such as along the beaches in northeastern Santo. Vanuatu has 158 species of orchid, of which about

COCONUT CRAB

The *krab kokonas* (coconut crab) has always been a part of local cuisine. It climbs palms and breaks off the coconuts, which split when they hit the ground. The crab scuttles down and feasts on the flesh. It's the world's largest land crab and matures very slowly, taking 15 years to reach harvesting size. Sadly, there's been a serious decline in crab numbers and strict conservation measures are in force.

Coconut crabs start life in the ocean, then move into shells on the shore. As hermit crabs they move into bigger shells until they are large enough to move inland. Adult crabs generally live in forested areas near the sea. Villagers catch them by fixing split coconuts to the ground, then going back with a torch at night. While locals can pick up the crabs without losing a finger, don't try it yourself.

40 are native. The best place to see them is in Aneityum in October and November. Also of interest are the ferns – all 250 species of them.

Less enchanting are the introduced weeds. Lantana and the widespread American 'mile-a-minute' vine are the worst. The latter was brought from the US as a camouflage plant during WWII; it's been left to overrun everything.

Environmental Issues

There are four official conservation areas in Vanuatu: Vatthe and Loru on Santo, the kauri reserve on Erromango, and the cloudforest area around Lake Manaro on Ambae. Marine Protected Areas (MPAs) include Ngunu-Pele off Efate, USS *President Coolidge* and Million Dollar Point off Santo and Uri-Narong Marine Park off Malekula.

Vanuatu is facing many environmental challenges, including invasive introduced species (such as the Indian myna bird), degradation of freshwater habitats, and the exploitation of many plant, animal and marine resources. The greatest problem, however, is the scarcity of fresh water on some islands, a problem exacerbated following Cyclone Pam (which destroyed rainwater tanks) and a prolonged drought.

Japanese longline nets are strung in Vanuatu's waters and Korean fishing boats help themselves. Owners of the waters and reefs stand helpless on the rocks, waving bush knives – there's no coastguard to call on.

Global warming is raising sea levels, which threatens arable coastal land, and climate change is throwing the seasons out of whack, resulting in reduced agricultural harvests and smaller-sized root crops.

The Vanuatu government has also allowed the multinational aquarium trade to collect tropical fish from Devil's Point on Efate. The area has been quickly ravaged. Disney's *Finding Nemo* added to the problem, with children everywhere desperate to own a clownfish. Shefa's council of chiefs stepped in to try and stop the trade but, sadly, it has continued. Grazing fish such as angelfish and sea stars keep the balance of algae correct, so the problem is far more than one of stock numbers.

Steps to help the environment include dedicating resources to the marine environment, fisheries and reforestation. A code of logging practice has been established and the country has joined the International Tropical Timber Organisation (ITTO; www.itto.int), a group that fosters sustainable forest management.

Organisations such as OceansWatch International encourage visiting yachties to monitor the waters and educate villagers about indicators for reef health. They keep an eye out for seagrass fields and crown-of-thorns starfish (a fast-spreading pest), and they monitor the diversity of reefs. Yachties have the unique position of being able to check out the country's less-visited villages. See www.oceanswatch.org for updates on the state of Vanuatu's coastal areas.

Traditional Village Culture

If you spend all of your time in Vanuatu around Port Vila or on a resort on Santo you'll see relatively little of Vanuatu's traditional village life. But you don't have to go far into the outer islands to experience *kastom* (traditional) village culture. Here, pigs are a valuable commodity and magic spirits inhabit everything from volcanoes to banyan trees.

Land Ownership

Land ownership is a big deal in Vanuatu, and it's even more life changing with the development of the tourism industry. If you own something as frequently visited as Santo's Champagne Beach, you'll reap the financial rewards when tourists pay to see it. In many ways, land ownership has allowed forests and natural areas to survive, as Melanesians believe the people are nurtured by their land in the same way plants and trees are. Families have the right in customary law only to occupy specific sections of land, not to sell them. These rights go back to the first ancestors who settled each district. The only way to acquire territorial rights outside one's own clan is to marry into another group. Although most *kastom* land is registered to males, there's no law forbidding women from owning land, and some do.

Rights to reefs and boat-landing places are similarly inherited. Fishing rights extend out from the beach or rocks as far and as deep as shoreside angling and free diving for seashells are possible. It's all *kastom* – the traditional ownership of a piece of land, object or stretch of reef and the associated cultural legacies, laws and ancient ancestral religions and customs.

Since independence, only *kastom* owners and the government are permitted to own land, although identifying the true *kastom* owner can be difficult. Other islanders and all foreigners may lease land for a maximum of 75 years for commercial use, which is the productive life of a coconut tree.

Village Life

Subsistence farming, with hunting and fishing, has traditionally kept villagers happy and healthy. The forests are a major resource, providing medicine, food, building materials, and timber for boats and artefacts. Water is often fresh, crystal-clear, bubbling from a deep spring and gravity-fed into the village through a plastic pipe. However, some areas rely on rainwater, which is almost always in short supply.

Islanders generally do not wear scant or revealing clothing, and women's thighs are always covered. Try to ensure that what you wear shows due respect.

Each village is a group of extended family members, their houses set around a *nakamal* (meeting house and kava bar). Before the sun rises, the wives light the family's fire, food is prepared, and then family members go to the gardens and the young children to school. Teenagers leave the village to attend boarding school, or to live with maternal uncles perhaps. Many young people head for Port Vila, but just as many move back to their traditional homes where they can grow food, hunt pigs and care for families.

School fees for secondary education are expensive. Private cargo boats time their trips around the islands to collect copra (coconut fibre) for just before the school fees are due every three months, because they know the islanders will have been working hard and crops will be plentiful. Coffee beans are also harvested from the bush just before the school fees are due, as are the cocoa and vanilla beans. School fees may be exempted in times of hardship, as they were following Cyclone Pam in 2015.

The other driving force for tending to cash crops is the need to provide a huge feast for boys' circumcision rites.

Who Does What?

In Vanuatu men acquire pigs so they can throw feasts in order to keep the people who eat at their feast beholden to them. Once, the ultimate challenge was to provide a human for the feast, creating a much greater debt for those who partook. Men, therefore, had to be powerful warriors to acquire the sacrificial feast components (and to avoid ending up as the main course themselves).

Women work hard, traditionally tending to the men, the children and the pigs. Most of the islands don't have electricity, so they struggle to prepare food and to keep their families clothed, fed and clean. They work as a group, outside the male bastion.

The children are responsible for the younger ones. They are safe in the villages, and their endless play trains them for later life. Watch a toddler with a bush knife, a young child leaping from a boulder into a pool, a preschooler with a baby on the hip.

Families share their children, raising a relative's child, sending their own to live on a different island, adopting a teenager. This creates a wide family network throughout the islands.

Tabu

Most locals will be delighted to have their photo taken, though there are exceptions, so always ask. Sometimes you'll be charged a fee; video cameras attract the highest fees.

This is where the English word 'taboo' comes from, and it means 'sacred' as well as 'forbidden'. In its simplest form, *tabu* can mean 'no entry' when written across a doorway. Failure to observe *tabu* could require the payment of pigs, or even the death of the transgressor.

Many *tabu* relate to traditional ceremonies and the particular parts that women and uninitiated men are barred from seeing. In some areas a woman may not stand higher than a male; nor may she step over a fire because its smoke – while she's standing in it – may rise higher than a man. Men may not deliberately place themselves below a woman.

Menstruation and birth are surrounded by *tabu*. Most traditional villages have an area set aside for both childbirth and menstruating women. For a woman in a *kastom* village to go fishing while pregnant is a serious breach of *tabu*. The penalty could be a hefty fine (paid in pigs to the chief) or expulsion from the village. In the past the transgressor would have been killed. It's forbidden for men to visit the women's *tabu* part of the village.

Magic & Spirits

Many ni-Vans believe their world to be populated by ancestral spirits and demons. The ghosts of the recently dead are considered especially potent as well as being potentially malicious, even towards their own family.

The practice of magic is generally *tabu* for women, but most adult men in the traditional parts of Vanuatu know a few useful spells. These may be used to further love affairs or to produce good crops. A practising

NAKAMALS

The village *nakamal* is a men's clubhouse or meeting house with two rooms: one room where men meet at the end of the day, and the other room that often contains ancestral skulls and other sacred objects. In most areas, the *nakamal* is where men meet at sunset to talk and drink kava. It may be an open-ended hut or as simple as a space beneath a banyan.

RAMBARAMP

About eight months to a year after a chief's death, the Small Nambas in south-central Malekula would give him a new body, or *rambaramp*. This was built by overmodelling – covering a frame with vegetable fibre and clay. To ensure the *rambaramp's* face looked like the dead man, the skull was removed from his decomposing body and overlaid with clay.

The *rambaramp* was painted all over in red, white and black, and fitted with armbands, feathers, armlets, a *namba* (penis wrapper) and a bark belt.

Finally it was displayed for one day only. The men danced before the *rambaramp*, dressed as spirits, covered with strands of smoked ferns, their heads shrouded in spider webs or green moss. Then the *rambaramp* was returned to the *nakamal* (meeting house and kava bar), where it remained until it fell apart.

The ritual of *rambaramp* died out with conversion to Christianity, although you'll find good examples on display in Port Vila's cultural centre.

magician is employed for more specialised tasks such as raising or calming storms, healing the sick, banishing spirits or controlling volcanoes.

Dances & Ceremonies

Watch the village dances; feel the earth vibrating under feet stamping to the beat. There are two types of dances. In the first, each dancer becomes an ancestor or legendary figure, not human, so the dance and dress are similarly nonhuman and involve elaborate masks or headdresses, such as in the Rom dances of Ambrym.

The second type of dance has themes such as gathering food, hunting, and war or death, as in the extraordinary Toka celebrations of Tanna.

All dances require constant rehearsals. The timing is exquisite, the movements regimented – everyone turning, leaping, stomping together – so harmony and cooperation develop between people and villages.

Male dancers perform wearing *nambas* (penis wrappers) or *mal mal* (T-pieces); women dancers wear grass skirts.

Always carry at least 500VT to 2000VT in cash with you to any activity, as you never know when a villager will ask you to pay a fee for swimming, fishing, walking on or looking at their property.

Initiations

Initiation takes a child straight into adulthood. Boys, usually aged from 10 to 12, are secluded in a special hut for several weeks, during which time circumcision takes place. When their wounds have healed, they return to their families amid much feasting.

Pig Kills

Grade-taking is a system of ceremonies and pig kills where a tribal man rises in the village hierarchy – ultimately, perhaps, becoming chief. The higher a man rises in his grades, the greater must be the number and value of the pigs he kills. To become valuable, a boar is first castrated and its upper teeth removed. Then it is hand-fed – and kept tied up to prevent it foraging or fighting – for seven years, until its tusks complete a circle and penetrate the jaw (very painful).

Village Chiefs

A ni-Vanuatu chief acts as a justice of the peace and as a delegate for the people of the village. His word is law. Even politicians must do what the chief says when they go back home.

The Malvatumauri (National Council of Chiefs) is an elected group of chiefs from Vanuatu's regions. Their role is to discuss matters relating to custom and tradition. However, their power in government is limited, as legislation doesn't have to be approved by them.

These days many of the village chiefs are elected, though in northern areas chiefs achieve this status through the *nimangki* system, which allows men who can afford to hold pig-killing ceremonies to gain village authority.

Art & Music

With 83 isolated islands, it's hardly surprising that Vanuatu's art and traditions vary from island to island, and this diversity contributes to the country's unique cultural identity. Ni-Vanuatu art focuses on the human form and traditional interpretations of what ancestral figures looked like. The most important ni-Vanuatu artefacts are made in preparation for *nimangki* grade-taking ceremonies.

Carving

The National Museum in Port Vila is an excellent place to learn more about the arts in Vanuatu.

While wood is the main material used for carving, objects are also formed from tree fern, stone and coral. Serious carving is almost entirely undertaken for ceremonies, while items for sale are usually small copies of the real thing. The best carvings come from north Ambrym.

Clubs & Weapons

War clubs are made to designs attributed to an ancestral cultural hero. To alter a basic shape is considered a breach of *kastom* (tradition). Pig-killing clubs are shaped like mattocks, with two stylised faces carved on either side. Carved bows and arrows, and traditional ceremonial spears can be found in the village of Mele and on the island of Ifira, both near Port Vila.

Bowls, Poles & Walking Sticks

Large platters and bowls are used to pound yams and kava in, or to serve *laplap* (a staple dish). Some, such as those from the Shepherd Islands, are carved like birds or fish.

Some chiefs use carved wooden staffs as badges of office and walking sticks are made with figurines in place of handles.

Canoes

Exquisite model canoes with sails fashioned from dried pandanus leaves come from Makura in the Shepherds. Atchin islanders (off Malekula) carve their miniature canoes complete with figureheads.

Fern Figures

Tall statues made from tree ferns, or black palms, are made on Ambrym, Malekula and Gaua. They represent both male and female ancestral figures and are carved for *nimangki* ceremonies. They're often painted in different colours, using tints extracted from vegetable dyes and crushed shells; the choice of colours depends on the grade being taken.

Ceremonial Masks

For a good overview of Vanuatu's developing contemporary music and arts scene, see www.furtherarts.org.

The island of Malekula produces some of the most colourful and dynamic ceremonial masks. Dancing masks worn by men of high rank are carved from tree ferns, as are masks for funerals, *nimangki* ceremonies or boys' initiations. Other ceremonial headdresses are built using a human skull for the base and surmounted by tall feathers. In the past, many headdresses were burnt after use.

Music

String bands developed during WWII, when ni-Vans were exposed to US soldiers playing bluegrass. Local lads added the bush bass, made from a converted tea chest; the bongo; the tambourine; and a ratchet made from bamboo. Some bands use a xylophone of water-filled bottles. The singing is done with a pinched throat, forming a high-pitched lyrical note. Songs are improvised about life. For example, when Nguna's local band sings, 'Poor Saykem, caught in a current, canoe is filling, sharks are swimming, Poor Saykem, Poor Saykem,' it captures a dramatic moment when an old fisherman had to be rescued. Book in for a Melanesian feast in Port Vila to guarantee a listen; these also usually feature *kastom* dancing.

Musicians have contributed to the country's economy and are getting recognition, with sound studios and training rooms being established on many islands, notably the charitable Canal Studio on Santo.

Contemporary music to listen out for includes Nauten Boys of Tanna ('Jewel in a Crown'); Vanessa Quai, an international award winner (see *The Best of Vanessa Quai*); Natano Pasifika, featuring Mars Melto; and Chocolate Strings featuring singer-guitarist Ofa Fanaika.

> The influence of reggae on Vanuatu's musicians (and young folk) is obvious; even the logo of Fest' Napuan (Efate's annual almost week-long outdoor celebration of Vanuatu's music) is in red, green and gold. See more about this festival at www.fest napuan.org.

ART & MUSIC MUSIC

Musical Instruments

Young ni-Van men make their own instruments, and join together to form local string bands. If you are fortunate enough to buy, say, a homemade guitar, you will be surrounded by interested strangers asking if they may play it for you at mostly every cafe, bus stop or airport. The downside is when your waiter tells you there's no fish on today's menu as the fishers have all left to play in a string band.

Ni-Van women have not, to date, been encouraged to play musical instruments, but the women of Gaua use the ocean to play water music. You can watch them play at Aver Bay, near Gaua airport. The Leweton Cultural Group have been travelling around the world, performing their amazing water dance; you can also see them on Santo at Leweton Cultural Village in Luganville.

Tamtam

Vanuatu's unique musical device is the huge *tamtam*, or slit-gong, from Malekula and Ambrym. It is a carved log with a hollowed-out slit that enables it to be used as a drum. Originally used to send coded messages as well as form drum orchestras for festivities and celebrations, it is traditionally made from the breadfruit tree, which gives the best sound.

> Follow music news and events on www.vanuatu music.com.

The typical *tamtam* has a representation of a human face carved above the drum part; some in north Ambrym have rooster faces. Faces on Malekulan drums are generally very simple, but those from Ambrym can be ornate and elaborately carved, and often valued by collectors worldwide. It takes about 160 hours to produce a 2.5m *tamtam* with a single face.

ANCIENT ART

Stumbling onto a scene of petroglyphs in Vanuatu is extraordinary. They're usually in an unlikely spot off the beaten track, such as on Maewo, near the Hole of the Moon cave. Your boatman stops the tiny boat, and the local chief, who you picked up at the previous village, encourages you to hop out. He leads you through prickly, stinging plants to a muddy spot beside a mossy, dripping cliff face. You squint and there they are: depictions of European ships in full sail, carved in the 18th century, alongside traditional patterns carved out of the overhanging rock wall. Pentecost, Aneityum and Malekula also have interesting petroglyphs accessible only with a local guide.

SAND ART

Many works of art are relegated to history, something seen only in museums and cultural centres, but the beautiful art of sand drawing endures in Vanuatu. Ni-Vans create intricate, temporary sand drawings that leave messages or illustrate local legends, songs or ceremonies. The most elaborate and picturesque versions are made on Ambrym.

The artist first draws the foundation design, usually a sequence of squares or rectangles, in the sand. Then he or she begins to circle with a finger, making many delicate loops and circles without raising the finger until the design is finished. Many are linked to games, songs, and dance or mask patterns; others depict objects.

At sand-drawing festivals and competitions, the artists tell the story as they complete the drawing, then repeat the pattern by using string twirled between the fingers.

On Ambrym designs belong to particular families and can only be used if a fee is paid. Some carvers have produced copies in Vila. Ambrym chiefs look out for such transgressors – they are no longer executed, but they are fined.

Flutes & Conch Shells

Panpipes, usually with seven small bamboo flutes, are found all over Vanuatu. Ambrym people play a long, geometrically patterned musical pipe, while in Santo a simple three-holed flute is used.

On many islands, large triton shells (a type of conch) are blown as a means of communication.

Santo supports local music through jamming sessions, workshops and the local version of Efate's Fest' Napuan, held at Unity Park in November. See more about Lukaotem Gud Santo festival at www.festnapuan.org.

Painting

Styles of painting practised in Vanuatu include bark art in the Banks Islands. Body painting is popular throughout the country as part of various traditional ceremonies.

Petroglyphs and rock paintings are the country's most ancient forms of pictorial art, though the meanings and traditions of the carvings have been lost. Apart from drawings depicting European ships from the 18th century, it is difficult to establish their age. Several islands have caves whose walls are decorated with hand stencils and paintings of animals.

Weaving

Mostly undertaken by women, weaving is always done by hand. Pandanus leaves and *burao* (wild hibiscus) stalks are the most favoured materials. Wicker, coconut leaves and rattan are used for more robust items.

Pandanus shopping baskets are made on a number of islands: the artisans of Mataso (in the Shepherds) and Futuna are noted for their intricate wares.

Locally made red pandanus mats are traditionally used as currency in Ambae, Maewo and northern Pentecost. These mats are presented at weddings, grade-taking ceremonies, births, funerals and for the payment of customary debts. They were used as everyday clothing, but nowadays are only worn during ceremonies.

Fish, bird and shellfish traps are also manufactured, as are furniture and Panama-style hats.

Vanuatu's Local Food

Vanuatu's tropical climate and fertile lands bless it with fresh seafood, succulent meats, organic tropical fruits and fresh-from-the-garden vegetables. However, the availability of foods can be affected by the vagaries of seasonal changes, cyclones, earthquakes, drought and transport difficulties. Food crops, including most of the fruit plantations, were damaged or wiped out by Cyclone Pam in March 2015, creating food shortages that have been worsened by drought and severe water shortages. Some estimates say it will take five years to fully recover.

Staples & Specialities

Ni-Van families have their first meal – a chunky slice of bread – around the open fire as the sun comes up. Bread is baked in the small metal wood-fired ovens that you see throughout the countryside, or in a pot over an open fire. Children take a banana-leaf-wrapped bundle of rice (which is mostly imported) with them to school. The evening meal will be vegetables from the family's garden. Village families live mainly on vegetarian or fish diets, eating meat when it's freshly available since there's usually no refrigeration. If the yield from the garden is inadequate, the family eats very little.

In times of plenty Futuna islanders wind-dry a mash of bananas or breadfruit, wrap it in *laplap* leaves and bury it in dry ground, which provides a food reserve during cyclones or drought.

Markets sell produce grown in village gardens, when available: look for coconuts, pineapples, bananas, pawpaw, yams, cucumbers, grapefruit, carrots and tomatoes, as well as cooked foods such as the national dishes *laplap* and *tuluk* (smaller parcels of *laplap*).

Laplap, Vanuatu's national dish, is made by grating manioc, taro roots or yams into a doughy paste. The mixture is put onto taro or wild spinach leaves and soaked in coconut cream. Pieces of pork, beef, poultry, fish, prawns or flying fox are often added. Leaves from the *laplap* plant (similar to banana leaves) are wrapped around the doughy mix, tied up with strands of vine and then placed in a ground oven, with hot stones above and below. *Nalot* is a dish made from roasted taro, banana or breadfruit mixed with coconut cream.

Local specialities found in restaurants on Port Vila include *roussette* (flying fox or fruit bat) and *nautou* (green-winged ground pigeon). *Roussette* and *nautou* are almost always edible when served *au vin* (in red wine). Poulet fish is common and delicious. River prawns are delicate, but best of all is Tahitian fish salad: the fish is marinated in lime juice, then sweetened with coconut milk. Beef, from those contented Charolais and Limousin cows wandering around the coconut plantations, is also excellent.

Coconut is naturally a ubiquitous staple. It is used in five stages of ripeness: the first (young coconut) is for drinking; the next has a tasty jellied flesh; the third, when the flesh is firm but succulent, is the best for eating; the fourth is for drying into copra (coconut fibre); and the fifth is when the nut sprouts while the milk inside goes crispy, making 'coconut ice cream'.

Other edible fruits include *nakatambol,* clustered cherry-sized fruits that turn yellow when ripe, and *naus,* which is similar to mango. You'll also probably see the rose-apple tree; its small pink-and-white fruit has

Nangae trees grow wild in Vanuatu, and their nuts, the *nangae* nut (or Canarium), are in worldwide demand for their oil. There's huge potential in Vanuatu for these nuts to generate much-needed income for communities – though getting the harvesting right is important. The Summit, in Port Vila, produces *nangae* oil for sale.

apple-like flesh beneath its skin. Villagers flavour their food with its blossom, known as the *kae kae flaoa* (food flower).

Several edible nuts are grown; these include cut-nuts, also called *narli-nuts* or island chestnuts, and *nangae,* an oval nut-containing fruit that tastes like an almond.

Drinks

Fresh coconut juice is a cheap and refreshing drink. If you want to drink coconuts straight off the tree ask the *kastom* (traditional) owner or your guide. They'll hold it in their open hand; whack, whack with the bush knife, and it's yours. Elsewhere they're available at markets or from street stalls in villages.

Look out for Tanna coffee, a strong brew grown on Tanna island and roasted in Port Vila. A few cafes in Vila and Luganville have European-style coffee machines; everywhere else it's instant coffee.

Vanuatu's main locally produced beer, Tusker, is a decent brew and widely available, from Port Vila's supermarkets to remote island stores and bungalows. Its sale may be limited to one shop in some towns. Spirits and wine are relatively expensive.

The major supermarkets carry a good range of French and Australian wines and spirits, and Australian and local beers.

Celebrations

A man taking a *nimangki* grade will provide a magnificent feast. He lines up scores of pigs and walks along, killing selected animals with blows to the head, touching others to show that they'll be slaughtered later. He then presents woven mats and sufficient yams and taro for the lavish meal.

KAVA CULTURE

It's called the peace drug. Its hallucinogenic properties make your mind happy and you feel clever. You love the rhythm of talk. Many people wouldn't consider a day complete without a couple of 'shells' of the stuff.

Kava has a pungent, muddy and slightly peppery taste. It looks like dirty dishwater, and many say it doesn't taste much better. But it's not *that* bad. Kava etiquette dictates that you should down the shell in one go (first-timers should opt for the half shell). Your lips will go numb and cold; your limbs become heavy; and you'll probably want to do nothing more than think about life. Also, your eyes become sensitive to light, so flashbulbs are intrusive.

Kava ceremonies are held to welcome visitors, seal alliances, begin chiefly conferences, and commemorate births, deaths and marriages. For such occasions, there are strict rules for preparing and drinking kava. On Tanna, for example, prepubescent boys prepare the roots by chewing them into a mush that is mixed with water and filtered through coconut fibres (don't worry, just ask which *nakamals* use a grinder). First the chief drinks, followed by any honoured guests, then other men in order of precedence. As noted, etiquette requires drinking each shell in a single gulp. Also, it's drunk in a quiet atmosphere.

Kava drinking is traditionally an exclusively male activity surrounded by all sorts of *tabu*. However, these days most islands have places where women are welcome to partake. If you're asked to join kava drinkers, consider yourself honoured, as the invitation amounts to a formal welcome.

Known botanically as *Piper methysticum*, a relation of the pepper plant, kava is grown in damp places, often around the edge of a taro paddy field, and is one of Vanuatu's major cash crops. Many islands claim to grow the best kava but Tanna's is said to be the most potent and Pentecost's some of the best.

Long-term use of kava can result in liver and kidney damage, and there's little doubt that its use also causes loss of productivity, though kava is never consumed before 5pm. You can recognise a kava bar by its single red or green light.

STOCKING UP

Local village stores on Vanuatu's outer islands – where they exist – may be limited to shelves full of tinned food, packet noodles, biscuits, a few sacks of imported rice and (with luck) some fresh bread. Stock up on snacks and treats in Port Vila or Luganville for those long truck rides or airstrip waits. Also seek out the local village market, where you can buy fresh produce and seafood.

For a lad's circumcision celebration, the father holds a grand feast. Villagers dress in wildly colourful costumes, with face and body paint, and amazing headpieces. Miles of bright material form shade-screens, and peacock feathers are used as decorations. Dancing lasts all through the night to celebrate the rite of passage of the boy. Adding to the colour are huge piles of gifts – food, mats and baskets – paid to the paternal extended family.

Feasts are prepared for every festival and anniversary, for a new house, for someone arriving or leaving, for births, deaths and many other reasons. The women work together throughout the day, preparing *lap-lap* and *nalot*. The men catch fish and a pig is slaughtered. For a large gathering, it might be a cow. Everybody calmly wanders around selecting food and sitting on the ground in small groups to eat it with their fingers.

One of Port Vila's oldest restaurants, L'Houstalet, is famous for its local delicacies: wild pigeon and stuffed flying fox.

Eating Out

Dining can be hit-and-miss in Vanuatu and variety lacking as a result of changing availability of ingredients, especially on the outer islands; but pick a winner (sublime crab perhaps, or perfectly cooked organic steak) and you'll remember it for months.

Port Vila is by far the best place in Vanuatu for eating out, although there are also some good restaurants on Santo and a few on Tanna. Resort dining is usually of a high standard. There are numerous independent cafes and restaurants in Vila and Luganville where you can get pizzas, burgers, local lobster or bouillabaisse. Most large resorts in Port Vila have at least one island 'feast night' weekly, when food is served buffet style accompanied by dancing and other entertainment.

Restaurants are hard to find in more remote regions, and many bungalows include meals with your stay for this reason. If you do see a local restaurant, call in. Some are surprisingly good despite the restricted menu, though with little refrigeration they may only remain open until the available food is gone.

If you're staying in a bungalow, you'll usually be eating what your host cooks up. It's worth keeping in mind that access to fresh food (and funds to buy it with) can be limited (this is especially the case since Cyclone Pam). Unfortunately, in the outer villages convenience has taken over from tradition and taste, and your stay in a bungalow might be accompanied by a meal of tinned beef mashed over instant noodles or a large pile of boiled rice. This can be a cost-saving exercise on behalf of the bungalow; if you're willing to pay a bit more, when you arrive ask your hosts about what they serve for dinner and make some suggestions, such as fresh fish or vegetarian dishes.

Island Edibles, by Judy MacDonnell, is an illustrated and informative work with great recipes (think island cabbage dolmades and Tahitian sushi) and translations from Bislama into English.

Dining at the bigger town or resort restaurants in Vila or Santo is rarely cheap; expect 3000VT plus for a main meal, particularly if it involves seafood. At local markets you can get filling, tasty meals for 400VT. Supermarkets in Vila and Luganville carry local and imported foods.

Where they exist, most bars and pubs have a fairly good Western-style food menu. BYO snacks to kava bars.

Vanuatu Directory A–Z

Accommodation

There's an impressive selection of luxury hotels and resorts in and around Port Vila and, to a lesser extent, on Santo and Tanna. Other islands have a varying range of budget or medium-priced bungalows or guesthouses. Here, meals are simple affairs and are often included in the room rate.

On the most isolated islands communication is by word of mouth, transport is by foot and there's no money to fix things that break. You'll be pampered in the locals' happy-go-lucky, warm style. If you've paid for everything back in your own country or are on a tour from Port Vila, take cash to cover all drinks, pay upfront for extras (such as *kastom* – traditional ownership – fees), and don't be surprised if your host has no money to give in change (always carry some small denomination notes). If you've booked island accommodation through an agency, be aware that your hosts may receive only a tiny portion of the payment

and, even then, they may not receive it until after you've gone. At the end of your stay, you'll be presented with a handwritten bill, which will probably include an itemised list. A lot of time and thought goes into preparing these bills, so it's not really something to quibble about unless you really disagree with a certain charge.

Bungalows

Outside of main towns, bungalows are the most common form of island accommodation; these are quaint, thatched bamboo or timber huts, usually with verandahs and plaited pandanus-leaf walls. Floors range from concrete slabs to sand or crushed shells. Owners usually take great pride in the bungalows, but it's hard to keep them spotless when only a few tourists arrive each year, if your extended family needs somewhere to sleep and there's a community of geckos living in the roof.

You might find communication difficult (mobile-phone coverage can be patchy on outer islands), and remote

island bungalows can be at the peril of cyclones, changing tides and arguing families. Get local advice (Port Vila's tourist office is the best source) or just head there regardless; you'll always find somewhere to stay.

Some hosts can't wait to show you all the treats the island offers; they'll catch fresh seafood for meals, and will head off at 4.30am for an hour's walk to the nearest boat so that it's waiting ready for you at 7am. Others may leave you to find your own way around, and offer only a loaf of bread and cup of tea in the morning.

Staying in a bungalow generally costs around 2000VT to 3500VT per person (not per room). This often includes meals, but check in advance as you may need to take your own food. Luxuries are rare: most island bungalows have only solar lighting and occasional generator power in the evenings, and often there's no running water, so expect bucket showers and long-drop toilets. Be prepared for hard beds, lack of warm bedding, holes in the mosquito nets and a chorus of roosters acting as your personal alarm clock from 4am. But the locations – on waterfront clifftops, in pristine jungle or in the shadow of a brooding volcano – along with warm family welcomes, make up for all of that.

For photos of remote bungalows, and how to get there,

BOOK YOUR STAY ONLINE

For more accommodation reviews by Lonely Planet authors, check out http://lonelyplanet.com/hotels/. You'll find independent reviews, as well as recommendations on the best places to stay. Best of all, you can book online.

SLEEPING PRICE RANGES

The following price ranges refer to a double room in high season:

$ less than 8000VT

$$ 8000–20,000VT

$$$ more than 20,000VT

visit **Positive Earth** (www.positiveearth.org/bungalows).

Camping

Most island bungalows and guesthouses will let you use their grounds and facilities for camping (around 1000VT per person). If you want to pitch your tent on a remote beach, the local chief will probably give his approval. Camping is popular on organised overnight hikes to the volcanoes of Ambrym or treks on Malekula and Santo; tents can be supplied. There's a camping ground in Havannah Harbour on Efate.

Guesthouses, Resthouses & Nakamals

It's unusual but possible to ask to stay in a women's meeting room or church hall, or in someone's house, though these days most communities that attract tourists have a formal bungalow set-up (to which you'll be directed).

Young males might be offered a spot in the village *nakamal* (meeting house and kava bar) in exchange for an evening's *toktok* (discussion). You'll need bedding and protection against mosquitoes (sometimes fleas and rats, too).

Resorts, Hotels & Motels

Port Vila dominates Vanuatu's tourist industry and has accommodation to match. Reasonable budget options start at 5000VT for a double,

and single rates are often half, or open to negotiation. Expect ceiling fans; air conditioning will be a bonus or will cost extra if you want it turned on.

Midrange options are priced between 8000VT and 20,000VT for a double room, and could include resort-style or motel-style rooms, usually with a swimming pool and restaurant. Top-end hotels and resorts start at around 20,000VT for a double or twin room and range from intimate beachfront places to full-blown family resorts with water sports and kids clubs.

You can usually negotiate a rate for long stays. If you're a walk-in traveller, ask about 'local rates', which can be substantially lower than those listed online, especially if it's quiet. Children under 12 are often free.

Customs Regulations

People over 15 years may bring the following into the country:

➡ 250 cigarettes

➡ 2.25L of wine and 1.5L of other alcohol

➡ 250mL of eau de toilette

➡ 100mL of perfume

➡ Other items up to a value of 50,000VT

Declare the following on arrival:

➡ Plants, fruit and seeds

➡ Meat, poultry and dairy products

➡ Fish and shellfish

Failure to declare these items can lead to prosecution and fines.

No firearms or ammunition may be brought into the country.

If taking home carved statues made of tree fern or palm, be sure they're fumigated and have a CITES (Convention on International Trade in Endangered Species) exemption form.

Electricity

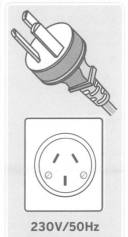

230V/50Hz

Embassies & Consulates

Australian High Commission (☑22777; www.vanuatu.embassy.gov.au; Winston Churchill Ave, Port Vila; ⊙8am-4.30pm Mon-Fri) High Commission based in one of the more impressive new buildings in Port Vila. Also handles Canadian consular services.

French Embassy (☑28700; www.ambafrance-vu.org; Lini Hwy) Also home to Alliance Française.

New Zealand High Commission (☑22933; www.nzembassy.com/vanuatu; Teoma St) Consular facilities and informative website.

Food

For information on food in Vanuatu, see p115.

LGBT Travellers

LGBT travellers will probably have to be discreet in Vanuatu. While homosexuality is legal, public displays of affection are not the done

---

EATING PRICE RANGES

The following price ranges refer to the price of a main meal:

$ less than 1500VT

$$ 1500–3000VT

$$$ more than 3000VT

---

thing, regardless of your sexual persuasion. There are no specifically gay bars on the islands.

Insurance

A travel insurance policy to cover theft, loss and medical problems is vital; note some policies specifically exclude 'dangerous activities', which can include parasailing, scuba diving, motorcycling and even trekking. Check that the policy covers ambulances and an emergency flight home.

Worldwide travel insurance is available at lonelyplanet. com/travel-insurance. You can buy, extend and claim online anytime, even if you're already on the road.

Internet Access

Numerous cafes and bars in Port Vila and Luganville have free wi-fi. There's a TVL internet cafe in Lenakel (Tanna) and Lakatoro (Malekula). Many hotels and resorts also offer wi-fi.

If you have a TVL or Digicel phone SIM with a 3G data plan you should be able to use the internet on your phone at main villages on all but the most remote islands.

Maps

It's difficult to get good maps in Vanuatu; you're best to buy one before you leave home. The **Hema Vanuatu Country Map** (www.hemamaps.com) 1:1,000,000 is a good start.

Tourism booklets have very basic tourist maps of Santo and Efate.

Money

Vanuatu's currency is the vatu (VT), which floats against a basket of currencies including the US dollar, so it is reasonably stable. It's easy to exchange Australian dollars and most major currencies in main banks.

Commercial banks in Vanuatu are ANZ (http://anz.com/vanuatu), Westpac (http://westpac.vu), the local National Bank of Vanuatu (NBV) and the French bank Bred (www.bred.vu).

ATMs

Banks have offices in central Port Vila and branches in Luganville on Santo. ANZ and Westpac have plenty of ATMs in Port Vila, and a couple each in Luganville. There are ATMs at the international airports in Santo and Port Vila.

Exchange rates vary between banks and you'll invariably be slugged with a fee at both ends, so it pays to use ATMs sparingly. The maximum you can withdraw is 44,000VT per day. At Port Vila's Sportsmen's Hotel there's an ATM that dispenses Australian dollars, which you can then change at the bar (or a bank) at a (supposedly) favourable rate.

Cash

Take plenty of vatu everywhere outside Port Vila and Luganville as there are only a handful of NBV banks that change foreign currencies; additionally, hours are limited, queues are long and banks may run low on cash. There are plenty of tales of travellers running out of cash on Vanuatu's islands. In remote areas it's useful to have coins and smaller-denomination notes.

Credit Cards

The major credit cards are accepted by hotels, car-rental agencies, airline offices,

most of the tourist-friendly shops and restaurants in Port Vila and, to a lesser extent, in Luganville. You can't use credit cards outside these two towns and Tanna's main resorts. The standard surcharge is 4% to 5% but this can still work out cheaper than ATM fees.

Money Changers

ANZ, Westpac and NBV all exchange major foreign currencies, including Australian and New Zealand dollars. Main offices are in Port Vila; branches are in Luganville on Santo. The NBV also has branches on major islands, including Lakatoro (Malekula), Lenakel (Tanna) and Pango (Pentecost), but these shouldn't be relied upon.

There are branches of Goodies Money Exchange in Port Vila, which offer good rates.

Tipping

In *kastom* terms, tipping is an obligation that the receiver must return so, to avoid embarrassment, keep your 'tip' to a smile of thanks. Restaurant staff in Port Vila are happy to accept a tip, though.

Travellers Cheques

Don't bother. Travellers cheques can only be changed in Port Vila and Luganville.

Opening Hours

Government offices Monday to Friday from 7.30am to 11.30am, and 1.30pm to 4.30pm; sometimes open on Saturday mornings.

Shops Monday to Friday from 7.30am to 5pm or 6pm; some close for midday siesta. Saturday shopping finishes at 11.30am, although Chinese-owned stores remain open all weekend.

Photography

It's polite to ask people before taking photos of them. Often the fee for taking photos of special performances (such as land diving or traditional dances) is included in the entrance fee, but there is usually an extra cost for recording footage.

Memory cards and other photographic equipment can be found in Port Vila and Luganville.

Post

Vanuatu Post (www.vanuatu post.vu) has the world's only underwater post office and volcano-side postbox; waterproof and volcano postcards cost 400VT, and can be posted anywhere in the world. Buy the volcano cards from Tanna's resorts or in Port Vila and bring them with you up the volcano.

There's no street postal-delivery service in the country; addresses are PO Box or Private Mail Bag (PMB). There's a poste restante service in Port Vila. All major centres have post offices. Outer-island mail is delivered to the main islands by plane; add the relevant airport to the address.

Public Holidays

When a national holiday falls on a weekend, there's usually a public holiday on the following Monday. Vanuatu's official national holidays include the following:

New Year's Day 1 January

Father Walter Lini Day (Remembrance Day) 21 February

Kastom Chiefs' Day 5 March

Good Friday & Easter Monday March/April

Labour Day 1 May

Ascension Day 24 May

Children's Day 24 July

Independence Day 30 July

Assumption Day 15 August

Constitution Day 5 October

National Unity Day 29 November

Christmas Day 25 December

Family Day 26 December

School Holidays

A stream of students return to their home islands during local school holidays (May, August and Christmas). They mainly travel by cargo or passenger boat, but it's a good idea to book domestic flights as early as possible at these times. Flights are also busier during Australian and New Zealand school holidays, but the tourist facilities will almost always have vacancies.

Safe Travel

Vanuatu is situated on the Pacific Ring of Fire and experiences relatively frequent earthquakes (some 2000 seismic events are recorded each year) and less frequent tsunamis. The country also has active volcanoes. The alert level on volcanoes can change rapidly, so check with local authorities prior to travelling to volcanic areas. Always be alert and check the Vanuatu Geohazards Observatory website (www. geohazards.gov.vu) for information about earthquakes, tsunamis and volcanoes.

Cyclone season in Vanuatu lasts from November until April. There's a high risk of strong winds, heavy rains and associated flooding, landslides and road closures. See the Vanuatu Meteorolog-

ical Services website (www. meteo.gov.vu) for current information.

There are sharks in the waters off Santo and Malekula in particular, so always check with locals before diving in.

In terms of theft and personal crime, Vanuatu is very safe, but it pays to take precautions, especially in Port Vila. Keep those wads of vatu well hidden; take taxis at night in main towns; and lock your bungalow with a padlock.

Telephone

There are no local area codes in Vanuatu.

International Calls

➡ International area code: ☑678

➡ International code for calls out of Vanuatu: ☑00

Using the national carrier TVL, calls to Australia, NZ, New Caledonia and Fiji cost 50/60VT per minute from fixed lines/mobile phones; calls further afield cost up to 150VT per minute. Calls to satellite phones are 500VT per minute. SMS to anywhere costs 12VT.

Landlines

Landlines that have been accidentally dug up or have melted away into nothing do not usually get replaced, meaning that many landline numbers are now no longer

---

GOVERNMENT TRAVEL ADVICE

The following government websites offer travel advisories and information:

Australian Department of Foreign Affairs (www. smarttraveller.gov.au)

British Foreign Office (www.fco.gov.uk/en/travel-and-living-abroad/travel-advice-by-country)

Canadian Department of Foreign Affairs (www. dfait-maeci.gc.ca)

US State Department (http://travel.state.gov)

in use, especially on outer islands. Vanuatu has had an exceptionally high take-up of mobile phones. Although new phone towers are regularly being erected (they were among the first things replaced on Tanna after Cyclone Pam in 2015), reception can be patchy on outer islands.

Public telephones are sometimes located at airports and in a public area in villages, but are rarely used.

Mobile Phones

Vanuatu is on GSM digital. Much of the populated archipelago is covered by two mobile phone networks: the red Digicel (www.digicelvanuatu.com) or orange TVL (www.tvl.vu) signs are the most ubiquitous form of advertising you'll see around the islands. A Smile SIM-card package is 3000VT, including 2500VT of calls, or you can get a Digicel SIM card for 2000VT. Coverage, service and pricing are similar but most islanders don't take any chances and have both SIM cards. If you intend to use 3G data (for email or web browsing), make sure you get a sensible mobile internet plan; topping up and paying for data as you go is ridiculously expensive.

Time

Vanuatu time is GMT/UMT plus 11 hours, one hour ahead of Australian Eastern Standard Time (AEST). Noon in Port Vila is 1am in London, 8pm in New York and 11am in Sydney. There's no daylight savings time (DST) in Vanuatu.

Time seems to move slowly in the South Pacific; after a while you get used to the unhurried pace of life. If you're travelling in rural Vanuatu you might spend hours waiting for planes, taxis, speedboats, guides...

Toilets

There are public toilets in Port Vila and Luganville, and at several airstrips, but that's about it. If you're travelling to the outer islands, take your own toilet paper, a torch and mosquito repellent, though the better bungalows now have attached bathrooms. Don't expect to find flush toilets on the outer islands.

Tourist Information

There are walk-in tourist offices in Port Vila (Efate), Luganville (Santo) and Lakatoro (Malekula), and a number of regions also maintain useful websites, including www.espiritusantotourism.com.

Malampa Travel (☏7748030, 48888; www.malampa.travel) The Malampa Travel office, near the police station in the upper part of Lakatoro, can book accommodation or organise treks and tours on Malekula, as well as to Ambrym.

Sanma Information & Call Centre (☏36616; www.santo.travel; Main St; ⊙7.30am-5pm Mon-Fri, plus weekends on cruise-ship days) Part tourist office, part private travel agency, Sanma (Santo and Malo) has helpful staff who can make local bookings.

Vanuatu Tourism Office (VTO; ☏22813; www.vanuatu.travel; Lini Hwy; ⊙8am-5pm Mon-Fri, 8am-noon Sat, 8am-2pm weekends on cruise-ship days) Helpful staff; free maps and information about accommodation, activities, tours and the outer islands.

Visas

Every visitor must have a passport valid for a further six months and be able to show an onward ticket. Entry visas are not required for nationals of the British Commonwealth and EU. On entry, you're allowed an initial stay of up to 30 days, extended for up to four months once you're there (or you can apply beforehand).

Nonexempt visitors should contact the **Principal Immigration Officer** (☏22354; immigration@vanuatu.gov.vu) to organise their visa application (3600VT). This must be finalised *before* you arrive.

Visa extensions for up to four months (6000VT) can be done quickly without the need to leave your passport and onward ticket with the immigration department. You'll need your passport and copies of your passport, onward ticket and current passport photos for the

---

PRACTICALITIES

→ **Electricity** Mains power is provided in Port Vila, Luganville, Lenakel and Lakatoro. Rural bungalows use generators in the evenings until 9pm, or solar power.

→ **Newspapers & Magazines** *Daily Post* (100VT; www.dailypost.vu) is available Monday to Saturday; *The Independent* (200VT; www.independent.vu) is available Saturdays; *Island Life* (300VT; www.islandlifemag.com) is a glossy Vanuatu-focused travel and lifestyle magazine published every two months.

→ **Radio** Radio Vanuatu offers trilingual FM, AM and SW services from 6am to 10pm, and international and local news bulletins (98FM; 1125AM); Capital FM107 has music news and talkback in English, Bislama and French.

→ **Weights & Measures** Vanuatu uses the metric system.

application, which can be made at the immigration office in Port Vila.

Volunteering

Volunteer organisations that can provide information include Go Abroad (www.goabroad.com) and Lattitude Global Volunteering (www.lattitude.org.au). The following organisations have projects in Vanuatu:

Australian Business Volunteers (www.abv.org.au) Projects from one to six months for volunteers with business skills.

Australian Volunteers International (www.australianvolunteers.com) Can arrange volunteer placements through the Australian Volunteers for International Development program funded by the Australian government.

Midwives For Vanuatu (www.midwivesforvanuatu.org) Experienced midwives can fill staff shortages by volunteering at Port Vila hospital.

Oceans Watch (☑9434 4066; www.oceanswatch.org) Yachties and others can volunteer on marine conservation projects with Oceans Watch.

Scope Global (www.volunteering.scopeglobal.com) Provides skilled volunteer placements with the Australian Volunteers for International Development scheme.

Voice Australia (http://voiceaustralia.org.au) Australian youth development and volunteer program with projects in Vanuatu.

Volunteer Service Abroad (NZ VSA; www.vsa.org.nz) This well-established New Zealand organisation offers volunteer placements for skilled workers.

Women Travellers

Vanuatu is considered a safe place for female visitors, but there are plenty of horror stories, so exercise caution.

Take taxis and stick to busy areas at night. Try not to swim or sunbathe alone at isolated beaches.

Women staying overnight alone in villages may risk being harassed by men known as 'creepers', who hang around making kissing and 'pssst' noises. They are unlikely to take matters further, but for peace of mind ask them very strongly to not look at you or your door anymore (an open door is an invitation) and to go away. The villagers will always 'lend' you a young woman to sleep in your bungalow if you are nervous.

Vanuatu is a bastion of male chauvinism and, although the locals are bemused and tolerant of Western women's behaviour and dress, it's considered disrespectful to wear skimpy clothing, especially on the outer islands which see few tourists.

In villages, women are not always welcome at *nakamals*. Ask locally.

Vanuatu Transport

GETTING THERE & AWAY

Air

The following airlines have regular scheduled flights to Vanuatu:

Air New Zealand (☑22666; www.airnewzealand.co.nz) Direct flights from Auckland (from NZ$250) to Port Vila.

Air Vanuatu (☑23848; www.airvanuatu.com; Rue de Paris, Port Vila) Air Vanuatu/Qantas (code-share) operates direct flights from Brisbane and Sydney to Port Vila. Return fares start from A$700. There are also direct flights to Espiritu Santo from Brisbane. From New Zealand, Air Vanuatu/Qantas flies direct from Auckland to Port Vila; and from Auckland via Nadi and Suva (Fiji), Honiara (Solomon Islands) and Noumea (New Caledonia).

Aircalin (☑22739; http://au.aircalin.com; Lini Hwy, Port Vila) Flights to Port Vila from Nadi and Noumea.

Fiji Airways (☑22836; www.fijiairways.com; Lini Hwy)

Flights to Port Vila from Nadi and Noumea.

Virgin Australia (☑22836; www.virginaustralia.com) Direct flights from Brisbane and Sydney to Port Vila. Return fares start from A$700.

Airports

Bauerfield International Airport Port Vila's airport is 6km from the centre. It has an ANZ ATM, an NBV branch for currency exchange, a cafe and duty-free shopping. It's adjacent to the domestic airport, which has a Westpac ATM, a cafe, mobile phone outlets, and a souvenir and book stall.

Pekoa International Airport Three kilometres from Luganville, Santo's airport has an ANZ ATM, cafe, mobile phone outlets, duty-free shop and free wi-fi.

Sea

Cruise Ship

Vanuatu is a very popular cruise-ship destination, with ships stopping at Port Vila (Efate), Santo, Wala (Malekula), Mystery Island in the remote south and Pentecost during land-diving season.

The ongoing construction of a new wharf at Luganville by Chinese company Shanghai Construction Group, expected to continue until 2017, has caused disruption to some cruise-ship berths in recent years; however, cruise ships are once again docking at Luganville.

Pacific Sun, Pacific Dawn, Pacific Jewel and *Pacific Pearl*, operated by P&O (www.pocruises.com.au), are the most regular visitors; *Sea Princess, Golden Princess* and *Carnival Spirit* also call in.

Yacht

The best source of general information on yachting matters in Port Vila is **Yachting World Vanuatu** (www.yachtingworld-vanuatu.com; Lini Hwy, VHF16). It has a sea-wall tie up and diesel dock, and can arrange customs and quarantine inspections to your buoy; also has hot showers and wi-fi.

The authorised ports of entry for touring yachts are Port Vila (Efate), Luganville (Santo), Lenakel (Tanna) or Sola (Vanua Lava). There are hefty fines if you make landfall in or depart from Vanuatu before customs and immigration have been cleared; 24 hours' notice is required for customs clearance. Port dues are 7875VT for the first 30 days and 100VT per day thereafter. Quarantine clearance is

---

THE LONG TRIP HOME

If you have chartered a boat to travel out to the islands and the date for your international flight home from Port Vila is set in stone, consider returning by air. Seas change too dramatically to guarantee meeting such a deadline.

CLIMATE CHANGE & TRAVEL

Every form of transport that relies on carbon-based fuel generates CO_2, the main cause of human-induced climate change. Modern travel is dependent on aeroplanes, which might use less fuel per kilometre per person than most cars but travel much greater distances. The altitude at which aircraft emit gases (including CO_2) and particles also contributes to their climate change impact. Many websites offer 'carbon calculators' that allow people to estimate the carbon emissions generated by their journey and, for those who wish to do so, to offset the impact of the greenhouse gases emitted with contributions to portfolios of climate-friendly initiatives throughout the world. Lonely Planet offsets the carbon footprint of all staff and author travel.

3000VT and immigration clearance 4800VT.

Port Vila Boatyard (☑23417; www.portvilaboat-yard.com) has many amenities and facilities in sheltered Pontoon Bay.

Useful websites for yachting info include Cruising Vanuatu (www.cruising-va-nuatu.com) and Vanuatu Cruising Guide (www.vanu-atucruising.info).

Cruising New Caledonia & Vanuatu by Alan Lucas gives details on many natural harbours and out-of-the-way anchorages.

GETTING AROUND

Ownership of land, ocean and reefs is the basis of Vanuatu society. For visitors, this means you can't wander off the beaten track without a local guide. If you're travelling independently, discuss your plans with a tour operator or the Vanuatu Tourism Office (VTO).

In remote areas – such as the east coasts of Maewo, Pentecost and Ambrym, and the west coasts of Santo and Malekula – the only access is by foot or speedboat. Many islands have no roads, and even if they do these roads can quickly turn back into jungle if they're not regularly used or are hit by heavy rain. For many places, contact with the outside world is via the small cargo and passenger boats that operate out of Port Vila and Luganville.

Air

If you want to see a few of Vanuatu's islands, chances are you'll fly at some stage. Outside of Efate, Santo and Tanna, 'airports' have grass runways; most don't have electricity or even chairs. Apart from Vila, Santo's Pekoa, Pentecost's Lonorore and Tanna's Whitegrass airports are some of the better equipped.

Flights from Port Vila to domestic destinations usually depart from the domestic terminal next to the Bauerfield International Airport. Check-in is open until 30 minutes before departure.

Bicycle

With roads on most of Vanuatu's islands not even suitable for cars or 4WDs, you'd have to be very keen to take on Vanuatu by bike. Still, mountain bikes can be hired in Port Vila and Luganville and are useful for getting around town on their respective sealed roads.

Boat

Canoe & Speedboat

When ni-Vanuatu talk of speedboats, they mean outboard-powered dinghies. These can take on short interisland travel if weather conditions are favourable. Make sure there are life jackets.

Speedboat prices are high (fuel is expensive), so it's best to wait for a scheduled service or combine with a group of other travellers rather than charter. In many places it's easier to travel by speedboat along the coast than by road, and in some places, including Ambrym, it's the only way to go.

Canoes are paddle-powered dugout craft with outriggers and can be used to get to smaller outlying islands.

Passenger Boat

Big Sista (☑5683622; 9000VT) Weekly service between Port Vila and Lugan-ville (9000VT, 25 hours) on a 33m passenger vessel. Departs Port Vila at 1pm on Mondays and stops at Epi (5600VT), Paama (6100VT) and Malekula (7600VT). Children go half-price. You can pay an extra 500VT to upgrade to business class (indoor air-conditioned seat with movies).

Vanuatu Ferry (☑26999; www. facebook.com/Vanuatu-Ferry-Limited-690422517676564/; Lini Hwy) Weekly service between Port Vila and Santo (8000VT), departing Vila at 9pm on Mondays and stopping at Malekula (6500VT).

Bus

Minibuses with a red 'B' on their number plates operate in Port Vila, Luganville and northeast Malekula. They don't run along fixed routes but zoom to your destination (if you're lucky; it can also be first in, first delivered). Flag them down by the roadside (150VT for short trips). In central Port Vila these minibuses can create traffic jams so are often slow for short trips.

There are informal but regular bus services around Efate (including some that depart Port Vila in time to connect with speedboats to Pele and Nguna). A service also departs up the east coast of Santo.

Car & Motorcycle

The only places you can hire self-drive cars, 4WDs and scooters are in Port Vila and Luganville.

The minimum age for renting a car is usually 21 (25 for a dune buggy); for a scooter it's 18.

Driving Efate's Ring Rd or Santo's East Coast Rd is easy, but off these routes you may be hampered by a lack of road signs, up-to-date road maps or any indication of where the road finishes and a ravine starts.

Driver's Licence

You don't need an International Driving Licence; a valid licence from your own country will suffice to drive in Vanuatu.

Fuel & Spare Parts

Petrol costs about 150VT per litre in Port Vila and Luganville. Outside these townships it is not possible to get spare parts and nearly impossible to find a mechanic, so it's important to check your hire vehicle before heading off and to ensure you have the phone number of the hirer.

THE WAY TO FLY

Flying with Air Vanuatu, much like Vanuatu itself, is one fantastic adventure. The propellers whizz while you skim over volcanoes, crater lakes, coral reefs, rugged coastlines and ocean carpet, before coming to a bumpy landing on a grass airstrip. You may be seated next to nervous men with bush knives on their knees and share the cabin with all manner of cargo.

Strange stories abound. Flights to Futuna were cancelled for a while as the grass on the airstrip was too long for safe landing but the island lawnmover needed a spare part – to be delivered by plane. And when a mate was needed for the crocodile living in Sulfur River on Vanua Lava, a tranquillised croc was loaded into the plane. A bit big for the small plane, its head went through into the cockpit and rested between the two pilots.

Planes are frequently cancelled or delayed and might fly to remote islands once a week, but if you're flexible, flying is a fast, affordable and fun way of getting around the islands.

Airlines

Vanuatu's domestic airline Air Vanuatu has offices in Port Vila, Luganville and Lakatoro.

Air Vanuatu's safety record is not great, though there have been only two fatal accidents since 1991. The domestic fleet ranges from the 70-seater ATRs to 19-seater Twin Otters.

You can download Air Vanuatu's domestic flight schedule from the website, but it's not always up to date, so check ahead. Some flights (including those to Tanna and Santo) can be booked online. For flights to other islands or to arrange a complex itinerary, email requests to reservation@airvanuatu.com.vu. Show your international flight ticket with Air Vanuatu to receive a 20% discount on domestic flights. Children under 12 years and students receive a 50% and 25% discount respectively (take your student card).

If your itinerary is tight, it can pay to book well in advance, but if you're flexible it's often possible to get on a flight with a day's notice.

A number of charter companies offer flights:

Air Safaris (☑7745207; www.airsafaris.vu) Runs tours and is available for charter.

Air Taxi Runs tours and is available for charter.

Belair Airways (☑29222, 5551290; www.belair.vu; Bauerfield International Airport) Vanuatu's newest scheduled airline with a single nine-seater plane.

Unity Airlines (☑7744475, 24475; www.unity-airlines.com; Bauerfield International Airport) Flies tour groups to outer islands and is available for charter.

Departure Tax

Domestic-flight departure tax costs 200VT per person, payable in cash at the airport before each departure.

Insurance

Insurance is always added to the car or motorcycle hire – at an additional cost – by law. Take a note of any dings or damage and check your tyres (and the spare) before setting off.

Road Rules

Port Vila and Luganville have a speed limit of 50km/h, which is easy to stick to given the number of super-slow taxis and minibuses you're sharing the road with. Elsewhere, speed is dictated by road conditions – it's usually not much more than 10km/h. Vehicles drive on the right; steering is on the left.

Hitching

Since most vehicle owners on the islands derive an income from delivering people and goods, hitching is really just catching 'public transport' (ie you'll have to pay).

Taxi

Taxis (marked with a red 'T' on their number plates) are mostly sedans in Port Vila and Luganville, but elsewhere they're 4WD trucks with open trays at the back. Charges depend on distance, but also on the state of the road. Ask your driver for a price. To charter the whole truck will be expensive but local taxi truck fares are cheap.

A short trip in Port Vila might cost 400VT, but a day charter will cost between 8000VT and 12,000VT. On 'cruise-ship days' prices can explode; leave your trip until the ship port is empty.

Local taxis (4WD trucks) meet flights at island airstrips, but may not be around on Sundays, public holidays, when there's no fuel on the island or when there's a major celebration happening.

Tours

Operators in Port Vila and Luganville organise tours and activities in and around Efate and Santo, as well as throughout Vanuatu. You'll find a range of inbound, locally run tour companies next to Port Vila's market.

Outside Port Vila, many of the places offering accommodation also run tours, such as guided walks or traditional dances, usually on private or customary land. You'll often pay a guiding fee as well as an entrance fee to the land owners.

New Caledonia

📞 687 / POP 270,000

Best Places to Stay

➡ Le Lagon (p137)

➡ Hotel Hibiscus (p151)

➡ Relais de Poingam (p152)

➡ Nëkwéta Fish & Surf Camp (p150)

➡ Refuge de Farino (p148)

Best Beaches

➡ La Roche Percée (p150)

➡ Baie des Citrons (p131)

➡ Baie de Kanuméra (p166)

➡ Fayaoué Beach (p161)

➡ Yedjele Beach (p156)

Why Go?

New Caledonia's dazzling lagoon surrounds it with every hue of blue, green and turquoise. The light and the space simply delight your senses. By becoming a World Heritage site, the lagoon has helped bring the people together to celebrate and protect it, from village level through to government.

New Caledonia isn't just a tropical playground. There's a charming mix of French and Melanesian: warm hospitality sitting beside European elegance, gourmet food beneath palm trees, sand, resorts and bungalows. Long gorgeous beaches are backed by cafes and bars, with horizons that display tiny islets to attract day trippers. Be lured into kayaks or microlights, rock climb, sail, dive into a world of corals, canyons, caves and shipwrecks, go whale watching or snorkelling, or relax on the warm sand of a deserted isle. Natural wonders and manmade delights are at your fingertips.

When to Go
Noumea

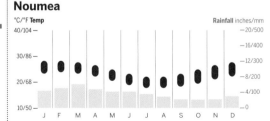

Apr–May Fresh from the heat and rains, the country is sparkling again.

Jul-Aug It may be cool for beachgoers, but that bodes well for hikers and whale-watchers.

Oct–Nov Catch life on the islands before folk head off on their summer vacation.

GRANDE TERRE

POP 245,000 / AREA 16,372 SQ KM

Orientated northwest to southeast, a chain of mountains sweeps down the middle of New Caledonia's main island, Grande Terre. Four hundred kilometres long, the island is 50km to 70km across for most of its length. To the west, in the lee of the mountains, are wide, dry plains dotted with country towns, while to the east, on the windward coast, lush vegetation descends to the sea.

The island is surrounded by its legendary World Heritage–listed lagoon, though this is not Grande Terre's only 'green gold'. The other is garnierite, a silicate rich in nickel that has fueled the country's economy since its discovery in 1864.

Administratively, Grande Terre is divided into two districts, Province Nord (the North) and Province Sud (the South). Île des Pins is officially part of Province Sud.

Noumea

POP 100,000

With its cheerful multi-ethnic community, New Caledonia's cosmopolitan capital is both sophisticated and uncomplicated, classy and casual. The relaxed city sits on a large peninsula, surrounded by picturesque bays, and offers visitors a variety of experiences. Diners can eat out at sassy French restaurants hidden in Quartier Latin, dine at bold waterfront bistros or grab a bargain meal from a nocturnal van in a car park. Meanwhile, shopaholics can blow their savings on the latest Parisian fashions or go bargain hunting for imported Asian textiles.

Central Noumea revolves around Place des Cocotiers, a large, shady square with landscaped gardens, a couple of blocks in from the waterfront. The main leisure area where locals and tourists hang out lies south of the city centre at Baie des Citrons and Anse Vata, with beaches, restaurants, bars and nightclubs.

While Noumea city has 100,000 residents, the greater Noumea area, including Le Mont-Dore, Dumbéa and Paita, is home to 164,000, or about 63% of New Caledonia's population.

☉ Sights

◎ City Centre

★ **Place des Cocotiers**   SQUARE
(Map p134) This is the heart of the city. The square slopes gently from east to west and at the top is a band rotunda, a famous landmark dating back to the late 1800s. Place des Cocotiers is the perfect spot to watch the world go by. Near the band rotunda there's a popular *pétanque* pitch and a giant chessboard. Down the other end it's like a lush botanical garden, with palms and large spreading trees. There's free wi-fi throughout the square.

Regular concerts and street markets are held in Place des Cocotiers. Held twice a month, the popular Jeudis du Centre Ville street market has a different theme each time.

★ **Le Marché**   MARKET
(Map p134; www.noumea.nc/en; ☉5-11am Tue-Sun) This colourful multi-hexagonal-shaped market is beside the marina at Port Moselle. Fishermen unload their catch; trucks offload fruit, vegetables and flowers; and there's fresh-baked bread and cakes, plus delights like terrines and olives. The arts and crafts section includes a cafe. On Saturday and Sunday live music keeps shoppers entertained. The market is busiest early in the morning.

★ **Musée de la Ville de Noumea**   MUSEUM
(Noumea Museum; Map p134; ☏26 28 05; Rue Jean Jaurès; admission 200 CFP; ☉9am-5pm Mon-Fri, 9am-1pm & 2-5pm Sat) The beautiful colonial-style Musée de la Ville de Noumea, which overlooks Place des Cocotiers, is dwarfed by towering palm trees. It features fascinating temporary and permanent displays on the early history of Noumea.

Musée de Nouvelle-Calédonie   MUSEUM
(Museum of New Caledonia; Map p134; ☏27 23 42; www.museenouvellecaledonie.nc; 42 Av du Maréchal Foch; adult 200 CFP; ☉9-11.30am & 12.15-4.30pm Wed-Mon) The Musée de Nouvelle-Calédonie provides an excellent introduction to traditional Kanak and regional Pacific culture. Local exhibits are displayed on the ground floor and regional artefacts on the mezzanine level.

Mwâ Ka   MONUMENT
(Map p134) Mwâ Ka is erected in a landscaped square opposite Musée de Nouvelle-Calédonie. The 12m totem pole is topped by a *grande case* (chief's hut), complete with *flèche faîtière* (carved rooftop spear), and its carvings represent the eight customary regions of New Caledonia. The Mwâ Ka is mounted as the mast on a concrete double-hulled *pirogue,* steered by a wooden helmsman, and celebrates Kanak identity as well as the multiethnic reality of New Caledonia.

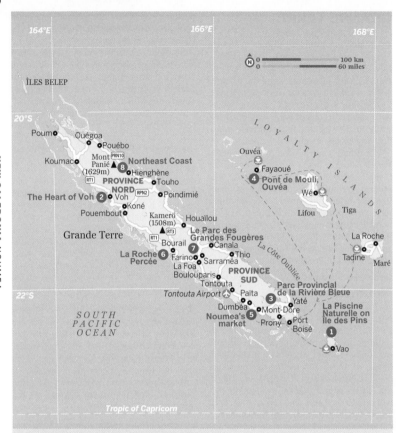

New Caledonia Highlights

1 Swimming with tropical fish at **La Piscine Naturelle** (p167) on Île des Pins.

2 Flying in a microlight over **The Heart of Voh** (p154) and the 'blue hole' in the lagoon from Koné.

3 Heading into the surprisingly isolated Far South for a hike in **Parc Provincial de la Rivière Bleue** (p143).

4 Admiring the stunning lagoon on Ouvéa and spotting turtles from **Pont de Mouli** (p161).

5 Drinking coffee with locals at Noumea's **market** (p129) while listening to a local Kanak band.

6 Checking out **La Roche Percée** (p150; Pierced Rock) and Le Bonhomme

(The Tubby Man) near Bourail.

7 Walking or biking among the great ferns at **Le Parc des Grandes Fougères** (p148) near Farino.

8 Riding the three-car ferry across the Ouaième River when driving up the stunning **Northeast Coast** (p152).

Cathédrale St Joseph   CHURCH
(Map p134; 3 Rue Frédérick Surleau) The cathedral was built in 1888 by convict labour and is one of Noumea's landmarks. It has beautiful stained-glass windows and an elaborately carved pulpit, altar panels and confessional.

The main entrance is sometimes locked, but you should find the side doors open.

Musée de l'Histoire Maritime   MUSEUM
(Maritime Museum; Map p133; ☎26 34 43; http://museemaritime.nc; 11 Av James Cook; adult/child 500/250 CFP; ☉10am-5pm Tue-Sun) Looking sharp after recent refurbishments, the

Musée de l'Histoire Maritime, down past the Betico ferry terminal, has a mix of permanent collections and temporary exhibitions. The focus is on the maritime history of New Caledonia and, in particular, the voyages of the great French Pacific explorer, Jean-François de La Pérouse (1785–1788). There are interactive exhibits for children.

Baie des Citrons & Anse Vata

★ Baie des Citrons   BEACH
(Map p136) Orientated north–south and less than 10 minutes from the city centre, trendy Baie des Citrons attracts locals and visitors alike. The beach is great for swimming, while the strip of restaurants, bars and nightclubs along the main road could well pull you in from breakfast until the wee hours.

★ Anse Vata   BEACH
(Map p136) Orientated east–west, this popular beach is a hotspot for visitors to Noumea, with hotels, restaurants, shopping and other attractions. Only 10 minutes from the city centre, the locals relax here too, especially on the *petanque* courts next to the beach. On a breezy day at Anse Vata, you can watch the colourful kite- and windsurfers skimming up and down the bay. It's only five minutes by taxiboat from here out to Île aux Canards.

★ Aquarium des Lagons   AQUARIUM
(Map p136; ☑26 27 31; www.aquarium.nc; 61 Promenade Roger Laroque; adult/child 1000/500 CFP; ⊙10am-5pm Tue-Sun; ⊕) This aquarium is stunning. Species found in New Caledonian waters – including nautilus, sea snakes, stone fish, turtles, sharks and stingrays – have realistic surroundings in their huge tanks. Living coral displays are surprising but don't miss the emperor of coral reefs: Napoleon fish.

Ouen Toro   VIEWPOINT
(Map p136) A sealed road winds up 132m Ouen Toro from just past Anse Vata beach. Two WWII guns still stand sentinel at the summit from where there are excellent views over Anse Vata and Baie des Citrons as well as the lagoon. Several trails weave through the wooded slopes of Ouen Toro.

Around the City

Tjibaou Cultural Centre   ARTS CENTRE
(Map p144; ☑41 45 45; www.adck.nc; Rue des Accords de Matignon; adult/child 500 CFP/free,

ℹ ONE PASS, SIX PLACES

On your first visit to a Noumea museum or site, ask about buying the 'Pass Nature & Culture'. It costs 1700 CFP but it gives you entry to three museums, the aquarium, the Tjibaou Cultural Centre and the zoo and botanical gardens.

guided tours 1000 CFP; ⊙9am-5pm Tue-Sun) The cultural centre is a tribute to a pro-independence Kanak leader Jean-Marie Tjibaou, who was assassinated in 1989. It sits in a peaceful woodland and mangrove setting on Tina Peninsula. Displays include sculpture, paintings and photographs representing Kanak culture, as well as other cultures from around the Pacific. The main buildings are a series of tall, curved wooden structures which rise majestically above the trees.

The harmony between this contemporary architecture (designed by Italian architect Renzo Piano, who also designed Paris' Pompidou Centre) and the surrounding landscape is amazing. Behind the main building are traditional *grandes cases*; Kanak dance shows are held every Tuesday and Thursday at 2.30pm (2500 CFP). City bus 40 and the Noumea Explorer bus run regularly to the centre.

Parc Zoologique et Forestier   ZOO
(Zoological & Botanical Gardens; Map p133; ☑27 89 51; Rte de Laubarède; adult/child 400 CFP/free; ⊙10.15am-5.45pm Tue-Sun, to 5pm May-Aug; ⊕) Wander along a network of paths through gardens of native shrubs and trees, cactus and forest with a changing backdrop of sea views in the distance. You'll come across native species such as the flightless *cagou, roussette, notou* pigeon and various parakeets right in front of you. Speed around the Parc Zoologique et Forestier on a **Segway** (☑86 46 83; per person 7500 CFP) for something different.

Offshore Islands

The waters around Noumea are sprinkled with beautiful islets and the clear waters surrounding them are great for snorkelling.

Amédée Islet   ISLAND
(www.amedeeisland.com) This islet, about 20km south of Noumea, is famous for its tall white lighthouse, **Phare Amédée** (admission 200 CFP), which was built in France, shipped out in pieces, and assembled on the postcard

One Week

Enjoy swimming at **Noumea's** beaches (Anse Vata and Baie des Citrons) and indulge in French pastries and bistro meals. Loll around the hotel pool, but emerge to visit the **market**, the gorgeous **aquarium** and, further out, the **Tjibaou Cultural Centre**. Ferry it to **Île des Pins**, pick up your awaiting rental car and explore the island, including visits to **Baie de Kuto**, **Vao** and **La Piscine Naturelle**. Walk in and along a river to a simple beachside restaurant where you can eat lobster. Return the car, catch the ferry back and dance like there's no tomorrow at an overwater nightclub.

Two Weeks

Follow the one week itinerary, then head north. Check out **Le Parc des Grandes Fougères** (Park of the Great Ferns), the beach and rock formations at **La Roche Percée**, and be sure to take a microlight flight over the **Heart of Voh** and the lagoon. Book ahead for a couple of magic days at **Relais de Poingam**, right at the tip, before heading down the east coast, discovering historical hotspots and buying up carvings and tropical fruits. Still time? Duck south and explore the **Parc Provincial de la Rivière Bleue** by canoe.

island in 1865. Climb up its spiral staircase to a narrow shelf with 360-degree views.

There's a snack bar and curio shop for visitors who come here on a day trip on the *Mary D*, which leaves from Port Moselle. Buy tickets at Palm Beach or Port Moselle.

Île aux Canards   ISLAND
(Duck Island; Map p136; www.ileauxcanards.nc; ☉8.30am-5.30pm, restaurant 11am-3.30pm; 🚹) Île aux Canards is a cute postcard-perfect islet sitting five minutes by taxi boat off Anse Vata. It's all here, including an underwater snorkelling path, rental gear, a restaurant, and a stunning beach with loungers, hammocks, beach umbrellas and even VIP Lounges. Head to the water-taxi booth about halfway along Anse Vata beach (return trip 1200 CPF).

Îlot Maître   ISLAND
Only 15 minutes by boat from Port Moselle or Anse Vata, the gorgeous little island of Îlot Maître makes for a great day trip. Get out there with L'Escapade (p138), which runs the island's resort, with Coconut Taxi (p143) or by taxi boat from Anse Vata. There's a beach and snack bar for day trippers, or ask the resort about using its facilities.

🏃 Activities

Diving

Abyss Plongée   DIVING
(Map p136; ☑79 15 09; www.abyssnc.com; Marina Port du Sud) Dives at many sites around Grande Terre and charges 7000 CFP for an intro dive and 11,000 CFP for a double dive, plus transport costs. It also offers PADI courses.

Alizé Diving   DIVING
(Map p136; ☑26 25 85; www.alizedive.com) Based at the Nouvata Park Hôtel in Anse Vata, Alizé Diving charges 13,000 CFP for an intro dive and 14,500 CFP for a two-dive package. Its boat leaves from Port du Sud Marina, but it includes transfers.

Amédée Diving Club   DIVING
(☑264 029; www.amedeediving.nc; 28 Rue du Général Mangin) Based on Amédée Island on the reef and in a marine reserve, these guys have some great options. Their Day Trip includes hotel transfers, boat transfers from Port Moselle, two dives and lunch. Departs 7am, returning 5pm, costing 15,000 CPF per person.

Water Activities

La Maison du Lagon   BOAT TOUR
(Map p134; ☑27 27 27; www.maisondulagon.nc; Port Moselle) This is a one-stop shop at Port Moselle for booking all your boat tours, whale-watching trips and anything else lagoon-and water-related.

Centre Nautique Vata Plaisirs WATER SPORTS
(Map p136; ☑78 13 00, 29 44 69; www.mdplaisirs.com) On the beach at Anse Vata, this place offers up all kinds of water-sports activities including stand-up paddle-boarding, windsurfing, wakeboarding, kitesurfing, boating and kayaking. Ask about the MD Plaisirs Card, which gives you 40% discount and is usable here and at its other base in Poé Beach.

Locajet   WATER SPORTS
(Map p133; ☑77 79 79; www.locajet.info; 5hr 26,000 CFP + fuel) In Nouville on the western

Noumea

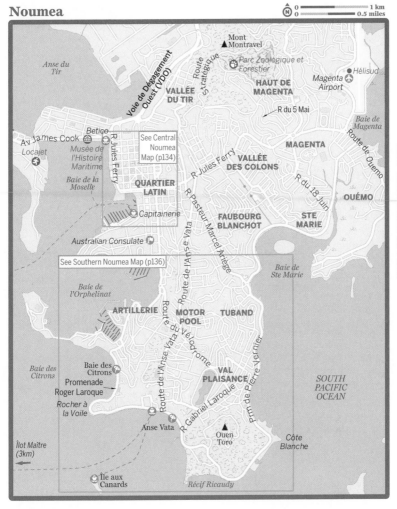

side of Baie de la Moselle, Locajet rents jet skis. Do a circular whiz from Baie de la Moselle to Île aux Canards, Îlot Maitre, a few more islets and back to the northern side of the Nouville peninsula.

Aquanature   SNORKELLING

(Map p134; ☑ 26 40 08, 78 36 66; http://aqua nature.nc; Port Moselle; half-/full day 7000/8500 CFP) Specialising in snorkelling trips, Aquanature heads out from Port Moselle on half-day and full-day trips to snorkel on the reef with equipment included in the price.

Noumea Kite School   ADVENTURE SPORTS

(Map p136; ☑ 79 07 66; www.noumeakiteschool. com; Port du Sud) Check out the website for all you need to know about kitesurfing and wakeboarding around Noumea.

Dream Yacht Charter   BOATING

(Map p134; ☑ 28 66 66; www.dreamyachtcharter. com; Port Moselle) Dream Yacht Charter offers skippered or bare-boat catamarans and monohulls for 'the best lagoon in the world'. It also has a catamaran in Koumac on the Northwest Coast.

Central Noumea

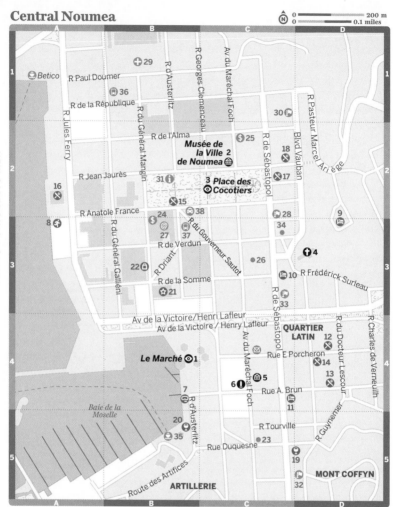

Land-Based Activities

You'll find all your favourite sporting activities are available in Noumea or around Grande Terre: golf, tennis, clay-pigeon shooting; just ask at the Office du Tourisme. It also has brochures for walks, cycling trips and climbs across islands, through forests and up creeks.

Noumea Fun Ride BICYCLE RENTAL
(Map p134; ☎ 26 96 26, 78 40 25; www.facebook.com/noumea.funride.7; Gare Maritime; scootcars 1/2hr 5500/7500 CFP; ▣) Based at the cruise ship quay, these guys rent wheels, including miniature cars, scooters, mountain and beach bikes. They also have helmets, child seats and roller blades. They're very busy when a cruise ship is in.

☞ Tours

Tchou Tchou Train TOUR
(☎ 26 31 31; http://amedeeisland.com/tchou-tchou-train-excursion; adult/child 2000/1000 CFP; ⊗10am Mon, 3pm Wed & Sat; ▣) Yes, that was a train you saw driving down the road. The bright yellow Tchou Tchou Train runs three times per week on entertaining and informative two-hour trips with an

Central Noumea

NEW CALEDONIA NOUMEA

English-speaking guide. Book at the *Mary D* at Galerie du Palm Beach. If you see it out on the road at other times you'll know a cruise ship is in!

Mary D BOAT TOUR
(Map p136; ☑ 26 31 31; www.amedeeisland.com; Galerie du Palm Beach, departs from Port Moselle, Anse Vata; tour 14,250 CFP; ☺ 7.30am-6pm Mon-Sat) It's a grand day on one of Mary D's launches out to Amédée Islet. Visit the lighthouse, snorkel offshore or from the glass-bottom boat, feed sharks on the reef, indulge in a luscious three-course buffet lunch, and see fun dance and cultural shows. Includes hotel transfers.

Hélisud SCENIC FLIGHTS
(Map p133; ☑ 26 96 62; www.helisud.nc; 30min flight 43,500 CFP) Helicopters fly a maximum of three people over Noumea's bays, the islets sprinkled across the lagoon, shipwrecks and the barrier reef. You can even fly to Île des Pins or north to see the Heart of Voh. Based at Noumea's Magenta Airport.

⚑ Festivals & Events

Noumea hosts a number of festivals through the year, including **Mardi Gras** in February, **Carnival** in August, **Régate des Touques** (Oil drum regatta) at Anse Vata in October, **Christmas Lights** in December and a major **New Year Fireworks** display.

In greater Noumea, there's a celebrated **Giant Omelette Festival** in Dumbea in April and a **Beef Festival** including rodeo in Paita in November.

🛏 Sleeping

Visitors need to make a conscious decision whether to stay in the middle of town or out at the beaches of Baies des Citrons and Anse Vata, a 10-minute drive away. The beaches offer up a lot more options.

🏙 City Centre

Auberge de Jeunesse HOSTEL $
(Map p134; ☑ 27 58 79; www.aubergesdejeunesse. nc; 51bis Rue Pasteur Marcel Ariège; dm/d 1800/4100 CFP; ◉ ⬤) This efficient and friendly hostel,

Southern Noumea

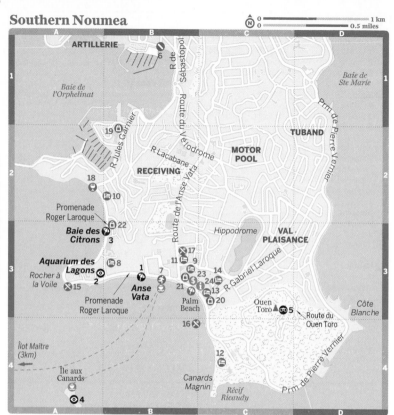

behind St Joseph's Cathedral, has a fantastic view of the city and Baie de la Moselle. The dorms and twin rooms share separate male/ female bathroom facilities, while there is a kitchen, wi-fi, a television lounge and a ping-pong table. From the centre of town, head up the 103 steps at the top of Rue Jean Jaurès.

Hôtel New Caledonia
HOTEL **$$**

(Map p134; ☑ 26 18 26; www.hotel-new-caledonia. com; 10 Rue Auguste Brun; d 9650 CFP; ❄ 🛜) Simple and central says it all for this 28-room hotel in Quartier Latin in the city centre. It's just inland from Port Moselle, close to the action, and rooms have kitchenettes. There's wi-fi in the lobby and rates include breakfast.

Hôtel Le Paris
HOTEL **$$**

(Map p134; ☑ 28 17 00; www.bestwesternleparis. com; 45 Rue de Sébastopol; s/d 11,450/12,350 CFP; ❄ 🛜) With 24-hour reception in the centre of Noumea, Hôtel Le Paris is only a short stroll from Place des Cocotiers and right next

to Best Cafe. Rooms are spacious and simple and staff can arrange airport transfers.

🛏 Baie des Citrons

⭐ Hôtel Beaurivage
HOTEL **$$**

(Map p136; ☑ 24 24 77; www.grands-hotels. nc; 7 Promenade Roger Laroque; r from 9200 CFP; 🅿 ❄ 🛜) Nicely refurbished and in a brilliant location just across the road from the beach, the Beaurivage is a great option. Le Nahalie's Bar, the popular onsite bar and *snack* restaurant is open 6am to 10pm daily and Baie des Citrons' restaurant strip is only a short stroll away.

Casa del Sole
HOTEL **$$**

(Map p136; ☑ 25 87 00; www.casadelsole.nc; 10 Rte de l'Aquarium; 1-bedroom apt from 12,150 CFP; ❄ 🛜 🏊) This hard-to-miss skyscraper houses spacious and modern apartments with bright kitchenettes, comfy furnishings and private

Southern Noumea

NEW CALEDONIA NOUMEA

terraces filled with views. It's a few minutes' walk from the beach, shops and restaurants.

🛏 Anse Vata

★ Le Lagon   HOTEL $$
(Map p136; ☎26 12 55; www.lelagon.nc; 149 Rte de l'Anse Vata; studio/ste 11,000/15,000 CFP; ❄@🛜🏊) Although back from the beach at Anse Vata, Le Lagon is the top boutique hotel in Noumea. An aquarium, lovely art and friendly staff welcome guests. The one-bedroom suites are double the size of the studios but all have modern kitchenettes, lovely king-sized beds and bathrooms with bath and shower. The pool's not huge, but the beach is nearby.

Nouvata Hôtel Complex   HOTEL $$
(Map p136; ☎26 22 00; 123 Promenade Roger Laroque; r from 9000 CFP; 🅿❄🛜🏊) In the middle of the tourist atmosphere at Anse Vata, this complex has all the facilities you could need. There are three hotels: Le Pacifique, Le Nouvata Hotel and Nouvata Parc Hotel. Among them there are all levels of rooms and suites. The lounging areas, pool area and restaurants are welcoming. Look online for deals.

Ramada Plaza   HOTEL $$$
(Map p136; ☎23 90 00; www.ramadaplaza-noumea.nc; Rue Boulari; studio/ste from 18,000/22,000 CFP; 🅿❄🛜🏊) With studios, suites and apartments at the twin-towered Ramada Plaza, the bases are covered. All are tastefully decorated in contemporary Pacific style and have racecourse or sea views. There's a gorgeous pool, a tropical garden, and the revolving restaurant features fine dining with fine views for all meals of the day.

Hilton Noumea La Promenade Residences   APARTMENT $$$
(Map p136; ☎24 46 00; www.hilton.com/Noumea; 109 Promenade Roger Laroque; r from 20,000 CFP; 🅿❄🛜🏊) A top spot on Anse Vata beach with gorgeous rooms ranging from studios to suites to apartments. The beach, restaurants and shopping are right outside. Exactly what you'd expect of a top-notch Hilton.

Le Méridien Noumea   RESORT $$$
(Map p136; ☎26 50 00; www.lemeridiennoumea.com; Pointe Magnin; r from 27,000 CFP; 🅿❄🛜🏊) Out on the point beyond Anse Vata beach, this stunning hotel has landscaped grounds, a hypnotic pool area (the best in town) and several restaurants. You have transport to all sights and activities, should you ever wish to drag yourself off the premises. Check out the special deals on the website.

Outside of Town

Tour du Monde
B&B $$

(Map p144; ☑84 96 54; www.tour-du-monde.nc; No 4 Les Fougeres, Col de Katiramona, Dumbea; s/d 6000/7000 CFP; ❄ 🛜 ⛩) It may seem a suburban location, and it is out of town, but you're in another world when you get through the gates. Each cabin is themed with pictures of the owner's travels, so take your pic of the Orient, Broussard (think cowboy) or Melanesian cabin. There's a hot tub and a small pool in a lovely communal area.

L'Escapade
RESORT $$$

(☑26 05 12; www.glphotels.nc; Îlot Maître; garden/beach/overwater bungalows from 18,000/24,000/43,000 CFP; ❄ 🛜 ⛩) This is overwater bungalows at their best on Îlot Maître, a couple of kilometres south of Anse Vata beach, only 20 minutes from Noumea by shuttle boat. There's a gorgeous restaurant, a pool bar and myriad activities. Beach and garden bungalows also await, and it's also possible to head out there for a day trip.

✖ Eating

Noumea has excellent restaurants specialising in French and international cuisine as well as seafood. There are some great new cafes in the city centre, plus plenty of options out at Baie des Citrons and Anse Vata.

✖ City Centre

Aux Délices de Noumea
BAKERY $

(Map p134; ☑27 25 24; 21 Rue Eugène Pocheron; ⊙5am-7pm Mon-Sat, to 12.30pm Sun) There's nowhere to sit, but come here to Quartier Latin for Noumea's best breads, cakes and pastries. Beautiful displays and friendly service.

★ L'Annexe
CAFE $$

(Map p134; ☑25 33 15; www.facebook.com/lannexe.noumea.7; Place des Cocotiers; ⊙6am-6pm Mon-Fri, from 7am Sat) A great cafe right on Place des Cocotiers that is perfect for a late break-fast, lunch or coffee break. Sit back and watch the world pass by with whatever tempts you.

Le Faré du Quai Ferry
CAFE $$

(Map p134; ☑20 67 60; www.cuenet.nc; ⊙6.30am-5pm Mon-Fri; 🛜) This little oasis with free wi-fi sits down at the cruise ship terminal on the waterfront. Chic tables and chairs spill outside under bright sun umbrellas and a gorgeous shade tree. Beverages include freshly squeezed juices, beer and wine, while the Bil' Burgers and crêpes are superb.

Chez Toto
FRENCH $$

(Map p134; ☑28 80 42; 15 Rue August Brun, Quartier Latin; mains from 2300 CFP; ⊙11.30am-1.30pm & 7.30-9.30pm Tue-Sat) Head to this buzzing little restaurant for terrific French meals; it is truly so Frenchy, so classically chic, and, not surprisingly, often full to the brim.

Zanzibar
RESTAURANT $$

(Map p134; ☑25 28 00; www.facebook.com/restaurant.zanzibar.noumea; 51 Rue Jean Jaurès; mains from 2300 CFP; ⊙11.30am-1.30pm Mon-Fri, 7.30-9.30pm Mon-Sat) It's all atmospheric timber and cloth, with a tiny upstairs verandah and a range of dishes like duck with lavender. It's famous for its desserts.

Best Cafe
CAFE $$

(Map p134; ☑25 01 01; www.cuenet.nc; 47 Rue de Sébastopol; mains 600-2950 CFP; ⊙6.30am-10pm Mon-Thu, to 11pm Fri & Sat) Don't be fooled by the look from the outside. Best Cafe is kind of funky and hits all the right spots, no matter the time of day.

La Chaumière
FRENCH $$

(Map p134; ☑27 24 62; www.facebook.com/RestaurantLaChaumiereNoumea; 13 Rue du Docteur Guégan; mains from 1730 CFP; ⊙10am-10pm Mon-Sat, to 2pm Sun) The atmosphere is warm and uncluttered in this old colonial building where fabulous fine dining makes it very popular. French favourites like fish soup or confit of duck come with traditional accompaniments that are hard to find elsewhere. Come for lunch, share the menu, whatever – just don't miss out.

Le Pandanus
CAFE $$

(Map p134; ☑29 75 75; 25 Rue de Sebastopol; ⊙6am-6pm Mon-Sat) With takeout bakery products such as sandwiches, cakes and tarts out front and a full sit-down restaurant out the back, Le Pandanus is a haven for weary feet just across the road from Place des Cocotiers. A top spot to stop for a coffee, brunch or lunch.

FOOD PRICE RANGES

The following price ranges refer to a standard main course.

$ less than 1000 CFP

$$ 1000–2500 CFP

$$$ more than 2500 CFP

Baie des Citrons

The electric strip at Baie des Citrons has an oft-changing line-up of restaurants clamouring to be noticed: Italian, seafood, steak – you name it. Wander along, join all the other people soaking up the atmosphere, enjoy a drink or two, then pick your spot. The recommended Baie des Citrons drinking establishments usually serve good food too.

Sushi Hana JAPANESE $$
(Map p136; ☑23 88 87; Mirage Plaza; mains from 2000 CFP; ☺11am-2pm & 6-10pm Tue-Sun) Cool, quiet and frequently booked out, this restaurant has Japanese food brimming with fresh flavour. The best sushi in Noumea.

 Anse Vata

Snack Ulysse FAST FOOD $
(Map p136; ☑28 69 28; 140 Rte de l'Anse Vata; sandwiches 5000-880 CFP; ☺11am-9pm) A popular *snack* that serves generously filled hot or cold sandwiches, burgers, chips and curry dishes. A good budget option. Eat in or take away.

★**Le Faré du Palm Beach** CAFE $$
(Map p136; ☑26 46 60; www.cuenet.nc; Galerie du Palm Beach; ☺6.30am-10pm; 🛜) In a garden setting streetside at the Palm Beach shopping centre, Anse Vata's version of Le Faré (the sister cafe is in town at the cruise ship quay) serves up tasty meals from early morning until late at night. The salads, burgers and crépes really hit the spot, and the people-watching opportunities aren't bad either. Free wi-fi.

Fun Beach Restaurant & Grill INTERNATIONAL $$
(Map p136; ☑26 31 32; www.cuenet.nc; mains 2000-4900 CFP; ☺11am-2pm & 6.30-10pm; 🛜) Out on the peninsula between Baie des Citrons and Anse Vata, Fun Beach serves up salads, pasta, steak and seafood on a deck and surprisingly large indoor restaurant right by the bay. A very pleasant spot for a drink in the evening.

Le Roof SEAFOOD $$$
(Map p136; ☑25 07 00; www.cuenet.nc; 134 Promenade Roger Laroque; mains from 3500 CFP; ☺11.30am-2pm & 6.30-10pm; 🛜) It would be hard to miss Le Roof in Anse Vata. Out on the pier, spacious and open, Le Roof offers elegant fine dining with amazing sunsets, a cool terrace and, if you're really lucky, views down

on visiting sealife such as dolphins or sharks. Not surprisingly, the speciality is seafood.

 Drinking & Nightlife

While there are places to drink in town, locals head out to the beaches, particularly the convivial bar and restaurant strip at Baie des Citrons, for a happy-hour beer after work.

City Centre

★**Art Cafe** BAR
(Map p134; ☑27 80 03; www.facebook.com/Artcafe-410011155804982; 30 Rue Duquesne, Quartier Latin; ☺6am-11pm Mon-Fri) Don't miss a drink at this terrific indoor/outdoor bar inland from the marina. You might chance upon live acoustic music while you eat pizza or drink cocktails on the terrace, and the crowd is friendly.

Le Bout du Monde BAR
(Map p134; ☑27 77 28; www.leboutdumondenoumea.com; 4 Rue de la Frégate Nivôse; ☺7am-11pm) Overlooking the Port Moselle marina, this is a pleasant place for a drink as well as a meal. It's open for breakfast, lunch and dinner, makes the most of the nautical atmosphere at the marina, and frequently has live music.

Baie des Citrons

★**Les 3 Brasseurs** BREWERY, BAR
(Map p136; ☑24 15 16; www.cuenet.nc; ☺11am-1am, to 2am Fri & Sat, to 10pm Sun) This brewery pub on the main drag in Baie des Citrons has it all; popular restaurant upstairs, brewery

NEW CALEDONIA NOUMEA

NOUMEA FOR CHILDREN

Face it, the children just want to stay on the beach, swimming and building sand castles at Anse Vata or Baie des Citrons. But if anything will drag them away, it's a ride on the **Tchou Tchou Train** (p134). A visit to the **aquarium** (p131) is a must: endlessly entertaining and the perfect introduction to a trip out in a glass-bottom boat.

There's a **children's playground** at Baie de l'Orphelinat off Rue du Général de Gaulle, and another next to the public swimming pool at Ouen Toro, just past Anse Vata. Or head to **Le Marché** (p129): there's a buzz of activity, plenty to buy, and opposite, in the car park, children's fair rides.

Northern Grande Terre

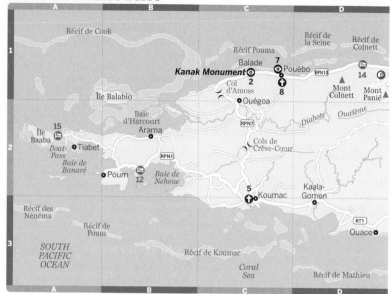

NEW CALEDONIA NOUMEA

and bar downstairs with five of its own brews on offer, daily half-price happy hour running 4pm to 7pm and regular live music. It even does beer cocktails.

La Barca Cantina y Taqueria   LOUNGE
(Map p136; ☑28 15 40; www.facebook.com/La-Barca-Noumea-506190522749625; ☺9am-3am; ☞) This fabulous spot transforms itself from quiet, relaxed lounge and cafe during the day to happy-hour pizza and beer 4pm to 7pm, to bar and nightclub later on with regular live music. Comfy couches, great decor and an extremely convivial atmosphere make La Barca a great place to hang out.

MV Lounge   LOUNGE
(Map p136; ☑78 97 67; www.facebook.com/mv loungenoumea; ☺10am-1am) At the city end of Baie des Citrons, MV Lounge sits so close to the water that waves are lapping the sand right in front of you. It's a relaxed and laid-back tapas-cocktail bar by evening; others turn up for breakfast, lunch and coffee by day.

🍷 Anse Vata

Code Bar   COCKTAIL BAR
(Map p136; ☑26 05 51; ☺10am-11.30pm) Streetfront at the Nouvata Parc Hotel complex, Code Bar offers up a lot more than a regular hotel bar. Things get going in the evenings with regular live music, salsa nights and Latin dance evenings.

Le Bilboquet Plage   WINE BAR
(Map p136; ☑26 46 60; www.cuenet.nc; Galerie du Palm Beach; ☺11am-2pm & 6.30pm-midnight; ☞) Upstairs at the back of the Palm Beach shopping centre, this brasserie serves tasty meals and snacks and has a spacious verandah that's a relaxing place for a drink amid plenty of greenery (as in potted plants).

Pop Light   CLUB
(Map p136; ☑26 27 25; www.facebook.com/pop. light; Anse Vata; ☺8.30pm-3am Tue, 10pm-3am Wed-Sat) This hugely popular venue in Anse Vata is fun, bright and as close to the water as you can get (without getting wet).

⭐ Entertainment

For the latest, check out the *NC Pocket* (www.sortir.nc) entertainment guide, plus snap up a free copy of the English-language *Weekly* (www.newcaledoniaweekly.nc).

Ciné City   CINEMA
(Map p134; ☑29 20 20; www.cinecity.nc; 18 Rue de la Somme; tickets 1200 CFP) Twelve theatres screen a large range of movies in French in central Noumea. During La Foa Film Festival

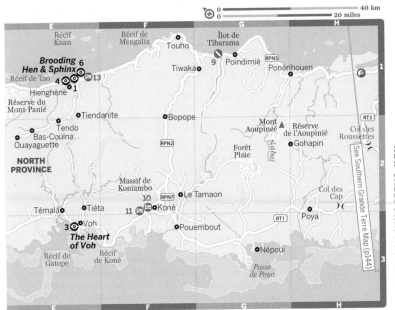

0 ——— 40 km
0 ——— 20 miles

Récif Kuan
Récif de Mengalia
Touho
Îlot de Tibarama
Brooding Hen & Sphinx 6
Récif de Tao 4 1 13
Hienghène
Réserve du Mont Panié
Tiwaka
9 Poindimié RPN3
Ponérihouen
Tiendanite
Bopope
Mont Aoupinée
Réserve de l'Aoupinié
Col des Roussettes
RT3
Tendo
Bas-Coulna
Ouayaguette
RPN2
Forêt Plate
Gohapin
NORTH PROVINCE
Massif de Koniambo
10 RPN7 Le Tamaon
Col des Cap
Témala
Tiéta
11 Koné
Poya
RT1
3 Voh
The Heart of Voh
Pouembout
Récif de Gatope
Récif de Koné
Népoui
Passe de Poya
See Southern Grande Terre Map (p144)

NEW CALEDONIA NOUMEA

(June/July) movies are screened, both here and at La Foa's Cinéma Jean-Pierre Jeunet, in their original language.

Théâtre de l'Île
THEATRE

(Map p144; ☑25 50 50; www.theatredelile.nc; 161 Ave James Cook) This popular theatre is housed in a renovated old building at Nouville that has had former lives as a warehouse, a dance hall, a cinema and a boxing venue. Now a historic monument, the theatre offers a varied program.

🛍 Shopping

In central Noumea you'll find shops selling French designer labels as well as prêt-à-porter outlets along Rue de Sébastopol, Rue de l'Alma and Rue Jean Jaurès.

Out of the centre, **Galerie Commerciale Port Plaisance** (Map p136; Baie de l'Orphelinat) is a pleasant mall on the way to the beaches, **Mirage Plaza** (Map p136) is at Baie des Citrons, and at Anse Vata **La Promenade** (Map p136), in front of the Hilton, and **Galerie du Palm Beach** (Map p136) have loads of boutiques and cafes.

Marine Corail
OUTDOOR, SPORTS

(Map p134; ☑27 58 48; www.marine-corail.nc; 26 Rue du Général Mangin; ⊗8am-6pm Mon-Sat) For everything for water activities, from diving, snorkelling and fishing gear to nautical maps, head to Marine Corail in central Noumea.

ℹ️ Information

INTERNET ACCESS

There is free public wi-fi around Place des Cocotiers and in a number of cafes and bars.

Cyber Nouméa Center (Map p134; ☑26 26 98; www.facebook.com/Cyber-Noum%C3%A9a-Center-872893476079877/; per 30min 250 CFP; ⊗7.30am-5.30pm Mon-Fri, 8am-5pm Sat) Internet, printing, photocopying, DVDs, CDs.... you name it, they can do it here.

MAPS

The Office du Tourisme has excellent free maps of Noumea, New Caledonia and individual maps of the main islands.

MEDICAL SERVICES

Pharmacies, identified by a green cross, are dotted all over Noumea. Weekend on-call pharmacies and doctors are listed in the Weekly.

Decompression Chamber (Map p134; ☑26 45 26) A Comex 1800 decompression chamber, the only one in New Caledonia, is next to the hospital, available 24/7.

Hôpital Gaston Bourret (Map p134; ☑25 66 66, emergencies 25 67 67; www.cht.nc; 7 Rue Paul Doumer) Noumea's main hospital, this is the main medical facility in New Caledonia.

Northern Grande Terre

MONEY

ATMs that accept major credit cards are outside most banks.

Banque BNP Paribas (Map p136; ☑ 26 21 03; www.bnpparibas.nc; 111 Promenade Roger Laroque) Usefully located at the heart of Anse Vata.

Banque Calédonienne d'Investissement (BCI; Map p134; ☑ 24 20 60; www.bci.nc; 20 Rue Anatole France) Good location near Place des Cocotiers in central Noumea.

Banque Société Générale (Map p134; ☑ 25 63 00; www.sgcb.nc; 44 Rue de l'Alma) Good location in the centre of Noumea; Western Union representative.

POST

Main Post Office (Map p134; www.opt.nc; 7 Rue Eugène Porcheron) The main office of the Office des Postes et Télécommunications (OPT) has a poste restante and fax service, and there's an ATM outside the building. There's also a post office on Route de Anse Vata, on the way to the beach. Buy SIM cards here.

TOURIST INFORMATION

First chance, pick up the free *Weekly* from airports, tourist sites, hotels, Office du Tourisme etc. Also get the monthly entertainment guide *NC Pocket* (www.sortir.nc) for the month's festivals, exhibitions, concerts and Jeudis du Centre Ville themes.

Office de Tourisme (Map p134; ☑ 28 75 80; www.office-tourisme.nc; Place des Cocotiers; ⊙ 8am-5.30pm Mon-Fri, 9am-noon Sat) The very friendly staff offer practical information in English or French. The office walls are layered with pamphlets about every activity and service and the website is very good.

Office du Tourisme, Anse Vata (Map p136; ☑ 27 73 59; 113 Promenade Roger Laroque; ⊙ 9am-noon & 1-5pm) It's a little smaller than the office in the city centre, but the service is just as good.

TRAVEL AGENCIES

Companies that organise transport, tours and accommodation within New Caledonia:

Arc en Ciel Voyages (Map p134; ☑ 27 19 80; www.arcenciel.nc; 59 Av du Maréchal Foch) Arranges tickets for travelling or touring anywhere, including day trips to the islands.

Caledonia Spirit (Map p134; ☑ 27 27 01; www.caledoniaspirit.com; Le Village, 35 Av du Maréchal Foch) Expect friendly and efficient service at this small agency in Le Village. It specialises in the islands and has an excellent website.

◎ Getting There & Away

AIR

Noumea's domestic airport is at Magenta, 4km east of the city centre.

Air Calédonie (Map p134; ☑ 25 21 77; www.air-caledonie.nc; 39 Rue de Verdun; ⊙ 8am-4pm Mon-Fri, to 11.30am Sat) Air Calédonie is the domestic airline, with flights to northern Grande Terre, Île des Pins and the Loyalty Islands. It also has a ticket office (☑ 25 03 82) at the domestic airport in Magenta.

BOAT

The friendly and efficient **Capitainerie** (Harbour Master's Office; Map p134; ☑ 27 71 97; www.sodemo.nc; ⊙ 8am-4pm Mon-Fri, to 11am Sat) is at Port Moselle's southern end.

Betico (Map p134; ☑ 26 01 00; www.betico.nc) Noumea is connected to the Loyalty Islands and Île des Pins by the fast Betico ferry.

◎ Getting Around

TO/FROM THE AIRPORT

Tontouta International Airport is 45km northwest of Noumea. Public buses (Line C) operated by Carsud run between the city centre and the airport. A number of companies, including **Arc en Ciel Voyages** (Map p134; www.arcenciel-voyages.nc), run airport transfers (one way 3000 CFP). Taxis into Noumea cost 11,000 CFP (shared).

Magenta domestic airport is serviced by Karuia Bus. A taxi to the city or beaches costs around 1700 CFP (shared).

BUS

Carsud (Map p134; ☑ 25 16 15; www.carsud.nc; Gare de Montravel, Rue Edouard Unger) Operates buses on 12 lines between Noumea and the greater Noumea region. It goes as far north as Tontouta (400 CFP), passing through Dumbéa (320 CFP) and Païta (360 CFP), and south to Plum in Mont-Dore (400 CFP).

Karuia Bus (Map p134; ☑ 26 54 54; www.karuiabus.nc; Rue Austerlitz) This is the local bus service around Noumea city with 18 numbered lines. The red-and-white buses operate from 6am to 7pm. The ticket office is opposite the Compact Megastore; tickets are 190 CFP when bought there; 210 CFP when purchased on the bus.

Line 40 runs from the city centre to Magenta domestic airport and Tjibaou Cultural Centre. Lines 10 and 11 run out to Baies des Citrons and Anse Vata beaches.

On Saturday and Sunday only, Karuia Bus runs a hop-on, hop-off bus from the Ferry Quai. Line 12 Culturelle heads out to Parc Forestier and back, while Line 14 Panoramique runs out to Ouen Toro via Baies des Citrons and Anse Vata.

CAR & SCOOTER

The Office du Tourisme has a comprehensive list of car- and scooter-hire companies. Car rental costs from 3500 CFP per day, including free 150km per day – go for unlimited if you plan to tour the north or south.

TAXI

Radio Taxis de Noumea (Map p134; ☑ 28 35 12; www.noumea.nc/taxi) Noumea's taxis are operated by Radio Taxis de Noumea. Head to the main taxi rank on Rue Anatole France, across from Place des Cocotiers. There's also one near the aquarium at Anse Vata. City centre to Baie des Citrons costs 1400 CFP.

TAXIBOAT

Coconut Taxiboat (☑ 75 50 17; www.coconuttaxiboat.com) Hop on the Coconut Taxiboat to any of 14 spectacular islands. Your choice! Get dropped off and picked up later, or share your adventure with your skipper.

The Far South

The far south feels like a remote wilderness. The vast, empty region is characterised by

---

ⓘ ROAD WARNING

Before heading out to explore the far south by rental car, pick up a map from the Office du Tourisme. While the road from Noumea to Parc de la Riviére Bleue and on to Yaté is in good shape, things gradually deteriorate between Yaté, Touaourou and Goro, then become decidedly dicey from Goro to Port Boise, on to Prony and then to Plum. On this southern section we're talking total lack of signage, potholes that are more like bomb craters a small rental car could disappear into, and a massive nickel processing plant spewing smoke. Fill up with fuel and provisions in Noumea, and if you're planning on tackling the Goro to Plum section of road, mentally prepare for an adventure.

---

its hardy scrub vegetation and red soil, and offers a wide range of activities including hiking, kayaking and mountain biking. While Blue River Park sees the natural environment treated with care, the presence of a massive nickel-cobalt mine has seen sediments and toxic metals discharged into the lagoon offshore.

⦿ Sights

Monts Koghis   MOUNTAIN
Monts Koghis are clad in rainforest and rich native flora, and they have several walking trails; pick up a free route map. Or take a treetop trail on swinging bridges and rope walks with **Koghi Parc Aventure** (Map p144; ☑ 82 14 85; koghiparcaventure.e-monsite.com; trail 3000 CFP; ⊘10am-4pm Sat & Sun, by reservation Mon-Fri). The turn-off to these mountains is on RT1, 14km north of central Noumea.

★**Parc Provincial
de la Riviére Bleue**   WILDLIFE RESERVE
(Blue River Park; Map p144; ☑ 43 61 24; adult/student 400/200 CFP; ⊘7am-5pm Tue-Sun, entry closes 2pm) Protected Blue River Park is a reserve for many bird species, including the *cagou*. The landscape is a mixture of the far south's scrub vegetation and dense rainforest, and includes gigantic kauri trees. Take well-maintained RP3 from La Coulée to get to the western end of the hydroelectric dam, Lac de Yaté. It's a 2.4km drive from there to the park entrance.

There is a **visitor information centre** by the entrance gate which has good displays in English and French on the park's flora and fauna. At the entrance you will also find free

Southern Grande Terre

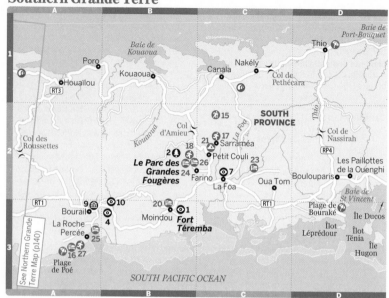

maps that outline the park's many walks, ranging from 30 minutes to six hours and from easy to difficult.

To the west and northwest of the park are Rivière Blanche and Rivière Bleue, Lac de Yaté's main tributaries. For the Rivière Bleue side, you can drive as far as Pont Perignon. A bus departs regularly (7.30am to 3.15pm, 400 CFP) from there to Vieux Refuge, taking 45 minutes each way. You can also walk, bike or kayak up the river. On the Rivière Blanche side, you can drive along the banks to the end of the road.

Le Site de Netcha   VIEWPOINT
(Map p144; day entry adult 400 CFP) Here, there are wooden platforms over the river and shelters and tables overlooking the water where you can picnic. You can camp here (500 CFP per tent) and rent canoes. From RP3, take the signposted road turning south at the eastern end of the Lac de Yaté. The 400 CFP entry fee also gets you into Chutes de la Madeleine.

Chutes de la Madeleine   WATERFALL
(Map p144; adult 400 CFP; ☺8am-5pm) This ladylike waterfall, with its wide apron of tinkling water, sits in a botanic reserve in the middle of a vast plain. Swimming is forbidden at the waterfall, but allowed back towards the main road.

Touaourou Church   CHURCH
(Église de Touaourou; Map p144) If you do any driving around Grande Terre, you're bound to be stunned by the number of old churches. It seems that every village has at least one. At Touaourou, south of Yaté, the church demands a photo. Backed by a wall of mountains and tall pines, the bright white and blue *église* sits next to a makeshift soccer field.

Cascade de Wadiana   WATERFALL
(Map p144) At Goro on the east coast the road passes beside Wadiana falls, which cascade down a rocky slope into a natural pool where you can swim.

Port Boisé   BEACH
(Map p144) Port Boisé is an isolated bay surrounded by a forest of Cook pines, 6.5km from the turn-off on the main road. The ecolodge here makes a good base for the walking tracks along the coast and to a lookout point. It's also a top spot for lunch. You'll have to drive through heavy mining territory to get here.

Prony   VILLAGE
(Map p144) Once a convict centre, Prony sits in a lush hollow surrounded by forest beside Baie de Prony. A stream runs through the village of corrugated-iron cottages and overgrown stone ruins. The first European

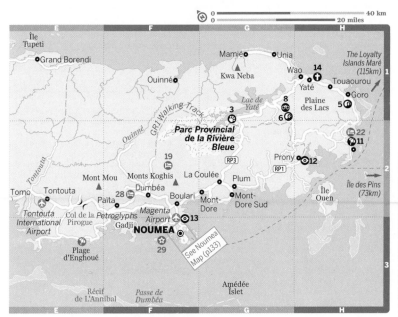

inhabitants were Captain Sebert and 29 convicts who landed here in 1867 to log timber for building materials for the growing colony.

The GR1 walking track starts about 500m south of the village at Baie de la Somme, which is part of the larger Baie de Prony.

🏃 Activities

There's a great range of activities waiting in the far south: canoeing, kayaking, mountain biking, walking, hunting or sitting by a stream.

Whale Watching   WILDLIFE WATCHING
(www.maisondulagon.nc) The whale-watching season runs from 11 July to 13 September, with great opportunities to head out and view humpback whales, especially in seas around the far south. La Maison du Lagon in Noumea can provide information on a dozen whale-watch operations that meet required industry standards. Expect to pay in the vicinity of 10,000 CFP per person.

GRNC1 Walking Track   HIKING
(Grande Randonnée 1; www.province-sud.nc/content/gr-nc1) The GR1 is a five-day (123.4km) hike from Prony through Parc Provincial de la Rivière Bleue and northwest to Dumbéa. This is a trek from the sea through plains, forests, hills, mountains and streams with huts to bunk down in along the way. Download the seven stages of the hike from the website.

Aventure Pulsion   KAYAKING
(📞 26 27 48; www.aventure-pulsion.nc) There are lots of outdoor adventure options with these guys including canoeing, kayaking and 4WD trips. They'll also do drop-offs and pick-ups for GRNC1 hikers.

Sud Loisirs   BICYCLE RENTAL
(📞 77 81 43; www.sudloisirs.nc) Hire a mountain bike, a kickbike, a kayak, or take part in a bike/kayak combo tour in Parc Provincial de la Rivière Bleue. Ask the ranger at the park entrance for directions to the kiosk.

Pacific Free Ride   ADVENTURE SPORTS
(📞 79 22 02; www.pfr.nc) All sorts of activities including hiking, canyoning and kayaking at various spots around the far south.

🛏 Sleeping

Accommodation places serve meals to nonguests but you must book in advance.

Site de Netcha Camping Site   CAMPGROUND $
(Map p144; 📞 46 98 00; camping 1000 CFP; 🅿) Roofed campsites, set by the river, have camp fires, tables and benches, plus there

Southern Grande Terre

are bathroom facilities. There's no electricity and you'll need to take drinking water.

Gîte Iya BUNGALOW $
(Map p144; ☎46 90 80; www.office-tourisme.nc/en/gite-iya; camping 1500 CFP, bungalows 7000 CFP; [P]) The rustic but comfortable bungalows are in a coconut grove beside a small private beach. Meals are from 2100 CFP. You can snorkel along the fringing reef not far from the beach. There's a signpost to the gîte, just south of Wao.

Auberge du Mont Koghi BUNGALOW $$
(Map p144; ☎41 29 29; koghiland@offratel.nc; Dumbéa; chalet/half-board 8500/17,500 CFP; [P]) Overlooking Noumea and its bays, 476m above sea level, the *auberge* has chalets and more remote huts about a 10-minute walk into the forest. The restaurant is open for lunch and dinner. It has a fireplace, warm timber interior, and specialises in melted-cheese *raclette*.

Loisirs Concept CAMPGROUND $$
(Map p144; ☎83 90 13; http://loisirsconcept.nc; entrance 400 CFP, camping 70,000 CFP) A somewhat weird concept, but these guys have tents suspended from trees a few metres off the ground in two locations at Parc Provincial de la Rivière Bleue. There are two tents at Pont Germain and three at Camp des Kaoris. You really need to check out photos on the website to get a handle on this!

Kanua Tera Ecolodge BUNGALOW $$$
(Map p144; ☎46 90 00; www.tera-hotels-resorts.com/hotel; bungalows with breakfast from 25,600 CFP; [P][☎][☎]) This place is seriously isolated and hard to get to, on the seafront overlooking Port Boise Bay. There are 18 bungalows, plus a restaurant and bar. If you like seclusion, this could be the place for you.

ⓘ Information

Visitor Information Centre (Map p144; ☺8am-12.30pm & 1.30-5pm Mon-Fri, 8am-12.30pm Sat) A small visitor information centre at Yaté (next to the market) has information on accommodation and activities, including walking-track brochures.

ⓘ Getting There & Around

You'll need to hire a car to explore the far south. Head east out of Noumea towards Mont-Dore.

The road forks when it reaches the mountain at La Coulée: take RP3 to get to Parc Provincial de la Rivière Bleue and Yaté.

La Foa & Around

On Grande Terre's central west coast, the settlement of La Foa is a neat little town, 111km northwest of Noumea on RT1. La Foa is often seen as a staging point for exploring the nearby hotspots of Park of the Great Ferns, Farino, Sarraméa and Moindou.

ⓘ Getting There & Around

Several buses a day from Noumea stop in La Foa, but if you want to see what the region has to offer, it would be best to have your own wheels.

La Foa

The township and countryside around La Foa has an intriguing history. Atai, the initiator of the 1878 revolt, came from here, then later, groups of free settlers, convicts, Malabar Indians, Japanese, Indonesians and Polynesians from Wallis and Futuna established communities. You'll know you're hitting town when you look right from the highway bridge and see the Marguerite suspension bridge, designed by the disciples of Gustave Eiffel and opened in 1909.

La Foa township has everything you'll need stretched out along RT1, including supermarkets, restaurants, visitor information and a modern pharmacy. There is a weekly market next to the tourist information centre on Saturday mornings from 7.30am.

◉ Sights & Activities

La Foa Sculpture Garden   GARDENS
(Map p144; ⊙6am-6pm) **FREE** The sculpture garden behind La Foa Tourisme features wonderful sculptures by artists from throughout New Caledonia. The garden is a pleasant place for a picnic, with a children's playground and public toilets.

🛏 Sleeping & Eating

Hôtel Banu   BUNGALOW **$$**
(Map p144; ☑ 44 31 19; www.office-tourisme.nc/en/hôtel-banu; r 4350 CFP, bungalows 8350 CFP; P ❄ 🛜 ☒) Right in the middle of La Foa on RT1, the Banu has both rooms and bungalows, though the latter, which are at the back near the refreshing swimming pool, are the best bet. The restaurant is open for all meals, or have a gourmet sandwich on the porch

(550 CFP) then try counting the 5000 caps on the bar's ceiling.

La Petite Ferme   BUNGALOW **$$**
(Map p144; ☑ 44 34 05; www.office-tourisme.nc/en/la-petite-ferme; B&B per person 8100 CFP; ⊙ Fri-Wed; P) For a farmstay experience about 12km east of La Foa township, head to La Petite Ferme, a 34-hectare ranch farming cattle and chickens. The bungalows with bunks are basic, but the reception is friendly and your English-speaking host, Jean Louis, runs 4WD night spins to see the deer. Meals are served in the garden, but book 48 hours ahead.

Dinner with wine is available for 4725 CPF.

Le Jasmin   CREPERIE, ASIAN **$$**
(Map p144; ☑ 44 55 70; mains from 1300 CPF; ⊙ 11am-1.30pm & 7-9pm Tue-Sun; 🛜) This bright and friendly spot on RT1 in the middle of La Foa specialises in Asian cuisine and Brittany-style crepes. The food is good and there's free wi-fi if you're starving to hook up.

☆ Entertainment

Cinéma Jean-Pierre Jeunet   CINEMA
(Map p144; ☑ 41 69 11; www.festivalcinemalafoa.com) A major event on New Caledonia's social calendar is the June/July film festival where international films, screened in their original language, are shown at La Foa's Cinéma Jean-Pierre Jeunet. Each year the festival is presided over by a famous person from the film industry.

ⓘ Information

La Foa Tourisme (Map p144; ☑ 41 69 11; www.lafoatourisme.nc; ⊙ 8.30am-4.30pm Mon-Sat, to 10.30am Sun) The friendly and efficient staff at La Foa Tourisme, the visitors information centre, can advise on accommodation and activities in La Foa, Farino, Sarraméa and Moindou.

Farino

Best described as a mountain village, Farino is only a 15-minute drive from La Foa, but it feels like a different world. New Caledonia's smallest district, Farino split from La Foa in 1911 and took its name from a synthesis of the name of a local Kanak clan and Farinole in Corsica, where many immigrants came from.

The road climbs steeply until you are presented with a majestic viewpoint over the plains and out to the lagoon from the Town Hall, at an altitude of 350m. Farino is known as the gateway to the Park of Great Ferns, but you'd better stock up in La Foa as there are no shops here. There is a market on the second Sunday of each month.

Activities

Sentier de la Petite Cascade FISHING

(Little Waterfall Walk; Map p144) **FREE** This popular and easy short walk starts at the parking area below Refuge de Farino. It's about 1½ hours (3.6km) return to the small waterfall. Rainforest and an abundance of birds can be enjoyed along the way.

⭐⭐ Festivals & Events

Festival of the Bancoule Worm FAIR

Held on the second Sunday in September: head to Farino to taste some fat, wriggling white worms. Becoming more popular by the year!

🛏 Sleeping

★ Refuge de Farino BUNGALOW $$

(Map p144; ☎44 37 61; www.office-tourisme.nc/en/le-refuge-de-farino; camping 800 CFP, bungalows 8900 CFP; P 🛜) On a hillside in Farino's forest, Florence's superb timber bungalows have a kitchenette and forest views from their decks. There are barbecues, a hot tub (from 1890 CFP to use), a playground and 24-hour wi-fi around the bar. Breakfast is 950 CFP. BYO food is the way to go for other meals. Camping is also a great option.

Les Bancouliers de Farino LODGE $$

(Map p144; ☎41 20 41; www.bancouliers.blog spot.com; Farino; camping per tent 1500 CFP, half-board per person 8000 CFP; P) A lovely timber

---

PARK OF THE GREAT FERNS

Le Parc des Grandes Fougères (Park of the Great Ferns ; Map p144; ☎46 99 50; http://grandes-fougeres.nc; adult/child 400 CPF/free; ⊙7.30am-5.30pm Wed-Mon) This 4500-hectare park, in the mountains above Farino, features tropical rainforest with rich and varied flora and fauna. As the name suggests, tree ferns are in abundance, and most of Grande Terre's native birdlife can be spotted. A number of well-signposted hiking tracks range from 45 minutes to six hours, plus there are trails for mountain-bike enthusiasts. Head 6km up the unsealed road from Farino to the park entrance, where you can pick up a trail map.

The park sits between 400m and 700m in altitude.

---

bungalow with a mezzanine looks out over a river and sleeps six, or stay in one of the brightly decorated rooms that are attached to the house. It's friendly, rustic and you'll love the homemade (and often home-grown) food. Camping is another option.

ℹ Getting There & Around

From La Foa, head north on RT1 for five minutes, then turn right onto RP5, a major road which crosses the island. The road to Farino is signposted on the left after a couple of kilometres.

Sarraméa

Sarraméa, 15 minutes' drive north of La Foa, sits in a lush valley surrounded by mountains. There are good walking, biking and horse-riding opportunities. On the main road, just past the Sarraméa turn-off, is tribu de Petit Couli, where a beautiful old *grande case* stands at the end of a row of araucaria pines.

There is a market on the fourth Sunday of each month. Sarraméa hosts a coffee festival at the end of August.

🏃 Activities

Sarraméa Randonnées OUTDOORS

(Map p144; ☎76 60 45; www.sarramearandon nees.com; ⊙8am-5pm) Near the end of the road in Sarraméa, these guys offer a number of outdoor activities including horseback riding (from 4500 CPF) and quad bikes (from 7700 CPF). They also have a track available to hikers and mountain bikers for 500 CPF.

Trou Feillet SWIMMING

(Map p144) At the end of the road in the Sarraméa valley, follow the signs for a five-minute walk to Trou Feuillet, a rock pool in a mountain stream that is popular for bathing.

Plateau de Dogny HIKING

(Map p144) This popular hiking course covers 16km and rewards walkers with great views from a high plateau. With a vertical climb of nearly 1000m, it is a strenuous walk taking six to eight hours. Hikers should be well prepared before heading to the trailhead near the end of the road in the Sarraméa valley.

Stock up on provisions in La Foa and pick up a pamphlet on the hike at La Foa Tourisme.

🛏 Sleeping & Eating

Camping de Sarraméa Decouverte CAMPGROUND $

(Map p144; ☎44 39 55; www.office-tourisme.nc/en/camping-de-sarramea-decouverte; tent 1500 CPF;

P) Right beside the road in the valley, this lovely shaded campground in tropical surroundings has shower and toilet facilities, plus tables and chairs. No shops, so bring your own food.

Hotel Evasion　　　　　　　　　　HOTEL **$$**
(Map p144; ☑44 55 77; www.hotel-evasion. com; r/bungalows incl breakfast 9350/19,600 CFP; ✳@🛜🌊) This upmarket eco-retreat has well-equipped rooms, plus smart bungalows with verandahs overlooking a stream at the end of the road in Sarraméa. There is a swimming pool, spa facilities, and an excellent restaurant that is open for breakfast, lunch and dinner. Meals (from 1860 CFP) are terrific.

❶ Getting There & Around

From La Foa, head north on RT1 for five minutes, then turn right onto RP5. The road to Sarraméa is signposted on the right after 8km.

Moindou

A 15-minute drive straight up RT1 north of La Foa, Moindou is a small village with a long history. Visit reconstructed Fort Téremba, then stay in the village's beautifully restored inn. There is a market on the first Sunday of each month.

◉ Sights

★**Fort Téremba**　　　　　　　　HISTORIC SITE
(Map p144; ☑44 32 71; www.fort-teremba.com; RM9 Moindou; adult/child 800/300 CPF; ⊙9am-4pm) Built in 1871, this historic fort originally held convicts brought to the area to build roads. Following a revolt by local Kanaks against French colonial rule in 1878, the fort was strengthened, then abandoned in 1898 when deportations came to an end. After years of neglect, it was restored from 1984 and is now classified as a historical monument.

The Fort Téremba Spectacle, held in October, features a play in period costume followed by fireworks. Explore the fort and view the interesting displays. It is 3km south of Moindou, signposted off RT1.

🛌 Sleeping & Eating

★**Auberge Historique
de Moindou**　　　　　　　HISTORIC HOTEL **$$**
(Map p144; ☑35 43 28; www.office-tourisme.nc/ en/auberge-historique-de-moindou; RT1 Moindou; d 6650 CFP; P🛜) Right in the centre of the village and on RT1, this hotel, built in the 1890s, closed in 1976, has been beautifully restored and re-opened as the Moindou Inn, with

guestrooms and dining. Lovely furnishings and old photos make staying here a delight. Breakfast 580 CFP, Plate of the Day 1680 CFP.

Bourail & Around

With its strong Caldoche community, Bourail township is rural and inland, on RT1, 163km northwest of Noumea. The town itself is not the attraction for visitors. Most turn up for the nearby beaches of Plage de la Roche Percée and Poé Beach. The main road crosses the Néra River bridge at the southern end of town, and the turn-off to the beaches is immediately after the bridge when heading north.

Bourail

Bourail township has everything you need, from ATMs and petrol stations to *snack* restaurants and a supermarket. Get what you need before heading out to the beaches. There is a market on Friday and Saturday mornings from 6am.

◉ Sights

Musée de Bourail　　　　　　　　MUSEUM
(Map p144; adult/student 250/100 CFP; ⊙9am-noon & 1-5pm Mon-Sat; P) An old stone building 500m south of the town centre houses the Musée de Bourail. Its displays include objects relating to the presence of US and NZ troops in Bourail during WWII and a guillotine complete with the basket where the decapitated head was placed. The guillotine was brought to New Caledonia in 1867.

New Zealand War Cemetery　　　　CEMETERY
(Map p144) Nine kilometres east of Bourail on RT1 is the well-tended New Zealand War Cemetery, where over 200 NZ soldiers killed in the Pacific during WWII are buried. NZ troops set up a hospital in the area during the war, and many locals received free medical care there.

A ceremony is held at the cemetery on the Saturday closest to Anzac Day (25 April) and local children place a flower on each grave.

Arab Cemetery & Memorial　　　　CEMETERY
(Map p144) Ten kilometres east of Bourail on RT1 is a mosque, an Arab cemetery and a memorial to Arabs, Kabyles, Algerians, Moroccans and Tunisians who were deported to New Caledonia between 1864 and 1896. Most took part in uprisings against French colonial rule in their homelands.

✦ Festivals & Events

Bourail Country Fair   FAIR

(admission 500 CFP) Bourail holds a hugely popular country fair, first held in 1877, over the weekend closest to 15 August: there are farm animals on display; produce, arts and crafts for sale; children's rides; food stalls; and, the highlight, a rodeo. Campsites are available, and 25,000 people are expected.

🛏 Sleeping & Eating

Hôtel La Néra   MOTEL $$

(Map p144; ✆44 16 44; s/d 8150/9150 CFP; ❄ ☎ ☎) This place has simple rooms with a river view, a pool and a children's playground, and is by the Néra River bridge. The cosy restaurant serves dishes such as deer curry, and you can head out on deer-hunting or cattle ranch tours.

ℹ Information

Bourail Tourism (Map p144; ✆46 46 12; www.bourailtourisme.nc; ☺9am-noon &1-5pm Mon-Sat; ☎) The town's helpful tourist information office is at the museum, on RT1 as you enter town from the south.

ℹ Getting There & Around

Long distance buses heading up the west coast stop in Bourail, but if you want to head out to the beaches, you'll need your own wheels. There is talk of a shuttle service starting up from Bourail to the beaches, so ask around for the latest news.

La Roche Percée

Only a 10-minute drive from Bourail township, La Roche Percée has two famous rock formations: **La Roche Percée** (pierced rock), a headland with a hole in it that you can walk through, and **Le Bonhomme**, a stand-up rock off the end of the headland that's shaped like a tubby man.

The surf at Plage de la Roche Percée is caused by a break in the fringing reef, so you don't have to go out to the reef to catch a wave. The best spot is at the mouth of the Néra river. The beaches around here are also known as a nesting spot for sea turtles, and nests are monitored and protected by locals.

There are a couple of *snack* restaurants here, but no shops. The long beach is a popular swimming spot.

🏃 Activities

Three Bay Walk   FISHING

(Sentier des Trois Baies) A walking track begins at the parking area at the base of the cliff near La Roche Percée headland, climbs the headland, then follows the coast past Baie des Tortues (Turtle Bay) to Baie des Amoureux (Lover's Bay). Allow 1½ hours for the 4km return walk.

There's a panoramic viewing point above Le Bonhomme where you can often spot turtles in the Baie des Tortues below.

Île Vert Eco-tour   ADVENTURE TOUR

(✆78 40 26; www.nekweta.com/english; tour 6300 CPF) This half-day eco-tour, run by Manu at Nëkwéta Fish & Surf Camp, involves a visit to the offshore island, Île Vert (Green Island), snorkelling, observations of fish and fauna, plus explanations of local myths. Pre-booking required. Manu also operates a taxi boat to Île Vert (3150 CPF per person return).

Surf Charter   SURFING

(✆78 40 26; www.nekweta.com/english; day trip 5250 CPF) Guided surfing tours out on the barrier reef run by Manu from Nëkwéta Fish & Surf Camp on a 7.4m banana boat. Opt for a four- to six-hour day trip or check out the website for full board and accommodation packages at Nëkwéta. Rental boards available.

🛏 Sleeping & Eating

★**Nëkwéta Fish & Surf Camp**   BUNGALOW $$

(Map p144; ✆43 23 26, 78 40 26; www.nekweta.com; d from 9150 CFP; ℗ ❄ ☎) One block back from the beach, Nëkwéta has a lovely tropical garden setting. Choose from an attractive *case* (bungalow) or one of the rooms in a two-storey building built from scratch by owner Manu. Meals are first class.

Plage de Poé

Plage de Poé is a beautiful, long white-sand beach 9km west of La Roche Percée. A 20-minute drive from Bourail township, Plage de Poé has *snack* restaurants, but no shops.

🏃 Activities

Poé Kite School   WATER SPORTS

(Map p144; ✆77 60 59; www.poekiteschool.com) While the name says Poé Kite School, this place, at the western end of Poé, has all sorts of things on offer. Learn how to kite surf (3½ hours 13,000 CFP), ride the glass-bottomed boat (1½ hours, 2500 CFP), or rent a kayak (1100 CFP per hour) or stand-up paddle-board (1100 CFP per hour). *Snack* restaurant **L'alizé** is also here on site.

Poé Plaisirs
WATER SPORTS

(Map p144; ☑ 75 00 01; www.mdplaisirs.com)
At the eastern end of Poé, these guys rent
out kayaks (1300 CFP per hour), windsurfers
(from 1500 CFP per hour) and stand-up
paddle-boards (1300 CFP per hour). Ask
about the MD Plaisirs discount card.

🛏 Sleeping & Eating

La Rêve de Némo
CAMPGROUND $

(Map p144; ☑ 46 44 64; www.lerevedenemo.
com; per person/tent 300/1500 CFP; ℗) With a
great location along the Poé waterfront, this
campground has a *snack* restaurant on site
and good facilities.

★ Auberge de Poé
HOSTEL $$

(Map p144; ☑ 41 82 08; www.aubergesdejeunesse.
nc; dm/d 2500/7500 CFP; ℗ ❄ 🛜) This new
purpose-built hostel is as good as it gets, just
back from the beach. All rooms have ensuite
facilities, there's a laundry, a fully equipped
kitchen, a television room, free wi-fi and free
use of kayaks and snorkelling gear.

Hotel de Poé
HOTEL $$

(Map p144; ☑ 44 22 00; www.facebook.com/hotel.
de.poe; d from 13,600 CFP; ℗ ❄ 🛜) This immaculate new hotel, a block back from Poé beach,
offers 14 fully equipped stylish bungalows
with bathrooms, refrigerators, TV and wi-fi.
The restaurant is open Thursday to Monday.
Highly recommended.

Sheraton Déva Resort & Spa
RESORT $$$

(Map p144; ☑ 26 50 00; www.sheratonnewcale
doniadeva.com; r from 16,000 CFP; ℗ ❄ 🛜 ⛱) At
Domaine de Déva, a five-minute drive west
of Poé Beach, the Sheraton has everything
you'd expect to find at a new five-star re-
sort hotel, including two restaurants, a golf
course, a kids' club, a gym, a spa, bicycles
and water sports such as kayaking, stand-up
paddle-boards and jet skis.

Northwest Coast

Much of the northwest coast and its rolling
plains are taken up by cattle ranches. The
towns up here may have made their money
from nickel, but there is still plenty of interest.

Koné & Around

Koné, the Northern Province capital, is on
RT1, 274km northwest of Noumea. It has
all you'd expect of a growing rural town, in-
cluding a post office, *gendarmerie,* a clinic,
a pharmacy, supermarkets and banks with
ATMs.

One claim to fame is that the term 'Lapita'
was coined by archaeologists during a 1952
excavation near Koné on the Foué peninsu-
la. On mishearing a word in the local Haveke
language, which means 'to dig a hole', the
terms 'Lapita' and 'Lapita pottery' became
commonly used in research on the early peo-
pling of the Pacific islands. So-called 'Lapita
sites' have been uncovered in Melanesia and
as far away as Tonga and Samoa.

🛏 Sleeping & Eating

★ Hotel Hibiscus
HOTEL $$

(Map p140; ☑ 47 22 61; www.hotelhibiscus.nc; ⊙ r
from 13,500 CPF; ℗ ❄ 🛜 ⛱) Be prepared for a
surprise. What doesn't look much from the
outside turns into an absolute oasis in the
middle of Koné township. Gorgeous swimming pool and gardens, immaculate bar, gal-
lery and restaurant, plus tasteful rooms make
the Hibiscus one of New Caledonia's top boutique hotels. Co-owner Jean-Yves is a master
baker so you'll love the buffet breakfast.

Hôtel Koniambo
HOTEL $$

(Map p140; ☑ 47 39 40; www.grands-hotels.nc; r
from 14,000 CFP; ℗ ❄ 🛜 ⛱) Named after the
nearby nickel-bearing mountain range, this
makes a very comfortable base to explore the
surrounding 'stockman's country'. There is a
heart-shaped pool, a restaurant and a *snack*
bar on hand. It's right next to the airport, just
north of town.

ℹ Getting There & Around

Air Caledonie (www.air-caledonie.nc) flies three
days a week, taking 40 minutes from Noumea's
Magenta Airport to Koné airport, just north of
town. Buses head daily up RT1 from Noumea,
taking four hours.

Europcar (www.europcar.com) has rental cars
available from Koné airport.

Koumac

Koumac, 100km northwest of Koné, has
prospered from mining, both chromium and
nickel. The Tiébaghi mine (1902–64) was said
to be the most productive chromium mine in
the world.

The gateway to the far north and a sizea-
ble town, Koumac has an attractive marina
and an airport with direct flights to Nou-
mea. There are supermarkets, banks with
ATMs and plenty of *snack* restaurants. The

NEW CALEDONIA NORTHWEST COAST

town hosts one of New Caledonia's biggest Agriculture & Craft Fairs in September.

◉ Sights & Activities

Église Ste Jeanne d'Arc   CHURCH
(Map p140) Located near the roundabout, eye-catching Église Ste Jeanne d'Arc was constructed in 1950 out of a WWII aircraft hangar.

Reve Bleu   DIVING
(Map p140; ☑97 83 12; www.revebleucaledonie. com) Head to Koumac's impressive marina, La Marina de Pandop, where the dive club, Reve Bleu, is geared up to provide a grand professional experience. Intro dives are 6000 CFP, two-tank dives 12,000 CFP.

🛏 Sleeping & Eating

Gite du Lagon   CAMPGROUND, CABIN $$
(Map p140; ☑42 39 49; www.mairie-koumac. nc/Gite-du-Lagon_a420.html; camping/bungalows 1000/8400 CPF; P🐾) This attractive spot, right on the water a five-minute drive from town, has bungalows and camping and is a good budget option. The whole site is covered by wi-fi.

Monitel Koumac   HOTEL $$
(Map p140; ☑47 66 66; www.monitel.nc; d from 10,750 CFP; P🌸🐾🏊) In the middle of town, Monitel Koumac has well-equipped clean rooms that look out on the pool with its inviting deck chairs. The restaurant meals (eat inside or out) are great and the service is friendly.

ℹ Information

Koumac Tourisme (Map p140; ☑42 78 42; www.mairie-koumac.nc; ◷9am-noon & 1-4pm Mon-Fri, 9am-noon Sat) Koumac Tourisme, the information centre, is at the northern end of town opposite the post office.

ℹ Getting There & Around

Air Caledonie (www.air-caledonie.nc) flies two days a week from Noumea's Magenta Airport to Koumac airport, just north of town. Buses head daily up RT1 from Noumea, taking 5½ hours.

The Far North

The remote region north of Koumac is known as the far north. Keep your eyes open for deer and wild horses, and if you're into bonefish fly-fishing, this is the place to set world records. Stock up on supplies before leaving Koumac, as there's next to nothing available in Poum.

🏃 Activities

New Caledonia Fishing Safaris   FISHING
(☑78 62 00; www.fishing-safaris.com) Richard Bertin's NCFS is for serious fishermen. Plan ahead for outstanding bonefish fly-fishing opportunities in the far north.

🛏 Sleeping & Eating

★ Relais de Poingam   BUNGALOW $$
(Map p140; ☑47 92 12; www.relais-poingam.nc; camping per person 900 CFP, bungalows 10,000 CFP; P🐾) On a long beach at the northern tip of Grande Terre, this place is a prime reason to fit the far north into your schedule. Comfortable bungalows have atmospheric 'outside' private bathrooms attached, there's a saltwater pool, and the restaurant serves wonderful dinners that include wine (3300 CFP). The camping area is right on the beach.

From the turn-off south of Poum, it's 23km to Poingam. The last 5km is on an unsealed road.

Hôtel Malabou Beach   HOTEL $$
(Map p140; ☑47 60 60; www.grands-hotels.nc; d bungalows from 12,500 CFP; P🌸🐾🏊) This family-friendly place at Baie de Néhoué has newly renovated, well-equipped upmarket bungalows. The main restaurant's grand buffet (3900 CFP) specialises in seafood straight from the lagoon and there are plenty of activities – kayaking, trekking, tennis, minigolf. The hotel is signposted on the main road.

ℹ Getting There & Around

Air Calédonie has flights from Noumea to Koné and Koumac. There are daily buses from Noumea. Life will be a lot easier with your own wheels.

Northeast Coast

The stunning, relatively untouched coastline here features lush vegetation, gentle rivers, fascinating rock formations, waterfalls, deserted beaches and small villages.

Poindimié and Hienghène are the two main towns on the northeast coast. Both have grocery stores, a post office, clinic, pharmacy, bank and ATM, and *gendarmerie*.

ℹ Getting There & Around

Air Calédonie flies three times weekly from Noumea to Touho, halfway between Poindimié and Hienghène. **ALV** (☑ tel/fax 42 58 00; www.office-tourisme.nc/en/alv-poindimie; Poindimié; car hire per day from 5000 CFP) can meet you at the airport with a hire car.

Buses from Noumea run daily to Poindimié and Hienghène.

Poindimié

The largest town on the coast, Poindimié has a picturesque coastline and, stretching inland, the peaceful valleys of Ina, Napoémien and Amoa River, where you can admire the natural bush or pretty *tribu* gardens. These valleys are delightful places for a walk or a scenic drive. There are a number of *snack* restaurants in town.

🏃 Activities

Tiéti Diving   DIVING
(Map p140; ☑ 42 42 05; www.tieti-diving.com; dives from 7000 CFP) As well as dives, Tiéti Diving, which operates from a base next to Hotel Tiéti, offers transfers to Îlot de Tibarama (per person full day 2000 CFP), a great spot to relax, snorkel and swim just offshore from Poindimié.

🛏 Sleeping & Eating

Hotel Tiéti Poindimié   HOTEL $$$
(Map p140; ☑ 24 24 77; www.grands-hotels.nc; r from 15,000 CFP; P❄️🛜🏊) At the northern end of Poindimié, this is the most upmarket place to stay on the northeast coast. There's a refreshing pool, renovated bungalows, a stylish bar and a topnotch restaurant, all right on the beach.

Hienghène

This serene village is tucked into the foothills on the shores of Baie de Hienghène, at the mouth of the Hienghène River. The area has fascinating rock formations, and it is known as the birthplace and home of Jean-Marie Tjibaou, New Caledonia's pro-independence leader who was assassinated in 1989. People speak of Tjibaou with great respect, and he is buried in Tiendanite, a *tribu* 20km up the Hienghène valley.

⊙ Sights & Activities

★Brooding Hen & Sphinx   LANDMARK
(Map p140) Hienghène's renowned Poule Couveuse (Brooding Hen) rock formation sits on one side of the entrance to Baie de Hienghène, facing the Sphinx on the other. You can view these two rock formations

from the signposted lookout, 2km south of the village. There's a better profile of the Sphinx about 1.5km north of the village.

Lindéralique Rocks   LANDMARK
(Map p140) The Lindéralique rocks are towering black limestone rocks that stretch to 60m in height in places and are topped by jagged, sharp edges. They are best seen beside the road about 6km south of town.

Centre Culturel
Goa Ma Bwarhat   CULTURAL CENTRE
(Map p140; ☑ 42 80 74) This cultural centre on the eastern side of the river houses exhibitions, a museum and a sculptor's workshop. Undergoing renovation at the time of research, it was expected to reopen in 2016.

Babou Côté Océan   DIVING
(Map p140; ☑ 42 83 59; www.babou-plongee.com) Go diving around unique cliff faces and sheltered coral massifs (intro/double dives 8000/12,000 CFP), join an island trip to Îlot Hienga, which includes walking and snorkelling (4200 CFP), or rent a kayak (1500 CPF). There is also camping here for 500 CPF per person with free wi-fi. It's 10km southeast of Hienghène township.

🛏 Sleeping & Eating

In the Hienghène valley there are many *accueil en tribu* (per person around 3000 CFP), traditional homestays with Kanak families. Visitors usually take part in everyday activities and meals. Book through Hienghène's visitor information centre at least a day in advance.

Babou Côté Océan Camping   CAMPGROUND $
(Map p140; ☑ 42 83 59; www.babou-plongee.com; camping per person 500 CFP, tent hire 1000 CFP; P🛜) About 10km southeast of Hienghène, on the coast, this is the best place to camp. The Babou Côté Océan dive club is based here. Bring your own food. There's free wi-fi around the base building.

★Ka Waboana Lodge   BUNGALOW $$
(Map p140; ☑ 42 47 03; www.kawaboana-lodge.nc; r/bungalows from 6500/10,500 CFP; P❄️🛜) Opposite the marina in Hienghène, this is a top place to stay. The smallest rooms with shared bathrooms meet requirements and are good value for the price, while the bungalows with kitchenettes perch in the forest above the restaurant and terrace. It's spotlessly clean and very tastefully done, with views of the bay.

DON'T MISS

HEART OF VOH AND THE LAGOON FROM THE AIR

The Heart of Voh (La Cœur de Voh; Map p140) North of Koné, near the township of Voh, there's a mangrove swamp which has developed some unusual natural designs. The most intriguing is a perfect heart shape, La Cœur de Voh (The Heart of Voh), which is on the cover of *Earth from Above*, a book of aerial photography by renowned photographer Yann Arthus-Bertrand. There's a track up Mt Kathépaïk to a viewing point at an altitude of 400m (two hours' return), but the Heart is best seen from the air.

Hotel Hibiscus ULM Flights (☑ 47 22 61; www.ulmnc.com; from 17,000 CFP) These microlight flights that depart from Koné airport not only fly over The Heart of Voh, but also take in the magnificent lagoon and let you look right into a 'blue hole', a 200m-deep hole in the coral reef. The flight is spectacular, with the the pilot flying low enough to spot stingrays, turtles and sharks in the lagoon.

Koulnoué Village Hotel BUNGALOW $$
(Map p140; ☑ 24 24 77; www.grands-hotels.nc/koulnoue; bungalows from 15,000 CFP; P ❋ ☎ ☎) Undergoing refurbishment at the time of research, this surprisingly large ex–Club Med complex was starting to regain some of its mojo. The bungalows are well equipped and have private porches out to the beach. Play tennis or *petanque*, canoe, or go horse riding. Meals are buffet style (breakfast 2100 CFP, dinner 4300 CFP). The turn-off is 8.5km south of Hienghène.

❶ Information

Visitor Information Centre (Map p140; ☑ 42 43 57; www.hienghene-tourisme.nc; Hienghène; ⊙ 8am-noon & 1-5pm Mon-Fri, 8am-3pm Sat) This efficient visitor information centre looks over the Hienghène marina. Staff can book accommodation in *tribus*, help you contact guides for trekking in the area, and arrange traditional meals and dances. Contact them before you go for accommodation and trekking enquiries.

North of Hienghène

This is the wildest and most stunning stretch of the northeast coast. It's covered in tropical vegetation, and waterfalls and streams rush down the mountains to join the sea.

It's a captivating journey. A three-car ferry carries vehicles across the Ouaïème River, 17km northwest of Hienghène. It's free, runs 24 hours a day, and the crossing is a highlight. Expect to see roadside stalls selling fruit and carvings outside local thatched dwellings. Take care on one-lane bridges and watch out for dogs and chickens.

The area around Pouébo and Balade is a fascinating historical hotspot with places that mark the first contact between the Europeans and local Melanesians. While the Ouvanou Memorial is carefully tended by local Kanaks,

other monuments celebrating European arrival and French annexation of New Caledonia have been left to virtually disappear in the undergrowth.

◉ Sights & Activities

The area north of Hienghène is an amazing drawcard for trekking enthusiasts and nature lovers. All activities, however, require a guide and authorisation for you to enter tribal territories. At the time of research, **Mont Panié**, New Caledonia's highest mountain, was closed to the public. Contact Hienghène Visitor Information Centre for the latest.

Pouébo Catholic Church CHURCH
(Map p140) Inside Pouébo's Catholic church there's a marble mausoleum where the remains of Bishop Douarre, who set up New Caledonia's first Catholic mission, are interred. The church complex, with school and grounds next door, is surprisingly large and impressive.

Ouvanou Memorial MEMORIAL
(Map p140) About 1km north of Pouébo, on the coast side of the main road, is a carefully tended, touching memorial to 10 local Kanak men who were guillotined by the French on 18 May 1868. They have very obviously not been forgotten, nearly 150 years on.

Balade Church CHURCH
(Map p140) The stained-glass windows in this cute little church tell the story from the first Catholic mass. In 1853 France officially laid claim to New Caledonia at Balade, the same year in which Bishop Douarre, who performed the first mass, died.

★ **Kanak Monument** MEMORIAL
(Map p140) Directly below Balade Church, this monument, a large Kanak flag, was

unveiled on 24 September 2011, 158 years to the day after France took possession of the colony at this exact spot, and a year after the Congress of New Caledonia voted to fly the Kanak flag alongside the French tricolor in the territory. Unlike the nearby Monument de Balade, which celebrates French possession, it is a call for Kanak and New Caledonian independence from France.

Next to the Kanak Monument is the original stone pillar erected by the French in 1853 when they took possession, though the commemoration plaque has since disappeared.

Mahamat Beach
BEACH, MEMORIAL

(Map p140) Captain James Cook became the first European to discover New Caledonia in 1774, on his second voyage. He landed at Mahamat Beach, and it was on climbing the mountains inland that he decided the new land reminded him of Scotland and called it New Caledonia. An altar at Mahamat beach commemorates the first Catholic Mass on Christmas Day 1843, though it may take some searching to find it. The turn-off to the beach is 1.5km north of Balade's church.

Monument de Balade
MONUMENT

(Map p140) This impressive monument was unveiled in 1913 to great fanfare to mark 60 years of French possession of New Caledonia. It has since been left to virtually disappear in the weeds. About 1km north of the Mahamat Beach turn-off, it sits atop a small hill that was the site for France's first fort in the colony, built in 1853. History buffs should look for a sign on the right, when heading north. Blink and you'll miss it.

🛏 Sleeping & Eating

There are a number of campsites along the coast where you can simply turn up. Allow for 1000 CPF per tent and stock up on groceries before you go.

Relais de Ouane Batch
BUNGALOW $

(Map p140; ☑ 42 47 92; www.gite-ouanebatch. com; camping 1100 CFP, bungalows with/without bathroom 5250/4200 CFP; 🅿 🛜) The bungalows and campsites that line the beach are simple at this friendly spot, but they do the trick. There's free wi-fi at the main building and meals are good (breakfast/dinner 950/2850 CPF). Activities include snorkelling and canoe hire (half-/full day 1500/3000 CFP). It's 20km north of the river ferry and 22km south of Pouébo.

LOYALTY ISLANDS

POP 22,000 / AREA 1980 SQ KM

Maré, Lifou and Ouvéa. Fairy-tale names for fairy-tale islands. In a line 100km off the east coast of Grande Terre, they're all sparsely populated with secluded beaches, hidden caves and deep holes. They all have large tracts of impenetrable bush, but their roads are so good that driving around is a dream.

Loyalty Islands? It is thought that British traders named them that at the end of the 18th century, perhaps because the people were so 'honest and friendly'.

The islands saw intense power struggles between Protestant pastors and Catholic missionaries in the 1840s, but the Protestants made greater headway, using indigenous languages while the Catholic missionaries preferred French. The Loyalty Islands still have a strong Protestant influence, English words in their languages and even a love of cricket!

The islands were only annexed by France in 1864, but, deemed unsuitable for intensive colonisation, they were left as a native reserve. The official language is French, but while it is generally spoken and understood, each island also has its own language.

The locals blend traditional and modern lifestyles with ease. You'll need to take cash (although each island has a bank with an ATM). You'll find a shop with limited groceries in each village. Dining is somewhat limited to your (or other) accommodation, or *snack*-type simple eateries.

✪ Festivals & Events

Loyalty Islands Fair
FAIR

(www.iles-loyaute.com) Held each year in early September, the islands take turns hosting this three-day extravaganza. Musical performances, dancing, art, agricultural stalls, fishing and everything Loyalty is on display.

ℹ Information

An excellent online source for information in English is www.iles-loyaute.com/en

ℹ Getting There & Away

AIR

Air Calédonie (☑ 25 21 77; www.air-caledonie. nc) Flies at least twice a day between Noumea's Magenta Airport and each island. It also has flights between Lifou and Ouvéa on weekdays.

Air Loyauté (☑ 25 37 09; www.air-loyaute. nc) Flies between the Loyalty Islands in small aircraft daily.

NEW CALEDONIA LOYALTY ISLANDS

BOAT

Betico (✆ 26 01 00; www.betico.nc) The Betico sails from Noumea to Lifou and Maré, once or twice a week.

ⓘ Getting Around

The islands have limited public transport so it's best to hire a car and have it waiting for you on arrival. Car-rental companies drop off vehicles at the airport, wharf or accommodation places for free.

Hitchhiking is common everywhere but it can take a while for a car to come along.

Maré

POP 7400 / AREA 641 SQ KM

With its scenic coastline, stunning beaches and coral cliffs, plus an interior that hides impressive sunken pools and a mysterious rock edifice, it is small wonder that Maré's geographical features have inspired legends.

The indigenous language is Nengoné, and while there are two small towns, Tadine and La Roche, most Maréans live in tribes associated with one of 29 chieftaincies. The coastal town of Tadine is Maré's main centre; if travelling by ferry you'll arrive or leave from the wharf there. Tadine has shops, a petrol station, a pharmacy, and a market on Tuesday and Friday mornings. The airport is near La Roche.

Maré proudly hosts three festivals: the **Avocado Festival** held in May; the **Ura Festival**, a celebration of agricultural and fishing abundance, in July; and the **Wajuyu (Snapper fish) Festival**, held in early November.

◎ Sights & Activities

Hotels and gîtes can organise tours of the island for around 3000 CFP per person.

Centre Culturel
Yeiwene Yeiwene   MUSEUM, RUIN
(Map p158; ✆ 45 44 79; ⊙ 7.30-11.30am & 1-4pm Mon-Fri) [FREE] Maréan Yeiwene Yeiwene was deputy to independence leader Jean-Marie Tjibaou and assassinated alongside him on Ouvéa in 1989. A statue of Yeiwene stands before the cultural centre, where there is a small exhibition of Kanak artefacts. Out the back are the stone ruins known as Hnaenedr wall, a mysterious rock wall that supposedly dates back to AD 250.

★ Yedjele Beach   BEACH
(Map p158) The southwest coast has several gorgeous beaches where you can swim or snorkel during the day and watch the glorious sunsets in the evening, but best of the lot is Yedjele Beach. There's an enclosed lagoon with turquoise water, coral outcrops and plenty of tropical fish.

★ Aquarium Naturelle   LANDMARK
(Map p158) About 3km south of Tadine is a large Aquarium Naturelle, a rockpool sunk in the cliffs and linked to the sea. Watch for Napoleon fish, perroquettes, picods and sometimes turtles swimming in the translucent water. It is signposted by a parking area beside the main road. No swimming.

Trou de Bone   CAVE
(Map p158) About 3km off the La Roche–Tadine Rd, on the road to Thogone, is Trou de Bone, a deep rock cavity that drops to a lush tropical garden and a pool. It's on the right-hand side of the road as you're heading to Thogone, about 1.5km from the turn-off. It isn't signposted, so look out for a metal guardrail beside the road.

La Roche   HILL
(Map p158) A huge limestone rock covered in vegetation near the coast gives the surrounding area of La Roche (the Rock) its name. The rock, known locally as Titi, rises above the impressive Catholic church. You can climb to the top of the rock with a local guide. Make enquiries in the *tribu*.

★ Le Saut du Guerrier   VIEWPOINT
(Warrior's Leap; Map p158) Seven kilometres east of La Roche by sealed road is this gap in the cliffs, 5m wide and 30m above the pounding surf. Legend tells of a warrior who escaped his enemies by leaping across the abyss. Try to imagine the jump as you look down at the rocks and pounding waves below.

Shabadran   HIKING
(Map p158) This isolated, exquisite sandy beach at the southeast corner of Maré is surrounded by cliffs and forest and makes a great day-hike. You must have a guide, so contact Damas Bearune (✆ 73 29 71) in Kurine, the *tribu* at the end of the road. Book in advance; allow for four hours walking, take plenty of water and wear sturdy footwear.

🛏 Sleeping & Eating

Chez Nath   BUNGALOW $
(Map p158; ✆ 45 10 93; Tribu de Kaewatine; camping/d 2000/3990 CFP; [P]) Head through the casual open-air restaurant (meals from 2000 CFP) and follow the coral paths to two smart traditional thatched-roof *cases* with an external shower and toilet block. There's

electricity, friendly faces and guides for local walks, though the beach is a good 40-minute walk away. Chez Nath is at Tribu de Kaewatine in the north of the island.

Seday
BUNGALOW, CAMPGROUND $
(Map p158; ☑84 86 42; camping 1200 CFP, case per person 2000 CFP; ℗) Up north, in the quiet *tribu* of Roh, is a little honeymoon bungalow (5600 CFP) set on a rock in the water, plus three thatched bungalows. Sit on the wooden platform over the water, or slither between the rocks where it's great to snorkel. The restaurant serves excellent meals (1800 CFP) based on fish and home-grown vegetables.

Waterloo
BUNGALOW, CAMPGROUND $
(Map p158; ☑87 05 93, 45 18 02; www.office-tourisme.nc/en/waterloo; Eni; bungalows/camping 4000/1260 CFP; ℗) There are two thatched *cases* here in pretty gardens beside the family home. Dinner is likely to be fish (2500 CFP), served with a delicious papaya salad. There are two bathrooms and shaded camping spots. Lovely Eni beach is a short walk away.

★ Gite Yedjele Beach
BUNGALOW $$
(Map p158; ☑45 40 15; www.office-tourisme.nc/en/yedjele-beach; bungalows from 9000 CPF; ℗) A top spot to stay right on the island's most gorgeous beach. These sturdy bungalows, with kitchenette and mezzanine floor, can accommodate up to seven and are ideal for families. You'll need a rental vehicle and a smattering of French. Meals available with advance notice.

Hôtel Nengone Village
RESORT $$$
(Map p158; ☑45 45 00; www.hotelnengone village.nc; bungalows/ste 15,900/31,000 CFP; ℗❋⊛⊠) The island's only upmarket hotel, Nengone Village has spacious and comfortable bungalows that feature local timbers along a boardwalk. There's a refreshing pool by the excellent restaurant. Rental bicycles and kayaks are available. The meals are first class and the restaurant is open to nonguests with a reservation. The only place with wi-fi. Airport/wharf transfers cost 2800/1600 CFP.

ℹ Information

BCI Bank (Map p158; ☑25 53 20; ◷7.15am-noon & 1.15-4pm Mon-Fri) In Tadine; has an external ATM.

Post Office (Map p158; ☑45 41 00; ◷7.45-11.15am & 12.15-3pm Mon-Fri) The main office is in Tadine, with a secondary office in La Roche.

Tourist Information Office (Map p158; ☑45 51 07; ◷7.30-11.30am & 1.15-4pm) In Tadine; this place is helpful with advice and maps.

ℹ Getting There & Away

Air Calédonie (Map p158; ☑45 55 10; www.air-caledonie.nc; ◷8-11am & 2-5pm Mon-Fri) The domestic carrier has an office at the airport.

ℹ Getting Around

You can try cycling around the island if you are fit but roads are long, straight and monotonous. Hôtel Nengone Village hires bicycles (half-/full day 650/1100 CFP).

The best way to get around Maré is by car, organised before you go.

ETTM (☑45 42 73; per day from 6300 CFP) Rental cars dropped off and picked up from the wharf and airport.

Golf Location (☑45 09 42; per day from 6300 CFP) Rental cars delivered to the wharf and airport.

Lifou

POP 10,320 / AREA 1207 SQ KM

Lifou is home to magnificent cliff-top views, sheltered bays with coral shelfs teeming with colourful tropical fish, secluded beaches, fascinating caves and a rich traditional culture. The indigenous language is Drehu.

The main centre in Lifou is Wé, where the Loyalty Island's provincial offices are based. Wé stretches for about 2km along the main road beside Baie de Châteaubriand. There's a market Wednesdays and Fridays, a good supermarket and a number of *snack* restaurants.

Lifou celebrates with a **Pahatr (Fern) Festival** in April, the **Sandalwood and Honey Festival** in August and the **Vanilla Festival** held in October.

⦿ Sights & Activities

★ Chapelle Notre Dame de Lourdes
CHURCH
(Map p160) At the large white cross at Easo, stay on the coast road to a parking area below the small Chapelle Notre Dame de Lourdes. Steps lead up the hill to the chapel from where there are fantastic views of Baie de Jinek to the west and Baie du Santal to the east and south. The chapel was originally built in 1898 to commemorate the arrival of the first Catholic missionaries in 1858.

Maré

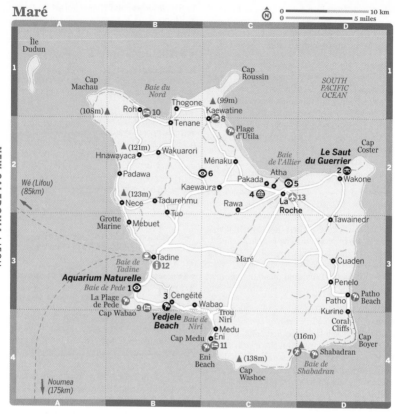

NEW CALEDONIA LIFOU

Peng BEACH
(Map p160) Don't miss the blissful, secluded beach at Peng on Baie du Santal, 3.5km off Wé–Drueulu Rd; turn off at the *tribu* Hapetra.

★Luengoni Beach BEACH
(Map p160) A stretch of fine white sand bordering a stunning lagoon. Locals boast that it is New Caledonia's most beautiful beach. The sheltered bay is a renowned turtle haunt.

Grotte les Joyaux de Luengoni GROTTO
(Map p160) Just west of Luengoni Beach are limestone caves both above and below ground; the underground caves have beautiful deep rock pools which shimmer emerald green when you shine a torch on the water.

Baie de Jinek SNORKELLING
(Map p160) At Easo, head down to Baie de Jinek, where steps from a wooden platform lead down to the water and an active snorkelling route in a fabulous coral-filled bay. The water teems with tropical fish in this popular snorkelling spot.

Jokin Cliffs SNORKELLING
(Map p160) Lifou's northernmost *tribu* sits on the cliff tops overlooking a vast bay with brilliant sunset views; the footpath to the left of the church here leads to about 150 steps that take you down under the cliffs to a perfect snorkelling cove.

Lifou Diving DIVING
(Map p160; ☑ 78 94 72, 45 40 60; www.lifoudiving.com; 2-dive package 11,000 CFP) Based at Easo, Lifou Diving has qualified English- and French-speaking PADI instructors and divemasters, and runs dive trips to spectacular spots around the island. It offers night dives (7000 CFP), and can organise accommodation locally for clients.

Maré

🛏 Sleeping & Eating

À La Petite Baie
BUNGALOW $

(Map p160; 📳45 15 25; www.office-tourisme.nc/
en/la-petite-baie-0; Tribu de Joj; bungalows per person 2100 CFP; 🅿) À La Petite Baie's *case*, in lovely gardens, is one of the best you'll find, and the dining room and bar is by the sea (organise your simple meals the day before). There's a kayak club here, and ask Annette about her outrigger trips.

★L'Oasis de Kiamu
RESORT $$

(Map p160; 📳45 15 00; www.hoteloasisdekiamu.
nc; r from 12,000 CFP; 🅿❄🛜🏊) This oasis right beside the main road and below limestone cliffs offers a variety of smart rooms, a swimming pool, a superb restaurant, a *snack* bar and its own beach just across the road. There's friendly service, free wi-fi, buffet breakfast (1850 CPF) and three course dinners (3500 CPF).

Chez Jeannette
BUNGALOW $$

(Map p160; 📳45 45 05; www.office-tourisme.nc/
en/node/1243; bungalows d 5600 CFP, case 2100 CFP; 🅿) Jeannette's homestay buzzes with energy as adventurers organise their day. It's right on the beach at the northern end of Baie de Châteaubriand. Follow the unsealed road in front of *tribu* Luecilla along the waterfront.

Faré Falaise
BUNGALOW $$

(Map p160; 📳45 02 01; www.office-tourisme.nc/
en/fare-falaise; camping 2100 CFP, d bungalows 5775 CFP; 🅿🛜) Perched on the very edge of the cliffs at Jokin at the northern tip of Lifou, Faré Falaise offers rustic bungalows and camping. The water is via 150 steps, but it's great snorkelling. Campers have a kitchen for cooking, while good meals are available. You can also rent bicycles and cars here.

Hôtel Drehu Village
BUNGALOW $$$

(Map p160; 📳45 02 70; www.hoteldrehuvillage.
nc; bungalows from 17,000 CFP; 🅿❄🛜🏊) Turn down towards Châteaubriand beach and you'll find Lifou's upmarket hotel where comfortable bungalows spread through to the grass and white-sand beach. The restaurant tables are romantically situated around a pool and under a *faré* (breakfast 2400 CPF; dinner from 3250 CFP).

ⓘ Information

BCI Bank (Map p160; 📳45 13 32; ⊙7.20am-noon & 1-3.45pm Mon-Fri) On the main road opposite the Air Calédonie office, it has an external ATM.

Post Office (Map p160; 📳45 11 00; ⊙7.45am-3pm Mon-Fri) Located behind the provincial offices in Wé.

Visitor Information Centre (Map p160; 📳45 00 32; ⊙7.30-11.30am & 12.30-4.30pm Mon-Fri) The main office is next to the *mairie* in Wé. There's also a booth at the airport with maps and stacks of info.

ⓘ Getting There & Away

Air Calédonie (Map p160; ⊙7.30-11.30am & 12.30-5.15pm Mon-Fri, 7.15-11am Sat) An office in Wé (📳45 55 50) and a desk at the airport (Map p160; 📳45 55 20; Airport).

ⓘ Getting Around

The best way to get around Lifou is by car, though you could take it on with a bike.

Alizée Locations (📳45 07 67) Rental cars delivered to the airport.

Loca V (📳45 07 77; locav@lagoon.nc; per day from 5700 CFP) Offers good rental cars delivered to the port or airport.

NEW CALEDONIA LIFOU

Lifou

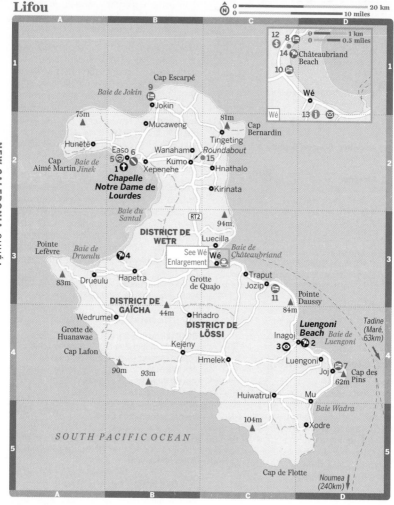

N ↑ 0 ————— 20 km
0 ————— 10 miles

Lifou map labels:

Cap Escarpé
9 Baie de Jokin
Jokin
75m
Mucaweng
81m
Hunëtë
Cap Bernardin
Easo 6
Wanaham Tingeting Roundabout
Cap Aimé Martin Baie de Jinek
5 1
Kumo 15
Xepenehe
Hnathalo
Chapelle Notre Dame de Lourdes
Kirinata
Baie du Santal
RT2
94m
DISTRICT DE WETR
Luecilla
Pointe Lefèvre Baie de Druelu
See Wé Enlargement
Wé
Baie de Châteaubriand
4
83m Drueulu Hapetra
Grotte de Quajo
Traput
Jozip
11
DISTRICT DE GAÏCHA
44m
Hnadro
Pointe Daussy
84m
Tadine (Maré, 63km)
Wedrumel
DISTRICT DE LÖSSI
Grotte de Huanawae
Kejény
Inagoj Luengoni Beach Baie de Luengoni
Cap Lafon
Hmelek
3 2
90m 93m
Luengoni
Joj 7
62m Cap des Pins
Huiwatrul
Mu
104m
Baie Wadra
Xodre
SOUTH PACIFIC OCEAN
Cap de Flotte
Noumea (240km)

Inset (Wé Enlargement):
12
8
14 Châteaubriand Beach
10
Wé
13
Wé

See Wé Enlargement

Ouvéa

POP 4360 / AREA 132 SQ KM

Think 25km of perfect white beach backed with grass, tropical flowers, and thick forest inhabited by the endemic and protected Ouvéa green parrot. Look out over an exquisite turquoise lagoon stretching as far as you can see. Add a chain of tiny islets, the Pléiades. Sound unreal? Ouvéa may leave you shaking your head in wonder.

The Ouvéa lagoon was one of six marine areas in the New Caledonian archipelago to be listed as a Unesco World Heritage site in 2008. It's stunning.

Ouvéa has two indigenous languages. Iaaï is of Melanesian origin, while Faga-uvéa is spoken in the south and north of the island by descendants of Polynesian migrants who arrived in the 16th and 17th centuries.

A thin sliver of land, Ouvéa has administrative centres at Wadrilla and Fayaoué. The facilities in these villages, however, are so spread out that nowhere can really be described as a centre. There's a bank with outside ATM, a clinic and a pharmacy near the airport.

Lifou

Ouvéa hosts its **Lagoon Festival** in June and the **Waleï (Sweet Yam) Festival** in August.

⊙ Sights

★ Fayaoué Beach   BEACH
(Map p162) The highlight of Ouvéa is its magnificent beach and lagoon. While the east coast of the island is mainly rough cliffs pounded by the Pacific Ocean, the west coast faces the protected lagoon and this gorgeous beach stretches from Mouli in the south, fully 25km to St Joseph in the north. Make the most of the swimming, kayaking, sailing, windsurfing and other watersport opportunities.

★ Ouvéa Memorial   MEMORIAL
(Map p162) The large memorial in Wadrilla is a tribute to 19 Kanaks who died in 1988, when French military personnel stormed a cave to free French *gendarmes* being held hostage by the pro-independence movement. Tragically, pro-independence leaders Jean-Marie Tjibaou and Yeiwene Yeiwene were assassinated opposite the memorial at the first-year memorial ceremony. The perpetrator believed they had ceded too much to France. The names and faces of the 19 are inscribed on the impressive memorial.

DON'T MISS

HEAVENLY BRIDGE

Pont de Mouli (Map p162) It may seem unusual to recommend a road bridge as a top sightseeing spot, but at Pont de Mouli, Ouvéa's tip, Mouli island, is cut off by a wide channel that flows out of Baie de Lékiny into the lagoon. From the bridge, the display of dazzling white sand and shades of turquoise is occasionally broken by outlines of sharks, rays, turtles and fish swimming beneath you (unless it's the weekend, when all you'll see are kids jumping off).

Trou à Tortues   LANDMARK
(Turtles Hole; Map p162) Up in the north near St Joseph, the Turtles Hole is down an unmarked dirt road, then along a 50m path through the bush. An immense hole in the limestone is full of water and connected underground to the sea. Sit patiently and turtles are bound to appear. This is also a great place to spot the protected Ouvéa green parrot.

Trou Bleu d'Anawa   CAVE
(Map p162) The deep Trou Bleu d'Anawa is sunk in the coral rock and connected to the sea underground. If you're lucky, you may see fish and turtles in the blue water. Turn left along a track just past the Anawa shop, where the road curves sharply away from the coast. The pool is behind some abandoned bungalows.

Ouvéa Soap Factory   FACTORY
(Savonnerie D'Ouvéa; Map p162; ☑45 10 60; ⊙8-11.30am & 1.30-3.30pm Tue & Thu) FREE Take a free visit to the soap factory, next to the ferry quay in Wadrilla. Using coconut oil, it produces household soap, soap perfumed with *niaouli* (paper bark tea tree) and even soapflakes for laundry detergent. There's soap for sale.

⚑ Activities

Plage de Tiberia   SNORKELLING
(Tiberia Beach; Map p162) At the north of Ouvéa and almost at its easternmost point of Pointe Escarpée, this superb snorkelling spot is down a set of stairs beside the road. There's a sandy beach and an easily accessible reef teeming with coral and fish.

Ouvéa

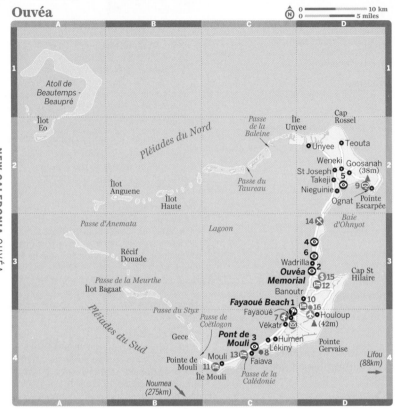

NEW CALEDONIA OUVÉA

Charly Aema Tours BOAT TOUR

(☑ 45 07 60; tour incl lunch 6500 CFP) Head out on a boat tour from Moague with Charly Aema. The trip heads out to Îlot Gee in the Pléiades du Sud where you can snorkel, fish and enjoy a picnic. Late each year sharks give birth in the warm shallow waters and with good timing you'll be able to see the 'shark nursery'. Book a day in advance.

Canio WATER SPORTS

(Map p162; ☑ 75 45 45; ⊙ 8-11.30am & 1-4.30pm Tue-Sat) The interesting catamaran-shaped building on the beach in Fayaoué is the sailing club. Canio rents per one/two hours windsurfers (1500/2500 CFP), hobie cats (from 2000/3500 CFP) and kayaks (1000/1700 CFP).

Mio Palmo Plongée DIVING

(☑ 84 47 38; www.facebook.com/miopalmo.plongee.1; 2-dive package 12,000 CFP) You'll potentially be swimming with green turtles, Manta rays, humphead wrasse, parrotfish, surgeon-fish and sharks with this scuba-diving club. Take an intro dive for 8000 CFP, or a PADI Open Water course for 49,000 CFP.

Les Falaises de Lekiny ADVENTURE TOUR

(Map p162) These grey cliffs, pitted with caves, are 12km south from Fayaoue. Explore them with guide **Felix Alosio** (☑ 92 55 12; per person 2100 CFP).

🛏 Sleeping & Eating

★**Moague** BUNGALOW **$$**

(Map p162; ☑ 75 08 89, 45 07 60; www.office-tourisme.nc/en/moague; Mouli; camping 2500 CFP, bungalows s/d 5500 CFP; P) This friendly beachside accommodation in Mouli is run by Charly Aema, famous for his boat excursions. There's camping, five thatched-roof bungalows, separate bathroom facilities with hot water, plus an excellent restaurant. Join the island or boat tours with prior bookings. Airport transfers are 3000 CFP.

Ouvea

Chez Dydyce   BUNGALOW **$$**
(Map p162; ☑ 94 78 21, 45 72 87; www.office-tour isme.nc/en/chez-dydyce; camping 2300 CFP, bungalows 5500 CFP; ℗ 🛜) This spot has a good camp kitchen, clean bathrooms and sunny camping spots. The restaurant Snack Champagne (complete with sand floor) is on-site, offering three-course dinners from 1575 CPF and free wi-fi. You can hire bikes (per day 1575 CFP) or join an excursion to the Southern Pleiades islets (7500 CPF).

Gîte Cocotier   BUNGALOW **$$**
(Map p162; ☑ 79 43 57, 45 70 40; www.office-tourisme.nc/en/cocotier; camping 2000 CFP, bungalows from 5500 CFP; ℗) Sammy has some good options at Cocotier, about 500m north of the church in Mouli. It's across the road from the beach, but you can pitch your tent on the beachfront. Hire bikes, go snorkelling or take an island tour for 3500 CFP. A set menu is 2200 CFP. Airport transfers cost 3000 CFP.

Hotel Beaupré   BUNGALOW **$$**
(Map p162; ☑ 45 71 32; www.hotelbeaupre. nc; bungalows from 14,900 CFP; ℗🛜) Lovely

bungalows, the restaurant specialises in seafood, plus you can join island and boat tours at this well-positioned place not far from the airport. No charge for transfers.

Hôtel Paradis d'Ouvéa   RESORT **$$$**
(Map p162; ☑ 45 54 00; www.paradisouvea.com; villas from 32,000 CFP; ℗ ✴ 🛜 🌊) Step out of your luxurious spacious villa onto the stunning white-sand beach, or lie on your private deck and think about swimming in the azure sea. The tropical restaurant is top class and has soaring ceilings. Relax by the pool, hire bikes or head out on an island tour (4100 CFP). Airport return transfers are 2200 CFP

O'kafika   SEAFOOD **$$**
(Map p162; ☑ 45 90 27; ⊙vary) In the village of Hanawa and right next to the road and beach, O'kafika serves everything from sandwiches to tasty seafood meals on an outside terrace. Sandwiches from 500 CFP, meals from 1200 to 2600 CFP. This place is perfectly positioned if you are on a road trip to the north.

ⓘ Information

BCI Bank (Map p162; ☑ 45 71 31; ⊙7.20am-noon Mon-Fri, plus 1-3pm Wed) On the road to the airport; has an internal and external ATM.
Post Office (Map p162; ☑ 45 71 00; ⊙7.45-11.15am & 12.15-3pm Mon-Fri) There's an ATM inside the office in Fayaoué.
Tourist Information (☑ 94 97 14; Wadrilla; ⊙7.30am-4.30pm Mon-Fri) The office is on the beach road in Wadrilla and has info on tours and accommodation.

ⓘ Getting There & Away

Air Calédonie (Map p162; ⊙7.30-11am & 1.30-4pm Mon-Fri) Has an office in Wadrilla (☑ 45 70 22; Office) and a desk at the airport (☑ 45 55 30; Airport).

ⓘ Getting Around

There's no public transportation. The best option is to get a rental car delivered to the airport, or arrange transfers with your accommodation.
Julau Location (☑ 45 45 30; per day from 6300 CFP) Delivers to the airport.
Ouvéa Location (Map p162; ☑ 45 73 77, 79 55 58; per day from 6300 CFP) Delivers to the airport.

ÎLE DES PINS

POP 2000 / AREA 152 SQ KM

Known as Kunié to the Melanesians, Île des Pins (Isle of Pines) is a tranquil paradise of

Île des Pins

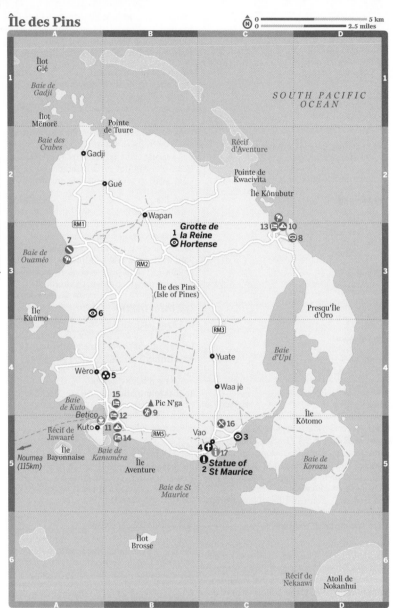

turquoise bays, white-sand beaches and tropical vegetation 110km southeast of Noumea.

According to legend, warriors of Tongan descent came from Lifou about three centuries ago and were invited to take over leadership of the island. Captain James Cook later named the island Isle of Pines when on his second voyage of Pacific exploration in 1774.

The 1840s saw the arrival of both Protestant and Catholic missionaries, and traders looking for sandalwood. The Kunies opted for the Catholic religion and thereby for

Île des Pins

French possession in 1853, though they may have regretted it 21 years later when their island became a settlement for 3000 political deportees from the Paris Commune. Nowadays the island is an indigenous reserve.

Administratively, Île des Pins is part of Province Sud. Vao is the administrative centre, while Kuto is the main tourist area. There's not much in the way of shops or restaurants and most people eat where they are staying. Restaurants attached to gîtes or hotels accept nonguests, but you'll need to book in advance. Seafood is popular, as are Île des Pins' *escargots* (snails), a local speciality.

The **Île des Pins Fair** is held in May or June over three days and features singing, dancing, crafts and gastronomic delights.

ⓘ Getting There & Away

Air Calédonie (☑ Vao 44 88 50, airport 44 88 40; ⊙7.30-11am & 2-5pm Mon-Fri, 7.30-11.30am Sat) Air Calédonie flies to Île des Pins from Noumea at least twice daily.

Betico (☑ 44 22 42; www.betico.nc) The Betico sails from Noumea at 7am for a day trip on Wednesday. It also departs Noumea on Saturday at 7am and returns Sunday, arriving back in Noumea at 7.30pm. It docks at the wharf in Baie de Kuto.

ⓘ Getting Around

It is important to arrange a hire car, transfer or tour in advance, so you're not stranded at the airport or wharf, especially if you're on a day trip.

Edmond Location (☑76 69 96; per day 7500 CFP) Will deliver rental cars to the port or airport.

Nataiwatch Rentals (☑46 11 13; www.natai watch.com) Rental mountain bikes/cars per day 2000/7000 CFP;

Vao

Île des Pins' main village and administrative centre, Vao, is a serene place with not much going on. There's a market on Wednesday and Saturday mornings.

⊙ Sights & Activities

Catholic Church   CHURCH

(Map p164) The attractive 19th-century Catholic church dominates Vao. It was established by the Marist priest Father Goujon, who managed to convert most of the island's population in just over 30 years following his arrival in 1848.

★**Statue of St Maurice**   STATUE

(Map p164) At Baie de St Maurice, this statue commemorates the arrival of the first missionaries on the island and is also a war memorial. There's a solemn line of wooden totem poles just above the beach.

Baie de St Joseph   BAY

(Map p164) Two kilometres east of Vao and also referred to as Baie des Pirogues, this is where the Pirogue Excursion (p166) leaves from daily. Locals build their traditional canoes here.

✕ Eating

Snack Kohu   CAFE

(Map p164; ☑46 10 23; dishes 750-1450 CFP; ⊙10am-3pm Mon-Fri) This is a pleasant place for lunch, just out of Vao on the road north towards the airport. There are tables under thatched shelters and everyone is very friendly. Meals include chicken or steak and chips, sandwiches from 450 CFP and a *plat du jour* (1650 CFP).

ⓘ Information

BCI Bank (Map p164; ☑46 10 45; ⊙8am-noon & 1-3.30pm Mon & Fri, 8am-noon Tue & Wed, 1-3.30pm Thu) Has an outside ATM.

PIROGUE EXCURSION

Its scenery aside, Île des Pins' most famous attraction is its wooden *pirogues* with their triangular sails. *Pirogues* leave Baie de St Joseph at 8am each morning, heading for the top of Baie d'Upi. A path from there, taking about an hour, leads through forest to magical *La Piscine Naturelle*. Laze on the sand or snorkel above a kaleidoscope of fish in its clear waters.

Pirogue excursions, including transfers to Baie de St Joseph and back from Baie d'Oro, cost around 4000 CFP all up. Book and discuss lunch options at your place of accommodation.

Post Office (Map p164; ☑46 11 00; ☉7.45-11.15am & 12.30-3.30pm Mon-Fri) Has a public telephone; there are other phones at the airport and wharf.

Visitor Information Centre (Map p164; ☑46 10 27; www.ile-des-pins.com; ☉8-11.30am Mon-Sat & 2-4pm Mon-Fri) Next to the bank. There's an information desk (☑46 14 00) at the airport which opens for flights.

Kuto & the West Coast

Kuto has two gorgeous aquamarine bays, separated by the narrow neck of Kuto peninsula. **Baie de Kuto** is the perfect place to lie on the beach or swim in the calm sea. For snorkelling go to **Baie de Kanuméra**, where coral grows not far from the shore. The ferry and cruise ship quay is on the north side of the Kuto peninsula.

◉ Sights & Activities

Convict Prison Ruins   RUIN

(Map p164) Just north of Baie de Kuto, beside the main road, are the crumbling, overgrown ruins of an old convict prison built in the late 19th century. Île des Pins was initially used as a place of exile for convicts, including Paris Communards and Algerian deportees in the 1870s.

Grotte de la Troisième   CAVE

(Map p164) About 8km north of Kuto, a signposted turn-off leads down a dirt road to the sunken Grotte de la Troisième. The cave is 100m down a path from the end of the road and if you climb into the wide opening, you can peer into its depth.

Nokanhui Atoll Boat Excursion   BOAT TOUR

(☑45 90 66, 77 28 50; www.facebook.com/iledes pins.plaisance; per person with/without lunch 9500/7500 CPF) This day excursion by boat from Kuto Bay, departing at 9am, lets you take in the magnificent Nokanhui Atoll, to the south of Île des Pins. Lunch follows, then there's time to explore Île Môrô before returning to Kuto Bay around 3.30pm. Book at your accommodation.

Pic N'ga Track   HIKING

(Map p164) Feeling energetic? Take a 45-minute climb up Pic N'ga (262m), the island's highest point. The path is mostly exposed, so it's best to go early morning or late afternoon. From the summit there are fantastic views over the entire island and its turquoise bays. The signposted path begins from the main road 200m south of Relais Le Kuberka.

Kunié Scuba Centre   DIVING

(Map p164; ☑46 11 22; www.kunie-scuba.com; intro/2 dives from 9200/13,300 CFP) Based at Ouameo Bay, 10km north of Kuto, these guys have been organising dives, PADI training and snorkelling trips around Île des Pins since 1974.

🛌 Sleeping & Eating

★ **Gîte Nataiwatch**   CAMPGROUND, BUNGALOW **$$**

(Map p164; ☑46 11 13; www.nataiwatch.com; camping 1800 CFP, bungalows 10,900 CFP, B&B s/d 9700/10,900 CFP; P ?) This is a popular gîte with a wide range of accommodation options in a wooded area towards the eastern end of Baie de Kanuméra. There's everything from camping to family bungalows, all with free wifi. Throw in a good restaurant, rental cars and mountain bikes, and a number of excursions on offer and you have a great spot to stay.

Relais Le Kuberka   BUNGALOW **$$**

(Map p164; ☑46 11 18; www.office-tourisme.nc/en/relais-kuberka; s/d 7500/9400 CFP, bungalows 12,400 CFP; P ? ☀) A short walk from the beach, this home-away-from-home has tidy rooms and bungalows set around a small garden and pool. The restaurant serves an excellent range of meals (dishes 2100 CFP). Airport/wharf transfers 1500/500 CFP.

Hôtel Kou-Bugny   HOTEL **$$$**

(Map p164; ☑46 18 00; www.kou-bugny.com; r/bungalows 22,600/26,600 CFP; P ✱ ? ☀) Kou-Bugny is right on Kuto beach, with rooms on the inland side of the quiet road and its restaurant almost on the sand. Sit on the terrace with a drink and catch the sunset. A great location with plenty of excursions on offer.

Ouré Tera Hotel RESORT $$$

(Map p164; ☑43 13 15; www.tera-hotels-resorts. com/hotel; r/bungalows from 36,900/45,900 CFP; P❄@☎☲) This top place is right on the water at Baie de Kanuméra. The open bar and dining room (mains 2800 CFP to 3600 CFP) open on to a spectacular curving pool area. Rooms are superb. If you're not staying here, consider booking to eat at the restaurant.

Baie d'Oro & Around

North of Vao the road climbs gradually onto a central plateau. Follow the signs out to beautiful secluded Baie d'Oro. At the end of the road is a parking area, plus a lunch *snack* restaurant run by the local *tribu*.

◉ Sights & Activities

★ Grotte de la Reine Hortense CAVE

(Map p164; admission 250 CFP) This impressive cave tunnels into a limestone cliff at the end of a path through wild tropical gardens. Queen Hortense, wife of a local chief, is believed to have taken refuge here for several months during intertribal conflict in 1855; there's a smooth rock ledge where she slept. The sealed road down to the cave is signposted.

★ La Piscine Naturelle SNORKELLING

(admission 200 CPF) A 20-minute signposted walk from the carpark at the end of the road, this pool of exquisite turquoise water is protected from the sea by a narrow waterway. The snorkelling is unbelievable and if you just sit in knee-deep water on the fine white sand, tropical fish will approach you! Highly recommended.

🛏 Sleeping & Eating

Camping/Restaurant

Le Kou-gny CAMPGROUND $

(Map p164; ☑70 25 35; camping 1000 CFP) This rustic campsite and restaurant is on the beach, five minutes east of Le Méridien. Tables are set under trees looking out over the water and it does a good trade serving lunch to Piscine Naturelle visitors. Try a dozen tasty Île des Pins snails here for 3100 CPF.

Le Méridien RESORT $$$

(Map p164; ☑26 50 00; www.lemeridienile despins.com; r/bungalows from 35,000/50,000 CFP; P❄☎☲) This is tropical luxury at its best. While the central lounge, bar and restaurant areas invite you to relax and enjoy, the rooms are as top-notch as you'll find in New Caledonia. The infinity pool is a stunner and there are plenty of excursion options on offer.

CRAIG MCLACHLAN ©

1. La Roche Percée (p150)
This unusual headland has a hole you can walk through.

2. Le Roof (p139), Noumea
Elegant dining and amazing sunsets are offered at this restaurant overlooking Anse Vata beach.

3. Fort Téremba (p149), Moindou
This historic fort comes alive in October for the Fort Téremba Spectacle.

4. Île aux Canards (p132)
Serious relaxation is offered on this island, a five-minute boatride from Noumea's Anse Vata beach.

DANITA DELIMONT / GETTY IMAGES ©

IAN WATT / ALAMY STOCK PHOTO ©

1. Baie de Kanumera (p166), Île des Pins
Coral close to the shore makes this one of Île des Pins' top snorkelling areas.

2. Brooding Hen (p153), Hienghène
The *Poule Couveuse* is one of New Caledonia's most striking natural sights.

3. Blue Hole (p154), near Koné
Microlight flights offer breathtaking views of this 200m-deep reef feature.

CRAIG MCLACHLAN ©

New Caledonia Today

The heat is on. As outlined in the Noumea Accord of 1998, a referendum on New Caledonia's self-determination must be held by the end of 2018. With that date drawing ever-nearer, squabbling is frantic between pro- and anti-independence groups as to who should be eligible to vote in the referendum.

Best in Print

The Kanak Apple Season (2005) Déwé Gorodé's collection of short stories about traditional aspects of Kanak life, the status of Kanak women and the struggle for Kanak emancipation.

Les Cœurs Barbelés (1999) Claudine Jacques' love story explores the cultural differences and similarities between Kanak and Caldoche lovers.

La Brousse en Folie (The Mad Bush) A popular comic-book series by Bernard Berger that follows the adventures of four typically Caledonian characters.

Jean-Marie Tjibaou, Kanak Witness to the World: An Intellectual Biography (2008) Eric Waddell's study of the life of arguably the most important post-WWII Oceanic leader.

The Kanak Awakening: The Rise of Nationalism in New Caledonia (2014) A study by David Chappell into events leading up to violent uprisings in New Caledonia in the 1980s.

Culture & Economic Divide

There is a huge cultural and economic divide between New Caledonia's Kanak and Caldoche (locally born descendants of Europeans) populations. In many ways, it's as if they are living in entirely different countries. Kanaks suffered terribly after the arrival of the Europeans in the 19th century, and the cuts still run deep. As well as their decimation after exposure to new diseases in the 1800s, many Kanaks were forced to leave their traditional lands to make way for European settlers. The brutal treatment of the Kanaks by their colonisers, which continued into the 20th century, has made it difficult for many to move on.

The European presence ensures that New Caledonia has good roads, quality infrastructure and 24/7 electricity – all things that its independent neighbour Vanuatu cannot claim. Noumea has a sophisticated air, with glitz and glam by the yacht-sprinkled waterfront, but it's not Kanaks who are lying back sipping champagne. As well as a cultural gap, there is an obvious financial gap. Young Kanaks are overrepresented in jail and their unemployment rate is four times higher than youths descended from Europeans. Only time will tell whether independence from France will help these two cultures move on from the past.

2018 Vote on Independence

In 1986, after bloody clashes, the UN put New Caledonia on its 'Decolonisation List' and France was required to take 'immediate steps' to ensure independence for its colony. Initially in the Matignon Accord of 1988, then in the Noumea Accord of 1998, a power-sharing arrangement and aims for the gradual transfer of power from France to the government of New Caledonia were outlined. This is to culminate in a referendum by the end of 2018 to decide on 'self-determination'. Should the independence vote fail, the Noumea Accord provides that two more referenda must be held in ensuing years.

With 2018 drawing ever closer, things are getting messy. In the 2014 elections, anti-independence parties won 29 of 54 seats, but pro-independence parties cleaned up in the Loyalty Islands and the Northern Province. Noumea remains the stronghold for anti-independence supporters. Recent squabbles between pro- and anti-independence groups centre on who should be eligible to vote in the 2018 referendum.

While pro-independence groups are organising for self-governance, they are split into factions, and on the other side anti-independence groups are also divided. The high stakes of potential independence from France are prompting panic and vitriol from anti-independence supporters, and continued inequality and discrimination against Kanaks provide impetus for supporters of a referendum. With the population 40% Kanak and 29% European, a 2015 electoral law stating that only indigenous Kanaks and persons enrolled in 1998 will be automatically eligible to vote in the 2018 referendum makes it appear that the country is destined for independence.

The Accord also encourages the building of a united destiny through the selection of symbols of national identity, such as a new flag. Loyalists did not want to lose the French tricolour, however, so in 2010 the Kanak flag was also adopted. This makes New Caledonia one of few countries with two official flags.

Resources

Having its lagoon listed as a Unesco World Heritage site in 2008 was a moment of pride for New Caledonia, but with the lagoon's listing came the huge responsibility to protect it. This is easier said than done when nickel mining provides most of the country's income.

Despite providing employment and income, nickel mining causes the loss of huge swathes of vegetation and dramatic landscape changes. The surrounding air, rivers and heritage-listed lagoon are at risk from the by-products of mining – in 2009 sulphuric acid leaked into a river that flows into a World Heritage buffer zone, killing around 3000 fish.

Kanak communities have fought the mines, citing concerns about their environmental and cultural impact. In 2006 there was a violent confrontation when local Kanak protesters tried to halt construction of a new nickel plant. Eventually local leaders signed an agreement stipulating that the plant's owner would provide funding for reforestation and community development projects. Although not supported by everyone, the promise of employment opportunities for local Kanaks was a strong persuader.

POPULATION: **270,000**

GREATER NOUMEA
POPULATION: **164,000**

LAND AREA : **18,275 SQ KM**

BIGGEST TRADING
PARTNER: **FRANCE**

PERCENTAGE OF WORLD'S
NICKEL RESERVES: **25%**

if New Caledonia were 100 people

40 would be Melanesian (Kanak)
29 would be European
9 would be Wallisian & Futunian
22 would be other

belief systems
(% of population)

60
Roman Catholic

30
Protestant

10
Other

population per sq km

NEW CALEDONIA   NEW ZEALAND   AUSTRALIA

= 3 people

New Caledonian History

This isolated island country in the South Pacific has had an intriguing history since the Austronesians turned up 3500 years ago. Since the 1770s, the British, the French, missionaries, traders, convicts, nickel miners and pro-independence activists have all played their parts – and now 'self-determination' is on the horizon.

Early History

The name Lapita comes from a site near Koné on Grande Terre, where elaborate, pinhole-incised pottery was discovered. 'Lapita culture' is now used in describing the peopling of the Pacific from west to east in the years 1600 BC to 500 BC.

About 1500 BC, Austronesians, later to be known as Lapita, arrived in the islands from Vanuatu. The Lapita were both hunter-gatherers and agriculturists. From about the 11th century AD until the 18th century groups of Polynesians also migrated to New Caledonia.

These early settlers cultivated yams, taro, manioc and other crops; the terraced fields they once worked are still visible in many places on Grande Terre, such as Païta, Bourail and Houaïlou.

Life centred around the *grande case,* the clan's largest (conical) hut, where the chief lived. The hut was topped by a carved wooden rooftop spear known as a *flèche faîtière,* which symbolised the presence of the ancient and highly worshipped ancestors.

European Arrival

The first Europeans arrived in New Caledonia in the late 18th century. At the time the indigenous population was estimated to be more than 60,000.

English explorer James Cook spotted Grande Terre in 1774 when midway through his second scientific expedition in search of *terra australis.* He named it New Caledonia because the terrain on the northeast coast where he landed near Balade reminded him of the highlands of Scotland (called Caledonia by the Romans).

Cook and his crew, aboard HMS *Resolution,* anchored off the northeast coast on 4 September 1774 and spent 10 days exploring the region,

TIMELINE	50,000 years ago	1500 BC	AD 1774
	New Caledonia separated from Australia 65 million years ago, reaching its current position 50,000 years ago.	The Lapita, New Caledonia's first inhabitants, arrive from Vanuatu.	European discovery of Grande Terre by James Cook. The country is named New Caledonia after the Scottish highlands.

where they were given a friendly reception. The *Resolution* then sailed down the east coast of the main island (without sighting the Loyalty Islands) until Cook came across the beautiful Île des Pins (Isle of Pines).

The First French

French interest in New Caledonia was sparked in 1785 when Louis XVI sent Jean-François de Galaup La Pérouse out to explore the world. But La Pérouse and his crew on the *Astrolabe* and *La Boussole* disappeared in a cyclone on the reefs off Vanikoro in the southeast of the Solomon Islands. A mission to find them set out from France on 28 September 1791. Led by Admiral Antoine Bruni d'Entrecasteaux and Captain Huon de Kermadec, the *Espérance* and *La Recherche* landed at Balade on 17 April 1793, having sailed past Vanikoro where, it is believed, survivors of La Pérouse's expedition were still living.

Shortly after arriving in New Caledonia, de Kermadec died. D'Entrecasteaux and members of his crew explored northern New Caledonia, crossing by foot from the east to west coast and back again. They stayed a month but were not given the same friendly reception as Cook. One theory for the different perceptions of the English and the French is that Cook and his crew had introduced new diseases that killed many locals. As a result, locals were much less welcoming to the new group of Europeans.

In 1793 d'Entrecasteaux made the first European sighting of Ouvéa, the northernmost of the Loyalty Islands; however, he died on the return journey to France. In the same year, the English captain William Raven on the *Britannia* sighted Maré, the southernmost of the Loyalty Islands, and reported the presence of sandalwood.

Noumea's original name, Port-de-France, was changed because mail addressed there kept ending up in Fort-de-France in Martinique, a French colony in the Caribbean.

Money Making: The Traders

British and American whalers were the first commercial seafarers to make landfall on the islands. By 1840 British whalers had set up an oil-extraction station on Lifou, the largest of the Loyalty Islands.

Next came sandalwood traders, who were the first Europeans to have any real impact on the islanders. Sandalwood was traditionally burnt as incense in Chinese temples. Between 1840 and 1850, traders operating out of Australia almost completely stripped first Île des Pins, then the Loyalty Islands and finally Grande Terre's east coast. The traders gave the islanders tobacco and alcohol or metal tools such as axes, nails and fish hooks in return for the sandalwood. With their ships loaded, they sailed to China, where the fragrant wood was traded for tea for Australia.

Later in the 19th century, many Kanaks were recruited to work on plantations in Australia. Some stayed on and their descendants still live there.

1793	1841	1840s	1843
French navigator Antoine de Bruni d'Entrecasteaux briefly explores New Caledonia.	The first Anglican Protestants set up a mission in the Loyalty Islands.	Whalers and sandalwood traders begin arriving and trading. Not all goes well, and in 1849 the crew of an American ship is killed and eaten by a local tribe.	The Catholic Marist Brothers missionary is established in Balade; it's later demolished by Kanaks angry at drought, starvation and a spate of new diseases.

Missionaries

During the 19th century both Catholic (French) and Protestant (English) missionaries arrived in New Caledonia. In 1841 two Samoan Protestant missionaries from the London Missionary Society (LMS) were the first to arrive on Île des Pins. Though soon driven off by unreceptive locals, the British missionaries successfully established themselves on Lifou in 1842. Meanwhile French Marists established a mission at Balade on the northeast coast of Grande Terre in December 1843.

With the introduction of Christianity, both polygamy and cannibalism eventually ceased. In addition to cultural changes, the Protestant missionaries also introduced cricket. It is still played today and is wildly popular.

French Annexation

In the early 1850s the French were looking for a strategic military location, as well as an alternative penal settlement to French Guyana in South America, whose unhealthy climate resulted in a high convict mortality rate.

HISTORICAL HOTSPOTS

Travelling on the northeast coast of Grande Terre, north of Hienghène, presents some great opportunities for history buffs. It's a bit like a treasure hunt, but if you look hard enough around Pouébo and Balade, you can find:

➡ **Mahamat Beach** (p155), where Captain Cook landed in 1774, climbed the inland hills and named the land he'd 'discovered' 'New Caledonia'.

➡ The remains of an **altar** (p155) where the first Catholic Mass in New Caledonia was held in 1843.

➡ Below **Balade church** (p154), you can see a stone pillar marking the exact place where France took possession of New Caledonia in 1853.

➡ The touching **Ouvanou Memorial** (p154) to 10 local Kanaks who were guillotined by the French in 1868.

➡ **Monument de Balade** (p155), in the undergrowth, unveiled in 1913, celebrating 60 years of French possession.

➡ A **Kanak monument** (p154) in the form of an independence flag, where Kanaks asked for their country back in 2011, 158 years to the day after France took possession at that same spot in 1853.

Tick them off as you find them!

1853	1856	1860	1864
Napoleon III orders the French annexation of New Caledonia on 24 September, predominantly as a possible site for a penal colony. It's now named Nouvelle Calédonie.	Melanesian uprisings indicate opposition to their lands being taken and the creation of a head tax. The first convicts arrive from France to the new penal colony.	The first postal stamps for New Caledonia are issued.	The first convoy of convicts arrives in the new penal colony at Noumea.

In 1853 Napoleon III ordered the annexation of New Caledonia, and the French flag was raised at Balade on 24 September of that year. Britain did not react; however, an article in the Australian *Sydney Morning Herald* criticised Britain for not beating the French to colonise New Caledonia, a strategic point on the trade route between Australia and China and the west coast of America. There was also a negative reaction to France's plans to establish New Caledonia as a penal colony after the recently won struggle to abolish convict transportation to Australia (1852).

The Penal Colony

The first convict ships arrived in May 1864 at Port-de-France (present-day Noumea) after an arduous six-month journey from France. Convicts carried out the colony's public works, including the construction of Noumea's Cathédrale St Joseph.

Between 1887 and 1895 the toughest convicts were sent to Camp Brun, where conditions were so harsh that it was known as 'the slaughterhouse'.

France continued to send convicts to New Caledonia until 1897; around 22,000 to 25,000 hard-labour convicts and petty offenders in total were transported. Once freed, the majority of ex-convicts were obliged to settle in the colony since hard-labour convicts sentenced to eight years or more were subject to 'perpetual residence in the colony' even after they had served their sentence.

Convicts faced a long journey from France to New Caledonia: 1864 – six months in a sailing ship via the Cape of Good Hope; 1897 – 1½ months in steamship via Suez Canal.

The Communards Arrive (Then Go Again)

In 1871, following the Paris Commune uprising, some 4300 political deportees or Communards were banished to New Caledonia. Unlike hard-labour convicts, Communards were not imprisoned but were restricted to certain areas. Most Communards were sent to Île des Pins. Among the more famous of these was Henri Rochefort, a newspaper editor who had been a member of parliament in 1869. Another well-known deportee was the feminist and anarchist Louise Michel.

By 1879 a series of pardons for the Communards was granted, allowing many of them to return to France (which most did).

The Revolt of 1878

In the 1860s and 1870s, aided by the discovery of nickel in 1864, a program was set up to bring settlers from France. Hostilities between the Kanaks and the French arose as the settlers encroached on tribal lands. The process of taking Melanesian land began in earnest under Governor Guillain (1862–70). Large tracts of land were taken over for cattle farming,

1864	1867	1878	1894
Engineer Jules Garnier discovers nickel in New Caledonia. It turns out the country has 25% of the world's supply.	The guillotine is first brought to the country. Some 80 people are beheaded over the next 21 years.	A Kanak revolt led by Chief Ataï against land appropriation by French settlers claims more than 1000 lives. The resulting system puts Kanaks outside common law; they become second-class citizens.	The penal colony is terminated by Governor Feillet, leading to waves of immigration from France and Indonesia. The new population staffs the mining industry.

destroying the Kanaks' taro and yam beds and wrecking their irrigation channels.

Some of the best land was taken from Chief Ataï for an extension of the La Foa penitentiary, which led to the revolt of 1878. The revolt, led by Ataï, broke out around La Foa and Boulouparis. It continued for seven months, involving clans all the way from Boulouparis to Poya. The French military eventually crushed the revolt with the help of allied Kanak tribes. In all, 200 French and 1200 Kanaks, including Ataï, were killed.

The Kanak Population Halves

The *indigénat* system, instituted by the French soon after the 1878 revolt, became the most damning aspect of colonisation. This system put Kanaks outside of French common law, legally giving them a subordinate status. The locals were forced into reservations in the mountainous highlands, which they could leave only with police permission. Interisland trading routes among Kanaks were halted and religious or ancestral ties to sites and places were ignored. They were forced to work for settlers or the colonial authorities.

KANAK DEPORTATION

In New Caledonia itself, the sentence for those of the Kanak population who were found guilty of political insurrection or activities hostile to French rule was exile to Île des Pins, the Loyalty Islands or deportation to penal institutions in other French colonies. In many cases, particularly those of mass exile or deportation, the damage to Kanak society as a whole was devastating.

Chiefs were invariably sentenced to deportation. In 1858 Chief Bouarate of Hienghène was found guilty of plotting against the French and of hostility towards French missionaries, and was deported to the Fort of Taravao in Tahiti. Nine years later, 13 Kanaks from Pouébo were sentenced to exile with hard labour on the island of Lifou. The 10 who survived were later deported to the prison of Poulo Condor in Cochinchina (now southern Vietnam); their Chief, Ouarébate, was deported to Tahiti. All had been found guilty of crimes committed during an uprising.

The Kanak revolt of 1878 was, for the most part, punished by internal exile to the Île des Pins or the Îles Bélep in the north.

And it wasn't only convicts and French political detainees who were shipped to New Caledonia by the French. If you are driving on RT1 southeast of Bourail, check out the **Arab Cemetery & Memorial** (p149). The memorial is dedicated to Arabs, Kabyles, Algerians, Moroccans and Tunisians who were sent to New Caledonia between 1864 and 1896. Most took part in uprisings against French colonial rule in their homelands.

1897	1899	1917	1942
Convict transportation ends after some 22,000 criminal and political prisoners have been transported from France.	A head tax is imposed on male Kanaks to encourage them to seek work with settlers and the colonial government.	Another Kanak revolt, this time to oppose forced recruitment into the French army during WWI.	US troops (some 50,000 of them) arrive when the US army sets up a WWII base in New Caledonia.

When the flow of convicts stopped in 1897, the settlers' free-labour supply was extinguished; Kanaks were soon brought in to fill the convicts' place. The metallurgical industry, whose mines had previously been worked by hundreds of convicts, faced the same labour crisis. The flow of foreign labour – mainly from Indonesia, Indochina and Japan – that began in the early 1890s increased.

The Kanak population began to decline, dropping from 42,500 in 1887 to only 28,000 in 1901. The *indigénat* system was reviewed every decade until WWII, with the French authorities deciding on each occasion that the natives hadn't reached sufficient moral or intellectual standards to run their own affairs. Not until 1946, when the system was abolished, were they allowed to leave their reservations without permission.

The World Wars

During WWI, 2145 men from New Caledonia, including 1005 Kanaks, were sent to the French and Turkish fronts. Nearly 600 died, including 382 Kanaks.

The Kanak soldiers had been volunteered by their chiefs under pressure from colonial authorities. This and other factors resulted in the 1917 Kanak revolt in the Koné-Hienghène area led by Chief Noël. Two hundred Kanaks, including Noël, and 11 French died in the uprising.

In 1923 the teaching of French in schools became compulsory and the practices of Kanak medicine men were outlawed, with the threat of jail for anyone practising 'wizardry'.

The US set up a military base on Grande Terre and, in early 1942, 50,000 American and a smaller number of New Zealand personnel arrived. The influence of the Americans, in particular, ushered in a new modern era for New Caledonia.

Much of Grande Terre's infrastructure was built by the Americans during WWII, including a number of airfields, roads and bridges around the island.

The Colony Ends

New Caledonia's status was changed from a colony to a French overseas territory after WWII. In 1946 Kanaks were given French citizenship and progressively, over the next decade, gained the right to vote.

In 1953 the first political party involving Kanaks was formed. Union Calédonienne (UC) was a coalition of Kanaks, white small-scale landowners, the missions and union supporters. The UC was to dominate the New Caledonian political scene over the next two decades. During this period, Roch Pidjot, the man who later became known as the 'grandfather of the independence struggle', became the first Kanak to be elected to the French National Assembly.

1946	1953	1969–72	1984–88
New Caledonia becomes a French Overseas Territory and Kanaks get the right to vote.	French citizenship is granted to Kanaks for the first time.	Nickel boom attracts 20,000 to 25,000 immigrants from France. For the first time the Melanesian population is a minority.	A period of violent confrontations known as Les Évènements occurs throughout New Caledonia between pro-independence and loyalist supporters.

The Independence Movement

Ouvéa, in the Loyalty Islands, has two indigenous languages. Iaaï is of Melanesian origin, while Faga-uvéa is spoken in the south and north of the island by descendants of Polynesian migrants who arrived in the 16th and 17th centuries.

A new political consciousness was raised by the first Kanak university students, who returned from France in 1969 having witnessed the student protests in Paris the year before.

With the evolution of independence in Fiji (1970) and Papua New Guinea (1975), new political groups formed and wanted more than the limited autonomy that the UC had previously aspired to. In 1975 the Kanak leader Yann Celene Uregei first spoke of independence. In the 1979 territorial assembly, the majority of Kanak parties united to form the Front Indépendentiste (Independence Front).

In 1977 the loyalist party Rassemblement pour Calédonie dans la République (RPCR) was set up by Jacques Lafleur. It became the main adversary of the pro-independence movement.

In 1983 round-table talks were held in France between the government and pro- and anti-independence leaders, at which France accepted the right of the Kanak people to independence. In turn, the pro-independence leaders recognised that other communities in the territory, principally the Caldoches (descendants of French settlers), were 'victims of history' and had as much right to live in New Caledonia as the Kanaks.

Les Évènements

The turning point for the independence movement came in 1984, the year that Les Évènements (the Events) began. In 1984 the Front Indépendentiste, along with other pro-independence parties, became the Front de Libération Nationale Kanak et Socialiste (FLNKS) with Jean-Marie Tjibaou at its helm.

The FLNKS immediately boycotted the forthcoming territorial election and proclaimed the Provisional Government of Kanaky, presided over by Tjibaou. Ten days later, mixed-race settlers killed 10 Kanaks near Hienghène. With the country on the brink of civil war, a referendum on independence and self-government 'in association' with France was proposed in January 1985; the independence movement rejected it.

France decided to usher in a new program of land reforms and increased autonomy for Kanaks. After the French legislative elections in May 1986, an uneasy calm prevailed as the new conservative minister in charge of the territory stripped the four regional councils of much of their autonomy and abolished the office that had been buying back land for Kanaks.

A referendum on the question of independence was scheduled for late 1987. The FLNKS wanted eligible voters to consist only of Kanaks and those people who were born in the territory with at least one parent also of New Caledonian birth. With a UN resolution backing this demand,

1986	1988	1988	1988
New Caledonia is placed on the UN's list for decolonisation, with France required to take immediate steps towards the 'complete independence and freedom' of the territory.	Nineteen Kanak separatists are killed after taking 27 people hostage in an Ouvéa cave and demanding independence.	Matignon Accords signed on 26 June, outlining a 10-year period of development and greater autonomy from France.	The country is divided into three regions: the Southern Province, the Northern Province and the Loyalty Islands Province.

the FLNKS decided, if France would not agree to it, that it would boycott the referendum.

In December 1986, the UN General Assembly voted in favour of New Caledonia's reinscription on the UN's decolonisation list. It was an important step towards independence, as it gave international credence to the territory's right to self-government.

On 13 September 1987, the referendum on independence was held and boycotted by 84% of Kanaks. Of the 59% of eligible voters (everyone who had lived in the country for more than three years, including the nickel-boom immigrants of the 1960s and 1970s) who cast a ballot, 98% were against independence. The referendum was viewed as a resounding victory by loyalists in the territory and the conservative French government.

The French National Assembly approved a new plan for the territory put forward by the government and called an election for 24 April 1988. The new plan redefined the four regional council boundaries so that the Kanaks were likely to lose one region and be left with the country's most underdeveloped and resourceless areas.

In April 1988, just before the French presidential elections, the Ouvéa crisis erupted, when members of a separatist group took 27 people hostage and demanded instant independence for New Caledonia. An attempt to end the situation resulted in the deaths of 19 hostage-takers and two members of the military. The Socialists were returned to power in France and a concerted effort was made to end the bloodshed in New Caledonia.

NEW CALEDONIAN HISTORY LES ÉVÈNEMENTS

MEMORIAL CULTURAL CENTRES

Pro-independence Kanak leader Jean-Marie Tjibaou and and his second in command, Yeiwene Yeiwene, were assassinated in 1989 on Ouvéa as they attended the one-year memorial of the 1988 Ouvéa crisis, in which 21 people died. They were killed by Djubelly Wéa, another Kanak, who believed they had given in to France and betrayed their people by signing the Matignon Accord.

In Noumea the spectacular **Tjibaou Cultural Centre** (p131), opened in 1998, the same year the Noumea Accord was signed, should not be missed. As a tribute to Tjibaou, and for its design by Italian architect Renzo Piano, who also designed Paris' Pompidou Centre, it is a must on any itinerary to New Caledonia.

On the Loyalty Island of Maré, the less-grand **Centre Culturel Yeiwene Yeiwene** (p156) is tribute to a hometown hero. His statue stands out front.

On Ouvéa, and well worth a visit, is a large, impressive **memorial** (p161) featuring photos of the 19 Kanaks who died there in 1988.

1989	1998	2006	2008
Jean-Marie Tjibaou, leader of the pro-independence FLNKS, is assassinated in Ouvéa on 4 May.	Noumea Accord signed on 5 May, establishing 15- to 20-year period of stability and growth towards possible independence; referendum on independence to be held by end 2018.	The French parliament approves plans to ensure that only long-standing residents of New Caledonia can vote in territorial elections, legislation that had long been desired by Kanaks.	New Caledonia's lagoons, including at Ouvéa in the Loyalty Islands, are designated a Unesco World Heritage site.

The Matignon Accord

In June 1988, the newly elected French prime minister, Michel Rocard, brokered the Accords de Matignon. This historic peace agreement was signed at the Hôtel Matignon, the Prime Minister's official residence in Paris, by the two New Caledonian leaders, Tjibaou and Lafleur.

Under the accords, New Caledonia was divided into three regions: the Southern Province, the Northern Province and the Loyalty Islands Province. The accords stated that a referendum on self-determination would be held in 10 years. In May 1989, Tjibaou and his second in command, Yeiwene Yeiwene, were assassinated on the island of Ouvéa by a Kanak extremist who found Tjibaou too moderate.

While the UN put New Caledonia on its decolonisation list in 1986, it will be 2018 before there is a referendum on independence.

The Noumea Accord

As per the Matignon Accords, a new agreement between the FLNKS, RPCR and French government was signed in Noumea in 1998. The Noumea Accord laid out a 15- to 20-year period of growth and development culminating in a referendum on independence.

As part of France's requirements when the UN put New Caledonia on its decolonisation list in 1986, the French state made a compromise with the pro-independence movement through the Noumea Accord of 1998, which mandates that a referendum on self-determination must be held by the second half of 2018. If the independence vote fails, the Accord provides that two more referenda must be held in following years.

The 2014 Elections

Elections were held in May 2014 and due to high Kanak populations, independence candidates won every seat in the Loyalty Islands and 18 of 22 seats in Province Nord (Northern Province). With settler strongholds in Province Sud (Southern Province) and Noumea, however, anti-independence sentiment prevailed. At the 54-member national Congress level, 25 members were pro-independence, while 29 members formed a coalition in fierce opposition to secession.

Those numbers are likely to mean little, however, as a new 2015 electoral law mandated that only indigenous Kanaks and persons enrolled in 1998 will be automatically eligible to vote in the 2018 independence referendum.

2010	2014	2015	2018
Congress votes in favour of a motion to fly the Kanak flag alongside the French tricolour in the territory.	Anti-independence groups win 29 of 54 seats at elections, but pro-independence groups start preparing for self-governance from 2019.	New electoral law mandates that only indigenous Kanaks and persons enrolled in 1998 will be automatically eligible to vote in the 2018 independence referendum.	A referendum on self-determination must be held by the second half of 2018.

New Caledonian Environment

Needless to say, this remote island country in the southwest Pacific, with its World Heritage-listed lagoon, has a stunning natural environment. It also has 25% of the world's nickel reserves, however, and playing off the country's economic and environmental needs against each other is a continuing problem. Mining keeps the economy afloat, but it also leaves terrible scars on the countryside.

Lay of the Land

Just north of the Tropic of Capricorn in the southwest Pacific Ocean, New Caledonia is made up of an archipelago comprising the main island, Grande Terre (16,350 sq km), Île des Pins (152 sq km), the Loyalty Islands (1980 sq km), the tiny Îles Bélep and various dependencies.

Grande Terre

This mountainous island is 400km long and 50km to 70km wide for most of its length. It is divided by central mountain ranges, the highest peaks being Mont Panié (1629m) on the northeast coast and Mont Humboldt (1618m) in the southeast. From this mountain chain, numerous rivers make their way to the sea, causing sudden floods in the wet season.

Grande Terre's east coast is wet, lush and mountainous, and has a shoreline cut by narrow but deep estuaries. In contrast, the west coast is dry and windy, with wide, grassy coastal plains and large but shallow coastal bays. The bays are lined with mangrove forests. The Far South is mainly an iron plateau, 250m high, with red earth, small natural lakes and marshes.

In contrast to many Pacific islands, Grande Terre was not created by volcanic activity. Rather it was part of Gondwanaland. Grande Terre and New Zealand broke away from eastern Australia about 140 million years ago and, 80 million years later, Grande Terre went its own way. It forms part of the Pacific Ring of Fire and is prone to earthquakes and tsunamis.

Grande Terre is rich in minerals and is one of the biggest nickel reserves in the world.

Offshore Islands

The Loyalty Islands and Île des Pins originated from a chain of submarine volcanoes, which have been inactive for the past 10 million years, situated on the eastern border of the Indo-Australian plate. The Vanuatu Trench, with depths of 7600m or more, passes to the east of the Loyalty Islands in a north–south orientation. All the islands are now highly porous uplifted coral islands, created after the old volcanoes sank and the reef rose around them. The islands are essentially flat, have no rivers, but plenty of caves. Fresh water is caught in water tables.

The Reef

New Caledonia has 1600km of reef, which is the second-longest in the world after Australia's Great Barrier Reef and has been placed on Unesco's World Heritage list. The main barrier reef encompasses Grande Terre. Its western side is 600km long, while the eastern flank extends for 540km. It creates a magnificent 23,500-sq-km turquoise lagoon, the largest enclosed lagoon in the world. It is about 25m deep on the west coast and averages 40m in depth on the east. In addition to the barrier reef, close-to-shore fringing reefs surround all the smaller outlying islands.

Flora & Fauna

Animals & Reptiles

Back in 1862, 12 rusa deer were introduced to New Caledonia. Today their numbers are estimated at more than 100,000.

Around 4500 species of terrestrial animal life have been identified in New Caledonia, predominantly birds, reptiles and some mammals.

Of the few land mammals in New Caledonia, only *roussettes* (members of the flying fox or fruit-bat family) are indigenous. There are four species; one, the rock flying fox, is endemic and endangered. These nocturnal creatures live in 'camps' in trees and fly at sunset, travelling up to 15km in search of food, before returning at dawn. They are a traditional Kanak food source, although hunting is restricted and illegal at nesting or sleeping sites.

New Caledonia's rusa deer is one of the largest of its species. The deer have now reproduced to such an extent that they are creating major damage to native plants and the environment in general. You can see deer farms on the west coast.

New Caledonia is home to 107 endemic reptiles, including the world's largest gecko, the rare *Rhacodactylus leachianus*. It's 35cm in length and lives in rainforest areas.

Birds

The *cagou* is an endemic bird whose call sounds like a dog barking. Ironically, dogs are its main predator since the *cagou* is flightless.

With an estimated 68 species of land birds, about 20 of which are indigenous, New Caledonia holds the interest of ornithologists and amateur bird lovers alike. The most renowned indigenous species is the endangered *cagou (Rhynochetus jubatus)*, New Caledonia's national bird.

Ouvéa, in the Loyalty Islands, is home to the endemic Ouvéa green parrot, back from the brink of extinction due to habitat loss thanks to community efforts to increase its numbers and raise awareness of its plight.

Marine Life

New Caledonia's waters are rich with sea fauna in an amazing spectacle of colour and form. Reef sharks, stingrays, turtles, dugongs, dolphins, colourful gorgonian coral, sponges, sea cucumbers and a multitude of diverse molluscs – including trocchus (*troca*, in French), cowrie and cone shells, giant clams, squid and the beautiful nautilus – all thrive in these waters.

You're likely to see the amphibious *tricot rayé* or banded sea krait – one of New Caledonia's 12 species of sea snakes – which is often sighted on the water's surface or on land. Well adapted to the sea, it has a flattened, paddle-like tail and airtight nostrils, and can stay underwater for up to an hour. Its poison is particularly potent. Although often curious, it is not aggressive unless deliberately provoked or when protecting its nest. It is numerous on the islets around Noumea and particularly on Amédée Islet.

Humpback whales frequent New Caledonian waters between July and September. For a close encounter with one of these magnificent creatures you can do a whale-watching tour off the Far South coast.

Plants

Of the 3250 flowering plant species in New Caledonia, 80% are native. A great deal of New Caledonia has been stripped of its virgin forest. At present 4000 sq km, or around 20% of the land, is still covered by indigenous forest.

Interesting trees include the *Araucaria columnaris,* a columnar pine that can stand an impressive 60m in height and has a diameter of 2m. The banyan *(Ficus prolixa)* has a wide canopy and big aerial roots. The houp *(Montrouziera cauliflora)* is an endemic slow-growing hardwood

THE NAUTILUS

Unchanged for more than 100 million years, nautili are living fossils, the only survivors of a family that was common 450 million years ago and also included ammonites (whirled shells like a ram's horn). It's a mystery why most of this group suddenly disappeared 70 million years ago. There are six remaining species of nautili living in the southwest Pacific, one of which, *Nautilus macromphalus,* is found only in New Caledonia.

The nautilus is a mollusc; however, it is the only cephalopod to have an external shell. It moves by water expulsion through a siphon and can vary its buoyancy by changing the levels of gas and air in the individual chambers. It avoids light and warm water, and usually lives on the external slopes of the barrier reef at extraordinary depths of up to 500m.

tree with bright red flowers, while the kauri *(Agathis lanceolata),* from the araucaria family, is a conifer heavily forested for its good-quality wood.

Parks & Reserves

The biggest boon for New Caledonia's environment was Unesco's inscription of the Lagoons of New Caledonia (in six clusters) as a World Heritage site in 2008.

Land

Three types of reserves exist: nature reserves, special botanical or fauna reserves, and provincial parks. The level of protection offered varies, but only nature reserves have strict measures limiting access.

Parc Provincial de la Rivière Bleue and Chutes de la Madeleine in the Far South are easily accessible and have good infrastructure, as does Le Parc des Grandes Fougères near La Foa in central Grande Terre.

Marine

The following six areas are inscribed as Unesco's Lagoons of New Caledonia World Heritage listing: Grand Lagon Sud (3145 sq km); Côtière Ouest (482 sq km); Côtière Nord-Est (3714 sq km); Grand Lagon Nord (6357 sq km); Atolls d'Entrecasteaux (1068 sq km); and Atoll d'Ouvéa et Beautemps-Beaupré (977 sq km).

Environmental Issues

Traditionally, Kanaks had a very sensible relationship with the environment, considering it their *garde-manger* (food safe), which meant the territory had to be managed properly in order to provide a sustainable food supply. This contrasts greatly with modern-day capitalist attitudes and practices such as mining, deforestation and cattle farming.

Open-cut nickel mining has caused deforestation, erosion, pollution of rivers, streams and lagoons, and reef damage. The last has occurred particularly along the midsection of the east coast of Grande Terre, as the run-off from the stripped mountains pours straight into the sea.

Emissions from Doniambo nickel smelter in Noumea are also a serious issue. International health agencies, such as the US Department of Health and Human Services, have classified nickel as an extremely hazardous substance and have recognised that it can induce asthma. Measures to analyse the air in the greater Noumea region were only introduced in 2005.

Vale Nouvelle-Calédonie's Goro nickel processing plant in the Far South has caused plenty of controversy with its chemical extraction methods; there have been reports of breaks in its equipment and leaks of diluted hydrochloric acid and dispersed solvents.

Bushfires, which cause erosion and desertification, are a huge problem, despite public-awareness campaigns calling for vigilance and responsible action. Fires are often deliberately lit to clear land for agriculture and for hunting wild pigs (in order to herd them into specific areas).

Driving around Grande Terre it's impossible to miss the nickel mines. It's a huge industry; about 80% of New Caledonia's foreign earnings come from the export of nickel.

Traditional Kanak Culture

In traditional life the clan, not the individual, was the important element in Kanak society. Life was based on communal principles achieved through village living. Village life ensured that nobody went hungry or was uncared for. In return, everyone reaped the rewards. The ancient Kanak code of *la coutume* kept this system alive and it provided a common bond and understanding between all Kanaks. This aspect of Kanak culture is very much alive today.

The People

The Kanaks, the indigenous Melanesian inhabitants of New Caledonia, make up about 40% of the country's population.

Kanak is the local name given to New Caledonian Melanesians. The term Melanesians refers to the group of people who inhabit the islands in the southwest Pacific.

The term 'Kanak' (or *canaque,* as the French originally spelt it) was invented by early Europeans living in Polynesia. It is probably derived from the word 'Kanakas', which was used for people from the South Pacific who were abducted by blackbirders (slavers) to work in Australia and other places in the 19th century. The word was viewed by New Caledonia's indigenous people as an insult and it eventually died out as the French colonial authorities preferred to use *indigène* (native). It wasn't until the early 1970s, when political consciousness and cultural revival were on the agenda, that New Caledonia's indigenous people proudly reclaimed the name Kanak.

The large majority live in clan communities known as *tribus,* inland or along Grande Terre's east coast, on Île des Pins and on the Loyalty Islands. In recent decades many Kanaks have left their traditional life in search of work and education in Noumea but they still maintain a strong attachment to their *tribus.*

The Clan

Some 300 clans are believed to have existed when Europeans first arrived. The missionaries coined the term 'tribe' to describe a clan or subclan (*la tribu,* in French). Each clan lived in its own *tribu* and had its own totem; clan names were often derived from its totem. The clan's lineage continued through the bloodline of one person and was linked or related to a spiritual ancestor. Relationships with these ancestors and the spirit world were strong, and were demonstrated by symbolic festivals and dances. Each clan had its own traditions and legends. Bridal exchanges and polygamy meant many villages were interrelated. The clan's activity centred on the largest hut, the *grande case,* where the chief lived.

The Chief

Men became chiefs either on a hereditary basis or were appointed for their skills. In this oral society, eloquence was highly revered and the greatest chiefs were those who could best use the power of words. The chief administered justice and, when necessary, declared wars.

Assistance was given to him through a council of elders, made up of the oldest men of each family in the clan. Today, the chief represents or speaks for the local community.

The Women's Clan

In Kanak culture a woman generally becomes a member of her husband's family after marriage, and children are named after the father. However, when a child is born, it is permanently linked to its mother's clan through the mother's brother, known as the 'maternal' uncle. The maternal uncle takes on a role in the child's life that is more important than that of the father, because he is the child's guardian and lifetime mentor.

The missionaries deemed the traditional grass skirts worn by women to be immodest and instead introduced the Kanak or 'Mother Hubbard' dress. This shin-length, loose-fitting dress, usually adorned with lace, is still the preferred dress of many Kanak women today.

There are 28 distinct Kanak languages, as well as many dialects, spoken in New Caledonia. These are out of the 1200 Melanesian languages spoken throughout the southwest Pacific.

Kanak Custom

La coutume (custom) is the essential component of Kanak identity. This code for living encompasses rites, rituals and social interaction between and within the clans, and maintains the all-important link with the ancestors. Nowadays, modernity often clashes with *la coutume.*

The exchange of gifts is an important element of *la coutume,* as it creates a much-revered network of mutual obligations. The one who offers a gift receives prestige from this action while placing an obligation, which is never ignored, on the receiver to respond. After a gift is given discussions relevant to the event (such as a marriage, mourning, a festival or the welcoming of visitors) are held.

When Kanaks enter the home of a chief, they offer a small token as a sign of respect and to introduce themselves: a few metres of cloth, money

THE GRANDE CASE

The *grande case,* or 'big hut', is one of the strongest symbols of the Kanak community. The same building pattern has been followed for centuries; it is the widest and tallest *case* in each clan settlement, and traditionally home to the chief. Today, the chiefs all have modern homes, called *chefferies,* located close to the *grande case,* where the tribal gatherings and discussions still take place.

In building a *grande case,* the central pillar, an immense trunk of a carefully chosen tree, is erected first. It will support the entire *case* and symbolises the chief (in a normal *case,* it represents the family's head). A stone hearth, where a fire is lit for warmth during the cool months, is laid between this post and the door. Smoke from the fire also helps keep the thatch waterproof.

The entrance to the *grande case* is via a low doorway flanked by wide wooden boards. These are often carved in the form of a face and called *katara,* meaning 'the sentinel who reports the arrival of strangers'. Inside, the walls and ceiling are lined with wooden posts or beams lashed to the frame with strong vines, all of which lean against the central pillar, symbolising the clan's close link with the chief. Finally, a *flèche faîtière* (carved rooftop spear) is erected on the roof and traditional money is hung or buried nearby, providing an important link with the ancestral and spiritual world.

Replicas of *grandes cases* from various parts of New Caledonia can be seen at the Tjibaou Cultural Centre in Noumea. It's possible to spend the night in *cases,* especially at gîtes on the Loyalty Islands and Île des Pins. The room will be swept, mats will be laid out and your bed (a mattress on the floor) will be made up in clean cotton sheets and placed on the floor. They're usually very comfortable, with lights and power points making them quite 21st century.

TIPS ON MEETING KANAKS

In rural areas, even if you're inside a vehicle passing pedestrians, you'll find you do a lot of waving.

The ancient Kanak customary law of offering visitors food persists. Arriving in a village, you may be invited to share a cup of tea or coffee, or even an entire meal in the house of someone you met only 10 minutes earlier. Nothing more than a 'thank you' is expected in return if you are just passing through. However, if you stay a day or so, out of politeness you should present your host with food or a 500 CFP or 1000 CFP note.

Do not enter a *tribu* (clan community) wearing just swimwear or revealing shorts. Women should make sure their skirts or pants are of a 'decent' length and men shouldn't be bare-chested. Dressing in revealing clothes is OK around the beach suburbs of Noumea, but everywhere outside the capital it's frowned upon. Going topless is fine on Noumean beaches but it's not accepted outside the capital.

Traditional Kanak cemeteries are the abode of the ancestors and, unless you have permission from tribal elders, you should not enter these places.

Visitors are expected to ask permission from local people before exploring forests, swimming in *trous* (deep rock pools) or wandering around any tribal areas.

and a packet of tobacco. If you're given the rare privilege of being invited to a tribal home, you should respect *la coutume* by bringing a gift as you would in most other cultures. When you want to camp on a clan's ground or visit a site, you should first introduce yourself to the chief or someone from the clan.

Kanak Money

Kanak ancient bead money was not a currency in the common sense of the word, for it was never used for buying or exchanging. Instead, it was given as a customary exchange of respect at a birth, marriage, funeral or other ceremonial event, and as a seal to support and maintain relationships and alliances that had somehow been previously damaged. The money needed long and careful preparation. It was made in the form of the ancestors, with a carved or woven 'head' from which hung a string of pendants, either of bone, shell or herbs, resembling the spinal cord. It was always presented wrapped in a tapa (bark cloth) pouch. Several examples of old Kanak money (and contemporary versions using plastic beads and wool) can be seen at the Musée de Nouvelle-Calédonie in Noumea.

Kanak Flag

Information on Kanak history and culture can be found at the Tjibaou Cultural Centre's website: www.adck.nc.

Chances are that visitors will see the Kanak flag flying all over the country during travels around New Caledonia. In 2010 the Congress voted in favour of a motion to fly the Kanak flag alongside the French tricolour in the territory; it is a common sight, and a call for independence.

The flag is composed of three horizontal stripes of blue, red and green: the blue symbolises both the sky and the ocean surrounding New Caledonia; the red symbolises the blood shed by the Kanaks in their struggle for independence, socialism and unity; the green symbolises the land itself and by extension the ancestors buried within it. One-third of the way along from the left-hand side is a yellow disc representing the sun. This 'sun' is circled in black and on it is a black *flèche faîtière*, a kind of arrow thrust through *tutut* shells, which adorns the roofs of Kanak houses.

Arts & Architecture in New Caledonia

Art in New Caledonia dates back to ancient Lapita pottery from 1500 BC. Today the main fine arts include both traditional and contemporary wood and soapstone sculptures, paintings (including sand and bark paintings), weaving and basketwork. Noumea's Tjibaou Cultural Centre, a splendid example of contemporary architecture, has temporary and permanent exhibitions featuring examples of both traditional and modern art.

Traditional Sculpture

Wood

Traditional Kanak wooden carvings resemble spirits, hawks, ancient gods, serpents and turtles. They were often carved from tree trunks and placed as a palisade or fence around important objects such as the *grande case* (chief's hut). An interesting and easily accessible example of these carvings surrounds a religious memorial near the village of Vao on Île des Pins.

The most important wooden sculpture is the *flèche faîtière,* which resembles a small totem pole with symbolic shapes. War clubs were carved from the strongest trees and were fashioned with a phallic head, known in French as a *casse-tête* (head-breaker). Others featured an equally lethal bird's-beak club, or *bec d'oiseau.*

In conflicts, spears made from niaouli trees were used; these were often lit and thrown into the enemy's hut to set it alight.

Today the art of wood sculpture is alive and well in New Caledonia and continues to embody the spirit of Kanak culture. Sculptures can be bought in Noumea, and from roadside stalls along the northeast coast. Prices are considerably cheaper at these stalls than in Noumea.

Stone

The most important stone artefact in New Caledonia is the ceremonial axe, a symbol of a clan's strength and power. It was generally used to decapitate enemies during a battle or to honour ancestors during *pilou*

PETROGLYPHS

Petroglyphs, or rock carvings, are found throughout the Pacific, including in New Caledonia and Vanuatu. There are more than 350 sites in New Caledonia, with more than 4500 designs. They are often geometric – spirals, ellipses, crosses and circles – and sometimes resemble animal or human shapes. The meaning or purpose of petroglyphs remains something of a mystery, as does their age. One theory is that these rock carvings were used to mark out territory at the beginning of the 1st millennium, when tribe numbers were increasing and battles became more frequent. They're not easily seen, apart from at the **Musée de Nouvelle-Calédonie** (p129) in Noumea. There is a site by the main road near Païta; otherwise, if you stay at a Kanak homestay you should ask whether there are any sites in the vicinity.

(traditional Kanak dance) celebrations. The stone of this axe, usually green jade or serpentine, is polished smooth until it resembles a disk. Two holes like eyes are drilled into the central area of the stone, and a handle made of flying-fox fur is woven through these holes and fastened. The bottom of the handle is adorned with stones and shells, with each pendant serving as a symbolic reference to a particular clan.

Soapstone carvings are commonly made and sold from curio shops in Noumea, as well as from roadside stalls along the northeast coast. Prices for a small piece depicting an ancestor's face range from about 700 CFP in *la brousse* (the bush) to 2000 CFP from a shop in the capital.

Frimeurs des Iles, by Niko and Solo, is a popular, long-running cartoon about two New Caledonian beach bums.

Bamboo Engraving

Between 1850 and 1920, anthropologists collected intricately engraved bamboo canes from Kanak communities. As most of these canes date from around the arrival of Europeans, it's unclear whether cane engraving was a form of traditional art dating back many centuries or simply a fad of the time.

The canes averaged 1m in length and were used by Kanaks in dance ceremonies or when entering a village. They contained magic herbs that warded off evil spirits and were covered with designs. The designs were mostly geometrical, although real images – ranging from the *pilou* dance to agricultural motifs and village scenes such as fishing or building a *case* (hut) – were also often portrayed. The canes were held over fire to give the engraved areas a black patina.

The Musée de Nouvelle-Calédonie in Noumea has a good collection of these old canes on display. Contemporary Kanak artist Micheline Neporon is well known in this field. She has held exhibitions in New Caledonia and has participated in international arts festivals.

Dance

There are many different styles of dance that are currently popular in New Caledonia including *pilou,* Tahitian, Vietnamese and Indonesian dance. Performances are held regularly at festivals and other public events such as the Jeudis du Centre Ville.

Literature

The website of the popular comic book series *La Brousse en Folie* by Bernard Berger (www. brousse-en-folie. com) has loads of information on New Caledonian society.

New Caledonia has several book publishers and many authors who make up a dynamic literary scene.

Prominent writers include Bernard Berger, a Caledonian cartoonist. His *Brousse en Folie* comic book series is immensely popular. Pierre Gope is a Kanak writer whose works include poetry and plays. Déwé Gorodey is a Kanak politician and writer who evokes the struggle for independence in her writing and gives a feminist view of Kanak culture. Claudine Jacques is a French-born fiction writer worth looking out for. Nicolas Kurtovitch is a Caledonian who writes poetry, short stories and plays, and Paul Wamo is a leading Kanak slam poet.

Traditional Music

Music-making is an important element of traditional ceremonies such as initiation, courting or the end of mourning, and always accompanies dance and song. Sometimes instruments are played simply for the clan's entertainment. Above all, however, Kanak music is vocal.

The following (with Anglicised names) are some of the instruments used in ancient Kanak culture:

Bamboo stamping tubes Struck vertically against the ground and played at main events.

Coconut-leaf whizzer A piece of coconut leaf attached to a string and twirled, producing a noise like a humming bee.

EXPLORING THE HISTORIC BUILDINGS OF NOUMEA

Ville de Noumea produces the booklet *Le Circuit Historique*, which includes information about the history of Noumea and a walking tour (with a map) of some of the more significant buildings. Many examples of colonial architecture remain, though their use has changed. For instance, the original Hotel de Ville (c 1874) is now the **Musée de la Ville de Noumea** (p129). Its basement is particularly evocative. The Ancien Commissariat de Police (c 1893), with its corner location and wide balconies, resembles a typical Australian pub.

Conch or Triton's shell Used like a trumpet on special occasions and played by a special appointee.

End-blown flute Made from a 50cm-long hollowed-out pawpaw-leaf stem. The pitch varies depending on the position of the lips and how forcefully the air is blown through the flute.

Jaw harp (*Wadohnu* in the Nengone language where it originated) Made from a dried piece of coconut-palm leaf held between the teeth and an attached segment of soft nerve leaf. When the harp is struck, the musician's mouth acts as an amplifying chamber, producing a soft, low sound.

Oboe Made from hollow grass stems or bamboo.

Percussion instruments These include hitting sticks, palm sheaths that are strummed or hit, and clappers made from a hard bark filled with dried grass and soft niaouli bark, that are tied together and hit against each other.

Rattles Worn around the legs and made from coconut leaves, shells and certain fruits.

Music Today

In addition to popular Western music and hip hop, reggae has a huge following. Throughout New Caledonia you can see Kanaks wearing reggae colours of green, yellow and red. The popular local music known as Kaneka is a mixture of reggae and traditional Kanak rhythms. For examples of Kaneka bands and other music from the Pacific see www.adck.nc.

A CD worth purchasing and popping into the hire car's player is *Carnet de Voyage*. It features 27 songs and poems from the different islands of New Caledonia.

Architecture

Colonial buildings with ornate wrought iron or wood trimming around their roofs and balconies are one of the most aesthetic elements of New Caledonia's architectural heritage. Noumea has some beautiful examples of colonial houses. The imposing Cathédral St Joseph was built in 1890 and the wonderful Bibliothéque Bernheim was built in 1900.

To see a traditional Kanak *case* in Noumea you will have to visit the Tjibaou Cultural Centre (p131) or Musée de Nouvelle-Calédonie (p129). In the Loyalty Islands, however, they are plentiful, especially on Lifou, where there is at least one *case* inside almost every family compound. If you detour off the main road you will also see them in many *tribus* (clan communities) on Grande Terre.

For contemporary architecture, the Tjibaou Cultural Centre is a must-see work of art. The centre sits on a peninsula that is surrounded by mangroves. Internationally renowned Italian architect Renzo Piano has blended his contemporary design harmoniously into its natural environment.

Not only is the Tjibaou Cultural Centre an amazing piece of architecture, it also has regular outdoor concerts featuring local artists and, inside, excellent changing exhibitions of art, with a focus on New Caledonia today and in history.

New Caledonia's Local Food

Eating in New Caledonia is an absolute delight. Outdoor markets burst with colour and life, and there's always a little surprise to be found, such as plump, just-baked chocolate cake for sale in a remote regional market. In restaurants and even fast-food snack bars, even the simplest-sounding dish will be a taste-sensation. As in most other Pacific countries, New Caledonia's staple foods are fish, coconut, banana, taro, sweet potato and yam.

Local Produce

Lobster, coconut crab, dugong and turtle are all traditional Kanak food sources. These days the number of turtles and dugongs that can be hunted for food is limited and their killing for commercial purposes is prohibited.

Various local recipes exist for cooking *roussette*, a fruit-eating bat, but most commonly it's boiled, the skin removed and the flesh cooked in coconut cream.

A variety of nuts – such as the candlenut (known as *'tai'* in Kanak) and pandanus nuts – are eaten, as are the seeds from breadfruit, pawpaw, watermelon and pumpkin.

One of the most famous nuts is the coconut, which grows on palm trees that can live for up to 80 years. Coconuts usually take a year to ripen – they're ready when you can hear the juice shaking around inside. The less developed the coconut, the sweeter the juice, which is why many people cut off the tops when the outside husk is still green and drink the milk. Even when young, the soft coconut flesh is tasty, although the flavour increases with age.

While there's a decent range of fruit, New Caledonia does not have the abundance of tropical delights you might expect on a Pacific island and, in large supermarkets, imported fruits usually outnumber local produce. Seasonal fruits include avocados, passion fruit, mangoes, pineapples, custard apples, watermelons and citrus fruits such as oranges and pomelos. Bananas, coconuts and pawpaws are available year-round.

The Avocado Festival is not limited to avocados; like most regional festivals, it's a celebration of all things edible. Expect to see stalls selling all sorts of local fruit, vegetables, seafood and meat.

Unripe pawpaw is used in New Caledonia for salads and in cooking. It is grated and sprinkled with a vinaigrette dressing to make a tasty side dish.

Breadfruit trees bear large starchy fruit containing a lot of sugar. As the name suggests, the fruit can be baked or roasted and can replace flour when dried and pounded. The seeds and young leaves of the tree are also eaten.

Guavas grow wild along the roadsides in New Caledonia. The ripe yellow fruit tastes a little like a tomato and has many hard little seeds to spit out. It breaks the record for vitamin content and also contains a lot of pectin (used for making jam).

Drinks

The preferred drinks in New Caledonia are *vin* (wine) and *bière* (beer). The local beers are Number One, Manta and Havannah, brewed at the Grande Brasserie de Nouvelle-Calédonie (GBNC). Heineken and Kronenbourg are also brewed locally. Les 3 Brasseurs (p139) at Baie des Citrons in Noumea is a great pub that brews several of its own beers. Of late in New Caledonia it has become popular to add a lemon taste to beer; one of Manta's most popular beers is Manta Citron.

French, Italian, Australian, New Zealand and Californian wines are all available in supermarkets, although French wine far outnumbers the others. Restaurant prices for wine are up to three times what you'd pay in a shop and, unfortunately, the concept of BYO (bring your own) has not caught on here. There are also typical aperitifs such as *porto* (port) and *pastis,* an aniseed-flavoured drink much loved in France. Mixed with about five parts water, it's strong and refreshing.

Throughout New Caledonia, except on Ouvéa, water is safe to drink. Should you prefer bottled water, several French brands are sold in shops, or there's a local equivalent bottled from a spring at Mont-Dore.

Cafes and restaurants usually serve coffee European-style (enjoy a quick espresso while standing by the bar) and some of the world's best beans are grown here.

> Marist missionaries introduced coffee seeds in 1860 and coffee production has since become an art. Small plantations grow 'Leroy,' or 'Laurina' beans, which are low in caffeine and command some of the highest prices in the world.

NEW CALEDONIA'S LOCAL FOOD DRINKS

Celebrations

Many festivals in New Caledonia are harvest celebrations based around a particular food. These are big public affairs, with food, and arts and craft or produce stalls; festivities usually include singing and dancing. The most important Kanak festival is the Festival of the Yam, which is considered a sacred food. During this, however, there are no public celebrations. Some of the food-related events that you can experience include the following:

➡ **Avocado Festival** May, in Maré

➡ **Prawn & Venison Festival** May, in Boulouparis

➡ **Mandarin Festival** July, in Canala

➡ **Beef Festival** October, in Païta

➡ **Seafood Festival** November, in Poum

➡ **Lychee Festival** December, in Houaïlou

STAPLE ROOT FOODS

Yam The yam is to Pacific islanders what the potato is to Westerners: an energiser. It has a high status in Kanak society and is treated with a reverence normally reserved for elders and ancestors. It's nutritious (particularly rich in vitamins B and C, and in minerals) and grows as a climbing vine. The long, edible roots can be roasted, boiled or used for fritters and in curries.

Sweet potato Originating in South America, this plant has tasty tubers and grows in many varieties. It is associated with the arrival of Polynesians in New Caledonia.

Taro This root plant spread from Southeast Asia long ago and is still widely used, although its cultivation is declining as the consumption of rice takes over. The plant has big, edible leaves and stocky roots about 30cm long. It is an energy booster and is full of fibre, calcium and iron.

Cassava Also called manioc or tapioca, this plant has five to seven lobed leaves. It grows where yam and taro fail. Both roots and leaves are eaten.

PREPARING A BOUGNA

Bougna is the main Melanesian dish in New Caledonia. It's served on special occasions such as traditional festivals, weddings or when welcoming visitors. It is a mixture of yam, sweet potato, taro, vegetables and meat, fish or seafood covered in coconut milk. All the ingredients are cooked together in tightly wrapped parcels made from banana leaves. The parcels are arranged among hot stones in an earth oven and covered with more hot stones. Green leaves are placed on top of the stones to keep in the heat and steam, and the meal is left to cook for 1½ to two hours. It is served piping hot and portions are usually so generous you can't finish them.

Most Melanesian-run gîtes or homestays can prepare a *bougna* but you must order it 24 hours in advance. Expect to pay from 2500 CFP to 4000 CFP per person.

Eating Out

New Caledonia has a wide variety of cuisines, but the most common restaurants you will find are French, Vietnamese, Chinese and Indonesian. There are also a few West Indian, North African, Mexican and Italian restaurants, but these are mainly in Noumea. Outside the capital, restaurants are somewhat scarce and they are usually attached to hotels. The islands and the east coast are your best bet for trying traditional Melanesian fare.

Thanks to the long break in the middle of the day, just as big a fuss is made about lunch as it is about dinner. Restaurants are generally open between the hours of 11am and 2pm, and from 7pm to 11pm. On Sunday many establishments are closed.

French Cuisine

Carpaccio de cerf is a typical Caledonian dish of thinly shaved raw venison sprinkled with olive oil and herbs.

French restaurants abound in Noumea and cover a range of styles. On one street corner there might be a little cafe with filling, but hardly what one would call fine, food and, opposite, there might be an extravagant restaurant specialising in local *fruits de mer* (seafood), *escargots* (snails) from Île des Pins, *venaison* (venison) and other French gourmet dishes.

The best value for money comes by ordering either a *plat du jour* (dish of the day) or a fixed-price, multicourse *menu du jour,* usually referred to simply as a *menu* (we italicise menu to distinguish it from the English word 'menu'). A *menu* generally entitles you to an entrée, main course, dessert, bread and chilled water (and sometimes a small carafe of wine and an espresso).

Melanesian Cuisine

Kanak cuisine is served in most homestays found outside Noumea. Such places often cater to Western tastes, however, so the food isn't necessarily authentically Kanak. *Bougnas* are prepared for tourists on the Loyalty Islands, Île des Pins and the east coast of Grande Terre.

Snacks & Cafes

The cheapest type of restaurant is called a *snack*. These establishments do a swift trade at breakfast and lunch and then close at about 2pm. Some reopen from the late afternoon until about 6pm or 7pm. Trendy French-run cafes don't fit this description, as they generally don't close in the afternoon; they stay open until late at night and their meals are more expensive.

There are a couple of multinational fast-food outlets in Noumea. Most *roulottes* (food vans) offer cheap, filling and delicious options. Noumea also has many sandwich bars, where you can order something quick and easy to take away.

New Caledonia Directory A–Z

Accommodation

There's a great range of accommodation in New Caledonia. Hotels will most certainly have glorious garden or ocean views, and even the most basic bungalows usually have pretty special vistas. Campsites are often beachfront and facilities are usually sparkling clean.

Many budget places on the islands close during the Christmas/New Year period – in some cases closures last for months. Make sure you've got a confirmed booking rather than taking chances around this time of year.

For top-end places, package deals organised before you leave home are often cheaper than booking your accommodation once you arrive.

Accommodation tariffs are firmly set; you'll find them clearly marked at reception desks or in common areas of bungalows or campsites; they're also published in book or brochure form; ask for them at the tourism office.

Accueil en Tribu

Accueil en Tribu or *accueil chez l'habitant,* in French, refer to accommodation offered within a family compound or set apart slightly within a *tribu* (clan community). They're frequently named after someone, for instance 'Chez Jeanne Forrest', which makes them fairly easy to locate when asking around. They are

the best way to meet Kanak people and learn about their culture. Most offer accommodation in *cases* (traditional Kanak houses – there's often just one or two on a property) or bungalows. In most *cases,* guests sleep on mattresses resting on mats on the floor. Some *cases* can sleep up to eight guests. Bungalows will probably have beds.

Homestays generally cost 1000 CFP to 6000 CFP per person per night. Meals (from about 2100 CFP for three courses) can be arranged; organise 24 hours in advance.

Camping

There are numerous campsites everywhere except Noumea. Given the good roads and reasonable hire-car costs, a camping trip around the country is a great way to explore. Many campsites have hot and cold showers, and access to electricity in the shower blocks (but not in the rest of the campsite).

Most gîtes and homestays also have somewhere that you can pitch your tent. Expect to pay a bit more than 1000 CFP to do so, with an extra charge per person (of around 200 CFP). In most cases, prices for camping given in reviews cover a tent and two adults.

Farmstays

Farmstays are the best way to meet Broussards (rural New Caledonians). Guests receive a warm welcome, copious meals and laughter-filled

anecdotes, and are welcome to join in farm activities such as feeding the animals, rounding up cattle or, at night, deer hunting. Farmstays usually offer accommodation in rooms in the family home or in bungalows. Meals are usually part of the experience, so cooking for yourself is often not an option – check beforehand. Rates start at around 8500 CFP per person or double including meals. You will need to order meals 24 hours in advance in most farmstays.

Gîtes

Gîtes (small, very modest hotels) are one of the most common types of accommodation outside of Noumea. They are typically small huts that sleep between two and six people with a separate shared bathroom. Standards range from rustic to very comfortable; either way you can expect the sheets to be fresh and for the space to have had a good sweep out before you arrive. There is usually a restaurant

---

SLEEPING PRICE RANGES

The following price ranges refer to a double room:

$ less than 5000 CFP

$$ 5000–15,000 CFP

$$$ more than 15,000 CFP

or a communal kitchen attached to the gîte. Prices range from around 4000 CFP to 12,000 CFP for one or two people. Bungalows should be booked in advance (they may be closed over certain periods). You'll also need to order your meals 24 hours in advance in most gîtes.

Hostels

Hostel's aren't common. Auberge de Jeunesse in Noumea is the cheapest place to stay in the capital, and it's popular. If it's full (and it often is) staff there can recommend other places to stay. A new purpose-built youth hostel opened at Poé Beach, near Bourail, in 2015.

Hotels

There is a wide range of midrange and top-end hotel accommodation in Noumea. In Grande Terre's larger towns and tourist areas there is usually a midrange hotel or two and there is one on each of the Loyalty Islands.

In Noumea the cheapest hotel rates start at about 5000 CFP for a single or double room, possibly with a kitchenette. At the top end, rates start at 15,000 CFP for a double and can go up to 56,000 CFP – higher if you want a suite.

Customs Regulations

➡ People over 17 years arriving from Europe, Africa, America or Asia may bring in 1000 cigarettes, 2L of wine and 1L of other alcohol.

➡ People over 17 years arriving from Oceania (including Australia) may

bring in 200 cigarettes, 2L of wine and 1L of other alcohol.

Electricity

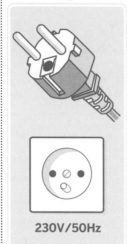

230V/50Hz

Embassies & Consulates

There is no US embassy in New Caledonia. The embassy responsible is in Suva, Fiji.

Australian Consulate (☑27 24 14; http://australian consulatenoumea.embassy.gov. au; 11 Rue Georges Baudoux, Noumea)

Dutch Consulate (☑24 21 21; consulat.pays-bas.noumea@ mls.nc; 33 Rue de Sébastopol, Noumea)

New Zealand Consulate (☑27 25 43; www.nzembassy. com/new-caledonia; 2nd fl, 4 Blvd Vauban, Noumea)

UK Consulate (☑28 21 53; www.gov.uk/government/

world/france; 14 Rue Générale Sarrail, Noumea)

Vanuatuan Consulate (☑27 76 21; 53 Rue de Sébastopol, Noumea)

Food

For more information, see New Caledonia's Local Food (p192).

LGBT Travellers

Homosexuality is legal in New Caledonia but, while there are some open-minded establishments, there are no specifically gay bars.

Insurance

A travel-insurance policy to cover theft, loss and medical problems is a good idea. Check that the policy covers ambulances and emergency flights home.

Worldwide travel insurance is available at www. lonelyplanet.com/travel-insurance. You can buy, extend and claim online anytime – even if you're already on the road.

Internet Access

Most hotels offer free wi-fi access, sometimes in guests' rooms and usually in the lobby. Internet cafes are few and far between. Places where you can get online in the Loyalty Islands are limited. Try the big resorts on the islands for wi-fi access for your laptop or smartphone.

Language Courses

French courses are organised by the Centre of International Cultural & Linguistic Exchanges in the Pacific (http://creipac.nc).

Maps

In Noumea and Anse Vata the Office du Tourisme has good free maps of New Caledonia

---

BOOK YOUR STAY ONLINE

For more accommodation reviews by Lonely Planet authors, check out http://lonelyplanet.com/hotels/. You'll find independent reviews, as well as recommendations on the best places to stay. Best of all, you can book online.

and detailed maps of specific regions.

Marine charts can be purchased at **Marine Corail** (📞27 58 48; 28 Rue du Général Mangin, Noumea).

Money

➡ The currency is the Pacific Franc (CFP), also used in French Polynesia and Wallis & Futuna.

➡ The 5% services tax is usually included in displayed prices.

ATMs

➡ Most banks have ATMs that accept major credit cards.

➡ There are ATMs around Noumea and other major towns and villages – though some are only accessible during the bank's business hours.

➡ Each of the Loyalty Islands and Île des Pins has at least one ATM.

Credit Cards

➡ Credit cards are accepted by hotels, restaurants, large shops and airline offices in Noumea, but not at budget places outside the capital.

➡ There's sometimes a surcharge.

➡ Don't expect to use them in too many places on the islands.

Money Changers

➡ Banks change money and travellers cheques.

➡ All major currencies are accepted, including US, Australian and New Zealand dollars, and euros.

➡ You can also change Vanuatu vatu.

Tipping

A tip is always accepted but it is not common practice.

Opening Hours

Hours may vary, especially in rural areas and outer islands.

Sundays are extremely quiet throughout the islands.

Banks 8am to 4pm Monday to Friday

Cafes 6am to 6pm Monday to Saturday

Government offices 7.30am to 11.30am and 1.30pm to 4.30pm Monday to Friday, some on Saturday mornings

Post offices 7.45am to 3pm Monday to Friday

Restaurants 11am to 2pm and 7pm to 11pm Monday to Saturday

Shops 7.30am to 6pm Monday to Friday and Saturday mornings; some close for lunch

Photography

It's polite to ask before taking photos of people and tribal buildings.

To help get the best out of your camera, get hold of Lonely Planet's *Travel Photography*. Written by internationally renowned travel photographer Richard I'Anson, it's full colour and is designed to be taken on the road.

Post

➡ Poste restante is available at the main post office in Noumea. To receive mail there, use the following address: Poste Restante, Noumea RP, 9 Rue Eugène Porcheron, Noumea, New Caledonia.

➡ Local SIM cards and IZI telephone cards are sold at post offices around the country.

Public Holidays

New Caledonia follows France in all its major public holidays.

New Year's Day 1 January

Easter Monday March/April

Labour Day 1 May

Victory Day 8 May

Ascension Day (40 days after Easter Sunday) May/June

EATING PRICE RANGES

The following price ranges refer to a main meal:

$ less than 1000 CFP

$$ 1000–2500 CFP

$$$ more than 2500 CFP

Whit Monday (The eighth Monday after Easter) May/June

Bastille Day 14 July

Assumption Day 15 August

New Caledonia Day 24 September

All Saints' Day 1 November

Armistice Day 11 November

Christmas Day 25 December

New Year's Eve 31 December

Safety

In general, New Caledonia is very safe for travellers.

➡ Always check that you're not walking or swimming in a taboo area, or on somebody's property.

➡ Along the coast or in the water, be aware of the various venomous sea creatures.

➡ When swimming, snorkelling or diving, don't underestimate the sea's current.

➡ New Caledonia is in a cyclone zone (from November to April) and experiences earthquakes and tsunamis. See www.meteo.nc for more information.

Telephone

There are no local area codes in New Caledonia. The international country code is 📞687. For directory assistance dial 📞1012.

Mobile Phones

➡ Local SIM cards cost 6195 CFP and include 3000 CFP credit; buy these from post offices (you need identification).

➡ Make sure you buy the correct recharge card (Liberté; 1000 CFP), which is available from post offices and tobacconists' stores.

➡ For assistance, dial ☑1000 (free call).

Phonecards

➡ Use IZI cards (1000/3000 CFP) to make local and international calls from a public phone box, a landline or a mobile phone.

➡ Available at post offices around the country and some tobacconists' stores.

Time

➡ GMT/UMT plus 11 hours, one hour ahead of Australian Eastern Standard Time (AEST).

➡ Daylight Savings Time (DST) is not used.

➡ New Caledonia uses the 24-hour clock; when written, the hours are separated from the minutes by a lower-case letter 'h'. Thus, 13h30 is 1.30pm, 20h15 is 8.15pm and 00h45 is 12.45am.

Toilets

➡ Temporary public toilets, signposted as *toilettes* or WC, are plentiful in Noumea, including on the beachfront at Anse Vata and several in Place des Cocotiers.

➡ There are public toilets at the *gare maritime* (boat terminal).

➡ It's best to use the toilets in *snacks* (inexpensive cafes), restaurants, (most) shops and supermarkets.

Tourist Information

The main visitor information office is the **Office de**

Tourisme (☑28 75 80; www. office-tourisme.nc; Place des Co-cotiers; ⊙8am-5.30pm Mon-Fri, 9am-noon Sat) in central Nou-mea. There are also branches at Anse Vata and at Tontouta International Airport, and you'll find small visitor information centres on the islands. Good websites include:

Loyalty Islands (www.iles-loyaute.com)

Office de Tourisme (www. office-tourisme.nc)

Tourism New Caledonia (http://visitnewcaledonia.com)

Visas

To verify the latest visa requirements, check the French government website for New Caledonia: www. nouvelle-caledonie.gouv.fr.

➡ EU, Canadian, US, Australian and NZ citizens are allowed entry into New Caledonia for three months without a visa.

➡ Some visitors, including citizens of Japan, are allowed entry for one month without a visa.

➡ Make sure your passport is valid for at least three months longer than your intended stay and that you have an onward ticket.

Women Travellers

Generally women travellers should have few problems getting around solo in New Caledonia. As in any place, of course, it is best to be cautious if you are on your own.

Work

Non-French citizens need a residency permit and a work permit to work legally in New Caledonia. There is a lot of paperwork involved in getting these permits. You can inquire through the Bureau des Étrangers in Noumea.

PRACTICALITIES

➡ **Drinking** The legal drinking and purchasing age for alcoholic beverages is 18. The blood-alcohol limit for driving is 0.05%.

➡ **Newspapers** *Les Nouvelles Calédoniennes* (www.lnc. nc) is the daily newspaper. *New Caledonia Weekly* (www. newcaledoniaweekly.nc) is a free English-language paper with information about what's on and helpful details for tourists.

➡ **Radio** Radio Nouvelle-Calédonie (http:// nouvellecaledonie.la1ere.fr/radio) is the national radio service. Other radio stations include indigenous station Radio Djiido (www.radiodjiido.nc); Radio Rythme Bleu (www.rrb.nc); Radio Océane (www.oceanefm.nc); and NRJ (www.nrj.nc).

➡ **Smoking** Illegal in enclosed public spaces, including restaurants, bars and nightclubs. Also banned in schools, hospitals, universities and public transport. Advertising of tobacco prohibited.

➡ **Television** Télé Nouvelle-Calédonie (http:// nouvellecaledonie.la1ere.fr) has one local channel, plus a number of French channels; all programs are in French. NC.TV (www.nctv.nc) is New Caledonia's first indigenous television station. Canal Satellite (www.canalplus-caledonie.com) offers a network of pay channels.

➡ **Weights & Measures** Metric system.

New Caledonia Transport

GETTING THERE & AWAY

Air

Airlines

The following airlines fly into New Caledonia. Air France flies code-share with Aircalin (Air Calédonie International). There are connecting flights all over the world with partner airlines, in particular, Air France.

Air France (www.airfrance.com)

Air New Zealand (www.air newzealand.co.nz)

Air Vanuatu (www.airvanuatu.com)

Aircalin (www.aircalin.com)

Qantas (www.qantas.com)

Aircalin has direct flights to:

Australia Sydney, Melbourne, Brisbane

New Zealand Auckland

Japan Tokyo, Osaka

Fiji Nadi

French Polynesia Papeete

Pacific Wallis, Futuna

Vanuatu Port Vila

Airports

Tontouta International Airport (www.tontouta-aeroport. nc) is 45km northwest of Noumea. Get there by public bus or shuttle. Tontouta has the following services:

➡ ATMs and a currency exchange office (exchange currency on arrival before clearing customs)

➡ Tourist information office

➡ All the big rental car outlets. There is no direct connection by public transport between Tontouta and the domestic airport (Magenta). Take a taxi or prearrange a shuttle.

Sea

Cruise Ship

An endless stream of cruise ships visit New Caledonia.

➡ Cruise ships dock at Noumea's *gare maritime* (boat terminal).

➡ A tourist information booth and a market opens at *gare maritime* on 'cruise-ship days'.

➡ Ships also often stop at Lifou and Île des Pins.

➡ P&O (www.pocruises.com. au) has regular services.

Yacht

New Caledonia welcomes thousands of yachties every year.

➡ All yachts arriving in New Caledonia should proceed to Port Moselle, Noumea. All entry formalities are now only handled in Noumea.

➡ Yachts are not permitted to stop or anchor anywhere in New Caledonian territorial waters before having visited Noumea and completed formalities.

➡ See www.noonsite.com for up-to-date details.

CLIMATE CHANGE & TRAVEL

Every form of transport that relies on carbon-based fuel generates CO_2, the main cause of human-induced climate change. Modern travel is dependent on aeroplanes, which might use less fuel per kilometre per person than most cars but travel much greater distances. The altitude at which aircraft emit gases (including CO_2) and particles also contributes to their climate change impact. Many websites offer 'carbon calculators' that allow people to estimate the carbon emissions generated by their journey and, for those who wish to do so, to offset the impact of the greenhouse gases emitted with contributions to portfolios of climate-friendly initiatives throughout the world. Lonely Planet offsets the carbon footprint of all staff and author travel.

WHERE AM I?

In New Caledonia it is easy to get confused with place names as locations often have more than one name or different spellings.

On the northeast coast of Grande Terre, road signs indicate two variations for each place name; the original Kanak name and the contemporary version (usually a French misrepresentation of the original). However, it is not uncommon for a place name to have three or four variations. We use the most common names and spellings.

➡ Visit www.cruising-newcaledonia.com for a good cruising guide.

GETTING AROUND

Air

Air Calédonie

Air Calédonie (☑25 21 77; www.air-caledonie.nc; 39 Rue de Verdun; ☺8am-4pm Mon-Fri, to 11.30am Sat), New Caledonia's domestic airline, flies out of Magenta domestic airport in Noumea.

Air Calédonie destinations include the following:

Northern Province Koné, Koumac, Touho

Southern Province Île des Pins

Loyalty Islands Lifou, Maré, Ouvéa

There are three levels of ticket prices: Promo Fare, Flexible Fare and Flexible fare with 20kg baggage. The earlier you purchase, the better the chance of getting a cheap fare.

Air Calédonie is very strict on weight for checked and cabin baggage. Expect cabin baggage to be weighed. Unless you have a 'Flexible fare with 20kg baggage' ticket, you are restricted to 12kg for checked baggage and 3kg for cabin baggage.

See the website for flight schedules, Air Pass details and booking facilities. Air Calédonie has agencies at all flight destinations, and a ticket office at Magenta domestic airport.

Air Loyauté

Air Loyauté (☑25 37 09; www.air-loyaute.nc) flies between Lifou, Maré, Ouvéa and tiny Tiga in the Loyalty Islands. It has smaller aircraft than Air Calédonie and is very competitive on price.

Airports

Noumea's domestic airport is **Magenta**, about 5km east of the city centre. It's accessed by bus 40 in 15 to 20 minutes. There is a cafe, ticketing office and information office on-site, but no wi-fi.

Each of the Loyalty Islands and Île des Pins has a small, but efficient airport with daily services to Noumea.

Air Passes

The Air Calédonie Pass offers a 32,800 CFP coupon deal for four domestic flight segments. This pass is sold through the **Air Calédonie** (☑25 21 77; www.air-caledonie.nc; 39 Rue de Verdun; ☺8am-4pm Mon-Fri, to 3pm Sat) office in Noumea. It's great in theory, however:

➡ There are a limited number of pass seats for each flight.

➡ You cannot buy extra coupons.

➡ You need to send a copy of your passport.

Bicycle

You'd have to be very keen to cycle around 400km-long Grande Terre. Drivers speed mercilessly, road-death rates are horrendous, and drivers are not particularly courteous to cyclists.

Ouvéa and Île des Pins, however, are ideal for cycling. Bikes can be transported on the *Betico* ferry.

Boat

Betico (☑26 01 00; www.betico.nc) fast passenger ferries sail from Noumea to Île des Pins, and to Maré and Lifou in the Loyalty Islands.

Tickets can be purchased online. The *Betico* often has special sailings that line up with holiday weekends and festivals held on the various islands. Check the *Rotations spéciales* page of the website.

To/From Île des Pins

Duration 2½ hours

Cost Adult/child one way 5450/2770 CFP, day trip 10,700/5320 CFP

Departures:

Wednesday Noumea–Île des Pins–Noumea

Saturday Noumea–Île des Pins

Sunday Île des Pins–Noumea

To/From Loyalty Islands

Duration Noumea to Maré (four hours); Maré to Lifou (two hours); Lifou to Noumea (five hours)

Cost Noumea to Maré or Lifou adult/child 7750/3600 CFP; Maré to Lifou adult/child 4260/2030 CFP.

Departures:

Monday Noumea–Maré–Lifou–Noumea

Thursday Noumea–Maré–Lifou

Friday Lifou–Maré–Noumea

Bus

Rai (Réseau d'Autocars Interurbain; ☑05 81 61; www.rai.nc) Nearly every town on Grande Terre is connected to the capital by Rai's extremely efficient 25-line bus system. There are several departure points around Noumea, depending on your destination. Check when you buy your ticket.

Carsud (☑25 16 15; www.carsud.nc; Gare de Montravel, Rue Edouard Unger) Operates buses on 12 lines between Noumea and the greater Noumea region. It goes as far north as Tontouta (400 CFP), passing through Dumbéa (320 CFP) and Païta (360 CFP), and south to Plum in Mont-Dore (400 CFP).

Karuia Bus (☑26 54 54; www.karuiabus.nc; Rue Austerlitz) Operates Noumea city buses with 18 numbered lines. These red-and-white buses operate from 6am to 7pm. The ticket office is opposite the Compact Megastore. Tickets cost 190 CFP when purchased there; 210 CFP on the bus. Lines 10 and 11 follow the beach roads to Baie des Citrons and Anse Vata. Line 40 goes to Magenta domestic airport and the Tjibaou Cultural Centre

On islands other than Grand Terre there are practically no buses. It's essential to prearrange transport (or hitchhike).

Car, Scooter & Campervan

Touring New Caledonia by car allows you to explore places off the beaten track that aren't easy to reach by bus.

➡ Car-hire rates are reasonable.

➡ Petrol costs the same no matter how remote you are.

➡ Major roads and most minor ones are sealed and in good condition.

➡ Off the main roads, road signs are sometimes missing or placed down the turn-off where they can't be seen, so a good map is essential.

➡ New Caledonians drive like the wind in a cyclone – very fast!

➡ Drink driving is common, so be very careful, especially at night.

Car Hire

Car-rental companies abound in Noumea and the larger ones have desks at Tontouta international airport. The big players such as Avis, Hertz, Budget and Europcar are here, plus local operators.

➡ Most companies rent small sedans from 4500 CFP including 150km per day. Extra kilometres cost from 23 CFP per kilometre. Car hire with unlimited kilometres costs from 7000 CFP per day.

➡ Look for deals such as one-week's all-inclusive rental from 28,000 CFP.

➡ In the Loyalty Islands and Île des Pins, prices start at 6500 CFP per day with unlimited kilometres (it's not like you can go far). There's no extra cost to get your car delivered and picked up from your port of arrival and departure.

Reliable local car rental companies in Noumea include the following:

AB Location de Voitures (☑28 12 12; ablocation@mls.nc; 36 Ave du Maréchal Foch, Noumea) Has a supply of smart and zippy white Peugeots for rent from 4100 CFP per day.

Point Rouge (☑28 59 20; www.pointrouge.nc; 96 Rue du Général de Gaulle, Orphelinat) Rents everything from small cars (3300 CFP, plus tax) to 4WDs (from 5500 CFP a day, plus tax).

Driving Licences

A valid licence from your own country will suffice to drive in New Caledonia.

Fuel & Spare Parts

➡ Petrol costs the same per litre no matter where you are.

➡ Roads are usually in excellent condition.

➡ Petrol stations sometimes close for lunch and often close for the day at 6pm.

AROUND GRANDE TERRE BY BUS

The following schedules are for services departing from Noumea. Fares range from 600 CFP to 2000 CFP.

DESTINATION	DURATION (HR)	FREQUENCY
Bourail	2½	Mon-Sat
Canala	3½	daily
Hienghène	6½	Mon-Sat
Koné	4	daily
Koumac	5½	daily
La Foa	1¾	Mon-Sat
Poindimié	5	daily
Pouébo	6½	Wed & Fri
Thio	2	daily
Yaté	2	Mon-Sat

→ Petrol stations can be few and far between, so make sure you have enough fuel to get you to the next major town.

→ Île des Pins has only one petrol station, so if you have to return your rental car full of gas, get organised!

→ Spare parts are possible to get; many petrol stations have a garage attached.

Insurance

Hiring a car on the islands is fairly informal, but inspect your car in case you need to make an insurance claim.

→ No extra insurance is required when hiring a car.

→ Some companies charge a security deposit of 100,000 CFP.

Road Rules

→ Driving in New Caledonia is on the right-hand side of the road.

→ The speed limit on a main road is 110km/h (though no one seems to pay attention to it) and in residential areas it is 50km/h.

→ Seat belts are compulsory.

→ The maximum permissible blood-alcohol concentration is 0.05%; random breath-testing is carried out.

Hitching

Hitching is never entirely safe, and we don't recommend it. Travellers who hitch should understand that they are taking a small but potentially serious risk. That said, here are our tips:

→ With little public transport on the Loyalty Islands, hitching is a viable way to get around – the locals do it.

→ Make sure your backpack isn't oversized, as cars are generally small.

→ As well as taking the usual precautions, avoid getting in a car with a drunk driver.

Taxi

Taxis are confined to Noumea, the larger towns on Grande Terre and a couple of islands.

→ In Noumea it's best to call and book (☑28 35 12), rather than stand on the side of the road and wait.

→ Taxis run on a meter.

Tours

Operators in Noumea organise tours and activities in and around the city, as well as throughout New Caledonia. Outside Noumea, many places offering accommodation run tours such as guided walks or horse treks, usually on private or customary land.

The **Office de Tourisme** (p198) has brochures for all kinds of optional tours, or try the following in Noumea:

Arc en Ciel Voyages (☑27 19 80; www.arcenciel.nc; 59 Av du Maréchal Foch) Arranges tickets for travelling or touring anywhere, including day trips to the islands.

Caledonia Spirit (☑27 27 01; www.caledoniaspirit.com; Le Village, 35 Av du Maréchal Foch) Arranges everything including accommodation and rental cars on the Loyalty Islands and Île des Pins.

Survival Guide

Health

BEFORE YOU GO

Planning before departure, particularly for pre-existing illnesses, will save trouble later. See your dentist before you go; carry a spare pair of contact lenses and glasses with you; and take your optical prescription. Bring medications in their original labelled containers, and a letter from your doctor describing your medical conditions and medications. If carrying syringes or needles, have a letter saying they're needed, or buy a prepared pack from a travel-health clinic.

Insurance

If your health insurance doesn't cover you for medical expenses abroad, consider extra insurance; see www.lonelyplanet.com/travel-insurance. Find out if your insurance plan will make payments directly to providers or reimburse you later; in both Vanuatu and New Caledonia private doctors expect payment in cash.

Make sure your insurance covers evacuation to the nearest major centre – the extra premium for this is usually not very much.

Recommended Vaccinations

➡ Hepatitis A
➡ Hepatitis B
➡ Measles, mumps, rubella (MMR)
➡ Tetanus-diphtheria
➡ Typhoid

Websites

Centers for Disease Control & Prevention (www.cdc.gov)

Fit for Travel (www.fitfortravel.scot.nhs.uk) User-friendly, up-to-date information about outbreaks.

Lonely Planet (lonelyplanet.com) A good place to start.

MD Travel Health (www.mdtravelhealth.com) Free travel-health recommendations.

Travel Doctor (www.traveldoctor.com.au) Australian site with user-friendly, up-to-date information.

World Health Organization (www.who.int/ith) The WHO's *International Travel and Health* guide is available free online.

Also consult your government's travel-health website:

Australia (www.dfat.gov.au/travel)

Canada (www.hc-sc.gc.ca)

UK (www.dh.gov.uk/policyandguidance/healthadvicefortravellers/fs/en)

USA (www.cdc.gov/travel)

IN VANUATU & NEW CALEDONIA

Availability & Cost of Health Care

New Caledonian health care is of a high standard; specialists in most disciplines are available and citizens of the EU have the same eligibility for government medical care as in France. Costs can be high, from AUD$4000 per day for an intensive-care bed.

In Vanuatu, Port Vila's lack of quality systems may mean the equipment or medication you need is not available, even for simple problems. Outside Port Vila, diagnostic and treatment facilities are rarely available, but volunteer doctors may be present in some hospitals. Santo has a program within which international junior doctors work at its hospital.

Private medical practitioners in both countries will expect payment in cash. Consultation fees, X-rays etc cost around the same as those in Western countries. Where hospital facilities exist, a cash deposit will be required; credit cards may not be accepted. Public-hospital outpatient services are free, but waiting times can be very long.

Commonly used drugs, including oral contraceptives and antibiotics, are available in Port Vila and throughout New Caledonia, and special drugs can be flown in. Diabetics may not be able to obtain their usual type of insulin preparation, so it's safer to have your own supply. Up-to-date anti-epileptics and anti-hypertensives may be hard to come by.

Private dentists practise in Port Vila and in the main towns in New Caledonia.

Infectious Diseases

Chikungunya Fever

New Caledonia reported its first cases of chikungunya in 2011. It's a viral disease spread by mosquito bites and causes fever and severe joint pain. It has signs that resemble dengue fever and can be misdiagnosed. There is no cure but symptoms can be treated.

Dengue Fever

Dengue fever, spread by mosquito bites, is mainly a problem in the wet season (from November to April). It causes a feverish illness with headache and severe muscle pains; a fine rash may also be present. Be obsessive about using insect repellents. Self-treatment includes paracetamol (do not take aspirin as this can have very dangerous side effects), fluids and rest. Danger signs are prolonged vomiting, blood in the vomit and/or a blotchy, dark-red rash.

Hepatitis A

This is a viral disease causing liver inflammation. Fever, debility and jaundice (yellow skin and eyes, dark urine) occur; recovery is slow, and it can be dangerous to people with other liver disease, to the elderly and sometimes to pregnant women. It is spread by contaminated food or water. Self-treatment consists of rest, a low-fat diet and avoidance of alcohol. The vaccine is close to 100% protective.

Hepatitis B

Like hepatitis A, hepatitis B is a viral disease causing liver inflammation, but it is more serious and frequently causes chronic liver disease and even cancer. It is spread, like HIV, by mixing body fluids, by using contaminated needles and by accidental blood contamination. Treatment is complex and specialised but vaccination is highly effective.

HIV/AIDS

The incidence of HIV infection is on the rise in West Melanesia and unprotected sex carries huge dangers. Condom use is essential. If you require an injection for anything, have your own needles or check that a new needle is being used.

Malaria

Malaria is a parasitic infection transmitted by mosquitoes that feed in dull light (ie at night, when it's overcast, in the jungle or inside dark huts). Since no vaccine is available you must rely on mosquito-bite prevention and taking antimalarial drugs before, during and after risk of exposure. No antimalarial is 100% effective.

There is no malaria in New Caledonia.

A few of Vanuatu's islands claim to be malaria free (including Aneityum or Futuna) and it is rare in Port Vila. In the rest of the country, however, take extreme care.

If you develop a fever during or after your visit to Vanuatu, first rule out malaria; most clinics will do a blood-smear check. If you have self-treatment malaria medication, still try to get a diagnosis and go to a major medical centre to confirm a cure.

This applies up to a few months after leaving the area. Malaria is curable if diagnosed early.

Typhoid Fever

This bacterial infection from contaminated food or water can be transmitted by food handlers and flies, or be present in inadequately cooked shellfish. It causes fever, debility and late-onset diarrhoea but is curable with antibiotics. Untreated it can produce delirium and is occasionally fatal. Vaccination is moderately effective; taking care with eating and drinking is important.

Traveller's Diarrhoea

Diarrhoea in the tropics is usually caused by bacteria or parasites in contaminated food or water. Drink plenty of fluids, especially rehydration solutions. If you have more than four stools a day, you should take an antibiotic (quinolone) and an anti-diarrhoeal agent (loperamide). If diarrhoea is bloody, persists for more than 72 hours or is accompanied by fever, shaking, chills or severe abdominal pain, seek medical attention.

Giardiasis

A parasite in contaminated water in Vanuatu, giardia produces bloating and a foul-smelling and persistent, although not 'explosive', diarrhoea. Taking one dose (four tablets) of tinidazole usually cures it.

Environmental Hazards

Bites & Stings

If you see the blue-coloured Indo-Pacific man-of-war in the water or on the beach, don't go in. Its whip-like sting is very painful. Treat with vinegar or ice packs. Do not use alcohol.

Coral Cuts

Live coral can cause prolonged infection. If you do cut yourself, treat the wound immediately, scrubbing it thoroughly with fresh water to get out all the coral, then with alcohol. Apply an antiseptic and cover with a waterproof dressing.

Coral Ear

This inflammation of the ear canal is caused when water activates fungal spores, leading to bacterial infection and inflammation. It usually starts after swimming but can be reactivated in a shower, especially if your wet hair lies over the ear hole.

It can be very, very painful. Self-treatment with an antibiotic plus steroid ear-drop preparation is very effective. Stay out of the water until the pain and itch have gone.

Diving Hazards

Strict depth and time precautions will be upheld by your dive operator. Temptation to stay longer at relatively shallow depths is great and is probably the main cause of decompression illness (the 'bends'). Any muscle or joint pain after scuba diving must be treated as suspect. Novice divers must be especially careful.

There are decompression chambers in **Port Vila** (☑26996, 25566; www.pro medical.com.vu; ☉24hr) and **Noumea** (☑26 45 26). Local planes fly patients in at a very low altitude. Check with **Divers Alert Network** (DAN; www.diversalertnetwork.org) about the current status and insurance to cover costs.

Food

Only eat fresh fruits or vegetables that have been cooked or peeled; be wary of dairy products that might contain unpasteurised milk. It's important to ensure restaurants you eat in have good standards of hygiene; food that comes to you piping hot

is likely to be safe. Be wary of salads and avoid buffet-style meals. In the outer islands, wash lettuce in vinegar to ensure any contamination from snails is removed.

Otherwise safe and edible fish can sometimes carry ciguatera. Poisoning causes stomach upsets, itching, faintness, slow pulse and bizarre inverted sensations – cold feels hot, and vice versa. Ciguatera has been reported in large carnivorous reef fish, including red snapper, barracuda and Spanish mackerel. There is no safe test to determine whether a fish is poisonous, but the locals know what to eat. Fish caught after any reef disturbance, such as a hurricane, are more likely to be poisonous. Deep-sea fish such as tuna are perfectly safe.

Leptospirosis

Also known as Weil's disease, leptospirosis produces fever, headache, jaundice and, later, kidney failure. It is caused by a spirochaete organism found in water contaminated by rat or bat urine. There is some concern that it can be contracted at Millennium Cave in Santo. If diagnosed early it is cured with penicillin.

Heat Exhaustion

This can be prevented by drinking at least 2L of water per day; more if exercising. Salt-replacement solutions are useful, as muscle weakness is due to salt loss and can be made worse by drinking water alone. The powders used to treat dehydration caused by diarrhoea are just as effective for heat exhaustion, or try a good pinch of salt to a half-litre of water. Salt tablets can give you too much salt, causing headaches and confusion.

Heatstroke

This is a dangerous and emergency condition, with muscle weakness, exhaustion

and mental confusion. Skin will be hot and dry. Reduce your temperature by lying in water and, if possible, with cold drinks. Seek medical help.

Sunburn

The time of highest risk is between 11am and 3pm, and cloud cover does *not* block out UV rays. Sunburn is likely to be a particular problem for those taking doxycycline as an antimalarial. Do the Australian and Kiwi 'slip, slop, slap' thing: slip on a shirt, slop on sunscreen and slap on a hat. Seek shade where possible. Treat sunburn like any other burn – with cool, wet dressings. Severe swelling may respond to a cortisone cream.

Women's Health

Tampons and pads can be obtained, but if it looks like they've been on the shelf for ages, check for evidence of cockroaches.

Vanuatu is not ideal for a pregnant woman. Malaria can cause miscarriage or premature labour, and pregnant women cannot take the antimalarial tablets recommended for Vanuatu.

Traditional Medicine

Local herbs, roots and leaves used by traditional healers often have effective ingredients; research institutions are currently investigating many of them. Extravagant claims (eg AIDS cures, aphrodisiacs) can be ignored, and it is best to avoid compounds made with animal ingredients. Tree-bark concoctions for fever are similar to aspirin.

Kava is a sedative and also has muscle-relaxant properties. It is drunk mainly in Vanuatu.

WANT MORE?

For in-depth language information and handy phrases, check out Lonely Planet's *French Phrasebook*, *Pidgin Phrasebook* and *South Pacific Phrasebook*. You'll find them at **shop.lonelyplanet. com**, or you can buy Lonely Planet's iPhone phrasebooks at the Apple App Store.

Language

In this chapter you'll find useful practical and social phrases in French (spoken in both New Caledonia and Vanuatu) and Bislama (the lingua franca of Vanuatu), as well as some basic phrases in Drehu, the most widely spoken of New Caledonia's Kanak languages.

FRENCH

The sounds used in spoken French can almost all be found in English. There are a couple of exceptions: nasal vowels (represented in our pronunciation guides by o or u followed by an almost inaudible nasal consonant sound m, n or ng), the 'funny' *u* (ew in our guides) and the deep-in-the-throat *r*. Bearing these few points in mind and reading our pronunciation guides as if they were English, you'll be understood just fine.

Basics

Hello.	*Bonjour.*	bon·zhoor
Goodbye.	*Au revoir.*	o·rer·vwa
Excuse me.	*Excusez-moi.*	ek·skew·zay·mwa
Sorry.	*Pardon.*	par·don
Yes./No.	*Oui./Non.*	wee/non
Please.	*S'il vous plaît.*	seel voo play
Thank you (very much).	*Merci (beaucoup).*	mair·see (bo·koo)

You're welcome.
De rien. der ree·en

How are you?
Comment allez-vous? ko·mon ta·lay·voo

Fine, thanks. And you?
Bien, merci. Et vous? byun mair·see ay voo

What's your name?
Comment vous appelez-vous? ko·mon voo·za·play voo

My name is ...
Je m'appelle ... zher ma·pel ...

Do you speak English?
Parlez-vous anglais? par·lay·voo ong·glay

I don't understand.
Je ne comprends pas. zher ner kom·pron pa

Accommodation

Do you have any rooms available?
Est-ce que vous avez des chambres libres? es·ker voo za·vay day shom·brer lee·brer

Can I see the room?
Est-ce que je peux voir la chambre? es·ker zher per vwar la shom·rer

How much is it per night/person?
Quel est le prix par nuit/personne? kel ay ler pree par nwee/per·son

Is breakfast included?
Est-ce que le petit déjeuner est inclus? es·ker ler per·tee day·zher·nay ayt en·klew

campsite	*camping*	kom·peeng
dorm	*dortoir*	dor·twar
guesthouse	*pension*	pon·syon
hotel	*hôtel*	o·tel
youth hostel	*auberge de jeunesse*	o·berzh der zher·nes

QUESTION WORDS

What?	Quoi?	kwa
When?	Quand?	kon
Where?	Où?	oo
Who?	Qui?	kee
Why?	Pourquoi?	poor·kwa

a ... room	une chambre ...	ewn shom·brer ...
single	à un lit	a un lee
double	avec un grand lit	a·vek un gron lee
twin	avec des lits jumeaux	a·vek day lee zhew·mo

with (a)...	avec ...	a·vek ...
air-con	climatiseur	klee·ma·tee·zer
bathroom	une salle de bains	ewn sal der bun
window	fenêtre	fer·nay·trer

Directions

Where's ...?
Où est ...? — oo ay ...

What's the address?
Quelle est l'adresse? — kel ay la·dres

Can you down write the address, please?
Est-ce que vous pourriez écrire l'adresse, s'il vous plaît? — es·ker voo poo·ryay ay·kreer la·dres seel voo play

Can you show me (on the map)?
Pouvez-vous m'indiquer (sur la carte)? — poo·vay·voo mun·dee·kay (sewr la kart)

at the corner	au coin	o kwun
at the traffic lights	aux feux	o fer
behind	derrière	dair·ryair
in front of	devant	der·von
far (from)	loin (de)	lwun (der)
left	gauche	gosh
near (to)	près (de)	pray (der)
next to	à côté de	a ko·tay der
opposite	en face de	on fas der
right	droite	drwat
straight ahead	tout droit	too drwa

Eating & Drinking

What would you recommend?
Qu'est-ce que vous conseillez? — kes·ker voo kon·say·yay

What's in that dish?
Quels sont les ingrédients? — kel son lay zun·gray·dyon

I'm a vegetarian.
Je suis végétarien/ végétarienne. — zher swee vay·zhay·ta·ryun/ vay·zhay·ta·ryen (m/f)

I don't eat ...
Je ne mange pas ... — zher ner monzh pa ...

Cheers!
Santé! — son·tay

That was delicious.
C'était délicieux. — say·tay day·lee·syer

Please bring the bill.
Apportez-moi l'addition, s'il vous plaît. — a·por·tay·mwa la·dee·syon seel voo play

Emergencies

Help!
Au secours! — o skoor

Leave me alone!
Fichez-moi la paix! — fee·shay·mwa la pay

Call a doctor.
Appelez un médecin. — a·play un mayd·sun

Call the police.
Appelez la police. — a·play la po·lees

I'm lost.
Je suis perdu/perdue. — zhe swee·pair·dew (m/f)

I'm ill.
Je suis malade. — zher swee ma·lad

It hurts here.
J'ai une douleur ici. — zhay ewn doo·ler ee·see

I'm allergic to ...
Je suis allergique ... — zher swee za·lair·zheek ...

Shopping & Services

I'd like to buy ...
Je voudrais acheter ... — zher voo·dray ash·tay ...

Can I look at it?
Est-ce que je peux le voir? — es·ker zher per ler vwar

I'm just looking.
Je regarde. — zher rer·gard

I don't like it.
Cela ne me plaît pas. — ser·la ner mer play pa

How much is it?
C'est combien? — say kom·byun

It's too expensive.
C'est trop cher. — say tro shair

Can you lower the price?
Vous pouvez baisser le prix? — voo poo·vay bay·say ler pree

There's a mistake in the bill.
Il y a une erreur dans la note. — eel ya ewn ay·rer don la not

bank	*banque*	bonk
internet cafe	*cybercafé*	see·bair·ka·fay
post office	*bureau de poste*	bew·ro der post
tourist office	*office de tourisme*	o·fees der too·rees·mer

Time, Dates & Numbers

What time is it?
Quelle heure est-il? kel er ay til

It's (eight) o'clock.
Il est (huit) heures. il ay (weet) er

It's half past (10).
Il est (dix) heures et demie. il ay (deez) er ay day·mee

morning	*matin*	ma·tun
afternoon	*après-midi*	a·pray·mee·dee
evening	*soir*	swar
yesterday	*hier*	yair
today	*aujourd'hui*	o·zhoor·dwee
tomorrow	*demain*	der·mun

Monday	*lundi*	lun·dee
Tuesday	*mardi*	mar·dee
Wednesday	*mercredi*	mair·krer·dee
Thursday	*jeudi*	zher·dee
Friday	*vendredi*	von·drer·dee
Saturday	*samedi*	sam·dee
Sunday	*dimanche*	dee·monsh

1	*un*	un
2	*deux*	der
3	*trois*	trwa
4	*quatre*	ka·trer
5	*cinq*	sungk
6	*six*	sees
7	*sept*	set
8	*huit*	weet
9	*neuf*	nerf
10	*dix*	dees
20	*vingt*	vung
30	*trente*	tront
40	*quarante*	ka·ront
50	*cinquante*	sung·kont
60	*soixante*	swa·sont
70	*soixante-dix*	swa·son·dees
80	*quatre-vingts*	ka·trer·vung
90	*quatre-vingt-dix*	ka·trer·vung·dees
100	*cent*	son
1000	*mille*	meel

Transport

I want to go to ...
Je voudrais aller à ... zher voo·dray a·lay a ...

At what time does it leave/arrive?
À quelle heure est-ce qu'il part/arrive? a kel er es kil par/a·reev

How long does the trip take?
Le trajet dure combien de temps? ler tra·zhay dewr kom·byun der tom

Does it stop at ...?
Est-ce qu'il s'arrête à ...? es·kil sa·ret a ...

Can you tell me when we get to ...?
Pouvez-vous me dire quand nous arrivons à ...? poo·vay·voo mer deer kon noo za·ree·von a ...

I want to get off here.
Je veux descendre ici. zher ver day·son·drer ee·see

boat	*bateau*	ba·to
bus	*bus*	bews
plane	*avion*	a·vyon
train	*train*	trun

a ... ticket	*un billet ...*	un bee·yay ...
1st-class	*de première classe*	der prem·yair klas
2nd-class	*de deuxième classe*	der der·zyem las
one-way	*simple*	sum·pler
return	*aller et retour*	a·lay ay rer·toor

aisle seat	*côté couloir*	ko·tay kool·war
first	*premier*	prer·myay
last	*dernier*	dair·nyay
next	*prochain*	pro·shun
ticket office	*guichet*	gee·shay
timetable	*horaire*	o·rair
window seat	*côté fenêtre*	ko·tay fe·ne·trer

SIGNS

Entrée	Entrance
Femmes	Women
Fermé	Closed
Hommes	Men
Interdit	Prohibited
Ouvert	Open
Renseignements	Information
Sortie	Exit
Toilettes/WC	Toilets

I'd like to hire a ...	Je voudrais louer ...	zher voo·dray loo·way ...
4WD	un quatre-quatre	un kat·kat
bicycle	un vélo	un vay·lo
car	une voiture	ewn vwa·tewr
motorcycle	une moto	ewn mo·to

child seat	siège-enfant	syezh·on·fon
diesel	diesel	dyay·zel
helmet	casque	kask
mechanic	mécanicien	may·ka·nee·syun
petrol/gas	essence	ay·sons
service station	station-service	sta·syon·ser·vees

Is this the road to ...?
C'est la route pour ...? say la root poor ...

(How long) Can I park here?
(Combien de temps) (kom·byun der tom)
Est-ce que je peux es·ker zher per
stationner ici? sta·syo·nay ee·see

The car/motorbike has broken down (at ...).
La voiture/moto est la vwa·tewr/mo·to ay
tombée en panne (à ...). tom·bay on pan (a ...)

I have a flat tyre.
Mon pneu est à plat. mom pner ay ta pla

I've run out of petrol.
Je suis en panne zher swee zon pan
d'essence. day·sons

I've lost my car keys.
J'ai perdu les clés de zhay per·dew lay klay der
ma voiture. ma vwa·tewr

BISLAMA

Also called *bichlamar* or *bichelamar* by French speakers, Bislama is the English-based pidgin (with a bit of French thrown into the mix as well) used throughout Vanuatu. It enables people from totally different areas of the country (with about 120 different first languages) to converse. It also allows the 40% of the population who have been educated in French-language schools to communicate with the 60% who have studied in English-language institutions. Most locals can speak Bislama with varying degrees of fluency, while the more educated also speak either English or French at least reasonably well.

Basics

Hello.	Alo./Alo olgeta.
Goodbye.	Bae./Ata.
See you.	Mi lukem yu.

How are you?	Olsem wanem?/Yu oraet?
I'm well, thanks.	I gud nomo, tankyu.
Please.	Plis.
Thank you (very much).	Tankyu (tumas).
Sorry.	Sore.
Excuse me.	Skiusmi.
Yes./No.	Olraet./No.
Do you speak English?	Yu tok tok Engglis?
I don't understand.	Mi no save.
What's your name?	Wanem nem blong yu?
My name is ...	Nem blong mi ...

Accommodation

I'm looking for a ...	Mi stop lukaot ...
guesthouse	reshaos
hotel	hotel

Do you have a ...?	Yu kat ... long ples ia?
bed	bed
single/double room	rum blong wan/tu

Do you have a house I can sleep in?	Yu gat haos blong slip?
for one/two nights	blong wan/tu naet
How much is it per night/person?	Hamas i blong wan naet/man?
Is breakfast included?	Hemia i blong brekfas tu?
Can I see the room?	Mi save luk rum?
Where is the toilet?	Tolet i stap wea?

Do you have (a) ...?	Yu gat ...?
clean sheet	klin kaliko blong bed
hot water	hot wota
key	wan kei
shower	ples/rum blong swim

Directions

How do I get to ...?	Bi mi go kasem ... olsem wanem?
Where is ...?	Wea ples ...?
How far is it from here?	Hamas farawe long ia?
here	long ples ia/long hia
there	longwe

What ... is this?	Wanem ... ia?
street/road	rod
village	vilej

beach	sanbij
bridge	brij
church	joj
coral reef	korel rif
island	aelan
lake	lek
river	reva
school	skul
sea	solwota
volcano	volkeno

Emergencies

Help!	Help!
Go away!	Gowe!
Call a doctor!	Singaot doctor!
Call the police!	Singaot polis!
I'm allergic to ...	Mi no save dring ...

Shopping & Services

Where is a/the ...?	Wea ples i ...?
bank	bang
clinic	haos meresin
hospital	hospitel
market	maket
post office	post ofis
public toilet	pablik tolet/smolhaos
restaurant	restoron
store	stoa
telephone	pablik telefon

I'd like to buy ...	Mi wantem pem ...
Can I look at it?	Mi save luk?
I'm just looking.	Mi stap lukluk nomo.
How much is this?	Hamas long hemia nao?
It's too expensive.	I sas tumas long mi.
I don't like ...	Mi no likim ...
Do you have another colour/size?	Yu nogat kalar/saes ia?

Time, Dates & Numbers

When?	Wanem taem?/Wataem?
What time is it?	Yu save wanem taem naoia?
It's ... o'clock.	Hemi ... oklok.
in the morning	long moning
in the evening	long aftenun

yesterday	yestede
today	tude/tede
tomorrow	tumoro
Monday	mande
Tuesday	tuste
Wednesday	wenste
Thursday	toste
Friday	fraede
Saturday	satede
Sunday	sande

1	wan
2	tu
3	tri
4	fo
5	faef
6	sikis
7	seven
8	eit
9	naen
10	ten
20	twante
30	tate
40	fote
50	fefte
60	sikiste
70	sevente
80	eite
90	naente
100	handred
1000	taosin

Transport

Can I go to ...?	Mi save go long ...?
I want to go to ...	Mi wantem go long ...
How long does the trip take?	Bae i longfela alsam wanem?
What time does it leave/arrive?	Wanem time em i leave/i kasem long ples ia?

boat	bot
plane	plen

I'd like to hire a ...	Mi wantem rentem ...
canoe	kanu/kenu
guide	tour guide
speedboat	spidbot/bot
taxi	taksi

KANAK LANGUAGES

More than 30 indigenous Kanak (Melanesian-Polynesian) dialects are spoken in New Caledonia alongside French, which is the official language. There are 28 distinct Kanak languages (not counting dialects) and all belong to the Melanesian branch of the Austronesian language family, except for Faga Uvea (spoken on Ouvéa), which is a Polynesian language. While all Kanaks know French and use it in particular situations, the majority of rural Kanaks use their own language within the sphere of their family and clan.

While many features of the various Kanak languages are similar, they don't have identical pronunciation. Keep in mind the pronunciation of the following sounds:

â	as the 'o' in 'on'
ë	as the 'an' in 'land'
ö	as the 'ou' in 'about'
ô	as the 'o' in 'long'
û	as the 'oo' in 'too' but shorter

c	as the 'ch' in 'cheque'
dr	as the 'd' in 'day'
g	as the 'ng' in 'camping'
hw	as a 'w' but with an audible puff of breath
ny	as the 'ny' in 'canyon'
x	as the 'ch' in the Scottish *loch*

Unlike neighbouring Vanuatu, New Caledonia has no unifying indigenous language. We've included the basics for Drehu, the most widely spoken Kanak language (spoken in the Loyalty Islands). It has some influences from Polynesian, French and English.

| Hello. | Bozu. |
| Goodbye. | Dréé. |

How are you?	Tune ka epun?
I'm well.	Kaloi.
Please.	Sipone.
Until tomorrow.	E lanyié.
Do you speak English?	Hapeu nyipë a qene papaale?
What's your name?	Dréi la éjé i éö?
What do you want?	Epun a aja nemen?
I'd like to buy ...	Eni a itö ...

banana	wshnawa
beach	hnangöni
bed	göhnë
boy	nekö trahmany
bread	falawa
dance	fia
dinner	xeni hej
eat	xen
English	papale
father	kem-kakaa
French	wiwi
language	qene hlapa
mother	thin-nenë
rain	mani
sky	hnengödrail
speak	ewekër
sun	jö
swim	aj
tree	sinöe
when	eu
where	kaa
which	kau
who	drei
why	némen

GLOSSARY

accueil – reception or welcome

Araucaria columnaris – columnar pine growing to 60m, found along New Caledonia's coast

atoll – low-lying coral islets and reef enclosing a lagoon

banyan – huge tree from the fig/rubber family, with a wide canopy and big aerial roots; also called 'nabanga'

barrier reef – long, narrow coral reef separated from the land by a lagoon; see also *fringing reef*

BCI – Banque Calédonienne d'Investissement

blackbirding – system where Melanesians worked in sugar cane fields in Australia and Fiji, and coconut plantations in Western Samoa

BNP – Banque Nationale de Paris

bougna – traditional Kanak meal of yam, taro and sweet potatoes with chicken, fish or crustaceans, cooked in an earth oven

boulangerie – bakery

breadfruit – large, starchy fruit; can be boiled, mashed, or fried like chips; the timber is used for making *tamtam*

burao – wild hibiscus

cagou – New Caledonia's national bird

caldera – large crater formed by the explosion or subsidence of a volcano

Caldoche – white person born in New Caledonia whose ancestral ties go back to the convicts or early French settlers

cargo cult – religious movement whose followers hope for vast quantities of wealth (cargo) through the generosity of supernatural forces

case – traditional Kanak hut, either conical or rectangular

cassava – popular staple root food, also called yuca or manioc; the starch, often called tapioca, is used as a thickener

cephalopod – class of mollusc that includes octopus, cuttlefish, squid and nautilus

CFP – Cour de Franc Pacifique; local franc

chefferie – house of a Kanak chief

ciguatera – type of poisoning caused by eating infected reef fish

clan – or tribe; people with a descent from a common ancestor

coconut crab – huge edible land crab

Communard – person who participated in the Paris Commune uprising of 1871; many were exiled to New Caledonia

copra – dried coconut meat, processed to make oil for margarine and soap

dugong – fully protected but endangered sea mammal; lives on sea grass. Nets, traditional hunting and motorboat propellers take a heavy toll on their numbers.

erpnavet – grade-taking ceremony

faré – large, often open-sided meeting house; thatched shelter

flèche faîtière – ornamental wooden spear seen on top of every *grande case*

FLNKS – Front de Libération Nationale Kanak et Socialiste; New Caledonia's main pro-independence political front, made up of several parties

fringing reef – reef found along the shore of an island or mainland coast without enclosing a lagoon; see also *barrier reef*

gare maritime – boat or ferry terminal

gare routière – bus station

gîte – small tourist hotel, usually run by Kanaks

grande case – conical-shaped hut where the tribal chiefs meet

houp – tree highly prized for its beautiful yellowish wood; its flowers are bright red

indigénat – used to describe the colonial authority's repressive system that forced Kanaks into reservations and required them to work for the authorities

kae kae – food

Kanaky – those who are pro independence for Vanuatu; also the name given to New Caledonia by pro independence Kanaks of New Caledonia

Kaneka – contemporary Kanak music

kastom – rules surrounding ancient ancestral legacies and customs

kastom ownership – traditional ownership of land, objects or reefs by individuals, families or clans

kauri – conifer giant of the forest, harvested for its wood

kava – mildly intoxicating drink

la brousse – bush or outback, encompassing everything outside Noumea; Caldoches from la brousse are sometimes called Broussards

la coutume – vital element of social and cultural life

lagoon – shallow water between land and ocean sealed off by reefs or sand-bars

Lapita – site close to Koné, on Grande Terre, where old pottery was found; it gave its name to the Lapita people, who inhabited much of Melanesia

laplap – Vanuatu's national dish; tightly wrapped doughy mix filled with meat or fish and cooked in a ground oven

ligne – bus route

maghe – grade-taking ceremony

mairie – city or town hall, also called 'hôtel de ville'

mal mal – T-piece, of cotton or tapa, worn by male dancers

man blong posen – sorcerer

manioc – see *cassava*

marché – market

Marist – person from the religious society, Société de la Propagation de la Foi, founded in 1836 in Lyon

Melanesian – people of New Caledonia, Papua New Guinea, the Solomon Islands, Vanuatu and Fiji

menu du jour – three-course meal with set price; often abbreviated to 'menu'

Micronesian – people of the northwest Pacific, of Malay-Polynesian origin

naghol – land-diving ritual practised on Pentecost

nakamal – clubhouse where men meet to talk and drink *kava*

nambas – penis-wrapper of dried pandanus leaves worn during ceremonies

nangae – fruit with a nut like an almond

nasara – chief's private room or area, where business decisions take place

naus – fruit similar to a mango

nautilus – chambered sea creature with a beautiful red-brown and ivory-striped shell; considered a living fossil

niaouli – trees from the dry west New Caledonia coast, forming a niaouli savannah

nimangki – status and power earned by taking a series of grades

ni-Vans – indigenous people of Vanuatu

ni-Vanuatu – more formal name for the indigenous people of Vanuatu

pandanus – tree found along the seashore; leaves are used for weaving mats and baskets

pawpaw – also known as 'papaya'; staple, sweet-tasting fruit

pétanque – type of lawn bowls played on a hard surface

petroglyphs – designs carved in stone and found throughout the Pacific

pilou – supreme Kanak dance, for important ceremonies

piper methysticum – botanical name for *kava*

pirogue – traditional outrigger canoe

Polynesian – people from Hawaii, Tahiti, Samoa, the Cook Islands and New Zealand

pomelo – also called 'pamplemousse'; large, sweet, juicy grapefruit with a pink interior

Quonset hut – half-moon-shaped shed built by the American troops in WWII

rambaramp – effigy of an important chief made a few months after his death to appease his spirit

récif – reef

roussette – flying fox

snack – inexpensive cafe

tabu – sacred or forbidden; can mean 'no entry' and can also apply to ceremonies, topics of conversation or other sensitive aspects of life

tamtam – slit-gong or slit-drum made from a carved

log with a hollowed-out section

tapa – cloth made from the bark of ebony, paper mulberry or breadfruit trees

taro – staple food all over the Pacific that can be boiled, crushed, baked or fried like chips; roots and leaves are eaten

toktok – discussion, chit-chat, conference

T-piece – piece of cloth which covers the groin area; see also *mal mal*

trocchus – 'Trochus niloticus', or 'troca'; a coiled, pink-and-white shell; the snail-like sea creature inside can be eaten

trou – waterhole

tuluk – small package of manioc dough wrapped in leaves and filled with meat or fish

yam – starchy tuber ('igname' in French); a staple food of Melanesians that can grow more than 1m long, and weigh 45kg; has important cultural significance

yuca – see *cassava*

Behind the Scenes

SEND US YOUR FEEDBACK

We love to hear from travellers – your comments keep us on our toes and help make our books better. Our well-travelled team reads every word on what you loved or loathed about this book. Although we cannot reply individually to your submissions, we always guarantee that your feedback goes straight to the appropriate authors, in time for the next edition. Each person who sends us information is thanked in the next edition – the most useful submissions are rewarded with a selection of digital PDF chapters.

Visit **lonelyplanet.com/contact** to submit your updates and suggestions or to ask for help. Our award-winning website also features inspirational travel stories, news and discussions.

Note: We may edit, reproduce and incorporate your comments in Lonely Planet products such as guidebooks, websites and digital products, so let us know if you don't want your comments reproduced or your name acknowledged. For a copy of our privacy policy visit lonelyplanet.com/privacy.

OUR READERS

Many thanks to the travellers who used the last edition and wrote to us with helpful hints, useful advice and interesting anecdotes: Antoine Boureau, Dave Rogan, David Gassman, Delphine Monnier, Delphine Teisserenc, Ed Minot, Emilie Servanin, Giandomenico Zingali, Marcus Feaver, Michael Gregora, Robert Scoliège, Vincent Ko.

ACKNOWLEDGEMENTS

Climate map data adapted from Peel MC, Finlayson BL & McMahon TA (2007) 'Updated World Map of the Köppen-Geiger Climate Classification', Hydrology and Earth System Sciences, 11, 163344.

Cover photograph: Baie d'Upi, New Caledonia. Stephane Frances/4Corners©

AUTHOR THANKS

Paul Harding

Many people helped with advice, information or just a good chat. Thanks in particular to Jack and Janelle, Kelson, Silas, Tom and Margaret, Sam and Helena, Sethrick and staff at Vanuatu Tourism Office in Port Vila. Thanks to Tasmin at Lonely Planet and my co-author Craig McLachlan. Most of all, and as always, thanks to Hannah and Layla for your love and patience.

Craig McLachlan

A hearty thanks to everyone who helped me out on the road, but most of all to my exceptionally beautiful wife Yuriko.

THIS BOOK

This eighth edition of Lonely Planet's *Vanuatu & New Caledonia* guidebook was researched and written by Paul Harding and Craig McLachlan. The previous edition was written by Jayne D'Arcy. This guidebook was produced by the following:

Destination Editor Tasmin Waby

Coordinating Editor Susan Paterson

Product Editor Joel Cotterell

Regional Senior Cartographer Diana Von Holdt

Book Designers Cam Ashley, Michael Buick

Assisting Editors Michelle Bennett, Andrea Dobbin, Bruce Evans, Anne Mulvaney

Cover Researcher Naomi Parker

Thanks to David Carroll, Laura Crawford, Andi Jones, Lauren Keith, Kate Mathews, Kathryn Rowan, Angela Tinson

Index

Map Pages **000**
Photo Pages **000**

INDEX C – M

NOTES

Map Legend

Sights

- Beach
- Bird Sanctuary
- Buddhist
- Castle/Palace
- Christian
- Confucian
- Hindu
- Islamic
- Jain
- Jewish
- Monument
- Museum/Gallery/Historic Building
- Ruin
- Shinto
- Sikh
- Taoist
- Winery/Vineyard
- Zoo/Wildlife Sanctuary
- Other Sight

Activities, Courses & Tours

- Bodysurfing
- Diving
- Canoeing/Kayaking
- Course/Tour
- Sento Hot Baths/Onsen
- Skiing
- Snorkelling
- Surfing
- Swimming/Pool
- Walking
- Windsurfing
- Other Activity

Sleeping

- Sleeping
- Camping

Eating

- Eating

Drinking & Nightlife

- Drinking & Nightlife
- Cafe

Entertainment

- Entertainment

Shopping

- Shopping

Information

- Bank
- Embassy/Consulate
- Hospital/Medical
- Internet
- Police
- Post Office
- Telephone
- Toilet
- Tourist Information
- Other Information

Geographic

- Beach
- Gate
- Hut/Shelter
- Lighthouse
- Lookout
- Mountain/Volcano
- Oasis
- Park
- Pass
- Picnic Area
- Waterfall

Population

- Capital (National)
- Capital (State/Province)
- City/Large Town
- Town/Village

Transport

- Airport
- Border crossing
- Bus
- Cable car/Funicular
- Cycling
- Ferry
- Metro station
- Monorail
- Parking
- Petrol station
- Subway station
- Taxi
- Train station/Railway
- Tram
- Underground station
- Other Transport

Note: Not all symbols displayed above appear on the maps in this book

Routes

- Tollway
- Freeway
- Primary
- Secondary
- Tertiary
- Lane
- Unsealed road
- Road under construction
- Plaza/Mall
- Steps
- Tunnel
- Pedestrian overpass
- Walking Tour
- Walking Tour detour
- Path/Walking Trail

Boundaries

- International
- State/Province
- Disputed
- Regional/Suburb
- Marine Park
- Cliff
- Wall

Hydrography

- River, Creek
- Intermittent River
- Canal
- Water
- Dry/Salt/Intermittent Lake
- Reef

Areas

- Airport/Runway
- Beach/Desert
- Cemetery (Christian)
- Cemetery (Other)
- Glacier
- Mudflat
- Park/Forest
- Sight (Building)
- Sportsground
- Swamp/Mangrove

OUR STORY

A beat-up old car, a few dollars in the pocket and a sense of adventure. In 1972 that's all Tony and Maureen Wheeler needed for the trip of a lifetime – across Europe and Asia overland to Australia. It took several months, and at the end – broke but inspired – they sat at their kitchen table writing and stapling together their first travel guide, *Across Asia on the Cheap*. Within a week they'd sold 1500 copies. Lonely Planet was born.

Today, Lonely Planet has offices in Franklin, London, Melbourne, Oakland, Dublin, Beijing and Delhi, with more than 600 staff and writers. We share Tony's belief that 'a great guidebook should do three things: inform, educate and amuse'.

OUR WRITERS

Paul Harding

As a writer and photographer Paul has been travelling around Asia, Australia and parts of the Pacific for nearly two decades, examining beaches and islands along the way. Vanuatu stands out though for its remote islands, pristine waters, friendly faces and ancient traditional culture. On this trip Paul climbed a volcano, drank too much kava and braved rough seas in very small boats. He has contributed to some 50 Lonely Planet guides.

Craig McLachlan

An island enthusiast from way back, Craig has covered such varying spots as the Greek Islands, Okinawa, Tonga, New Caledonia and Oahu for Lonely Planet. A Kiwi with a passion for exploring, he loves New Caledonia, in particular the Loyalty Islands and Île des Pins. A 'freelance anything', Craig has an MBA from the University of Hawai'i and is also a pilot, karate instructor, tour leader, hiking guide, Japanese interpreter and budding novelist. See www.craigmclachlan.com.

Published by Lonely Planet Global Limited
CRN 554153
8th edition – Dec 2016
ISBN 978 1 78657 220 2
© Lonely Planet 2016   Photographs © as indicated 2016
10 9 8 7 6 5 4 3 2 1
Printed in China

Although the authors and Lonely Planet have taken all reasonable care in preparing this book, we make no warranty about the accuracy or completeness of its content and, to the maximum extent permitted, disclaim all liability arising from its use.

All rights reserved. No part of this publication may be copied, stored in a retrieval system, or transmitted in any form by any means, electronic, mechanical, recording or otherwise, except brief extracts for the purpose of review, and no part of this publication may be sold or hired, without the written permission of the publisher. Lonely Planet and the Lonely Planet logo are trademarks of Lonely Planet and are registered in the US Patent and Trademark Office and in other countries. Lonely Planet does not allow its name or logo to be appropriated by commercial establishments, such as retailers, restaurants or hotels. Please let us know of any misuses: lonelyplanet.com/ip.